THE EVOLUTION OF
SOVIET OPERATIONAL ART
1927–1991

VOLUME I

CASS SERIES ON THE SOVIET STUDY OF WAR

(Selected Translations)

Series Editor: David M. Glantz

This series examines what Soviet military theorists and commanders have learned from the study of their own military operations. Separate volumes contain annotated translations of Soviet works analysing their own experiences, as well as the works of important Soviet military theorists and collections of Soviet articles concerning specific campaigns, operations or military techniques.

1. Harold S. Orenstein, translator and editor, *Soviet Documents on the Use of War Experience*, Volume I, *The Initial Period of War 1941*, with an Introduction by David M. Glantz.
2. Harold S. Orenstein, translator and editor, *Soviet Documents on the Use of War Experience*, Volume II, *The Winter Campaign 1941–1942*, with an Introduction by David M. Glantz.
3. Joseph G. Welsh, translator, *Red Armor Combat Orders: Combat Regulations for Tank and Mechanized Forces 1944*, edited and with an Introduction by Richard N. Armstrong.
4. Harold S. Orenstein, translator and editor, *Soviet Documents on the Use of War Experience*, Volume III, *Military Operations 1941 and 1942*, with an Introduction by David M. Glantz.
5. William A. Burhans, translator, *The Nature of the Operations of Modern Armies* by V. K. Triandafillov, edited by Jacob W. Kipp, with an Introduction by James J. Schneider.
6. Harold S. Orenstein, translator, *The Evolution of Soviet Operational Art, 1927–1991: The Documentary Basis*, Volume I, *Operational Art, 1927–1964*, with an Introduction by David M. Glantz.
7. Harold S. Orenstein, translator, *The Evolution of Soviet Operational Art, 1927–1991: The Documentary Basis*, Volume II, *Operational Art, 1965–1991*, with an Introduction by David M. Glantz.

THE EVOLUTION OF SOVIET OPERATIONAL ART 1927–1991:
The Documentary Basis

In two volumes
VOLUME I
OPERATIONAL ART, 1927–1964

Translated by
Harold S. Orenstein

With a foreword and introduction by
David M. Glantz

FRANK CASS
LONDON

First published in 1995 in Great Britain by
FRANK CASS & CO. LTD.
Newbury House, 900 Eastern Avenue,
London, IG2 7HH

and in the United States of America by
FRANK CASS
c/o ISBS,
5804 N.E. Hassalo Street, Portland, Oregon 97213-3644

Copyright © 1995 Frank Cass & Co.

British Library Cataloguing in Publication Data

Evolution of Soviet Operational Art,
1927–91: Documentary Basis. – Vol.1:
Operational Art, 1927–64. – (Cass Series
on the Soviet Study of War; No.6)
I. Orenstein, Harold S. II. Series
355.00947

ISBN 0-7146-4547-8 (cloth)
ISBN 0-7146-4228-2 (paper)

Library of Congress Cataloging in Publication Data

The evolution of Soviet operational art, 1927–1991.
    p.   cm. — (Cass series on the Soviet study of war ; 6–7)
    Includes index.
    Contents: v. 1. Operational art, 1927–1964 — v. 2. Operational
art, 1965–1991.
ISBN 0-7146-4547-8 (v. 1) — ISBN 0-7146-4548-6 (v. 2) (cloth)
ISBN 0-7146-4228-2 (v. 1) — ISBN 0-7146-4229-0 (v. 2) (paper)
    1. Operational art (Military science)—History—20th century.
2. Soviet Union—History, Military.   I. Series.
U162.E96   1995
355.02—dc20   94-39330
                                                                CIP

esetting, London
Britain by
Bookcraft (Bath) Ltd, Midsomer Norton

Contents

List of Figures and Sketches   vi

Foreword   vii

Translator's Notes   xi

Introduction   xiii

1. The Formative Years, 1927–40   1
   Strategy and Operational Art   A. A. Svechin (1927)   5
   Strategy in an Academic Formulation   N. Varfolomeyev (1928) 33
   The Evolution of Operational Art   G. Isserson (1932)   48
   Operational Prospects for the Future   G. Isserson (1938)   78

2. The Test of War, 1941–45   91
   Closing Speech at a Military
      Conference   S. K. Timoshenko (1940) 94
   The Nature of Modern Battles   P. D. Korkodinov (1941) 124
   The Development of Operational Art
      According to the Experience of
      Recent Warfare   N. Talenskiy (1945)   143

3. The Stalinist Postwar Years, 1946–53   166
   Concerning Soviet Army Operational   V. Zlobin and
      Art   A. Vetoshnikov (1947)   168
   Operational Art and its Place in Soviet
      Military Art   A. Vetoshnikov (1949)   206
   The Triumph of Soviet Operational
      Art in the Great Patriotic War   V. Zlobin (1950)   218

4. On the Eve of Revolution in Military Affairs, 1954–59   237
   The Operation, its Essence, and its
      Significance in Modern Armed
      Struggle   A. Tsvetkov (1955)   239
   Operational Art as an Integral Part
      of Soviet Military Art   V. Vasil'yev (1956)   256

On Modern Soviet Military Art and
   its Characteristic Features   *P. Rotmistrov* (1958)   269

5. The Revolution in Military Affairs, 1960–64   285
   Some Questions of Modern Operational
     Art   *B. Golovchiner* (1961)   287
   Formation and Development of the
     Theory of Operational Art
     (1918–38)   *I. Mariyevsky* (1962)   298
   Tactics and Operational Art of the
     Workers' and Peasants' Red Army
     at a New Stage   *A. I. Yegorov* (1963)   315

Index   329

List of Figures and Sketches

System of criteria of basic characteristics of warfare   xiv–xv

Army defensive region (one variant)   103

Main (basic) defense sector (one variant)   104

Force defensive zone in an army defensive region (one variant)   105

Front offensive operation (variant: attack on a narrow front)   110

Front offensive operation (variant: attack on a broad front
   or operations by adjacent *fronts*)   111

Front offensive operation (variant: several army penetrations
   along various operational axes)   112

Army formation in an offensive operation (one variant)   113

Formation of a mobile shock group of forces for the
   penetration (one of the possible variants)   115

Different variants of an army offensive against a defending enemy   120

Foreword

Since the mid-1970s, U.S. (and Western) military theorists and armies have been preoccupied with defining and mastering what they term "the operational level of war." Discovery by these theorists of the operational level, which they came to define as an intermediate level of combat between the more traditional levels of strategy and tactics, was sudden, and soon all-engrossing. This new arena of military thought, appearing at a time when the arms race was reaching its peak, provided focus to U.S. military thought and action.

The reasons for this discovery and the receptivity of U.S. theorists to seemingly radical new concepts were many and included the following:

- frustration over perceived poor performance of the U.S. Army in Vietnam, where simple tactical approaches failed to produce positive strategic results;
- dissatisfaction with inherently passive, defensive, and often politically motivated approaches to solving military problems; for example, forward defense in NATO and active defense as U.S. military "doctrine";
- perceived bankruptcy of the intellectual base of U.S. military thought, and atrophy and dissatisfaction with the performance of military educational institutions.

Given this unpleasant situation, the U.S. Army officer corps and leadership were particularly receptive to fresh ideas and approaches suited to igniting a renaissance in thought and action in the U.S. military.

As is often the case in military affairs, thought precedes action. So it was in the revolution which would ensue. Reform of the U.S. military educational system, begun in the late 1970s and accelerated in the 1980s, unleashed in the service of reform the force of military research, in particular, the study of foreign armies. One of the initial products of that research was discovery of a "new" combat concept, which, ironically, had been developed in the camp of the principal U.S. global opponent, the Soviet Union. That concept was termed by the Soviets the operational level of war, whose explanation and justification was found in the realm of operational art.

By the early 1980s, the operational level, well-defined in Western research on Soviet military theory, found its way into U.S. military field manuals and the minds of U.S. military theorists. One could argue that this step conditioned the subsequent renaissance, intellectual and practical, which characterized U.S. military development throughout the 1980s. It is indeed ironic that U.S. adoption of a predominantly Soviet concept undergirded the U.S. military renaissance, provided focus and purpose to the subsequent U.S. military buildup, and became one intangible contributory factor in the U.S. and the West's victory in the Cold War. Intellectual vigor in military theory, long a hallmark of the Soviet system, became a tool for Western victory when Western theorists mastered that theory and translated it into practice, while simultaneously, as many former Soviet theorists lament, Soviet research and theory atrophied during the Brezhnev period.

Many Western works have appeared on the subject of Soviet operational art. The articles of John Erickson in the 1960s and 1970s introduced the term to Western military writers. Similar practical work by Peter Vigor, Christopher Donnelly, and their associates at the British Soviet Studies Research Centre, Sandhurst, deepened Western awareness of the vital area of Soviet military art and its component fields: strategy, operational art, and tactics. By the early 1980s, Soviet operational art was a major subject of study at the U.S. Army Command and General Staff College (CGSC) and soon at the U.S. Army War College as well. A growing number of detailed studies on Soviet operational experiences added meat to the theoretical study of operational art, and by 1982 the premier U.S. army doctrinal manual, *Field Manual 100–5*, included the operational level as a valid category for the study, planning, and conduct of war.

Early Western study of Soviet operational art was a demanding task. First, it involved knowledge of the Russian language, for virtually all sources were written in Russian. Second, it involved overcoming skepticism concerning the validity and truthfulness of Russian sources in general. Finally, it involved painstaking collation of Russian open sources with foreign archival materials (principally German and Japanese) to test the accuracy of what Soviet theorists wrote about their operations.

As Soviet historiography became more candid, however, and the archival and documentary base expanded in the 1970s, the research task became easier. If German and Japanese archival data helped to illuminate, validate, or refute the details of Soviet operational art in the 1970s, it was Soviet archival materials themselves, released from the mid-1980s, that finally permitted fuller elaboration of the framework, essence, and details of Soviet operational experiences and Soviet operational art. Available only in driblets in the late 1970s, the amount of archival materials reached flood proportions in the late 1980s. All of these materials fueled keener and more accurate Western appreciation of the subject.

These volumes represent a major effort to exploit newly available archival materials, Western and Soviet, and form a comprehensive explanation of the roots, nature, and evolution of Soviet operational art. An earlier volume, written as a survey of Soviet operational art, appeared in 1990 and was entitled *Soviet Military Operational Art: In Pursuit of Deep Battle*. These volumes contain that first volume's documentary basis. They consist of previously untranslated and unpublished articles and documents on operational art written by those major Soviet military theorists who themselves developed the subject. The selections have been taken from the pages of formerly classified or controlled Soviet books and journals, in particular, the Soviet General Staff journal *Military Thought* (*Voyennaya mysl'*).

These two volumes trace the development of operational art from its inception in the 1920s to the tumultuous changes of the early 1990s. The selections document how operational art emerged as a key element of Soviet military art, and how it subsequently evolved. In that sense they are historical in nature. They also ponder where operational art may go in the future. In that sense, they have relevance as a new beginning. If, as I believe, the nature and tenets of operational art have changed in dialectical fashion, then what has been will provide necessary context for what will be. There is no doubt that the process which these volumes describe will continue in the future. If we hope to understand what the future may offer, it is critical to reflect on the roots and context of that process as it has occurred in the past.

Translator's Note

Languages are subtle means of communications unique to the people who speak them. Words possess multiple meanings depending on the context in which they are used, and those meanings frequently change over time. Often words have no precise counterpart in another language – they simply cannot be directly translated. In both of these respects, Russian is like every other language. Therefore, it is incumbent upon the translator, if he wishes to be accurate, to explain how he has translated those words which have multiple meanings or whose meaning has changed over time. That is the purpose of these notes.

Just as the term "military operation" emerged as a distinct concept in the twentieth century, the terminology used to describe it also evolved. In time a hierarchy of terms emerged to encompass the range of combat based on scope and intensity. Prior to the 1920s this hierarchy consisted of three terms to describe combat at the strategic and tactical levels. War (*voyna*) consisted of the large-scale battle (*bitva*), the engagement (*srazheniye*), and the smaller-scale battle or combat (*boy*). By the late 1920s the operation (*operatsiya*) joined the hierarchy to describe combat at the operational level. Generally, the operation was conducted by *fronts* and armies, as operational level entities, but during the Great Patriotic War, operations could be conducted by groups of *fronts* as well. Thus, the operation described combat at both the strategic and operational levels. By this time, the term *bitva* also had strategic meaning being used to describe the major battles at Moscow, Stalingrad and Kursk.

The Russians also employ the generic term *deistviye* to describe combat in more general terms. This term translates as "action," "operation," or "activity." In this volume *deistviye* is translated as "action" when it refers to combat in general and when it describes combat at the tactical level. When used to describe specific combat instances or arenas at the strategic and operational levels it is translated as "operation." Therefore, the Russian *teatr voyennykh deistvii* is translated as "theater of military operations." The term *deyatelnost'* is then translated as "activity."

The Russian term *udar* also challenges the translator. It translates as "blow," "attack," "thrust," or "strike." Likewise, *kontrudar* means "counterblow," and "counterstroke." In this volume *udar* is translated as "blow" or "attack" at the strategic, operational, and tactical levels, while strike refers to actions by aviation and artillery (particularly nuclear in nature). The Russian word *ataka* (attack) is seldom used, and when it is, it invariably refers to tactical level attack. In a defensive sense, we employ here the hierarchy of *kontranastupleniye* (counteroffensive), *kontraudar* (counterstroke), and *kontrataka* (counterattack) to describe actions at the strategic, operational, and tactical levels, respectively. The term *nastupleniye* is routinely translated as "offensive."

Another set of confusing terms are *zona,* meaning "zone," "area," or "belt"; *poloca* meaning "region," "zone," "belt," "strip," or "sector"; and *uchastok* meaning "sector," "area," or "zone." Here based on context, we have translated *zona* as "zone," as in operational and tactical defensive zones. The term *poloca* is translated as "sector" when it refers to a distinct linear portion of a front (for example, 3d Army's offensive or defensive sector), and as "belt" when it refers to territory occupied in depth (for example the first, second, and third defensive belt). *Uchastok* is left simply as "sector," roughly synonymous with *poloca* in a linear sense.

The term *rubezh,* meaning "boundary," "line," or "position," is also given meaning by context. Here we have translated the term as "boundary" when referring to the separation of distinct attacking or defending forces, as "line" when describing the specific definition of a linear objective, and as "position" when referring to the location of a force which has both width and depth.

The Russian word *maskirovka* encompasses a series of concepts, including masking, camouflage, and deception. Its proper translation also depends on context and the adjective used to describe it. Thus, it means deception at the strategic and operational levels and either deception or camouflage when used at the tactical level. Because no single English word embraces the total concept, we have opted to use the Russian term *maskirovka* itself. Similarly, *razvedka,* means "intelligence" or "reconnaissance," depending on context.

Finally, we have elected to translate the Russian *soyedineniye* and *ob"yedineniye* as "formation" and "large formation" respectively. The translation problem here lies in the fact that the former may refer to a formation at the operational, operational-tactical, or tactical level, while the latter may refer to a formation at the strategic, operational-strategic, operational, or operational-tactical level, depending, once again, on the context.

This by no means exhausts the list of words with multiple meanings. The others, however, are less vexing and require no comment.

Introduction

The Soviets (and Russians today) consistently viewed history as a process of dialectical change in nature and society. The discipline of history was a science, which, in their view, "studies the development of human society as a single natural process, regular in all of its great variety and contradictions."[1] This process often produced war, a socio-political phenomenon characterized as a continuation of politics by violent means. Anticipating the possibility of war, nations created armed forces to use as "the chief and decisive means for the achievement of political aims, as well as economic, diplomatic, ideological, and other means of struggle."[2]

Given the importance of war, the Soviets approached its study scientifically and systematically within the framework of what they term "military science," one of many sciences which helped explain the historical process. System informed the development of Soviet military thought as well as military practice. Over time, Soviet military theorists created a hierarchy of concepts and terms associated with a complex range of issues extending from national-level military policy and military doctrine to finite battlefield tactics (see Figure 1). The entire semantic and intellectual hierarchy, beginning with military policy, originated from, reflected, and received official sanction from Communist Party dogma and decision. Although that dogma and the Party which propagated it were discredited in the revolution of 1991, the military conceptual hierarchy will likely endure in the future, whether or not ideology remains discredited.

At the apex of this hierarchy is military policy (voyennaya politika), the military facet of national policy associated with the use or threatened use by states of the military instrument to achieve national objectives. The actual use of the armed forces in war and definition of the nature of war is the purview of military doctrine (voyennaya doktrina), which, in turn, examines two fundamental components: political-social and military-technical. Military doctrine, so defined, has encompassed "scientifically founded views" of military science with official party sanction, in so doing uniting the objective findings of military analysis with perceived objective truths of socialism.[3] In the broadest sense, outside a socialist context, future military doctrine will likely reflect those political realities which condition political, economic, and social development of all states of the former Soviet Union.

Figure 1. System of criteria of basic characteristics of warfare

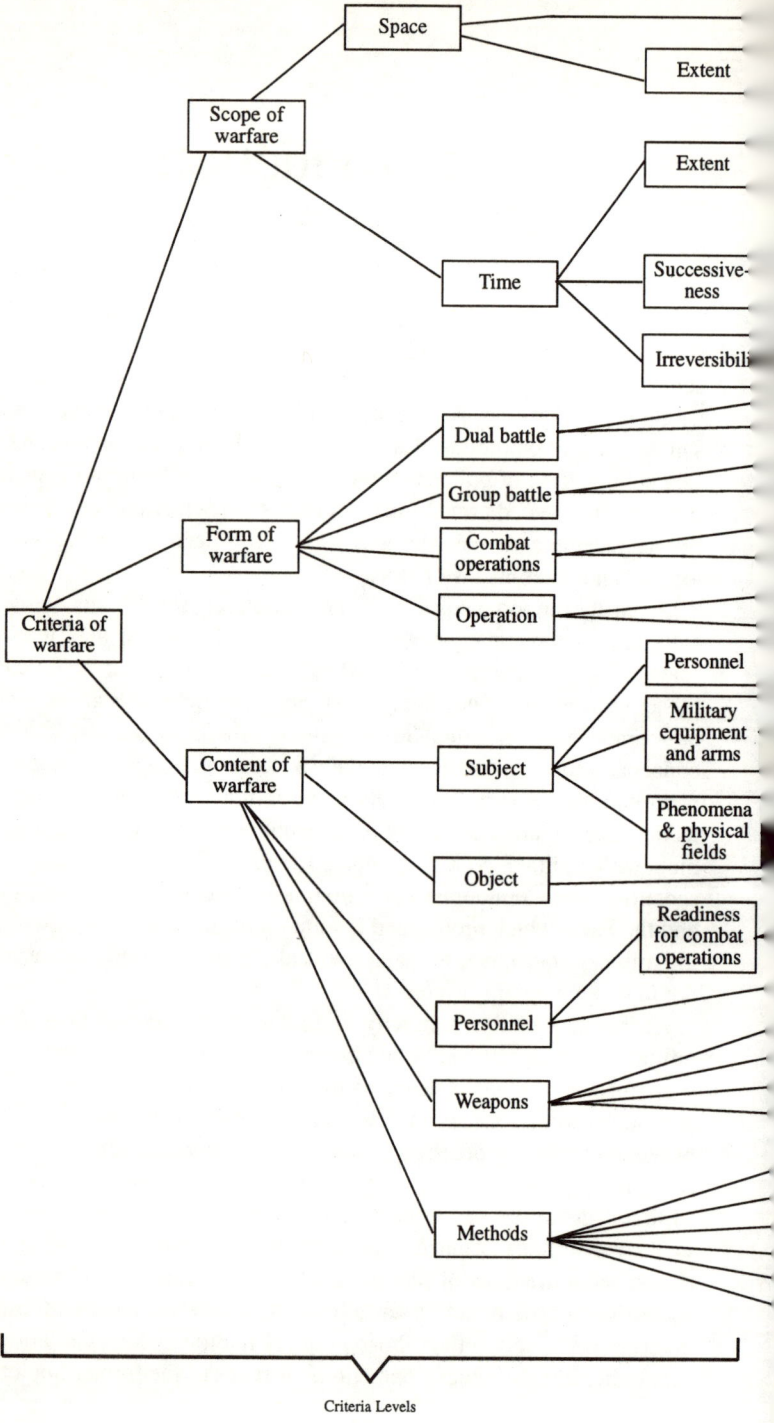

Criteria Levels

Criteria	Indicators
er of spheres	Single sphere / Dual sphere / Multiple spheres / Fraction of unit
lation of range of reconnoitering a target and reach of weapons	Fraction of unit
e of achievement of depth of tactical, operational and strategic zones of responsibility by :aneous operations	
of preparation for initiation of military operations	Minute, hour, day
of "reconnaissance-target designation-engagement" cycle in tactical, operational and gic zones	Second, minute, hour
of "engagement" cycle	Second, minute, hour
ee of simultaneity	Simultaneity / Succession
ee of continuousness	Discreteness / Continuousness
ee of synchronism	Time difference / Synchronism
e for building up "critical mass (threshold value) of losses"	Second, minute, hour
ure of weapon effect	One type / Comprehensive
d of effect	Single / Multiple
ure of interworking of weapons	One type / Combined-arms
d of effect	Single strike (fire) / Group strike (concentrated fire) / Deliberate effect
ure of coordination of forces	Single arm / Combined-arms
nd of effect	Group strike / Massive strike / Deliberate effect
ture of coordination of troops	Independent / Combined-arms
nd of effect	Group strike / Massive strike
le of man in warfare	Degree
otection	Degree
umber of types of military equipment and arms participating in warfare	Units, tens, hundreds
ontribution of each type of military equipment and arms to corresponding potential of force ouping	Fraction of unit
umber of phenomena and physical fields whose properties are realized in process of warfare	Units, tens
ontribution of each phenomenon and physical field to corresponding potential of force grouping	Fraction of unit
Role of destruction of particular potential in achieving success in warfare	Degree
ype of force element	Full strength / Reduced strength
Level of combat effectiveness	Fraction of unit
Nature of table of organization structure of troop units of all levels	Single arm / Combined-arms
Degree of influence of type of weapons of warfare on results of combat operations	Fraction of unit
Density of combat formations	Units, tens/km^2
Degree of mutual influence of weapons and troop units	Fraction of unit
Importance of individual and collective protection	Degree
Level of automation and robotization	Fraction of unit
Level of capability for surprise beginning of battle	Fraction of unit
Degree of mutual penetration of methods of operations	Fraction of unit
Arsenal of methods for beginning combat operations	Units, tens
Degree of integration and simultaneity of effect	Fraction of unit
Degree of systemization and centralization	Fraction of unit

Criteria

Indicators

Within the context of military doctrine, military science (*voyennaya nauka*) is "a system of knowledge concerning the nature and laws of war, the preparation of the armed forces and nation for war, and the means of conducting war."[4] Its basic subject is the investigation of armed conflict in war, and, while the state's political leadership manages war, the military leadership and General Staff play a more significant role in the conduct of armed conflict.

Military art (*voyennoye iskusstvo*) is the main component of military science, and is concerned with "the theory and practice of preparing for and conducting military operations on land, at sea, and in the air."[5] The growing complexity of warfare in the twentieth century dictated the necessity for further refinement of terminology describing the levels and scope of military art. This refinement led the Soviets to subdivide military art into the closely interrelated fields of strategy, operational art, and tactics, each field describing a distinct level of warfare measured against such standards as mission, scale, scope, and duration of military actions. Since, "the state of military art depends on the levels of the development of production and means of armed conflict, as well as the nature of social structures," and reflects "the historical and national characteristics of a country, its geographical conditions, and other factors," the definition and relative importance of its subordinate fields of strategy, operational art, and tactics changed over the years since the formation of the Soviet state and will continue to change in the future.[6] A central feature of Soviet military art is basic, yet evolving principles governing the nature of armed conflict, which have developed in consonance with those influences affecting military art in general.

Since the 1920s Soviet military theorists have considered military strategy (*voyennaya strategiya*) to be the highest level of military art "embracing the theory and practice of preparing the nation and armed forces for war, planning and conducting strategic operations and war as a whole."[7] Military strategy dominates the other components of the art of war, and it defines their tasks and the methods of force operations on an operational and tactical scale. In turn, military strategy relies upon operational art and tactics, taking into account their capabilities, and exploiting their achievements in the performance of strategic (war-winning) tasks.

The second level of military art is the operational level, identified by the Soviets in the 1920s, and used since then for the analysis of armed conflict as an intermediate link between tactics and strategy. Operational art (*operativnoye iskusstvo*) encompasses the theory and practice of preparing for and conducting combined and independent operations (*operatsiya*) by large formations of the armed forces. "Stemming from strategic requirements, operational art determines methods of preparing for and conducting operations to achieve strategic goals." In its turn, operational art "establishes the tasks and direction for the development of tactics."[8]

Tactics (*taktika*), as the lowest level of military art, studies problems relating to battle (*srazheniye*) and combat (*boy*), the basic building blocks of operations. Tactics "investigates the rules, nature, and contents of battle and works out the means of preparing for and conducting battle."⁹ Tactics is dialectically interrelated with operational art and military strategy. Strategy determines the nature and methods of conducting future war and the place of combat in warfare, while operational art determines the specific tasks tactics must address. Conversely, tactics influences operational art and military strategy.

This well-articulated system for the study of war emerged in the 1920s and has persisted for the ensuing 70 years. In that time the basic relationships within the system between the levels of war have not changed. However, the scope and importance of each level has varied according to political and military circumstances, and, most importantly, to technological changes in the implements of war. Moreover, definitions of operational art and retrospective analysis of operational art in past periods of history have been altered to accord with contemporary and future circumstances. This constant process of analysis and redefinition of the past both reflects and conditions contemporary interpretations of operational art and paves the way for definition of operational art in the future. Today, midst a period of uncertainty regarding the future nature of operational art, it is particularly important to maintain perspective on what operational art has been, is, and may be in the future.

This two-volume work captures, in the words of Soviet military theorists themselves, the process by which operational art was created and has evolved during both peacetime and wartime. It contains works or selections from works by those who formulated the basic concepts of operational art (such as Svechin, Varfolomeyev, and Isserson), as well as those who reflected on the earlier evolution of operational art and pondered how it would evolve in the future (such as Zakharov, Cherednichenko, and Savushkin). As such, it contains the thoughts of both creators and interpreters, and, from the varied interpretations, the reader can track a broader process of change in Soviet military thought.

Although the work is arranged in two volumes, primarily for publishing convenience, each volume represents a unity unto itself. Volume I details the creation and evolution of operational art from its inception in the 1920s through the turbulent prewar, wartime, and Stalinist postwar years. It ends in the early 1960s when technological changes associated with the advent of nuclear weaponry (a first postwar technological revolution) caused a virtual revolution in military affairs and prompted Soviet theorists to question the very basis and importance of operational art.

Volume II traces the rebirth of operational art in the late 1960s and the methods by which the Soviets attempted to accommodate operational theory to the realities of a nuclear age. It then reflects on how operational art evolved in the face of a second technological revolution, which produced new generations of high-precision weaponry and threatened to alter again the face of combat. Finally, Volume II addresses the future by relating how Soviet and Russian military theorists have altered operational art to match the realities of the stormy political and economic changes which have wracked the Soviet Union and Russia in the 1990s.

The time frames embraced by each chapter reflect the Soviets' own interpretation regarding the logical periodization in the development of military theory and practice. These periods have withstood the test of time and have been embraced by most theorists. Naturally, the most recent periods are subject to the most discussion and are most prone to reinterpretation.

The editor's and translator's intent is to permit the words of the Soviet military theorists and analysts to speak for themselves. Therefore, there is little or no editorial comment within each chapter or each selection. The short introductions which precede each chapter simply identify the military and political trends which provided context for the period, highlight points of interest or controversy which characterized each period, and, where required, identify significant facts regarding each author. Unless otherwise indicated, all end notes are taken from the original texts.

In essence, these volumes provide an organic, comprehensive view regarding how Soviet operational art has evolved midst the complexities of the twentieth century. While this work attempts to capture the past and chart how operational art has reached its present state, most importantly it strives to capture the essential process by which change has occurred. It is an understanding of that process by which we can receive hints as to what the future may hold for operational art, and for warfare in general.

NOTES

1. "Istoriya" [History], *Sovetskaya istoricheskaya entsiklopediya* [Soviet historical encyclopedia], Vol. 6 (Moscow: Izdatel'stvo "Sovetskaya Entsiklopediya," 1965), pp. 578–90.
2. D. A. Volkogonov and S. A. Tiushkovich, "Voyna" [War], *Sovetskaya voyennaya entsiklopediya* [Soviet military encyclopedia, hereafter cited as *SVE* with appropriate date, volume and page], Vol. 2 (Moscow: Voyenizdat, 1976), p. 301.
3. *Slovar' osnovnykh voyennykh terminov* [Dictionary of basic military terms] (Moscow: Voyenizdat, 1965), translated and published by U.S. Air Force, 1977, No. 37. See also "Doktrina voyennaya" [Military doctrine], *SVE*, 1976, Vol. 3, pp. 225–9.
4. A. A. Grechko, "Voyennaya nauka" [Military science], *SVE*, 1976, Vol. 2, pp. 183–4.
5. S. P. Ivanov and A. I. Evseyev, "Voyennoye iskusstvo" [Military art], *SVE*, 1976, Vol. 2, p. 211.
6. "Voyennoye iskusstvo" [Military art], *Voyennyy entsikopedicheskiy slovar'* [Military encyclopedic dictionary] (Moscow: Voyenizdat, 1983).
7. N. V. Ogarkov, "Voyennaya strategiya" [Military strategy], *SVE*, 1979, Vol. 7, p. 555.
8. V. G. Kulakov, "Operativnoye iskusstvo" [Operational art], *SVE*, 1978, Vol. 6, p. 53.
9. I. G. Borets, "Taktika" [Tactics], *SVE*, 1979, Vol. 7, pp. 628–34.

CHAPTER ONE

The Formative Years, 1927–40

INTRODUCTION

Operational art emerged slowly as a distinct category of military art in the twentieth century. The changing nature of war and its increasing complexity rendered traditional definitions of strategy and tactics less relevant to contemporary and future war. As understood by nineteenth century military theorists, war, as a series of battles (or large single engagements) was the object of study for strategy, and battle was the object of study for tactics. Successful battle, which destroyed or incapacitated an enemy's forces, permitted successful achievement of strategic war aims.

Forces unleashed by the political, social, and economic turmoil of the French Revolution and the Age of Napoleon altered the nature of war. Emerging multiple mass armies, economic mobilization of the state for war, and less limited wartime objectives (often involving the outright destruction of opposing political, economic, and social systems) complicated the traditional framework for analyzing and studying war. Technological innovations of the nineteenth and early twentieth centuries facilitated mobilization and employment of ever larger armies and application of increased firepower on the battlefield. This, combined with a "democratization of war" and emergence of mass armies, produced the carnage of mid- and late-nineteenth-century and early twentieth-century wars. Nineteenth-century military theorists recognized and wrestled with these changes. Clausewitz surfaced such new concepts as "absolute war" and "moral elements of war." Jomini attempted to capture war's increased complexity by describing a new realm of "grand tactics." Military operations matured to a grander scale and took the form of a series of consecutive and mutually related battles fought over a more protracted period of time. Nonetheless, military leaders (like Schlieffen) still planned for and sought to conduct the single battle of annihilation designed to produce decisive strategic results. Single battles of annihilation, however, failed to produce strategic results, for the destruction of single armies no longer ensured war termination. While some commanders learned this hard fact in the midst of war (Grant), it took the appalling human and materiel losses of the World Wars to bring this fact home to most European military theorists.

The Soviets claim credit for having been the first nation to recognize the changing nature of war and the first to adjust their military art to meet the new realities:

> To its credit, Soviet military theoretical thought, having first succeeded in seeing these tendencies in the development of military affairs, correctly perceived and revealed the new component of military art – operational art.[1]

Operational art, as a distinct field of study, emerged in the 1920s and evolved throughout the 1920s and 1930s as Soviet military theorists pondered the nature of modern war and solutions to the dilemmas of the World War, the most important of which was how to restore mobility and maneuver to a stagnant battlefield and to harness those means to the achievement of strategic aims. Within the framework of major doctrinal and strategic debates, Soviet military theorists, many of them ex-Tsarist officers, tapped their repository of military experiences (the Russo-Japanese War, the World War, and the Civil War), thoroughly read and studied past and contemporary Western theorists, and shaped a new understanding of the nature of modern war.

The debate over strategy was most fruitful. Spurred on by traditional military thought, now tinged with ideological ardor, M. Tukhachevsky and others advanced a strategy of annihilation, whereby modern forces equipped with modern weaponry could crush an enemy and quickly achieve strategic ends. Others, including A. Svechin and N. Varfolomeyev, cautioned restraint and adoption of a strategy of attrition to cope with and better equip the state (especially a technologically backward one) to survive the appalling destructiveness of modern war. Although this debate is beyond the scope of this volume, it was within its context that operational art emerged from the pens of Svechin, Varfolomeyev, and others from both contending strategic schools.

Operational art, as a new and more sophisticated realm, embraced new concepts of war at the operational level, which themselves matured throughout the 1930s. The theory of successive operations, a focal point of analysis by both strategic schools in the 1920s, matured in the 1930s into the twin concepts of "deep battle" (*glubokiy boy*) and "the deep operation" (*glubokaya operatisiya*), concepts which remained "ideals" of Soviet operational art for the ensuing 60 years.

The renaissance in Soviet military thought, which gave birth to the field of operational art and the concepts of "deep battle" and "the deep operation," continued until 1937. The persistence and originality of these ideas was remarkable, given the political repression which swept across the Soviet Union in the 1930s. In 1937, however, this repression struck the military in the form of the purges, which crushed originality of thought and claimed the lives of many of the Soviet Union's most imaginative military theorists. The purges accentuated an already existing truth in Soviet (and perhaps Russian) development – the tendency for practice and reality to lag significantly, and often disastrously, behind theory. For while operational art emerged as a vibrant new field of military study, most of the operational concepts associated with it were stillborn or only partially developed. The Red Army would discover this truth and suffer mightily as a result of it during the opening months of war in 1941.

The selections which follow reflect accurately the scope, promise, and inherent limitations of Soviet military thought in the interwar years. Aleksandr Svechin was an ex-Tsarist general staff officer and preeminent military thinker whose thought drew heavily on European (and Russian) military intellectual traditions. His perceptive study of (and participation in) the Russo-Japanese War and the World and Civil Wars uniquely equipped him to emerge as a premier strategist and virtual creator of the field of operational art. Having joined the Red Army in March 1918, he soon became Chief of the All Russian Main Staff. After the First World War he joined the faculties of the Frunze and General Staff Academies, where he was professor of staff service, strategy, and military art. His important works included *Strategiya* [Strategy] (1923 and 1927), in which he provides the first and clearest definition of operational art; *Strategiya v trudakh voyennykh klassikov* [Strategy in works of military classics] (1927); *Klauzevits* [Clausewitz] (1935); and *Strategiya XX veka na pervom etape* [Strategy of the Twentieth Century in its first stage] (1937). Svechin became a victim of the purges after 1937. The following excerpt from his book *Strategy* provides one of the most succinct definitions of operational art and an unsurpassed explanation of the context in which operational art was born and would evolve.

N. Varfolomeyev, also an ex-Tsarist officer, served in the Red Army from 1918 as chief of an army staff and deputy *front* chief of staff, and later as co-worker with Svechin in the Frunze Academy's Department of Strategy. He shared many of Svechin's strategic and operational views, and was an active writer of military theoretical books, including *Udarnaya armiya* [The shock army], and articles in the military journal *Voyna i revolyutsiya* [War and revolution]. Varfolomeyev focused on German Army operations in 1914 and, in particular, in 1918, and his work provided the basis for the emerging Soviet concept of successive operations. In this selection, Varfolomeyev explains how and why operational art evolved as a distinct field of military study from the strategy curriculum of the Frunze Academy.

Finally, G. S. Isserson was a survivor, one of the few theorists of operational art and the deep operation to survive the purges and was alive in the 1970s, when his purged comrades were rehabilitated and their ideas restored to their former state of grace. Isserson was a prestigious theorist and prolific writer, who produced several major books, including *Evolyutsiya operativ-nogo iskusstva* [The evolution of operational art], published in 1932 and 1937; *Novye formy bor'by* [New forms of struggle], published in 1940; and *Osnovy oboronitel'noy operatsii* [The basis of the defensive operation], published in 1938. He was Chief of the Operations Department of the Frunze Academy, and later, Chief of the Operations Department of the General Staff Academy. Why he was able to write advanced and visionary works as he did and survive in the process is still a mystery. But survive he did. As a survivor, in the 1970s he wrote several retrospective articles critiquing the work of Soviet military theorists of the 1930s and exposing the dearth of imaginative work done after 1937. In these selections, Isserson explains the essence of the operational level and the requirements for operational success in future war, namely the capability for conducting deep battle and the deep operation.

The three theorists whose works appear in this chapter display both the imaginativeness and the futility of Soviet operational theory in the interwar years. Their descendants today have not forgotten the lesson of what occurs when political folly renders irrelevant imaginative military thought.

NOTE

1. V.G. Kulakov, "Operativnoye iskusstvo" [Operational art], *SVE*, 1978, Vol. 6, p. 55.

Strategy and Operational Art

A. A. SVECHIN[1]

Operational Art. Tactical creativity, in its turn, is regulated by operational art. Combat actions are not self-contained, but rather the basic material from which an operation is assembled. Only in very rare instances can one count on achieving the ultimate aim of military operations by means of a single procedure. Normally, this path to an ultimate aim is broken up into a series of operations; the latter are separated in time, more or less, by considerable pauses, are composed of various sectors of the territory in a theater of war, and are quite sharply differentiated from one another by the difference in their intermediate aims, for the achievement of which troop efforts are temporarily being directed. We call an operation that act of war in the course of which troop efforts are directed, without any interruption, to a specific region in a theater of military operations to achieve a specific intermediate aim. An operation is a conglomerate of quite different actions: compilation of a plan of operation, material preparation, concentration of forces at the staging area, preparation of defensive structures, completion of marches, and conduct of battles resulting, either by means of an immediate envelopment or a preliminary penetration, in encirclement and destruction of hostile units and driving back other units, and in winning or holding a specific line or geographic region. The material of operational art is tactics and administration; success in developing an operation depends on both force resolution of individual tactical problems, and on forces being supplied with all materiel necessary to conduct the operation continuously until the operation's aim is achieved. Proceeding from the operational aim, operational art advances an entire series of tactical problems and assigns a number of missions for rear area activity. It cannot indiscriminately use any tactical means. Depending on available materiel, time which can be allocated for resolving various tactical problems, forces which can be deployed for battle on a specific front, and, finally, the nature of the operation itself, operational art dictates to tactics the basic line of its conduct. We cannot acknowledge the complete dominance of objectively existing battlefield conditions over our will. Combat actions are only a part of a higher whole which is represented by the operation, and the nature of our combat actions must be subordinated to the nature of the planned operation. Nivelle[2] in April 1917 and Ludendorff[3] in March

1918, deciding to penetrate the Western Front to destroy the enemy's positional front, attempted to change most sharply the tactics of their forces in accordance with the nature of the planned operation.

Strategy as Art. Victory in a separate operation is not, however, the final aim being pursued when conducting combat actions. The Germans were victorious in many World War operations, but they lost the final one and, hence, the entire war. Ludendorff, who demonstrated outstanding achievements in operational art, was not able to combine several of his operational successes so as to achieve even the slightest positive results in concluding a peace for Germany; in the final analysis, all his successes were of no service to Germany.

Strategy is the art of combining preparation for war and a grouping of operations to achieve the aim put forth by the war for the armed forces. Strategy resolves issues associated with the use of both the armed forces and all of a country's resources to achieve the ultimate military aim. If operational art must take into account *front* rear area capabilities, then the strategist must take into account the state's entire rear area, his own and that of the enemy, with all its political and economic potentials. The strategist will be successful if he has correctly assessed the nature of the war from various economic, social, geographic, administrative and technical data.

Strategy cannot be indifferent to operational art. The nature of war, with which the strategist conforms, must not remain a concept isolated and separated from military activities. The strategist must subordinate actual forms of operations which we undertake, their scope and intensity, their aims, and their consequence and their relative significance to his understanding of the possible nature of war. It is also necessary for the strategist to dictate the fundamental line of conduct of operational art and, in case the primary operation has extraordinary significance, even to concentrate its direct guidance in his own hands.

But, similar to the tactician and operational art specialist, the strategist also is not completely independent in his field. Just as tactics is a continuation of operational art and operational art is a continuation of strategy, so strategy is a continuation, a part of politics. War is not a self-contained phenomenon, but only a superstructure over the peaceful life of nations. War is undertaken for specific political aims, and its main features are determined, as we will see below, by politics. A special phase of our research is devoted to the interrelationship between politics and strategy which emerges from this.

We very often encounter such terms as strategy of the air fleet, naval strategy, strategy of colonial war, etc. Such terminology is evidently based on a misunderstanding. We can speak only of naval operational art, inasmuch as the armed forces at sea receive an independent operational aim. We can say the same about the air fleet with even greater reservations: in view of the close association between air force, army ground, and naval actions, only independent bombing operations can be the subject of air fleet operational art. However, inasmuch as such actions do not yet have independent significance and are one, albeit rather essential, component of the overall operation, we should view bombing actions just like reconnaissance and air fleet combat actions, that is, only as part of overall operational art. One cannot speak of strategy here, since it would be a misuse of the term. In just the same way there can be no strategy of colonial war: here one can only speak of features of strategic art in the struggle of imperialist states against an unequal, technically and culturally backward enemy in a situation of a colonial theater of war.

Strategy as a Theory of Art. Strategy as practical art, which represents a most important part of a commander's activity, has existed since prehistoric times, when human society began to wage wars. But the development of a theory of strategy began only 150 years ago, simultaneously with a scientific approach to the development of political economy. The Englishman Lloyd,[4] a contemporary of Adam Smith,[5] both of whom received a similar education, served in the Austrian, Prussian, and Russian armies. On the basis of the experience of the Seven Years' War, Lloyd began working on problems which had distinctly arisen from the limits of the conventional tactical outlook of military men.[6] His works opened a new period of development in military thought, which was already providing a number of profound research works on strategy, characterized, however, either by their incompleteness or by their intellectual one-sidedness. Considerable time and attention were spent on the question of whether strategy was a science or a theory of art. In its essential features, the answer depended on the scale of demands on science which characterize our conceptions about it. Clausewitz, Willisen,[7] and Blume,[8] who viewed strategy as art, proceeded from the requirement of apodictic (incontestable) precision for "science proper" as claimed by Kant.[9] The conclusions of military theory do not offer indisputable precision. But Kant attached the name of science to any systematic theory which embraced a particular field whose knowledge is regulated according to certain fundamentals and principles. Such theories were a kind of second-class science. In order to include strategy among them, many prominent strategic writers focused particular attention on confirming the presence of eternal, unshakable strategic principles upon which they structured their works. At present, our views on science have become considerably broader. We tend to understand science as any system of knowledge which facilitates our understanding of life and practical experience. The theory of all military art, including strategy, undoubtedly falls within such a broad definition of science . . .

FORMS OF CONDUCTING MILITARY ACTIONS

Initial Position. We reduce the entire essence of the strategic art of command in military operations to an understanding of the logic of a grouping of operations structured to achieve the aims of the war.

Military operations can take various forms: annihilation and attrition, defense and offense, maneuver and static. Each of these forms substantively affects the strategic line of conduct. Therefore, we begin our exposition with the study of these forms. Later we will acquaint ourselves with the major influence they have on the form of strategic action. Then we will briefly examine what modern operations with limited aims present, in the grouping of which strategic actions are included. Finally we will set about examining issues which are part of the concept of the strategic line of conduct itself.

Annihilation. Speaking about the war's political aim, we concluded that the political leadership, after attentive discussion with strategists, has the duty to orient an armed front's action toward either annihilation or attrition. The contradiction between these forms is much deeper, more important, and fraught with more substantive consequences than the contradiction between offense and defense.

The mission of strategy is substantially simplified if we or the enemy attempt to bring the war to an end by means of an annihilating blow, as exemplified by Napoleon and Moltke. Works on strategy which have in mind exclusively a strategy of annihilation were treated, in essence, in operational art tracts, and G. A. Leer was completely correct in placing a second title, "Taktika teatra voyennykh deystviy" [Tactics in a theater of military operations] under the title "Strategiya" [Strategy] on the title page of his works.[10] The predilection of strategists from the old school for analysis of Napoleonic campaigns was natural: in these an entire campaign was often reduced to only a single operation in the main theater; strategic problems presented no difficulties and consisted only of a definition of the main theater; the grouping of forces between the main and secondary theaters was done according to the principle of a decisive preference of interests of the main theater;[11] assignment of an aim for a single operation in the main theater cannot raise doubts, since in the strategy of annihilation this is reduced to the destruction of personnel deployed by the enemy in the theater. Thus, in the majority of instances the study of Napoleonic campaigns was reduced to a study of operational and not strategic art. It is natural that Jomini considered the issue of strategy simpler than that of tactics.[12] In no way does it follow from what has been said that we do not acknowledge Napoleon for strategic greatness; however, in the face of procedures for waging war at that time, it was immersed with politics: we can examine the wars of 1805, 1806, 1807, and 1809 in a single overall perspective, as separate gigantic operations against enemies brought forth by Britain on the Continent, and what will strike us is the correct assignment of an aim for each war, the correct moment for the commencement of military operations, and the extremely skillful conclusion of each campaign at the necessary moment. Undoubtedly, even during the Napoleonic era annihilating operations did not always lead to a finale (for example, in the wars of 1796–97, 1812, 1813), and in such cases Napoleon had to work on strategic problems. However, Napoleon's military historians today are still historians of his separate operations, and only political history has somewhat opened for us a perspective for embracing his strategic art.

Three fundamental elements of an operation – force, time, and expanse – are always combined in the strategy of annihilation in such a way that gaining time and space is a means, while the defeat of the bulk of a hostile army is the aim. Everything is subordinated to the interests of the general operation, and in the latter everything depends on a decisive point. This decisive point for the strategy of annihilation is somewhat like a compass needle, which determines all maneuvering. There is only one pure line of annihilation; there exists only one correct decision; in essence, the military commander is deprived of choice, since his duty is to understand the decision dictated to him by circumstances. The notion of annihilation compels us to recognize all secondary interests and trends, and all geographic objectives as insignificant. Pauses in the development of military operations contradict the notion of annihilation. If we see such a pause, lasting six weeks, between the battles at Aspern and Wagram, then this was the result of thoughtlessness on the part of Napoleon in preparing the first crossing of the Danube, and subsequent failure. Unity of goal, time, place, and action characterizes the strategy of annihilation. Its models are, in reality, classical in style, simplicity, and harmony. Theorists of annihilation chuckle at the fencing of seventeenth century strategy. In reality, in comparison with the game of strategic pricks and defenses of Turenne, the blows of Napoleon and Moltke are reminiscent of the shafts which with one blow smash a skull.

The strategy of annihilation requires yet another prerequisite: extraordinary victory. A geographic point can be the objective of an annihilating offensive only when enemy personnel have become phantoms. Until then, it must aim for the complete disorganization of enemy personnel, their complete destruction, the splintering of communications between fragments which remain intact, and the seizure of the most important lines of communication (most important for the armed forces, and not for the government as a whole).

A campaign of annihilation places attacking armies under such disadvantageous material conditions, so weakens them for the benefit of protecting the flanks and rear, and requires such efforts to supply these armies, that protecting oneself from ultimate failure is possible only by winning a number of outstanding operational victories. Hundreds of thousands of prisoners, destruction of entire armies to a man, and the capture of thousands of cannons, depots, and transports are necessary for successful annihilation. Only such successes can avert complete inequality in the final reckoning. There were no such victories in Galicia, nor in the "border engagements," nor in the Red Army offensive in 1920. Everywhere we dealt with ordinary victories, with driving the enemy back and inflicting somewhat greater losses than the attacker had. This was completely inadequate.

The necessity of an extraordinary victory in annihilation presents special requirements in selecting the form of operation. The enemy's main mass must be encircled or pressed to the sea or to a neutral border. Of course, the assignment of such an aim is associated with risk. If available means do not at all correspond to such an assignment, then it is necessary, in general, to reject annihilation . . .

An annihilating offensive under complex conditions is a series of successive operations which, however, have such close internal ties that they fuse into one gigantic operation. The initial position for the following operation emerges directly from the aim achieved in the operation which has just ended.

Currently we associate the strategy of annihilation with a successive series of operations having a constant direction, the series of aims of which has one direct logical line . . .

The significance which is given to the general operation for destroying an enemy in the strategy of annihilation seriously narrows the perspective of strategic thinking. The day after completing an operation we will stand face to face with completely new circumstances; extraordinary events in an operation radically change the situation and necessitate a complete reassessment. With the strategy of annihilation, which attaches such singular and exclusive significance to the result of a combat encounter with the enemy, the situation attains the nature of a kaleidoscopic spectacle: one flick of a decisive operation and a completely new, unexpected picture is created which was impossible to foresee. In the strategy of annihilation, tomorrow's operation is cloaked in a dense shroud of twilight. Only if he has an enormous superiority in forces, as did Napoleon in 1806 or Moltke in 1870, can the strategist of annihilation avoid losing sight of the ultimate aim by orienting himself on the "decisive point" by means of his compass needle. In general, the "decisive point" of an operation exercises almost complete sway in the strategy of annihilation, and any disruption of its dictates can be viewed as a dangerous deviation or "inclination."

Weighty circumstances which make annihilation difficult are advanced by contemporaneity. The first of these is the absence of long range modern operations, which compels a return to the "five transition" system, about which we will speak in the next chapter. It is necessary to split the operation into parts, temporarily halting the advance of a *front* to repair railroads in the rear. These pauses contribute to turning the fight into a positional one. The second circumstance is that in our time the beginning of a war is not the culminating point of strategic intensity. Military and economic mobilization advance the second and third echelons of mobilized and outfitted personnel. In the face of the armies improvised by Gambetta, Moltke the Elder dealt with the second echelon of quite unprepared French mobilization in 1870.[13] The standing French armies were destroyed in one month, and he had to "mess about" with the second echelon for four months. It seems to us that this experience also forms the basis of Moltke's views on Germany's future war on two fronts, as well as on the attrition struggle. The Marango Operation alone (1800) gave Napoleon all of Italy, while the Jena Operation (1806) made it possible to eliminate all of Prussia to the Vistula. Under our conditions Napoleon would have to conduct successive operations with increasing difficulty against new forces amassed by the state.

The Advisability of an Operation. The growth of the significance of a general operation in the strategy of annihilation leads to an operation being no longer described as one of the means of conducting war, but rather itself eclipsing the ultimate military aim and acquiring self-contained significance. The question of the advisability of an operation withdraws to the background. Operational and tactical considerations acquire preponderance. It is all the same where and when the enemy is beaten, only that the blow has an annihilating character. It is important that tactical actions of forces be directed against the line of least resistance. Therefore, from the point of view of the strategy of annihilation, one should not reproach Ludendorff for choosing Amiens, the least important strategic axis at the junction of the French and British armies, for the decisive blow in March 1918. In annihilation, the issue of direction [axis] is secondary in comparison with the scope of the attack. The mistake of the German command was in attempting to reduce risk, maintain a continuous front, and reject a fanciful mixing of its own and enemy forces into one ball of dough, which would have happened if they had advanced, ignoring sectors which continued to be occupied by the enemy; the Germans should have striven to increase enormously the area of the operation, keeping in mind that the units and means of both sides, which had become entangled here, in the final analysis would have been under the authority of the victor. On the contrary, Ludendorff's subsequent offensive attempts in new sectors, associated with new deployments which had a partially demonstrative character, sharply contradicted the strategy of annihilation. This was already the fencing of attrition, fencing which tied down the will of the enemy immeasurably less; and inasmuch as the situation in which Germany found itself in 1918 would have justified an attempt at annihilation, the manifestation of attrition activity was inappropriate.

Nowhere was the necessity of maintaining a sharp line between a strategy of annihilation and a strategy of attrition so telling as in questions concerning the advisability of an operation (formerly, a general engagement). G. A. Leer, all of whose thinking was structured in the spirit of annihilation, made, in our opinion, a serious mistake in logic when he advanced the question of the advisability of an engagement which crowned an operation. Of course, for Napoleon this issue and these doubts did not exist, since a general engagement was the ideal, the desired aim toward which he strove. And Leer, to support his concepts, which violated the style of annihilation, naturally had to turn to the ideas of attrition theorists, to the observation by Maurice of Saxony that engagements "are the everyday refuge of illiteracy";[14] to the observation by Frederick the Great that "battle is a means of feeble-minded generals," and that one should become engaged in battle only when the expected gain is higher than what is being risked.[15] Leer even cited a speech of the Duke of Alba,[16] a mid-sixteenth century military commander, whose purpose was to cool the dust of his assistants, who were demanding battle against the French, addressing their discretion and their composure: one cannot put on the map an entire kingdom against only one French general's embroidered coat; he falls back so, and in battle risks losing only his carts. Victory can be bloodless; an engagement should be fought: (1) to disarm an important fortress; (2) if reinforcements are proceeding to the enemy, which could give him a decisive superiority; (3) at the beginning of the war to produce a political impression on allies and secret enemies; (4) when the enemy is completely dispirited and can no longer offer resistance; (5) when we are so restricted that it remains only to die or to be victorious.

The arguments of Maurice, Frederick, and Alba are very curious, but do not at all square with the strategy of annihilation. Strategic theory can give meaning to the question of the advisability of an operation only after having established a dialectical difference between annihilation and attrition.[17]

Attrition. The term "attrition" very poorly expresses the variety of nuances of the different strategic methods lying beyond the bounds of annihilation. The "potato war" (the war for Bavarian succession) and the campaign of 1757 (the second year of the Seven Years' War), both creative products of Frederick the Great, relate to the category of attrition, since they do not include decisive movement to an ultimate aim; there was no notion in them of a campaign against Vienna. However, one campaign proceeded in a completely bloodless maneuver, and another numbered four general engagements – Prague, Kolin, Rossbach, and Leuthen. The variety manifested is characteristic for attrition.[18] One type of attrition very closely verges on the strategy of annihilation, which makes it possible for the Prussian General Staff, inconsistently, in truth, to even state that Frederick the Great anticipated Napoleon's annihilation techniques; the opposing view may consist of the formula "neither peace nor war" – a simple lack of recognition, a refusal to subscribe to peace, a single threat of the possibility of actions on an armed front. Between these two extreme views is a whole gamut of intermediate ones. The strategy of annihilation is isolated, and each time allows for only one correct decision. However, in the strategy of annihilation the intensity of the conflict on an armed front can be varied, and, correspondingly, each degree of intensity has its own correct decision. It is possible to clarify the degree of intensity required by a given situation only by means of very attentive study of economic and political preconditions. Wide bounds are open to political action; strategy must exhibit great flexibility.

The strategy of attrition in no way negates, in principle, the destruction of enemy personnel as the aim of an operation. However, it sees this only as a part of an armed front's task, and not the entire mission. When rejecting annihilation, the significance of geographic objectives and secondary operations increases multifold. The distribution of forces between main and secondary operations is a very complex strategic problem; the "decisive point" – the compass needle which each time makes it possible easily to base a decision for annihilation – is absent in the strategy of attrition.[19] It is necessary to think through thoroughly not only the orientation of efforts, but also their "dosage."

French strategic thought studied these issues very poorly during the World War. It remained deluded that even after the wreck of the Schlieffen Plan the French front was still the major and decisive one, and that everything had to be oriented on it, despite the shift of the war into the attrition framework. The French maintained that Germany, as before, was the most important enemy, and it was worth expending efforts only against her. Moreover, if, from the point of view of the strategy of annihilation, Austria-Hungary was a secondary enemy, then, from the point of view of attrition, she was even more important than Germany. If annihilation had to search for an operational line of least resistance to defeat Germany's main personnel forces, then the strategy of attrition had to search for a strategic line of least resistance in the alliance of central powers, and this, after defeats imposed on the Austrians by Russian forces, passed through Austria-Hungary. In 1915, as soon as a shift appeared in the center of gravity of German actions to the Russian front, Britain and France were obliged, to the fullest extent allowed by the development of communications on the Balkan front, to support Serbia; the deployment of an Anglo-French Army numbering half a million on the Danube would have forced Bulgaria to maintain neutrality, driven Romania forward, severed any communications between Germany and Turkey, made it possible for the Italians to storm across the border mountains, relieved the Russian front (which could have been held in Poland), and significantly accelerated the breakdown of Austria-Hungary. The duration of the World War would have been shortened by at least two years . . .

The strategy of attrition, as with the strategy of annihilation, offers a search for material superiority and a struggle for it, but this search is not restricted only to an attempt to deploy superior forces in a decisive sector. It is still necessary to create prerequisites so that a "decisive point" can exist in general. The difficult path of the strategy of attrition, which leads to greater losses than a short, annihilating blow to the heart of the enemy, is generally chosen only when a war cannot be brought to an end by a single procedure alone. Operations in the strategy of attrition are stages for developing material superiority, which in the final analysis would deprive the enemy of prerequisites for successful resistance, rather than immediate stages for the achievement of the ultimate military aim.

In reality, within the framework of the strategy of attrition all operations are characterized, above all, by the fact that they have a limited aim; war unfolds not in the form of a decisive blow, but rather as struggles for positions on the military, political, and economic front from which the delivery of this strike would ultimately be possible. However, in the process of this struggle there occurs a complete reassessment of all values. A main theater in which, after an expenditure of enormous forces and means, the struggle ends in a draw gradually loses its prevailing significance. The decisive point – this war-horse of the strategy of annihilation – turns into a costly but empty trinket. On the contrary, geographic points, personifying political and economic interests, acquire predominant significance. Operational and tactical issues play an increasingly more subordinate and technical role in strategy. Instead of the annihilation logic of Paris–Berlin, the attrition logic of Paris–Salonika–Vienna–Berlin is advanced. On 14 November 1918, the Entente would have occupied a decisive position not on the Lotharingian front, as Foch stated, but on the Danube.

A boxer concentrates his efforts on protecting the lower jaw from a blow, since such a blow can lead to his loss of consciousness and a fall; protection from a decisive blow is the first rule of any fight. The strategy of annihilation, which includes continuous attempts to land a knockout punch on the enemy, ties down enemy movement, and forces him to orient his actions against ours. The limited blows inflicted by the strategy of attrition tie down the enemy to an incomparably lesser degree. Separate operations are not directly connected with the ultimate aim, but are only building blocks which poorly subject the will of the enemy to themselves. Each such block requires a special operational deployment. The enemy is completely capable of pursuing his own aims in this game of operational deployments.[20] Napoleon's "operational line" was a single axis around which the events of the war unfurled; the operational desires of his enemies had to be, on the whole, subordinated to the will of the great annihilator. With the strategy of attrition, lack of coordination is completely possible: in 1915, one could have conceived of such a development of events, under conditions of holding Germany's main forces on the French front, that Ludendorff would have gradually consolidated in the Baltic provinces, while the Russian Army would have captured the outlets from the Carpathians to the Hungarian plain.

In the strategy of annihilation, uniformity of actions is completely unnecessary; if in the first weeks of the World War France became a theater of German annihilation efforts, then the Russians were unarguably obliged to commence, regardless of any considerations, an invasion of East Prussia, which relieved France promptly. However, if the idea of annihilation fades, then such a collateral subordination of operations can be allowed only very conditionally. The pursuit of limited aims makes it possible for each operational building block to maintain a certain degree of independence. In order to make it difficult for the enemy to use his reserves consistently, periods of activity in various theaters should, in general, coincide. But there was no necessity for tying our March offensive in 1916 at Lake Naroch to the defense of Verdun,[21] or, since the French were rather successfully continuing the Somme operation, which reckoned on attrition, for continuing the Brusilov operation. Instead of collateral subordination, with attrition it is necessary that each operation, in and of itself, leads to an actual operational achievement.

Under attrition conditions, the general operation does not form an impenetrable curtain which cuts off our thinking from the subsequent development of the war. Echelons of military and economic mobilization enter completely into the strategy of attrition and are alien in spirit to the strategy of annihilation. Attrition is guided more by distant goals than by preparation for an immediate large operation. The conduct itself of an operation, which under attrition conditions cannot produce decisive results, often had to be preconceived in the case of attrition, that is, its guidance had to be subordinated and adapted subsequently to resolved missions. Under attrition conditions, strategic problems, to a considerable degree, were complicated as a result of a growth in width and depth. It is not sufficient for the strategist to assess correctly the most important direction of operations in order to make a correct decision; rather, it is necessary to be aware of the entire panorama of war. An example of a decision emerging from such a panorama is the Kitchener Program of new formations for the British Army, calculated for four years, and Britain's limited assistance to the French during the first years of the war.

In the strategy of annihilation, a reasonable place is held only by operational reserves, that is, those reserves which can, in a decisive moment, hurry to a decisive operational sector. Annihilation, which recognizes the decisive role of a general operation, cannot recognize any strategic reserves whatsoever which do not take part in a decision within the framework of the time and space presented by the operation. However, the strategy of attrition can and should take into account such reserves (the Asian Russian Corps in 1914, militia formations, subsequent mobilization echelons, colonial contingents, a belated allied advance) and adapt one's line of conduct to them.

The strategy of annihilation brings an operation to a close with the achievement of the ultimate war aim. Under attrition conditions, sometimes the situation occurs where the attacking side has achieved its limited military aim, but the war continues, since resolution has not been reached on the political and economic fronts. This was so in the Russo-Japanese War: Japan's ultimate military aim was the destruction of the Russian Pacific Fleet, the capture of Port Arthur (its base), and the expulsion of Russian armies from southern Manchuria. This aim was achieved at the moment the Russian armies were defeated at Manchuria. However, the war continued for another half year. Russia's vital center was beyond the range of Japanese attacks, and Japan had to bide its time until the revolutionary movement in Russia. The last half year of the Eastern War had passed in such circumstances: Sevastopol was cleared of Russians on 9 September 1855, and at that moment the Allies had achieved their ultimate military aim – the destruction of our Black Sea Fleet and its base; yet, the Congress of Paris opened only on 13 February 1856. These periods of war, very meaningful with respect to events on political and economic fronts, are distinguished by a lull on the military front, which is interrupted only by a gesture of despair (Tsusima),[22] or by petty undertakings (the attack of Kinburn in 1855,[23] and the Sakhalin Expedition of 1905).

Strategic Defense and Offense. Every operation is a fundamental combination of defensive and offensive moments. Despite this, we distinguish offensive and defensive operations, depending on whether strategy advances a positive or negative operational aim. The advance of a number of positive aims characterizes a strategic offense, while a number of negative aims characterizes a strategic defense.

We do not agree with the statement that any delay on an armed front necessarily acts to the detriment of the side pursuing positive aims. A political offensive aim can also be associated with a strategic defense; a conflict can be underway on both the economic and political fronts, and if time is working to our advantage, that is, the balance of pluses and minuses unfolds in our interest, then the armed front can gradually strive for an advantageous change in the correlation of forces, even if this means marching in place. If a war has a blockade character, as the Russians blockaded Shamil's Dagestan,[24] or the British blockaded Napoleon's France or Wilhelm's Germany,[25] then an armed front gains much from time working against the enemy. Strategic defense, which unfolds from a number of operations with a negative aim, can, in general, pursue a positive ultimate aim . . .

Pursuit of negative aims, that is, fighting to maintain completely or partially the existing position, requires, in general and on the whole, fewer expenditures of forces and means than pursuit of positive aims, that is, fighting to capture or to advance. To hold what exists is easier than to gain something new. Naturally, the weaker side turns to the defense.

These statements are indisputable, both in politics and in military art, but only preconditioned by a certain stability and defensive capability of both sides in the existing situation. As sea waves grind coastal pebbles against each other, so does historical struggle round off state formations which are amorphous in nature, erase too winding borders, and cultivate the stability necessary for defensive capability . . .

A defensive form of actions is usually associated with certain territorial losses. It attempts to postpone a decision until the last moment. Consequently, for success in defense it is necessary to be able to lose territory so that time can work for our benefit. These conditions are more likely to be observed in a large state, which can more easily bear the temporary loss of several tens, even hundreds of thousands of square kilometers of territory, and which, delaying a decision, acquires the possibility of using a new portion of its resources, spread over enormous expanses. Small states are not independent in a defensive respect, and can exist only inasmuch as there exists hope of assistance from without. Nevertheless, vastness of territory far from guarantees successful defense: a decisive government and a strong internal posture are necessary in order to be able to bear material losses associated with an enemy offensive, and to force time to work for our benefit, and not for the benefit of the enemy. It is necessary that war leadership display sufficient firmness and not squander the combat capability of personnel, necessary for the moment of crisis, to defend various geographic "valuables."

A strategic offensive requires considerable expenditure of forces; it removes us from our base and compels us to allocate large forces for the organization and protection of lines of communications with the base. A precondition of a protracted offensive is a continuous flow of fresh forces. Unavoidable offensive expenditures lead to its development under normal conditions, when there are no forward bases, weakening the attacker. Hence, if the offensive is viewed theoretically as limitless, one must recognize that its successes must reach a higher culmination point of development; then its decline sets in, caused by material weakness. The most skillful strategic offensive leads to a catastrophe if available means are inadequate to achieve fortuitously the ultimate aim, which guarantees us peace.

Because of this offensive property, the attacker must select his ultimate military aim no farther than that line, beyond which, if we were to cross it, our successes would begin to go downhill. When establishing the ultimate political aim of the war, the politician should listen attentively to the advice of the strategist, since the ultimate military aim will also issue specifically from the political aim.

The primary strategic idea of defense also should be built on this offensive characteristic: where is the boundary at which one can place the end to the development of offensive success? This idea is dominant in strategic, operational, and tactical art. The enemy has overrun our forward line and is spread throughout the depth of our combat disposition: in order not to expend forces drop by drop, the tactician must attempt immediately to make himself aware of where and when he can deploy his reserves, stop the enemy, and go over to a counterattack. If the line has not been penetrated, but rather the deployment front placed under a great threat, the same question is basic for operational leadership. If it is necessary to wage a defensive war, then again the idea of the strategist must be, above all, to stop on that line in time and space on which he can count on a turning point for the course of the war, bring about a crisis, and shift from negative to positive goals . . .

An offensive which goes beyond its culmination point very swiftly becomes a gamble, and any further development of it only turns out to be the most complete preparation for the enemy to shift from the pursuit of negative to positive aims, which can acquire the greatest scope . . .

Hence, it is understood how important it is to estimate opportunely the limit beyond which an offensive turns into a gamble and begins to turn into preparation for an enemy counterattack. This is a very broad question, whose decision requires taking into account the enemy's political and economic resistive capacity to failures, the ability he has to maintain the army's combat capability after prolonged defensive operations and retreats, and the increase of forces which ensues as a result of further echelons of military and economic mobilization. In a war of annihilation, both the offensive culmination point and the ultimate defensive line are determined mainly by a spatial line: Napoleon's army perished after having reached Moscow, 2,000 kilometers from the French border. In a war of attrition, this line often shifts into a temporal category: during the fourth year of the war, the combat capability of the central powers' armed forces began to weaken sharply.

The attacker must remember that simple forward movement only weakens him and is a very conditional plus: the distance to the culmination point is reduced, and along the extent of this distance he can reap the harvest of his successes. Each kilometer the German forces advanced after the border engagement on the Marne without achieving noticeable tactical successes was an apparent loss.

Until the moment of crisis, a strategic defense must carefully "dose out" its efforts; on the one hand, it is necessary, if possible, to limit our territorial losses and force the enemy to advance not by simple marches, but rather by executing a number of large operative procedures – regrouping, bringing up hundreds of thousands of pounds of supplies to the front line, and forcing operationally difficult lines; on the other hand, it is necessary to maintain the army's combat capability at a certain level, below which it would generally be necessary to think about only avoiding contact with the enemy; it is necessary to provide oneself with the possibility of an ultimate turning point. To fail to escape without battle and to avoid being carried away by battle – this difficult task is often within the power of only highly qualified armies.

Position and Maneuver. If both sides promote positive operational aims, then extremely mobile operations, often meeting operations, occur. The Civil War of 1918–20, which afforded such opportunities for pursuing positive aims, was also an unusually mobile war. If both sides promote negative operational aims, military operations acquire a positional character. When conducting coalition war, negative aims are usually more widespread, since the egotistical interests of each ally motivate him so that others are granted the honor of attacking the enemy while he himself carefully protects what he has and maintains his forces until the last minute, to ensure that his interests are considered when concluding peace.[26] Therefore, coalition war adopts a positional nature more often than a conflict between two states. France and Britain had already assimilated these simple truths in autumn 1914, while Russia began to consider them only by autumn 1916; therefore, she was in a very disadvantageous position.

While both sides pursue negative aims, a positional lull dominates. Personnel losses and materiel expenditures are reduced on the front, which argues most favorably for successive mobilization echelons. Therefore, if preparation by both sides is quite inadequate, and, in particular, if prepared materiel reserves are inadequate, then one can expect with great probability that the war will assume positional forms . . .

Small states are least capable of positional war. In reality, fronts which they would have to occupy are reduced to a much smaller size than the territory which, using their own resources, must sustain their resistance; in a similar contour of two states, if the front of one is eight times shorter, then the territory will be 64 times less. More than 1,000 square kilometers of smoothly working rear area are necessary to maintain one linear kilometer of a positional front. All these mathematics are very conditional, since economic conditions in a territory have substantial significance. However, there is no doubt that Great China was necessary for the creation of the Great Wall of China, and that it is impossible to armor a ship having the tonnage of a torpedo boat.

The alluring efficacy of withdrawal is very considerable in maneuver war; a strong will and awareness of control are necessary so that forces do not immediately disperse to a region being vacated by the enemy. In a positional struggle, the front of each side positively strives to rely on the enemy's front. Reality somehow does not tolerate empty space between the forward units of each side; an exaggerated assessment of the significance of terrain, arising from losses which are the cost of an advance of several hundred meters, compels fronts to draw together. The mutual illusion of preparing for an offensive lies at the essence of a positional war pursuing a negative aim; therefore, in the majority of cases a positional front is tactically characterized as the staging area for an attack, and not as the most advantageous position for the defense. The best positions are abandoned if there is a possibility of advancing several kilometers. For years forces stand in trenches filled with water, under fire, in low places, sometimes all of two–three kilometers in front of sound, dry, elevated terrain. Positional struggle where equipment is so widely introduced, where control is strictly centralized, and where the war takes on such material forms and is organized, at first glance, by scientific methods, is, in reality, a wide field for elemental phenomena. Judicious command, free from illusion, can master the primordial process and achieve great results: having systematically concentrated its forces in advantageous sectors, it can force the enemy to deploy most improperly on an expanse of hundreds of kilometers.

When maneuver is denied, a reassessment of the significance of various sectors occurs; the geographic value of occupied terrain advances to the forefront. A rich industrial center, an important communications center, or the nearness of a highway valuable for castling require that a sector be occupied more firmly; poor terrain lacking valuable geographic objectives will not be covered as well. However, this difference will not be as significant as in maneuver war; secondary sectors in general acquire their own significance. The most important sector of the positional front in France and Belgium in 1914 came to be La Manche [adjacent to the English Channel], since capturing the northern coast of France would have provided great advantages to the Germans in organizing an underwater blockade of Britain. The front in Lotharingia and the Vosges, which was studied in such detail before the war by the French General Staff, became secondary, since here there were neither lines of communication important for France, nor industrial centers (with the exception of Nancy).

It is easy to be drawn into a positional struggle, even despite one's will, but getting out of it is associated with great difficulties. No one succeeded in this during the World War. If a positional front has limited size, then one can achieve extremely advantageous results by enveloping an open flank. In peacetime the French had already prepared elements for creating a positional front, upon commencement of the World War, on the Franco-German border. The envelopment of this front through Belgium was the basic idea of the Schlieffen Plan. In its invasion of East Prussia, Russia's 10th Army at the beginning of 1915 occupied a positional front, but did not extend its right flank to the Baltic Sea. Because of this, it was possible for Ludendorff to maneuver advantageously into an envelopment of the Russian right flank, which led to an encirclement of the center of Russia's 10th Army in the Augustow Forests. The threat of catastrophe to the entire positional front, which this maneuver threatened from beyond the flank, forced the Russians to extend the positional front to the entire width of the theater of military operations, and to anchor its flanks on reliable obstacles – to the sea or a neutral state capable of ensuring its own armed neutrality.

Such was the essence of the "race to the sea," the operation which followed the Marne in 1914. We do not see in it a pursuit of a positive aim by both sides – the envelopment of the enemy flank – but rather the pursuit of a negative aim – countermaneuver against such a possibility of envelopment. The "race to the sea" forms the base of a strategic defense, but not an offense.

Positive aims, which one begins to pursue after organizing and setting up in the process of positional conflict, can be of two types: either they will seek to develop pressure on the enemy without abandoning the framework of a positional war, after which a positional operation results (Verdun and the Somme in 1916, Flanders in 1917); or they will be directed to break off from a positional war and shift to a maneuver war. With a positional front which crosses the entire theater, the latter can be achieved in three ways: by penetration (attempts in the World War – Brusilov's offensive in 1916, Nivelle's offensive in April 1917); by envelopment, achieved by violating the neutrality of or entering into a coalition with a new ally (Romania in August 1916); or, finally, by withdrawal, whose purpose is to achieve a general shift. The latter method is based on the alluring efficacy of a withdrawal. It is possible to withdraw in some sectors only, in order to create a broken front which neither side would be capable of defending. Some sectors can be quite cleared, and it may be more feasible to gather reserves ready to go over to the offense behind those being held. An enemy advance ought to fulfill the function of preparing such an offensive. Similar proposals arose several times during the World War, but they were not disseminated by significant strategists. Apparently, on rich terrain cut by railroads, such a notion is purely theoretical, a proposition which is not implemented. Withdrawal leads to sacrifices of economic and communications interests, which are too important. However, one cannot help but observe that in the Belorussian–Polish Theater prospects are most favorable for such a maneuver.

In future wars one must take into account that some positional front sectors will be organized from the very beginning, during the period of operational deployment. If the border extends a few hundred kilometers and is based on solid geographical lines, then the emergence of an uninterrupted positional front can be expected already from the beginning of the war. The bulk of materiel required for conducting war and the necessity of waiting for the results of industrial mobilization and subsequent military echelons will in the future, for example, in a Franco-German engagement, make a temporary renunciation of pursuing positive military aims quite possible. In a maneuver war it will hardly be possible to protect our entire Western Theater immediately. Of course, a positional struggle can adopt more moderate forms, for example, those created on the Russian front in winter 1914–15 and permitted rather considerable maneuver in the gaps between positional sectors; positional fronts do not coincide with one another everywhere (for example, there was considerable space for the Prasnysh Quadrille between

Narva and the Prussian border). But it is necessary to prepare for positional war. Under certain conditions it is impossible to avoid the emergence of a positional front. Perhaps it is necessary to prepare for the possibility of shifting to maneuver on a wide scale, if enemy attempts to create a positional front have been overcome . . .

OPERATION WITH A LIMITED GOAL

The Evolution of an Operation. Studying methods of conducting an operation is the task not of strategy, but of operational art. While devoting several pages in our work to a sketch of the operation, we do not intend to fill in a perceptible gap in the theory of operational art. Strategy, which defines its mission in the conduct of military actions as a grouping of operations to achieve an ultimate goal, is not only interested in assigning an operational aim, but also sets forth certain requirements and methods for their achievement. All branches of military art are closely associated with one another: tactics takes the steps from which an operational leap is formed; strategy points out the path.

We understand an operation in military art as the sum of various actions directed toward the achievement of one of the aims advanced by strategy. Several operations joined by time and place form a campaign; the totality of campaigns in the course of an entire year is called a theater campaign.[27] One or several theater campaigns lead to that final situation in which both sides acknowledge the program of violent actions to be exhausted and establish a truce. Operational deployment is not an independent operation, but an essential element of any operation.

Thus, we reject subdividing operations into main and preparatory. Formerly, mobilization was understood as preparatory; however, the latter is not a direct act of conducting military operations, but rather one rear area operational action, and it is improper for us to disseminate such operational terminology. We consider the term "march-maneuver" to be archaic, and are discarding it.

Until the end of the nineteenth century, an operation was clearly divided into two parts: maneuver, the purpose of which was to place our forces in the most advantageous position for the moment of decisive contact; and the engagement itself.

Of course, the customary theories based on the experience of the Napoleonic Wars envision a third phase of operations as well – pursuit. How many fine words have been said in theory about this necessary act of developing success! It is difficult to remain within the logical confines of annihilation, having rejected the idea of pursuit as a colossal broadening of achieved successes. However, from Napoleon up to and including the World War, in military history we do not encounter a single pursuit which veers from a narrow tactical framework. The wars of 1854–56, 1859, 1861–65, 1866, 1870, 1877–78, 1899–1902, 1904–05, and 1914–18 do not provide a single example of pursuit. And since we are striving to use only currently existing concepts, we exclude pursuit from our discussion. Here we encounter a chain of bewilderments arising from the fact that the theory was often based not on reality, but rather on what appeared to be desirable, and in contemporary minds the concept of strategic pursuit almost materialized . . . Pursuit is possible only in an atmosphere of complete collapse of the enemy's state system, his complete political bankruptcy in the final minutes before the elimination of armed resistance. The increased might of the modern state, its enormous resources, new mobilization echelons, railroad maneuver, telegraph – all hinder pursuit today. To gather the harvest on an armed front before the enemy is politically disorganized is possible today only within the limits of the operation itself; pursuit today expresses not a military but a political victory.

In the Napoleonic era, maneuver was sometimes extended over dozens of marches and more (1806). The broad appeal of Napoleonic maneuver led to the French, having created their own terminology for the study of Napoleon's theater campaigns, still calling the operation a "maneuver."

With the appearance of railroads during the Moltke era, maneuver for initial operations began to be partially carried out by railroad, in the form of the initial operational deployment. Both sides deboarded relatively close to one another, and part of the maneuver, which was executed in march formation, was somewhat shortened during the initial operation. Subsequent operations (Sedan) were conducted according to the Napoleonic model.[28]

Currently, every operation is preceded by a special operational deployment, relying to a considerable degree on railroads. Owing to difficulties in separating armies a considerable distance from railroad stations, it is important to execute operational deployment as close as possible to those regions where the operational aims can be achieved.

Thus, in their initial stage all modern operations recall Moltke's initial operations. But in the concluding stage they completely differ from Moltke's operations, since in actual modern actions there are no general engagements or battles – completely concrete phenomena in the historical past; if these terms are still used, then it is only as a convention, an expression stating a preference for the figurativeness of the concept over the precision of its formulation. Today, a general engagement has merged with a significant part of the operation.

A nineteenth century engagement consisted of a series of battles over a short period of time covering a relatively small area, with the adversaries in close contact with one another. An engagement's overall duration was only a little greater than that of a separate battle. Clausewitz considered the engagement, from a strategic point of view, as a point in time and space.

Clausewitz's strategy rested from the moment the cannons began to fire until the end of the engagement, having transferred all leadership to tactics. During an engagement, forces did not change or regroup; there were no replenishments or rest. Except for these forces, only tactical reserves could take part in resolving an engagement. All these preconditions were still operative during the Moltke era; however, beginning with the Russo-Japanese War, conditions began to change.

The front of the encounter began to grow; centers of battles were splintered and scattered a considerable distance from one another. If during the Napoleonic epoch an advance two–three kilometers into the depth of the enemy's combat formation already led to the latter's collapse, currently a depth of even 60–70 kilometers does not always produce such results (Galicia Operation in August 1914, the German offensive in March 1918, etc.). A whole combination of battles in succession, and the completion of several marches with successful battle are required to break enemy resistance. The overall duration of these encounters is measured not in hours, but in weeks. The extent in time of a general encounter has no correlation whatsoever with the duration of a separate tactical encounter, which sometimes exhausts all the energy of the military unit. It is necessary to replace forces, permit them rest, and replenish them with personnel and materiel during the very development of the encounter; there is a possibility of regrouping forces, bringing up new reserves from afar, and supplementing and correcting the initial deployment by means of new railroad maneuver. One blow is splintered into many blows; one combat encounter is separated from another sometimes by entire marches, inasmuch as the modern battle arena has expanded. March movement, battles, rest, offense, defense, reconnaissance, security, supply, replenishment – all these separate actions alternate among one another, comprising the content of a modern operation. Formerly we were able to draw a precise boundary between engagement, rest, and march movements.

Quantity shifts to quality. Formerly an engagement had only a barely noticeable cleft separating it from separate battles. An increase in the extent of an engagement in time and space led to the breakup of the engagement into several pieces connected only in an entire operation.

If formerly an operation was divided into maneuver and engagement, then now we must establish other limits; now there is maneuver partly by rail, partly in the very whirlpool of events in the attempt to group separate battles to achieve the operational aims. Maneuver has been partly withdrawn into operational deployment and partly sandwiched between separate battles.

Operational Defense and Offense. Our pursuit of positive aims in an operation and desire to exploit surprise to achieve them lead us to the deployment of our forces and means; this is receiving wide development. On the contrary, pursuing negative aims forces us to delay the completion of deployment so as to retain the ability to concentrate efforts along axes which turn out, during the course of the operation, to be the most important. In the first case, a grouping draws near to the front; in the second, it is more deeply echeloned. It is not the greater or lesser per cent of offensive or defensive battles which characterize an offensive or defensive operation, but rather forestalling the enemy in deployment (offense) or being late in deployment (defense). The attacker is the first to be fully armed on the fields of the operation. Full deployment requires swift utilization; in the opposite case, the enemy is expected to direct his attacks against the most sensitive points of our grouping (for example, against the flanks). An indecisive, wavering offensive which is halted at critical moments provides the enemy with the most advantageous opportunities . . .

Thus, despite an operation entangling tactical defense and offense most capriciously, we establish the necessity of drawing a most strict line between operational defense and operational offense, and of not mixing together the logic of the one and the other. An offensive posture should not be adopted at a moment when there is no offensive, since this does not meet the elementary requirements of the defense, and for this one may suffer a severe penalty.

From this the conclusion follows that during intervals between operations, as well as at a moment of preparing an operation, it is necessary to adhere to defensive logic and group forces accordingly. Any offensive deployment before the moment an operation is developed should answer defensive needs. The gradual shift from an existing force grouping to the required operational deployment must be thought out in full detail. When we make our decision, we should weigh attentively the possibility of swiftly, covertly, and success-fully executing an operational deployment without being subjected to special risk. Those ideas about covering a deployment not only relate to the initial deployment, but also are applicable in each operational preparatory period.

In order to judge changes in the front's defense capability during the preparation period and to make a rational choice of the moment to begin the operation, a strategist should have at his disposal a chart of the proposed plan for gradual accumulation of forces and materiel in the operational deploy-ment region. It is desirable to express the preparedness of forces and the operational rear in percentages. Such preparatory work was formerly conducted mainly in the initial operational deployment plan; now it is un-deniably necessary to extend all aspects of preparation for this deployment to remaining aspects of the latter as well.

Tactical interpretation of the defense leads us to passivity, to a notion of repelling the enemy on an occupied line. Dynamism of the defense in tactics means going over to offensive actions. It is in no way possible to transfer these tactical concepts of defense and offense to operational art.

An operational offensive forestalls deployment, planned for the delivery of an attack calculated to overcome any resistance on a specific axis, and the implementation of this attack. A late-deploying defense would function least economically, piling up forces in front of the head of the attacking side, or occupying a series of successive lines along the attack axis. Those defensive maneuvers, which expend an armed force piecemeal under conditions for which the enemy has most prepared, are unfortunate. Every offensive has a flank; a grouping of defense forces, its engineer preparation, and a combination of strong and weak sectors; the execution of an envelopment or penetration along specific axes should intensify the issue of offensive flanks; only in rare cases does the attacker succeed in fully covering them with reliable positions. Defensive maneuver should consist predominantly of a flank counterstroke; thus, directed efforts, even if they have not achieved their aim, disadvantageously alter conditions for the development of the enemy offensive: he will have to stop or shift to another undesirable and unprepared axis. Only completely destroying defense forces operating on the flank will make it possible to continue the offensive, since this was intended. Ludendorff answered the threat of a Russian offensive against Silesia with an attack from Torna–Kalisha to Lodz. The Russians, going over to the defense, were able to respond, albeit weakly, with a Warsaw–Lodz (Berezina) attack, which was also a flank attack, and which placed the Germans in a difficult situation.

If conditions temporarily prevent the defense from responding with countermaneuver, then the most economical means of stopping the offensive without exhausting our remaining forces will consist of withdrawals [jumps back] which count on the unwieldiness and massiveness of modern tactical procedures. It is possible to execute such withdrawals on a tactical and operational scale. Tactical preparation for an attack, reconnaissance of our dispositions and approaches, artillery organization, and the approach itself require considerable time. After withdrawing the distance of a half-march, we gain a certain amount of time by forcing the enemy to repeat his tactical preparation from the beginning. But operational preparation to attack a reinforced front requires even more time, making it necessary to develop communications and concentrate combat supplies, measured by the capacity of dozens of trains, in the immediate rear area. Withdrawing by two–three marches, we will force the enemy to repeat his operational preparation, repair damaged roads, and transport along them tens and hundreds of thousands of tons of combat supplies by means of animal-drawn and motor vehicle transport. Of course, operational and tactical withdrawals achieve their aim only if they are carried out before the enemy has successfully completed his material preparation for battle.

Plan of Operation. Considerable force superiority facilitates the compilation of a plan; with such superiority, the details of the plan can come a little later. The plan, which clarifies the operational aim, determines its form, and thinks through the occupation of the staging area, should foresee the stages of its development in a certain perspective, without, however, becoming too fixated on time schedule. This is especially necessary in the compilation of separate operational plans for various services. Judicious rear area organization requires the establishment of several approximate norms concerning time, space, and intensity, and specification of the necessary outfitting of communications routes, quantity of required transports, supply and outfitting of reserves, evacuation of wounded, organization of occupied territory, etc. If the development of an operation requires special technical means (for example, to set up crossings over a large river or to capture permanent fortifications), either special force supplies (for example, packs for column transports which must cross mountains), or the inclusion of a large number of specialists (skiers under conditions of deep snow in the winter, political workers to organize large centers), or special reserves (capture of a large hungry town), then the plan must consider all the requirements beforehand and prepare to satisfy them to the degree possible.

The immediate steps of an operation, before large-scale encounters, can be envisioned much more precisely than its subsequent development. However, it is necessary to refrain from the temptation of going into too great detail for these first preparatory actions. Even the methodology of actions can be recommended only within certain boundaries, since enthusiasm for it delays both the preparation and development of the operation, and makes it difficult to utilize favorable circumstances. Experience attests that too great an involvement in preparatory work usually coincides with a slow tempo of development of actions . . .

The plan should establish the first stage in approaching the operational aim and subdivide the overall mission at this stage into a number of separate missions for the main subunits of the *front* (or army) conducting the operation. In the offense, the plan should clearly note the decisive axes [directions] along which major efforts must be concentrated. In the defense, if all actions do not amount to only gaining time, but include an attempt to bring the conflict to a crisis, then the plan's primary mission precisely amounts to indicating the position where decisive resistance must be rendered to the enemy, and where the plan envisions an advantageous turning point in the development of the overall operation.

The basic issues of the plan for achieving the established operational aim are associated with the necessary form of the operation, and with the occupation of the staging area – the operational deployment of armed forces and materiel, whose achievement includes material preparation of the operation.

Operational Forms. Operational forms – operational encirclement, penetration, envelopment, flank strike – are not selected arbitrarily, but are dictated by the correlation of forces and means, existing groupings, the capacity of various main roads, and the configuration of the theater of military operations and its main lines. Under modern conditions of the *front's* desire to partition off the entire theater of operations, the penetration often will be only an auxiliary device to achieve another form . . .

The form of an operation should be in accordance with the qualities of the command: one can rely on distinct actions of separate groups as a measure of the soundness with which the work of their chiefs has been coordinated (Zhilinskiy,[29] Samsonov,[30] and Rennenkampf[31] during the invasion of East Prussia by two armies from different directions). The form of an operation should also correspond to the given forces' features: if the main force of the army (French) includes the bulk of engaged technical means, it is not good if the form of the operation requires a prolonged stop and establishes decisive points a considerable distance from the main railroad stations; if an army has a purely positional character (the British in 1916–18) and is capable of executing only short, direct offensives, it is not good if the operation relies on complex maneuver, with meeting battles predominating; if the preponderance of our forces consists of artillery and cavalry, it is not good if the operation is resolved in forested regions, etc.

The form of an operation should, to the degree possible, be selected so as to place our forces in a favorable tactical position; if the enemy has at his disposal an entire system of prepared positions and solid lines, then it is advantageous for the operation to lead not to a frontal attack, but to an envelopment, forcing the enemy to regroup, deploy on a new, unprepared front, and engage in battle under disadvantageous tactical conditions.

At the same time, the form of an operation should be as simple as possible. Any addition of extraneous combat and maneuver strata to the operation is unacceptable, and not only because it extremely complicates the problem of control: any superfluous maneuver, any battle which is unnecessary to achieve the operational aim conceals the greatest of dangers – luring us away from the aim onto a false path. Large advance guards, battles at forward positions, demonstrations, and local battles, even when successful, can cause us great damage. Nothing should be superfluous in an operation; it must embody purposefulness. The form of an operation in its measure, its clarity, and the orderliness of its lines should remind us not of rococo scrolls, but of the strict rectangular features of a Grecian temple.

From this point of view, defense utterly wins if the ultimate line planned for the achievement of decisive results coincides with our forward line, and in this way we avoid a number of rearguard battles, which could completely divert us from our aim. The ideal of an operational defense is to bide one's time until the approach of an enemy, only to bring fire down upon him (Austerlitz).[32]

Operational Deployment. Operational deployment should precisely correspond to the planned aim and form of an operation. If the operation pursues an offensive aim, then forces should be grouped in accordance with anticipated offensive routes. *Front* sectors should be ready to regenerate columns of forces corresponding to our decision. The absence of long range contemporary operations forces us to occupy a staging area as near as possible to the enemy; therefore, during the preparatory period for offensive operations, defensive motifs advance to the foreground of the plan. If it is a matter of defense, then the force grouping should permit the most rapid concentration of the main bulk of efforts to repel the enemy along the most important axes with the least possible loss of territory. At the same time, secondary axes should be supported to such a degree that events on them do not turn into major ones. With the exception of the case of a preconceived solution, the defense needs several days to complete its deployment, which does not end in the staging area: the choice of axes does not depend on the defense. Attentive surveillance of the enemy, wide use of fortifications, echeloning in the depth of the force grouping, solid operational reserves partially on rails, and greatest of care for "castling" routes – as we have seen, these are the natural methods saturating the preparatory phase of the offensive to which an operational defense will turn. The main thought of an operational defensive deployment and preparatory work should be striving to organize a counterattack. Sometimes it is advantageous to form two or more compact groupings connected only by a weak screen and mutually flanking one another (Stalyupenin in August 1914, on a small scale).[33] A well-developed network of "castling" routes will be the best guarantee of the timely occurrence of a flank counterstroke.

The density of an operational deployment can be quite varied . . .

Of course, concentration of a grouping in the most important sectors, especially where we presume to achieve positive results, is extremely desirable; however, one should not forget that certain prerequisites are necessary for this. The presence of solid local barriers and fortifications along part of the front facilitates the possibility of thinning out forces here. The enemy's weakness and his passivity also facilitate the construction of a ram attack . . .

An offensive is conducted primarily along parallel routes. If possible, it is desirable that the operational deployment frontage be wider than the front along which an encounter with the enemy is expected. This makes it possible to march along somewhat concentric axes. A greater number of railroads, more dirt roads and more populated areas can be used, and the rear area will be grouped more advantageously. Despite the brevity of marches from the staging area to contact with the enemy, which characterizes the modern operation, and the general parallel position of the fronts, such advantages may be achieved in an attack sector by means of an oblique axis of delimited lines, so that as one closes with the enemy the attack sector frontage narrows and the frontage in secondary sectors widens. In this way, the attack sector will have at its disposal a maximum of routes and, moreover, it will be more difficult for the enemy to discover our attack axis beforehand.

The Commencement of Preparation of an Operation. Days of pauses between operations, necessitated by modern conditions, are never periods of inactivity. During this time the next operation is prepared, and its staging area is occupied. When ending one operation, we must be aware of the next. Strategy should view an advance by our forces after a successful operation and their withdrawal after an unsuccessful one from the standpoint of regrouping forces for a new operation. The aim of a new operation is, of course, coordinated with the results of the one just ended. Do we pursue the enemy or does the enemy pursue us? These actions – inasmuch as the resistance of neither side is broken once and for all – are only elements of the new operational deployment and its cover. Therefore, the new operational plan already begins to be implemented in the order for pursuit, for cessation of the offensive, or for withdrawal. At this moment the future operational plan will very often be shaped only in the most general terms; however, to avoid a loss of time as a result of useless troop movements and inadequate orientation of rear services, the development of the next operational plan cannot be postponed for an extended period of time. The withdrawal of the French Army in 1914 after the border engagement, which kept the right flank adjoined to the Lotharingian Fortified Front and sent the left flank east of Paris, already included a considerable portion of the elements of the Marne operation. The staging area for the following operation is also the line where forces mass after completing an operation; it orients all actions, and a strategist must, first and foremost, comprehend this.

If we reject the pursuit of a positive aim, it is necessary to begin to prepare a defensive operation swiftly: commencing the withdrawal of part of the forces into a deeply echeloned tactical and operational reserve, erecting a system of fortified positions, and materially preparing a countermaneuver.

A period of operations is characterized by a rapid tempo of force expenditure; a period of pause and preparation should be a period for amassing them. It is necessary not only to replenish depleted personnel and materiel, but also to spare troop strength in every way possible. Marches should be as limited as possible, and transport means should be used not only to save time in transferring troops, but also to provide troops with maximum comfort. A hut-type camp construction or reinforced dugouts are often necessary to improve deployment conditions.

Concern for troop material comforts is, at the same time, concern for the moral element and for increased command authority. An army judges its organization and control foresight by the comfort provided to its troops and by the system and concern of the rear for its soldiers. The psychology of a soldier who has spent several days in the line or who has been in a wet trench for a week is ready to react to any material trifle, as is the psychology of a man who has been discharged after suffering a serious illness.

NOTES

1. A.A. Svechin; this excerpt is taken from the 2d edition (1927) of *Strategiya* [Strategy].
2. R. Nivelle (1856–1924) – French general under whose leadership Anglo-French forces in April–May 1917 attempted to break through German positions on the front from Arras to Reims.
3. Erich Ludendorff (1865–1937) – German general. He, jointly with Hindenburg, directed German Army combat actions in the First World War from 1916 to the end of the war. He authored works on the First World War and on the theory of total war.
4. Henry Lloyd (1729–83) – English military writer, he was in the Russian service during the war against Turkey (1768–74). He authored the works, *The Philosophy of War, The History of the Seven Years' War*, and others.
5. Adam Smith (1723–90) – well-known English economist, one of the creators of classical bourgeois political economy.
6. Seven Years' War (1756–63) – war in which Prussia and England fought against a coalition consisting of Austria, France, Sweden, Russia, and Saxony for the repartition of Central Europe and for colonies.
7. Willisen (1790–1879) – a nineteenth century Prussian general and military writer.
8. Wilhelm Blume (1835–1919) – Prussian general and military writer. Works: *Strategy, The Army and the French Revolution, 1789–1793, The Initiative of a Military Commander in War*, and others.
9. Emmanuel Kant (1724–1804) – philosopher, the father of German idealism of the second half of the eighteenth and beginning of the nineteenth centuries.
10. Genrikh Antonovich Leer (1829–1904) – general of the Russian Army, professor, and chief of the military academy; military writer and theorist.
11. Concepts of annihilation undoubtedly induce passivity in personalities in a secondary theater; this is true in both strategy and politics.
12. Henri Jomini (1779–1869) – general in the French, and later Russian service, military theorist and historian. His work *Essays on Military Art* was translated into Russian.
13. Leon Gambetta (1832–82) – minister of internal affairs of the "National Defense" government during the Franco-Prussian War of 1870–71.
14. Maurice of Saxony (1696–1750) – French marshal. Author of memoirs on military art.
15. Frederick the Great (1712–86) – Prussian king from 1740–86.
16. Duke of Alba (1507–82) – Spanish military commander and statesman.
17. There are nearsighted critics who view the shift of the World War to the rails of the strategy of attrition as the consequence of errors and lack of foresight on the part of the general staffs. Such a critic is, of course, lacking in "object consciousness." We view the form of attrition in the World War as an historic necessity.
18. We allow the justification of the reproach that our categories of annihilation and attrition are not two opposites, i.e., not black and white, but white and not-white. However, in our opinion here there is no philosophical or logical blunder. The changing tension of an armed conflict characterizes a whole series of gradations of attrition, and achieves its end in annihilation. Only for this end are some principles of strategy absolute; they are conditional, and sometimes even completely false for other gradations of conflict.
19. However, as we will show later, it would be erroneous to view the shift from annihilation to attrition as going from the dominance of necessity to the dominance of arbitrariness.
20. After the border engagement in August 1914, Moltke the Younger considered the matter of annihilation already won. But the French were far from being tied down by the Germans on the entire front, and were capable of beginning a new operational deployment by means of transporting corps from the right flank to the center and the left flank. It was namely this capability of a new enemy operational deployment which ruled out the logic of annihilation.
21. Naroch Operation (1916) – an operation of Russian Army Western Front forces in the region of Lake Naroch in March 1916. During the operation, the Russians suffered great losses, but attracted to themselves a considerable number of German reserves, thereby

easing the position of the French at Verdun.

22. Tsusima – a group of islands in the Korean Straits with an area of 700 sq. km. In May 1905, there occurred a naval battle in these islands between 2d Russian Pacific Ocean Squadron (commanded by Vice Admiral Rozhdestvenskiy) and the Japanese Navy (commanded by Admiral Togo). It ended with the defeat of the Russian squadron.

23. Kinburn – the last point on the Kinburn Spit, near which the Turks built a fortress. Kinburn Fortress was twice occupied by Russian forces: in June 1736, and in the Russo-Turkish War of 1768–74. In the Russo-Turkish War of 1787–91, Suvorov defeated a large Turkish assault group at Kinburn; he himself was wounded twice in hand-to-hand combat.

24. Shamil (born around 1798; died 1871) – leader of the national liberation movement of Dagestan and Chechen mountaineers.

25. Wilhelm II (1859–1941) – emperor of Germany, king of Prussia (1888–1918).

26. Coalition war – war which is waged by the armed forces of several states joined by an agreement and having common interests.

27. Translator's note: the terminology here is, admittedly, problematic. Svechin differentiates between *kampaniya* (here translated as "campaign") and *pokhod* (literally, "crusade," but in a modern sense "campaign" as well, but on a larger scale), the latter being a higher level than the former. To maintain the author's distinction, Russian *kampaniya* will be translated as "campaign," and Russian *pokhod* will be translated as "theater campaign" unless otherwise noted.

28. Sedan – city in northeast France in the Ardennes Department; during the Franco-Prussian War in 1870 in the region of Sedan, the French Army, commanded by Marshal MacMahon, was routed and taken prisoner.

29. Yakov Grigor'yevich Zhilinskiy (1853–1918) – general of the old Russian Army, chief of the Russian General Staff (1911–14). During the First World War (1914) he was the Commander-in-Chief of Northwestern Front forces.

30. Aleksandr Vasil'evich Samsonov (1859–1914) – general of the Russian Army. 2d Russian Army commander in 1914.

31. Pavel Karlovich Rennenkampf (1854–1918) – general of the Russian Army. 1st Russian Army commander in 1914.

32. Battle of Austerlitz – between the Russo-Austrian and French armies at the end of 1805; it concluded in a victory for Napoleon's forces.

33. Stalyupenin – town in East Prussia, in the region of which on 4 (17) August 1914 there occurred a battle between part of the 1st Russian Army and I Corps of 8th German Army.

Strategy in an Academic Formulation

N. VARFOLOMEYEV[1]

I

In the list of academic disciplines comprising the 1918 program at the Red Academy of the General Staff, first in order was strategy. Under a somewhat different name, specifically, "Fundamentals of Modern Strategy," this discipline also occupied first place in the list of sciences taught in accelerated courses at the academy during the first academic year (1918–19).

However, it would be a mistake to conclude from this that dominant significance was given to strategy at the dawn of academic studies. If one were to use as a criterion only the amount of time allotted to study, then in this instance strategy could not brag about the excess of time devoted to it: out of 625 lecture hours in the academic plan, only 28 were given to strategy, while tactics and strategy together received 196 hours; this meant that the share of two fundamental and very important military sciences amounted to only one-third of the overall time.

Under these conditions, one cannot speak either about an existing monopoly of such a "high" science as strategy, or of a more utilitarian one, that is, tactics. Indeed, only in the later period of the academy's existence did tactics and strategy gradually earn a fitting place in the academic plan.

The development of the academic program for strategy proceeded on a winding path. This was conditioned by vacillations in exactly determining the very purpose of the Military Academy.[2]

With the elimination of *fronts*, the academy faced the task of studying the experience of the Civil and Imperialist wars and reworking it for Red Army use under conditions of prospective wars by attentively following contemporary events.

This task, naturally, was to place its imprint on both the content and the method of instruction of these sciences, including strategy. Above all, a broadening of the program commenced. Strongly unbalanced in favor of its theoretical, predominantly operational portion, the strategy program hardly touched upon the very essential issues of materiel support of the operation – the study of the work of the rear. The 1920 summer campaign against the White Poles, which concluded with our withdrawal from the Vistula to the initial position, obviously demonstrated the importance of correctly structured and well-guided work in the materiel support of success. This stimulated the focus of greater attention on materiel matters, since in 1921 the "feeding of the active army," where the rear structure and service were examined, was already a substantially large component part of the strategy program. However, in this period the cycle of strategy courses strived more to develop the students' overall military outlook than to cultivate practical skills. Therefore, to treat a number of issues of practical importance for the army more thoroughly, new sections (rear control, staff work, etc.) were in later years included in the strategy program. In addition to the Department for the "Study of War," which treated strategic questions, a Department for "Conduct of Operations" was created, which treated questions concerning operational art. The establishment of this department, whose program considered various issues associated with work in the all-round support of an operation, played a large role in bringing the cycle of strategy courses closer to the Red Army's practical requirements.

II

In the history of teaching strategy, the entire first five years of the academy's existence (1918–23) can be characterized as a transitional period, when attempts were made to create a specific course. Implementation of this was hindered, however, for a whole series of subjective and objective reasons. In searching for the proper course content, academic teaching practices, on the one hand attempting to reflect living questions, and on the other hand being influenced by the person in charge of the cycle at the given moment, underwent a number of changes.

The accelerated course of 1918 (the first academic year) provided its students, in the briefest of accounts, with only an overall basic understanding of strategy; there were no details or thorough analysis.

In the next year (1919–20), the course, in comparison with the previous year, was not distinguished by anything especially new. In addition to "strategy," such areas as "philosophy of war," "naval affairs," and "engineer preparation of the defense of the state" were studied. Studies in all areas of a single lecture cycle essentially were not consolidated, ideologically or organizationally, by overall guidance. As a result there was both ideological and methodological disorder.

The 1920–21 academic year brought the first changes in both the program and teaching methods. Strictly speaking, program changes did not relate to the strategy curriculum itself, which remained unchanged; however, "war economy" was introduced into a number of areas, which by rights should have been combined in the strategy cycle. Thus, as early as seven years ago the academic program was already acquainted with "war economy." Since then, from year to year, this area, included now in military administration, now in strategy, has appeared in academic plans first as a supplemental (and then a third) academy course. Until now, however, including the last academic year (1927–28), it could not be acknowledged as fully satisfactory in its development. There are many reasons, the main one being the absence of developed materials; in addition, in the attempt to delineate a concrete purpose it was impossible to make public many issues closely connected with the USSR's defense.

As for teaching methods, for the first time, with the formation in 1921 of the supplementary academy curriculum, the course was directed not only by way of giving lectures, but also by way of independent work on the part of the student on the so-called "third strategic theme" (later this theme was called "operational"). This nomenclature defined an entire group of work, both operational (combat actions) and administrative (supply). The scale was that of armies or corps.

The overall aim, pursued by the formulation of a strategic theme guiding the entire academic preparation, consisted of establishing, by means of independent student work, how regularly and solidly the theory and practice of troop control were assimilated. The theme fell into three areas: operational, military-administrative, and military-geographic and strategic. To pass the theme, the student made a report to a committee, which analyzed the work done.

In the course of three academic years, the "strategic theme" made up the supplementary curriculum of the academy. Transferred mechanically from old academy practice, under new conditions it degenerated into a lifeless "written language," of significant scope, but of little practical use. Far from reality, cumbersome, often poorly coordinated with respect to its component parts, these themes, while taking up much time and effort, were, nevertheless, of small benefit in practice. Students of the preceding theoretical course were poorly prepared for such critical independent work and, therefore, gave shallow treatment which, understandably, had a superficial, stereotypical, and often simply inept character. In the final analysis, work on the strategic theme did not justify the expenditure.

A fundamental reform took place in the following year (1921–22), which was a turning point in the life of the academy.

The impetus for this reform was provided by the reform of the Red Army itself, which had shifted to planned training. Strong ties which knitted the academy and Red Army together necessitated a radical restructuring of all scientific-academic work in full accordance with trends taking shape in the Army. Inasmuch as in the first years of the academy's existence all attention, forces, and means were absorbed by the Revolution and the Civil War; inasmuch as it was necessary to be satisfied with what was at hand (in particular, with respect to teaching personnel); inasmuch as the course of academy teaching was more and more detached from army life – under existing conditions of a breathing space, they could and had to analyze all shortcomings, reorganize, and start out on a new path.

The General Staff Academy was renamed the Military Academy. Tukhachevsky, then commander of Western Front forces, was named chief. On his suggestion a number of his comrades who had augmented their experience in the Imperialist War with Civil War experience, were recalled from the front and assigned to the academy as instructors. A new posture for the Military Academy was worked out and confirmed, in accordance with which it was tasked with preparing qualified *genshtabisty* [general staff officers] to lead the troops in war and to guide their peacetime training. At the same time, the Military Academy, as a military-scientific center, was to follow attentively contemporary events and study the experience of the Civil and Imperialist Wars, processing this for the Red Army. Henceforth, all teaching at the academy was to be permeated by the fundamental strategic and tactical ideas adopted by the Red Army.

Thus, close coordination with the concrete conditions of the existence and struggle of the *RKKA* [Workers' and Peasants' Red Army] and a consideration of Civil War experience formed the basis of the academic system. The academy, taking part in working out Red Army doctrine, was to keep pace with the Army.

In accordance with the overall reorganization, significant changes were also introduced in the strategic cycle. Their essence boiled down to increasing attention focused on questions concerning the materiel side of war and the conduct of operations (this concerned theory); in addition, instead of a "strategic theme" in the supplementary curriculum, it was proposed to develop applied work for thorough and detailed study of the organization of modern operations. The existing theoretical strategy course had focused principal attention on the operational side; only a comparatively insignificant crumb fell to studying the enormous area of materiel support.[3]

However, only in 1924–25, in fact, were they able to shift to the aforementioned reform. Before this time, for a number of reasons the strategy cycle continued to remain, for the most part, an operational cycle, since soon after sections which had taught the rear area structure, military communications, medical service, etc. withdrew from it (into the military administration cycle). "Techniques of Staff Service" (the former "Service of the General Staff") was included in the strategy cycle instead of these sections.

The overall task which confronted the cycle of strategy courses consisted of teaching students the correct understanding of the fundamentals of modern war. Here, it was considered that a thorough understanding of strategy could be obtained only by persistent independent work through the study of the history of military art, in particular, the history of wars. The academy's strategy curriculum would do its job if it were able to prepare students for such independent work; for this it had to illuminate the multi-sidedness of the foundation on which a strategic decision is based, by means of studying the most important questions concerning war preparation and army leadership.

Here we see that in the study schedule, attention is given to both strategy (war) and operational art (operations). Below it will be shown that, in reality, study was diverted to the side of investigating operations.

The academic program pursued two aims: to illuminate the nature of modern war, encompassing strategic, political, economic, tactical, technical, and administrative issues which condition it; and to analyze the work of higher operational organs (high command – *front* – army) for studying war preparation and methods of controlling troop masses.

This was, in a brief and general outline, the evolution of the teaching of strategy during the first five years of the academy's existence. Experiencing the direct influence of various changes in the overall course of academic life, the strategy program significantly changed more than once during this period. Commencing in 1918 with a modest course, "Foundations of Modern Strategy," this program, gradually modified and supplemented, had attained significant scope in volume on the threshold of the second five years, and adopted content which was varied in nature. In the first years the program's expansion was directed primarily toward the path of expanding its theoretical operational portion. It would be correct to state that in this period the strategy cycle focused its main attention on illuminating theoretical "foundations," avoiding, somewhat, an applied, technical bias.

Of what, then, did the content consist, and what determined the understanding of "strategy" itself? In the course of academy teaching, strategy as a concept was divided into lower (the study of operations or higher tactics), higher (the study of war), and peacetime (the study of preparing for war and compiling a war plan) strategy. Thus, here we have higher tactics equalling lower strategy. "Higher" tactics penetrated into the realm of strategy, managing operations in a theater of military operations; strategy descended to tactics, in truth becoming "lower." This uncomplicated "dialectic" was clearly unsuitable. It was difficult to be reconciled to the fact that the two-part formula "strategy – tactics," which had been simplified, meeting conditions of the nineteenth century, and the first half of the Napoleonic campaigns in particular, but not including the entire content of the art of conducting military operations under modern conditions, had been put into circulation as before.

Up to the recent past, tactics was understood as the study of the engagement. In the Napoleonic era, battle and engagement were essentially one and the same; strategy, having initiated the engagement, ceded control to tactics; at the end of the nineteenth century the engagement was now a group of battles, unfolding, however, in the immediate vicinity of the adversaries, and comparatively restricted with respect to time and space. Under these conditions, strategy, limited to the use of armed forces outside the field of engagement, became the "tactics of the theater of military operations."

The situation has been essentially changing since the beginning of the twentieth century (the Russo-Japanese War); now huge armies, numbering millions and supplied with massive equipment, operate along a front of hundreds of thousands of kilometers and into the depth; maneuver has become possible not only before, but also during the engagement itself; mistakes in initial deployment, formerly fatal, are now corrected by means of railroad and automobile maneuver; control has, to a great degree, become complex, completely beyond the capacity of a single commander-in-chief. The engagement has been divided into separate parts, that is, battles, the grouping of which is directed toward achieving the aims of the engagement. As a result, battle was sharply delimited from the engagement; the "engagement" of the past shifted to the "operation" of the present. Research on the operation emerged from the framework of tactics, the destiny of which was to research the separate battle, but not the group of them. In grouping battles, the modern operation is a complex act; it is understood as the totality of maneuvers and battles on a given sector of a theater of military operations directed toward achieving the overall aim established as the ultimate one in a given period of a campaign. Tactics is not up to the conduct of operations. This has become the lot of *operational art*. Hence, the former two-part formula, "tactics–strategy," has now turned into a three-part formula:

tactics/battle – operational art/operation – strategy/war.

Thus, in the academy, what as recently as 1922 was called *lower strategy* (or higher tactics) is now called *operational art*.[4] Strategy is understood as the study of war, broadly encompassing all issues of organizing the struggle on an armed front in full accordance with political indicators and economic conditions.

Thus, battle is the means of an operation, and tactics is the material of operational art; the operation is the means of strategy, operational art is the material of strategy. This is the essence of the above-mentioned tripartite formula.

In the period 1918–23, academy teaching posed the problem differently from that stated above. Conduct of operations occupied a greater place in the "strategy" curriculum. Strictly speaking, there was no strategy in the sense of a broad study of war in its modern understanding. Only in the following academic year, 1923/24, did this course make its appearance, as given by A. A. Svechin.

III

The first year of the *RKKA* Military Academy's second five-year period, 1924/25, was marked by a sharp turn in the history of the academy's teaching of strategy. In this year it succeeded in carrying out those measures for improving the teaching program and methodology which had been "theoretically" adopted two years before. Apart from this, in general, the strategy department almost completely restructured its training system.

In 1924, the Chief of Staff of the *RKKA*, Comrade M. N. Tukhachevky, was named the Main Director for Strategy for all military academies. The result of this measure was quickly felt by the strategy cycle in the Military Academy.

A differentiation occurred between teaching strategy (the study of war) and operational art (the conduct of operations). Accordingly, with respect to organization, the strategy cycle was divided into two departments: study of war and conduct of operations. Thus, *operational art* entered into scientific-academic use at the academy, both as a specific scientific concept and as an academic discipline.

The Department for the "Study of War" posed for itself the task of illuminating all basic issues associated with preparing for and conducting war as a whole. The curriculum program encompassed a wide circle of issues concerning the organization of the struggle of an "armed nation" on all fronts of modern war: political, economic, and military. In the 1924/25 academic year, seminar classes, which pursued as their goal a more thorough acquaintance with classical strategic thought and that of the most prominent modern military authors through their works, were held for the first time in addition to lectures. Therefore, only those sections having printed materials were presented for study. Two parts of *Strategiya v trudakh voyennykh klassikov* [Strategy in the works of military classics], compiled by A. A. Svechin, appeared in this manner.[5]

In the course of subsequent years and up to the present, the department's aims and missions have remained the same. Changes have taken place only in the amount of time allotted for this and in the method of teaching. Beginning in 1926, "study of war" has been expounded only by means of lectures. Seminars in the military classics were not resumed. Apart from the course, which set forth the theory of conducting war, there was also a "War Economy" Section, whose aim was to illuminate the problems of materiel preparation for war. This course, extremely interesting in its topical significance and importance, was to provide proper definition in the field of studying the influence of war on the national economy, and methods and tasks of economically preparing the country for war (development of an economic plan). Issues encompassed by this program were extremely significant and vast. Based on the experience of the Imperialist and Civil Wars, a correct analysis was to be provided of the influence, which the national economy as a whole, and its various branches in particular, would be subjected to under conditions of modern warfare. Furthermore, proceeding from these prerequisites and taking into consideration the probable nature of forthcoming wars, it was necessary to establish basic trends in the system of economic preparation for war on the basis of the USSR's actual economic substructure.

The tasks confronting the department, regarding the above-mentioned section, were, in truth, great. A particular difficulty was the lack of printed handbooks or texts on this problem. For the most part, it was necessary to teach and learn by auditing the teachers' lectures. The abundance and variety of issues required the work of a collective, which made homogeneous teaching difficult and created a certain lack of coordination. In many sections it was impossible to find qualified lecturers. Finally, the secrecy of much of the data required that many issues be illuminated in too general a form. The totality of the cited reasons, in sum, led to the fact that the "War Economy" Section is still at this time in an embryonic state.

Speaking of the Department for the "Study of War," it is necessary to recall the very interesting attempt to include in the overall course the section "Politics and War in the Era of Imperialism." Established for the first time in 1926 and repeated during the last academic year, this course, given by B. I. Gorev, immediately attracted attention by its detailed analysis of the military policy of the imperialist era, bringing to light, in accordance with twentieth century war experience, a picture of political preparation and political servicing of war. The exposition concluded with an illumination of postwar imperialist politics according to the experience of national liberation and colonial wars fought since the World War. In general, this course assigned itself (and resolved) the task of concretely clarifying, on an analysis of the political history of the most important wars of the twentieth century, the interrelationships between war and policy in the era and on the basis of imperialism; policy is viewed here both as the overall aim of the war for which war is only a means, and, conversely, as a means for preparing to serve the needs of war itself in the field of foreign and domestic policy.

We turn now to the "Conduct of Operations" Department. It was recreated in 1924; having had no past experience (or, more correctly, having had adverse experience), it was unable to be guided by a verified model, and had to search for new paths completely independently. In no way are we inclined to view this as bad; on the contrary, it seems to us that the absence of a stereotypical pattern created a favorable prerequisite for unfettered development.

The year 1924 was the first of a three-year period, 1924–27, which has been characterized as a period of broad military reforms and fundamental reorganization in the development of the Armed Forces. The first years of the breathing space which followed the Civil War's conclusion and the elimination of fronts were immediately devoted to putting the army apparatus in order and implementing a series of transformations of a local character. This daily activity, which required constant attention from the army's entire leadership stratum, put off for a time the possibility of attending to more radical reorganization of the army in all fields, reorganization which bore a more general character. This year was marked by the beginning of this reorganization, the basic principles of which were rooted in the experience of the Revolution and Civil War.

The several years since the day of the immediate conclusion of the war also made it possible to crystalize specific opinions in the field of the theory of military art. The Red Army, guided by the experience of its military past, was ideologically armed, proceeding along the path of establishing a military doctrine. As early as 1922 an animated discussion on the issue of military doctrine took place in the center and in the provinces; the discussion, however, was not brought to a conclusion, and instead of clarity it introduced confusion. It is, however, doubtless that the political, economic, and geographic peculiarities of the status of the first workers' republic could not fail to condition a specific influence on certain initial data in the field of preparing for war, as well as in the matter of training and educating the Red Army. Meanwhile, at this time the army still had no regulations and had little military-scientific literature, which inadequately served the military community. It was necessary to plan and establish landmarks on the path of developing uniformity of opinions; it was necessary to develop regulations and provide the troops with them; it was also necessary to establish a specific foundation, appropriate to the work spirit fostered in the army, concerning the training of command personnel among those who, upon completion of their training within the walls of the Military Academy, would proceed to the troops with the mission of energetically participating in army preparation and training. Accordingly, the program of the "Conduct of Operations" course received specific and solid orientation. Its content fully reflected Civil War experience, in particular the 1920 summer campaign against the White Poles.

What, then, were the accepted views in the field of operational art?

Briefly characterizing them, it is possible to reduce them to the following two basic tenets:

(1) Operations are conducted to destroy enemy armed forces personnel. However, under conditions of conducting modern combat operations involving mass armies very capable of maintaining their combat capabilities, it is difficult (with the exception of rare instances) to count on destroying the enemy in a single operation. A correct calculation of the situation will necessitate (while technology provides the capability) breaking off and disengaging from an inflicted strike: the enemy will

attempt to slip away. But in detecting this, the attacking side should organize pursuit, attempting to attack and defeat the withdrawing enemy at positions and times inconvenient for him. However, taking into account the possible failure of these attempts, it is necessary over the entire period of pursuit to be ready for a decisive operation at positions which the enemy cannot abandon. Here, it is necessary to attempt to place oneself in an initial position favorable for oneself and unfavorable for the enemy; this should be the result of preceding activities. Thus, the path to victory under modern conditions lies on the zigzag of an entire series of operations, successively developing one after another, logically connected to one another, united by the commonality of the ultimate aim, each one achieving limited intermediate aims which in their totality represent an operational pursuit, in the process of which the attacker attempts to use both his physical and moral–political advantages simultaneously with the entire sum of separate strikes and so-called intermediate failures to disrupt the enemy more, forcing him to enter a decisive operation under unfavorable conditions which are already inescapable. Consequently, the basic plan is characterized as follows: aims of operations – defeat and complete rout of enemy personnel; method of operation – continuous advance; means – prolonged operational pursuit, avoiding pauses and halts, implemented by a series of successive operations, of which each is an intermediate link on the path to the ultimate aim, achieved in the final decisive operation.

(2) The success of a "prolonged" offensive, a continuous, deep pursuit (series of successive operations) is directly related to the successful fight against the consequences of accompanying operational exhaustion.

The Civil War provided clear examples of prolonged offensive operations conducted under peculiar conditions, very different from those of the previous Imperialist War. In pursuing Kolchak, our army covered more than 2,500 kilometers in three and a half months, a daily average of 20–25 kilometers. It would seem that such a prolonged offensive should have suffocated; however, in this operation we not only were not exhausted, but we confront the fact of an increase in strength. The reasons lie in the ability to make use of forward bases; the army found almost everything necessary, including ammunition, in place. Losses were replenished from the Ural workers and the rebelling Siberian peasantry. Areas rich in grain provided food. Warehouses of captured goods provided munitions and uniforms. In sum, the Red armies were independent of their rear, in particular of railroad deliveries. While continuously and interminably advancing behind the withdrawing enemy, there was the possibility of not only not becoming exhausted, but, on the contrary, becoming enriched. There was no need for pauses or halts. A similar picture was observed in the liquidation of Denikin and Wrangel.

The experience of operations on the Eastern and Southern Fronts in 1919 resulted in several conclusions, which made it possible to view optimistically the potential for continuous, deep pursuit without particular fear of experiencing the consequences of operational exhaustion. It was considered possible for small armies to gain large territories and have a rear supported by the establishment of the dictatorship of the proletariat; the attacker, reinforced continuously (at a time when the withdrawing enemy was weakened because of desertions), had the opportunity to develop a swift advance (possible norm of 200 kilometers per week) in connection with the facility of establishing a rear. Local transport was sufficient for supply: divisions did not depend on the railroads. Hence the conclusion: move boldly forward and do not fear exhaustion; everything necessary will be at hand.

These views suffered a fiasco in the 1920 Warsaw operation.

Combat conditions on the Western Front for the most part substantially differed from those on the Eastern and Southern Fronts. Basically this was determined by the difference in the features of Belorussia and eastern Poland from the features of the Ukraine, Donbas, and Siberia with respect to political and materiel support for the operation. Practically speaking, we were convinced of this difference soon after the commencement of our offensive from the line of the Berezina River.

The mood of the local inhabitants was not uniform for the entire region of our offensive. Where the Belorussian and part of the Lithuanian peasantry were clearly sympathetic to the Red Army, the Polish peasantry under the best of circumstances was passive. Volunteers poured into the army in Belorussia, but in Poland we had no volunteers. In general, we could not use the local population for replenishment.

The rapid advance of our armies from the Berezina to the Vistula soon resulted in isolation of the troops from the railroads; more correctly, there was not isolation here (the distance did not exceed 60–180 kilometers for the entire operation), but rather a rupture between the forces and rail supply. Roads were re-established rapidly – 12–20 kilometers per day – so that later this led to unwarranted optimism in solving the difficult problem of restoring railroad lines destroyed by the enemy during his withdrawal; in general, it could be considered that the railroads did not lag behind the troops. This circumstance did not, however, save the situation: the absence of proper organization and the lack of adjustment of servicing military roads and mobile army supply installations (intermediate and main depots) on the one hand, and the insufficiency of rolling stock, mainly steam engines, on the other, resulted in an actual lack of supply of necessary goods to the forces at the necessary time. In sum, disorientation in regular supply from the rear caused a shift to local means, the organized use of which, however, we were not handling; moreover, these means were inadequate.

With our approach to the Vistula, the situation in the rear was not very gratifying: the rear areas were stretched out; large railroad centers were obstructed; many reserves were on wheels but did not get to the troops; reinforcements were also on wheels; mobile troop installations could not escape the common lot and were also jammed in the rear (division artillery depots); in searching for a way out of the existing situation, the forces fell back on local transport, using an enormous number of carts. Soon they were running out of ammunition, and it was necessary to resort to strict rationing. Losses over one and a half months of pursuit were strongly felt, divisions arrived at the Vistula having no more than 2,000–3,000 bayonets; reinforcements were bogged down in the rear.

Thus, if in our fighting on the Eastern and Southern Fronts we should have reckoned with the operational influence of the rear to a relative degree, then in our 1920 summer fight against the White Poles the rear weighed us down with the burden of its *lack of structure*. We were not in any condition to cope with either its organization or the appropriate Sovietization of the rear, the results of which we felt in full measure with the approach to the Bug River.

The conditions of our offensive from the Berezina to the Vistula in no way allowed for strategic growth; on the contrary, they led to strategic exhaustion. In the final analysis, at the moment preceding the decisive operation, a situation was created in places of a tendency to halt for a while on the line of the Bug to organize a rear area and add to the thinning ranks of reserves. The higher command rejected this delay, and the troops continued without a pause from the Bug to the Vistula. As is generally known, we withdrew again from the Vistula to the Bug, and further to the Berezina and the initial position. Our calculations of local assets were not justified. Our rear area did not cope with its task, and our "prolonged" offensive, expressed by a number of successive operations, was not crowned with success. Therefore, the question of the possibility of similar offensives under conditions quite obviously different from the favorable conditions of the Southern and, in particular, Eastern Fronts was posed. In order to answer this question, one of life or death for the theory of "prolonged" offensives, it was necessary to clarify if the rear, with appropriate organization, could support the necessary depth of the uninterrupted advance of pursuing forces. From here the obvious necessity to create the foundations of this organization, to refine the details of this work, and to establish the appropriate principles for rear control became clear.

In summer 1920 we were far from being fully armed with correct ideas regarding structuring a rear area and controlling it. We suffered not from a lack of reserves of necessary types of supplies or trained reinforcements – they were in storage depots and bases, in reserve units, and simply in echelons far behind – but we were unable to deliver them, that is, there was an evident gap here in the organization of the rear; in this area we did not have the necessary homogeneity of views, and each "service" worked independently, predominantly espousing its own interests, without close mutual adjustment and often without coordination. We worked amateurishly. The fact that in other cases the command and staff let the reins of control out of their hands resulted in considerable inadequacies and mistakes in rear operation. The rear was sometimes assigned tasks completely beyond its power, or, on the contrary, command was influenced by rear conditions. In general, inadequate technical knowledge of the organization and service of the rear's various branches was obvious; this resulted in such problems as cited above in the field of operational control of the rear.

The 1920 summer campaign demonstrated that we were not able to organize the rear or control it: hence the conclusion that this must be studied. It is necessary to be able to structure the rear in such a way, correctly assigning missions and using assets, so as to support the possibility of a "prolonged" offensive by means of planned rear operations without being tempted to rely on local assets. One cannot be limited to faith alone in the miraculous force of some kind of super-brilliant operational decisions; it is necessary to take into consideration all materiel conditions and to "fit the legs into the clothes." Under modern conditions the operation (even more so, a successive series of them) has the right to count on success only if the ability to execute the adopted operational plan is supported not only by the correlation of forces, correct choice of aim, and direction, but also by materiel. For this, cold calculation for each branch of the rear is needed above all.

The two prerequisites cited above were established as the foundation of the "Conduct of Operations" course. The regularity of "prolonged" offensives and their fundamental possibility were acknowledged. However, the actual possibility of their implementation was directly dependent on the organization of materiel support of the operations. Therefore, the center of gravity of the curriculum's content consisted of the all-round study of the organization of an army operation; a significant portion fell to its materiel support. All work was structured on the purely practical study of the issue. Here, not only a clear understanding and knowledge, but also acquisition of specific practical skills were required. In this connection, a method of study was organized. It was adopted as completely independent work on the students' part, with subsequent class analysis of this work. The lack of exhaustive texts made this work somewhat difficult. This lack was compensated for by lectures.

The study of the army operation by the applied method, evidenced in the decision of the primary operational mission, which from 1924 replaced the "strategic theme," pursued as its goal practical experience for the students in the all-round and thorough preparation of an operation. Students had to make an operational decision and then support the overall success in operational, political, and materiel respects. In this connection, students worked successively in the roles of army commander, army chief of staff, and then chiefs of combat arms and chiefs of "services." On the basis of a theoretical acquaintance with the technical resources, organization, and service of all forces and means being used, the multi-sided practical work in supporting the operation was revealed. In the operational respect, issues concerning the organization of reconnaissance, communications, *maskirovka*, use of artillery, organization of air defense, and, finally, engineer support of the operation were studied. Materiel support of operations was studied by means of frequent, very painstaking research of the supply service, military communications service, medical and veterinary services, and manning. Finally, in the field of political support of the operation, appropriate aspects of the Main Army Directorate's work were brought to light. In sum, the students received a complete idea of the totality of measures connected with all-round preparation of an army operation. In addition to this general result, practical experience in work at various roles imparted thorough knowledge and skills regarding operational techniques of various branches of the rear and of their control. The accepted method of study – independent work with pencil in hand, everything based on calculation, nothing based on faith – allowed for solidity in assimilating the subject on the one hand, but burdened the student with technical work on the other. Operational "arithmetic," here understood as the entire calculative aspect, made itself felt. For example, in studying the organization of communications in an army operation, not only were organizational principles as applied to the given concrete situation examined, but also a calculation of the necessary assets (wire, insulation, posts, etc.) was done. And this was so for each problem. The goal pursued was to keep both feet on the ground and heads out of the clouds, and to maintain the framework of available capabilities. This approach to every decision represented the positive aspect of operational "arithmetic." A shortcoming, perhaps, was some excess detail in calculations, which, undoubtedly, increased the "arithmetic" at the expense of theory.

Nevertheless, it seems to us that basically the approach taken is the correct one. Irresponsible operational "deviations," which are especially harmful, will disappear when encountering the trend for materiel calculation of the operation. It is probable that it is necessary to reduce somewhat the scope of applied work. Perhaps it is not necessary that every academy graduate knows well the technical details of the work of, for example, the chief of the army medical unit. Perhaps it is sufficient here to limit oneself only to familiarity with the fact that the unwarranted flowering of "applicativeness" will proceed to the detriment of theory. All this is true, and all this should be taken into consideration and corrected in the future. Nevertheless, the fact cannot be discounted that increasing attention toward the materiel basis brought about a decided increase in competency in the field of organizing the army operation on the whole and in various branches of its operational, political, and materiel support. We must always and everywhere be able to consider and strictly calculate each step. In this lies the guarantee of our success.

NOTES

1. N. Varfolomeyev, "Strategiya v akademicheskoy postanovke," *Voyna i revolyutsiya* [War and revolution], Book 11 (Gosudarstvennoye Izdatel'stvo, 1928), pp.78–93.
2. This issue is brought to light in the article by Ye. Shilovsky, *Evolyutsiya akademicheskoy podgotovki* [Evolution of academic preparation].
3. A significant part of the work in studying the foundations of materiel support was done in the large departments which existed independently, i.e., not connected with the department of strategy. Now, with the formation of course cycle there was the opportunity of consolidating all these related disciplines under an overall leadership, having collected them into a single cycle of strategic courses; this, above all, eliminated harmful discord and provided close coordination of the study of the issues of troop leadership and rear operation. The course cycle consolidated the following disciplines: strategy, strategic operations of cavalry, feeding of the active army, strategic preparation of communications, engineer preparation of the state, and naval affairs.
4. The terminology belongs to Military Academy professor A.A. Svechin (*Strategiya* [Strategy], second edition, p. 14 and following), who gave the course on strategy in 1923–24.
5. At these seminars, the following themes were developed:

    (1) Positional Strategy (text: Leval, *Introduction to the Positive Part of Strategy*).
    (2) Aims (text: Verdi, *On the Object of an Operation*).
    (3) Overall and Operational Basis (text: Verdi, *Operational Basis*).
    (4) Flexibility of Strategy (von der Holtz, *Strategy and Army Leadership*).
    (5) Basic Views of Clausewitz on Strategy (Clausewitz, *Foundations of Strategic Decision*; Svechin, *Istoriya voyennogo iskusstva*/History of military art).
    (6) Plan of the Campaign (Foch, *Conduct of War*; Svechin, History of military art).
    (7) Schlieffen's Plan for Germany's War on Two Fronts (Hans Kuhl, *The German General Staff*).

The Evolution of Operational Art

G. ISSERSON[1]

I. PATHS OF DEVELOPMENT OF OUR OPERATIONAL ART

Modern operational art, as the study of the conduct of an operation, faces a number of new problems.

Much still remains that has not been researched or resolved in this field.

Enormous changes in equipment, weaponry, and combat formations, reflected in the evolution of tactics, have still not been considered on the scale of conflict on an armed front as a whole.

Conduct of a modern operation under completely different socio-political conditions and on a completely different materiel-technical base still lacks a sufficiently concrete perspective on the structure of combat actions and development of their operational forms.

All experience of the most recent wars, so rich in the tactical respect, is far from adequate in revealing problems of the nature of the future operation.

This situation is exacerbated by the World War, in essence, not providing a single operation which could be rightly considered an operational solution to the problem of achieving victory.

Separate operations, which achieved their aim of actual defeat of the enemy (for example, the defeat of Samsonov's army) did not play a very significant role in the war's overall context.

And 1918, with its grandiose, deadly close engagements, did not solve the problem of overcoming a front on an operational scale, and was the apotheosis of the dead end which the military art of the era of imperialism had achieved.

The Entente's victory was achieved along other lines of political and economic significance.

The World War came to an end under the omen of insurmountable difficulties in organizing and conducting an offensive operation.

These difficulties turned on the enormous defensive strength of a positional front, the absence of political stimuli in soldiers for overcoming this, superiority of defensive over offensive means, the necessity for concentrating enormous means of suppression, complexity in organizing and conducting offensive actions, etc.; that is, in a military-technical sense they were localized completely in the realm of *tactics*.

This had enormous influence on the conduct of all operations in 1918.

Ludendorff says that it was necessary to place tactics above strategy. And, in actuality, the Germans attacked not where it was required according to concepts of operational expediency, but rather where it was possible with respect to tactical conditions. They developed an attack not in the direction which promised an operational result, but in the direction where the front could be, tactically speaking, more easily crushed. The March 1918 German offensive is the most striking example. The positional reality of war determined operational perceptions. It was beyond their power to overcome new conditions of struggle.

The main thing was that the soldier lacked sufficiently convincing positive political motives to resolve this mission with his blood.

It was necessary to awaken class will in the masses, and for class contradictions to pour out into open, armed class struggle; it was necessary that the imperialist war turn into a civil war so that a new soldier would appear, one who found in himself sufficient strength to overcome enemy resistance in an open offensive.

Our Civil War of 1918–21, with its crushing, *deep* attacks up to the final enemy defeat, undoubtedly marked the beginning of a new era in the history of military art, and sharply changed the entire nature of armed conflict. Clausewitz said of the wars of the French Revolution: "Revolutionary wars turned all old things upside down and drove from Chalons to Moscow itself."

One need not be a Clausewitz to understand, after shifting the latter words from east to west, the entire mobile nature of our revolutionary-class war.

The operational content of the newly arrived era is still far from being revealed, with respect to techniques for leading large military masses richly outfitted with modern equipment.

Changes which have occurred since the end of the Civil War are immeasurably significant.

These conditions compel us to pose in a different way the question of the correlation of the qualitative strength of means for defense and offense.

The problem of overcoming a fiery front acquires new significance for us, with the possibility of breaching its entire depth.

All our creative thought in the field of military affairs essentially addresses the resolution of this problem.

Both in capitalist countries after the World War, and in ours after the Civil War, the evolution of military art on a different class basis proceeded under the aegis of searching for new offensive tactical forms and employing new technical combat means.

During the brief period following the World War, which is an entire era in the field of military art, tactics have experienced greater changes than during the half century before the World War. During this time, all regulations have been reworked and newly published, and new tactics have been created in a few years.

It is not without interest to note that this was for the first time in the history of the development of military affairs.

Prussia entered the wars of 1866 and 1870 with regulations published in 1847, and replaced them only in 1888.

Germany entered the World War with 1888 regulations.

Thus, over a long 70-year period, Germany changed its regulations only once.

In our rapid period of socialist development, we published temporary Field Regulations in 1925, and then replaced them with permanent Field Regulations in 1929; in 1932 we were once again on the eve of reworking them, that is, at the end of seven years we were already working on our third field regulations.

This rapid tempo of creativity in regulations, natural under enormously progressing technological conditions, is a general phenomenon in the development of post-World War military affairs. In addition, it predetermined the evolution of military art, mainly on a tactical plane.

Problems of struggle on an armed front as a whole, and conducting military actions on an operational scale were pushed into the background and attracted the attention of military-scientific research to a considerably lesser degree.

It is true that general questions of conducting war within the framework of politics, strategy, and economics elicit great literary interest.

However, practical questions concerning the conduct of military operations on an armed front and techniques of conducting a modern operation are most weakly and poorly reflected.

Under restricted conditions of the Versailles military system, the German press is proceeding no further than an analysis of World War operations. Having developed a rich military theory after the 1870–71 war, they still keep repeating Schlieffen's teachings over and over again.

It is true that their author Groener provides much that is interesting in this respect, but hardly much that is new.

In France, the country where the military system of imperialism is most concentrated, Kuhlman's *Strategy* has appeared, considered in capitalist countries to be the last word in the study of the operation.

Nevertheless, Kuhlman does not develop an entire operational system, but elucidates only a series of individual related problems; his main perspective on the future quite incompletely examines an interpretation of everything new on an operational scale.

As for a whole series of bourgeois military writers (Ludendorff, Immanuel, Metsch, Recken, Fuller), who replaced any scientific formation of a theory of conducting operations by largely unsubstantiated fantasies in the realm of perspectives on future war, their writings, which reflect the entire class nature of the contradictions of modern capitalism, best of all still demonstrate how poorly scientific theory is investigating problems of modern operational art.

Our literature, in this respect, has an evident advantage.

Comrade Triandafillov's work, *Kharakter operatsii sovremennykh armiy* [The nature of the operation of modern armies] unarguably occupies a prominent place in literature concerning the modern operation.

With respect to the volume of questions touched upon and the way in which they are posed, this work develops an entire operational system, which resolves a series of important problems in their practical context.

However, it is necessary to bear in mind that before his tragic death Comrade Triandafillov sharply changed his views on a series of principal questions.

His inquisitive mind formed a different, far-reaching perspective on the basis of our new achievements.

A cruel occurrence prevented him developing his new system of operational views. Nevertheless, life went on.

To sum up, the study of the modern operation today is at a quite unsatisfactory level, and remains the least-developed branch of military art.

The circumstance that this is not the first time in history hardly serves as consolation.

In military affairs, under capitalist conditions, theory systematically lagged behind practice, and this was reflected, in the first order, in operational problems. Tactics is, to a considerable degree, practice which is verified by exercises and maneuvers. The conduct of an operation is more a theory in peacetime, which is not subject to experimental verification. Of course, it is much easier to employ a new means in its independent action than to organize its mass use in all production processes. Therefore, tactics has more than once outstripped operational art. But at the modern stage, the position of the latter is least permissible. Completely altered conditions of fighting on an armed front, new human material, and new means of struggle have authoritatively advanced requirements of their new use on a massive operational scale, at the level of which quantity shifts to a completely different quality.

Before the age of imperialism, with a comparatively restricted quantity of armed forces (the Prussian Army in 1870 numbered 500,000 men), the question of conducting an operation had not acquired the significance of an independent theoretical discipline, since, on the whole, they were resolved within the framework of the development of a given concrete war plan.

All problems confronting Moltke in preparing for the 1870 war were resolved in his practical development of deployment against France.

Now, with massive armies and extremely complex equipment, the enormous depth of columns and difficulty in deploying them into combat formation, and rear area complexity and a whole series of complicating factors, the conduct of an operation promotes problems, whose solution does not fit into the framework of a given concrete deployment plan, but requires laying a general theoretical base.

In his practical work, the operations specialist now requires a specific theory for conducting an operation.

Operational art as the study of an operation is, therefore, acquiring the significance of a most important discipline for the practice of operational work and direction of large military formations.

The currency of problems of operational art is conditioned by other factors as well. It is completely obvious that profound changes in the field of equipment and tactics are causing no less profound changes in the field of conducting an operation.

Clausewitz says:

> Changes in the nature of tactics must affect strategy as well. If tactical phenomena in a given instance have a different character than in another instance, then strategic phenomena must change as well; otherwise they will not be consistent or logical.

This obvious natural law was not always understood. In Moltke's time, with new fire weapons and altered tactics, they, nevertheless, still approached the conduct of battle from the point of view of Napoleon's operational art.

Moltke was, in this respect, a great reformer, having understood the new conditions and requirements of his time.

In 1914, however, the conduct of operations in form and method had not moved far from Moltke's era. All factors of armed conflict grew quantitatively, and this means qualitatively as well. However, their operational control did not undergo fundamental qualitative changes.

Even now, if one considers the structure of an operation as usually represented, it is difficult to see any fundamental changes.

Corps are formed up in one line, offensive sectors are assigned, and missions are delegated by lines, but this was also done in 1914, and, if we look into it further, it was also done in Moltke's time.

Operational art is unbearably conservative. Nevertheless, the conditions of our time and those of 1914, not to mention those of Moltke's time, are completely incommensurate.

The entire arsenal of basic factors of armed struggle has changed.

New weapons, new tactics, and a new soldier – all this is inevitably causing large-scale fundamental changes in the realm of conducting an operation.

After all, it is completely obvious that change in factory equipment and exploitation of new machines fundamentally alter the entire production process and the organization of all production.

This, of course, also predetermines a different organizational structure of military organisms.

Conduct of a modern operation, in this respect, is subject to most serious reexamination.

However, this is necessary not only with respect to material factors of conflict and the new soldier. This would be completely inadequate. The operation is a tool of strategy, while strategy is a tool of politics. Therefore, an operation is not the culminating factor of armed conflict. It is itself an element subordinate to war as a whole.

From a study of Clausewitz, Comrade Lenin wrote: "From new phenomena in the field of military art, only the most insignificant part must be ascribed to new inventions and new ideas; the majority is ascribed to new social principles and new social conditions."

Thus, the entire sum of factors with completely new qualitative content – different socio-political conditions, a different arsenal of technical combat means, new tactical combat forms, and, finally, the enormous practical significance of the theory of and urgent practical need for conducting an operation – determine the initial foundations for the development of our operational art.

It should be kept in mind that operational art, as the study of the conduct of an operation, is an extremely young discipline. In essence, it originated in the most recent period, following the World War, when it occupied an independent place.

Before the World War, military art defined its scope by two basic branches: strategy, as the study of war, and tactics, as the study of battle.

This bipartite system once again reflected how greatly military theory lagged behind practice.

The evolution of forms of armed conflict during the second half of the nineteenth century did not fit into the concepts of strategy and tactics alone, but grew from them. Armed conflict gave birth to a whole line of combat events spread out along a front and dispersed into the depth, which grew beyond the framework of battle and, therefore, could not be encompassed by the content of tactics; however, they also did not include the phenomenon of war as a whole and, therefore, could not be viewed by strategy as the study of war.

Thus, there occurred a large gap in theory between strategy and tactics, which, however, in the practice of armed conflict had already long been filled by phenomena of enormous scale and content.

These phenomena required a new concept, called operational art, which only after the World War occupied its own independent place as the study of the operation in a new tripartite system of dividing military art into strategy as the study of war, operational art as the study of the operation, and tactics as the study of battle.

But having been recently formed into an independent discipline, operational art at its current stage of development has the mission of fundamentally reexamining all study concerning the conduct of the operation.

As so often happens in the evolution of military affairs, the youngest, just born, is already obsolete.

Our operational thought cannot stop at the experience of the World War. The exhausting system of battles of attrition did not resolve the problems of an operational breach of a front; the creeping tempos of the offensive, which required of the Allies four months in 1918 to drive back the Germans a total of 100 kilometers, cannot serve as a basis for structuring our theory for conducting an operation.

Proceeding from the revolutionary-class content of our future war as a decisive encounter of worlds which exclude one another, we must proceed much further and require considerably more of our military theory.

The approaching new era of proletarian revolutions, building of socialism, and revolutionary class wars also predetermine the approach of a new era of military art.

Engels says, "The actual liberation of the proletariat, complete obliteration of all class differences, and the complete socialization of all means of production . . . presume the creation of a new method of conducting war."[2]

Before our operational doctrine stand great tasks, which were not and could not have been resolved by the Imperialist War. These are overcoming the frontal nature [of actions], conducting a deep offensive which breaks through and fractures the combat [literally, "fire"] front to its entire operational depth, and, finally, delivering swift, annihilating blows for the purpose of decisively and completely routing the enemy.

Under these conditions, the mission of our operational art is *to substantiate and form a theory of a deep annihilating operation.*

II. THE EVOLUTION OF OPERATIONAL ART UP TO THE WORLD WAR

The problem of forming a theory of operational art is extremely complex with respect to the ways in which this can be done.

Schlichting says, "A new strategic method is never born like Minerva out of Jupiter's head; it emerges from conditions of the time and available combat means."

All contemporary factors of socio-political, economic, and military-technical significance thus provide the initial material for determining the nature of an operation in a future war.

These factors, however, cannot be examined only in the stasis of the current era.

Their developmental tendencies, important for determining the nature of armed conflict, can be seen and understood only within the dynamics of its historical process.

To clarify for oneself the concrete nature of the modern operation, it is necessary to determine prerequisites and conditions which have caused its genesis and determined its evolution until our time. This historical approach also clarifies prerequisites determining the further evolution of operational forms of armed struggle at the present stage of their development.

Schlichting says: "In military affairs, it is best to base one's opinions concerning the future on the study of the immediate past."

In an historical context, the phenomenon known today as the operation very clearly reveals those of its primary features which determine the evolution of its character.

The military art of the Napoleonic era schematically consisted of two basic stages, far from equivalent in space and time. These stages were a great, long approach, which engendered a long operational line, and a short, final engagement in a single area, which, with respect to the long operational line, is a single point in space and a single moment in time.

Clausewitz expressed this figuratively as follows: "The field of battle in the face of strategy is no more than a point; in precisely the same way the duration of a battle reduces to a single moment."

This era of military art can rightly be christened the "era of a single point strategy," since the entire mission of a military leader was reduced to concentrating all his forces at one point and throwing them into battle as a one-act tactical phenomenon.

Such a sketch of Napoleon's military art has, of course, its own material prerequisites.

At that time fire was not very effective, and its specific weight was insignificant. The primary material factor of pressure against the enemy was an immediate attack by personnel. This required concentrating the entire mass of forces before the battlefield in one continuous mass of deep attack columns, which the French Revolution engendered with its new soldier, burning with enthusiasm for fighting.

It is completely understandable that from such a concentrated position only a massive attack along internal lines was possible, which smashed Frederick's linear combat formation as well.

However, such concentration before the battlefield at that time was also caused by material means of armament.

The characteristic distinction of combat conditions in Napoleon's era was that at that time they saw further (normally three–four kilometers) than they shot, since a rifle shot about 200 meters and a cannon about 1,200 meters.

The range of fire was considerably inferior to the range of vision. Under these conditions, the opposing sides would converge on the battlefield and examine one another, but they still could not fire, since the range was insufficient.

This circumstance also explains why in Napoleon's time the meeting battle, which developed directly from the march, could not occur, since this required opposing sides to have the ability to employ fire as soon as they caught sight of one another during the approach.

Thus, the pause between the march and the battle in the Napoleonic era was conditioned by the limited range of fire, and prompted preliminary marshalling into combat formation before the start of an operation and in front of the battlefield.

This defined the extremely important and characteristic distinction of military art during the Napoleonic era.

It consisted of the fact that the battle, as an end point which crowned a long operational line that was in no way predetermined by the latter, did not organically result from it, and was played out as a separate tactical episode. This can best be seen in the Italian Campaign, which concluded with the unique Battle of Marengo, and in the 1812 Campaign, crowned by the Battle of Borodino.

Thus, battle in the Napoleonic era was a one-act tactical phenomenon; it had no measurement in space, because its scale remained a point; it had no measurement in time, because its scale remained a moment; it had no depth because it was conducted in place; finally, it was played out as an independent tactical episode which did not issue organically from the campaign as a whole. Under these conditions, Napoleon's military art did not yet acknowledge the operation in the contemporary understanding of this word.

Undoubtedly, the fundamental indicators of the operation were absent.

Battle was within the competency of tactics alone as an independent combat exercise.

In truth, each historical era is pregnant with something new and already manifests rudimentary aspects of tendencies and new forms.

Thus, in the Napoleonic era one can already see the first signs of new forms of armed conflict, which emerged from the framework of the single battle.

This is evident from the examples of Ulm, Regensburg, Leipzig, and 1814.

It was not these new manifestations, however, that were characteristic for the Napoleonic era.

For this era, a long operational line, crowned by a point as an independent tactical episode, was characteristic.

And under these conditions, strategy had its own fundamental mission of simultaneously concentrating all forces on one battlefield, and ceded its place to tactics when this battle commenced.

Clausewitz expressed this situation as follows: "As soon as the enemy approached so as to give a general, decisive battle, strategy was over, and it could rest."

This situation, influential for a long time, played a large, conservative role under completely altered conditions, and fundamentally contradicted the phenomenon of the operation, which arose shortly thereafter.

In the second half of the nineteenth century, all conditions which had shaped Napoleon's military art radically changed.

The flowering of industrial capitalism, the introduction of compulsory military service on the basis of new production relations of bourgeois society, and technical progress on the bases of developed industry created new prerequisites for the evolution of the military system.

The introduction of rapid-fire, rifled weapons had enormous significance.

Armed with Dreyse rifles, the Prussian battalion of Moltke's time could already shoot 4,000 bullets per minute. It is true that the range was still limited (300–400 meters), but shortly thereafter it increased to 1,000 meters and 1,300 meters (French Chaspeaux).

The introduction of the rifled Krupp cannon immediately increased the range of fire power to 3.5 kilometers.

Under these conditions, the specific weight of fire grew considerably, and fire became the primary material factor for pressuring the enemy, marking the beginning of the era of fire destruction.

However, fire tactics greatly contradicted Napoleon's deep column, which made it impossible to employ all fire means and also presented a very large firing target. If the principal combat factor was fire, then this required the largest possible number of fire units to advance in a single line, so that they could be used.

The entire evolution of tactics in the second half of the nineteenth century proceeded from developing the deep column into a broad firing line [*liniya ognya*] and, subsequently, into a skirmish line [*strelkovaya tsep'*].

Concentration of the mass in front of the battlefield into deep closed attack columns resolved itself into a broad linear deployment, but already on a new qualitative basis of fire power.

Nevertheless, conservative tactics still strove for a long time for a close accumulation of masses in a narrow space. However, as Engels says, "the soldier was more sensible than the general, and, using common sense, arrived at the wide firing line."

This tactically significant circumstance soon affected the nature of armed struggle as a whole, which resulted in striving for a wider combat formation.

Moltke was already teaching that

> More is lost in the depth than is won by narrowing the front; two divisions which are proceeding next to each other, 7–10 kilometers from

one another, mutually support one another more easily and better than if one division is proceeding behind the other.

However, at the same time another enormously significant factor in the nineteenth century led to the widening of operations: this was the railroads, which accelerated army concentration in the theater of military operations; in addition, they inevitably gathered the army in different regions along a considerable front.

In 1886 against Austria, Moltke deployed in three separate armies on a front of 400 kilometers those 300,000 men whom Napoleon easily led and marshalled in a single concentrated mass. This was, it is true, conditioned by the line of the railroad network and the configuration of the Bohemian border. However, in 1870, the deployment of the Prussian Army against France occupied at the staging area a front of up to 100 kilometers, which then, with a forward advance, increased to 150 kilometers.

At that time, this widening of the front line was completely implausible and strongly criticized by Moltke's enemies. Conservative military theory elevated the foundations of Napoleon's military art to an unshakable canon and eternal principle, and could not understand the conditions and requirements of the new era.

Moltke's enemies, Benedek and the French marshals (Bazin and MacMahon), continued to attempt to squeeze their armies into narrow spaces in compact masses, and each time were dealt with mercilessly by the wider Prussian fire front. In national wars of the second half of the nineteenth century, two eras of military art and two military schools were, in essence, struggling. Predominance, of course, went to the one which took into account the new conditions of its time.

This could, however, be significant only because wars waged by Prussia in the second half of the nineteenth century had an historically progressive character, and the "War of 1870–71 was a continuation of bourgeois progressive politics (lasting for decades) for the liberation and unification of Germany. This liberation hastened the defeat of Napoleon III and his overthrow."[3]

From that time, military art turned to a wide deployment of forces in one line, and armies began to arrive at the theater of military operations in a wide linear front.

This was the dawn of a new era in the evolution of military art – *the era of linear strategy.*

Here it was not the numerical growth of armed forces which led directly to wide deployment, for the Prussian Army of 1866–70 in no way exceeded in numbers Napoleon's Army; rather it was superiority in new material factors – means of struggle and the railroads.

New fire means are the initial factor resulting in a wide line and a turn to wide deployment and linear strategy. This is the best corroboration of Engels' position that "nothing depends on economic conditions to such a degree as the army and navy"; that "armaments, personnel, organization, tactics, and strategy depend, above all, on the degree of production attained at the given moment, and on the means of communication."

With the arrival of the era of linear strategy, a number of new phenomena, which no longer fitted into the framework of one battlefield as a single point and so grew beyond the scale of tactics, were introduced into the scheme of events played out in the theater of war.

Inasmuch as armies began to engage in battle on a wide line, combat efforts were dispersed along the front, and battles began not at a single point, but at various points of the extended front.

The fundamental difference in the nature of armed conflict in the second half of the nineteenth century was that the single point of the Napoleonic era broke up into a series of separate points spread out in space.

In truth, this was still not a continuous front but an interrupted front of separate points where combat efforts were applied.

The War of 1866 began with three separate battles (Gitchin, Trautenau, and Nachod) spread out along a front of 100 kilometers.

The War of 1870 began with two large-scale battles (Spichern and Werth) simultaneously played out at a distance of 60 kilometers from one another.

Moltke the strategist was faced with a completely new problem of coordinating and directing combat efforts, tactically dissociated and dispersed in space to achieve the overall aim of defeating the enemy.

This situation was the first characteristic sign of the phenomenon which is known in modern terminology as the operation.

And as is known, Moltke coped with this phenomenon to a very small degree. Schlichting says, "This greatest of strategists did not have a full enough understanding of how to coordinate separate army operations in a theater of war."

Moreover, it was not only their dissemination along a front that was new in combat phenomena of the second half of the nineteenth century.

Together with the spatial dimension there appeared the first signs, in truth, in rudimentary form, of the temporal dimension, that is, in depth, with which the Napoleonic era was completely unfamiliar, since at that time battles were played out literally in place and lasted a few hours.

The appearance of a second, temporal, dimension of combat operations had its specific objective prerequisites.

In the second half of the nineteenth century, in light of a significantly increased distance of fire power, the range of fire compared to the range of vision. It was possible to strike the enemy with fire as soon as he became visible, for under average terrain relief conditions visibility amounted to three to four kilometers, and the new rifled cannon had similar range (3.5 kilometers).

This circumstance created completely new conditions for the commencement of combat.

Since a fire strike was already possible during the approach, there was no longer a break between the approach and the battle, and preliminary concentration for battle, such as in Napoleon's time, was unrealizable.

All battles began directly from the march. This also explained the emergence of the meeting battle, which became possible, in its modern understanding, precisely during the second half of the nineteenth century, when increased range of fire compared to range of vision.

In truth, this was not understood for a long time; conservative Prussian generals in 1866 carefully kept artillery at the tail of the column, in the position of a transport, and wanted to marshal for combat initially according to Napoleonic principles. Conditioned by new weapons, however, the objective course of events was stronger, and the initiative for commencing battle shifted from the general to the forward security detachment. In addition, combat arising from the march began to occur not in place, but in motion after having received its first signs, in truth, at a still insignificant depth.

However, a more important circumstance was that this tactical depth immediately grew beyond the framework of battle and acquired the features of operational depth.

In the second half of the nineteenth century the short-term strike battle turned into a drawn-out fire battle, and acquired a significantly larger temporal dimension.

Battles in Moltke's era lasted 10–12 hours. They did not provide a decisive outcome, as in the Napoleonic era. Fire turned out to be incapable of resolving the mission in a single combat act and on one line. At the end of a single battle the enemy was still not completely defeated; he successively withdrew, organized on a new line, and undertook a new battle.

Thus, the line of combat efforts spread into the depth.

In the War of 1870, three battles (Colombey-Nuilly, Mars la Tour, and Gravelotte and Saint Privat) took place successively (in time) around Metz. The course of events lasted six days in all, and during this time 2d Prussian Army wheeled around the left flank, having covered 90 kilometers in all.

The war consisted of separate combat efforts which Moltke had to unite in space and time to achieve the overall aim.

The Sedan march-maneuver, which lasted ten days and required passage to a depth of up to 150 kilometers, also had the same character.

Thus, in the second half of the nineteenth century a new depth dimension of combat phenomena was disclosed, although still in its rudimentary form.

The War of 1870, until the fall of the Second Empire, numbered in the depth a total of four combat links of independent battle (Spichern-Werth,

Metz, Sedan, and Paris). This was still a line of separate combat efforts not connected with one another. Their finale, for the most part, was still one battle which, in its scale, had considerable kinship with the battlefield of the Napoleonic era. A series of points, distributed in space, often still led to a single, general point (Koenigratz and Sedan). Strategy was still able to consider its primary mission to be the simultaneous concentration of all available forces at a single place. The difference, however, was that this concentration occurred from a wide deployment, that is, from various directions, leading to a concentric envelopment of the enemy.

Concentric maneuver along external converging lines, which gave birth to a "Cannae" on an operational scale, became characteristic for the era of linear strategy.

It is true that this maneuver from various directions still led to a single battle. However, the combat finale of Moltke's era already contained a fundamental difference from the past century.

It was not yet played out as a separate tactical episode, independent of the long operational line.

When combat began to be engaged from the march, and the interval between them fell, battle began to emerge organically from the march-maneuver and was predetermined by its formation.

The march made the transition directly into combat, and march-maneuver naturally developed into battle. The plan of the latter was concealed in the former.

Those Prussian corps, which when deployed in 1866 occupied the extreme flank position, 400 kilometers from one another, were those which at Koenigratz closed an envelopment and approached each other at four to five kilometers. Under these conditions, the deployment plan already contained the plan for forthcoming operations. And since possibilities for changing the initial grouping were very limited, the line of marshalled corps could not be substantially changed during the offensive.

While Napoleon was able to structure his march without taking into account the forthcoming battle, since he had the possibility before engagement to adopt the appropriate combat formation, Moltke already had to have a specific plan for defeating the enemy as the basis of his deployment and march-maneuver.

At this time, the structure of military operations required perspectives and foresight with respect to battle, that is, it attached to it that character which is inherent to the concept of the modern operation.

Moltke already had to structure the deployment perspective inclusively right up to the battle.

The boundary between the march and combat, march-maneuver and battle, between strategy as the tactics of a theater of military operations and tactics as the conduct of battle was erased for his era's command skills.

Leading an army in a theater of military operations had to develop directly into the conduct of battle, that is, it had to embrace that sphere of competence which modern operational art includes.

In addition, a feature of strategy of the Napoleonic era – resting after the battle began – disappeared, being in sharp contradiction with new conditions for leading forces.

For a long time this still could not be understood. Napoleon's fundamentals of military art had taken root too strongly, having been elevated to an unshakable principle.

On the eve of the Battle of Sedan, army control fell from Moltke's hands, and only the initiative of subordinate leaders crowned the march-maneuver with a decisive battle outcome.

Because of conservatism in military theory, new phenomena and new conditions of the second half of the nineteenth century still did not penetrate into consciousness for a long time. At the beginning of the twentieth century, Leer was still building his dogmatic system of strategy on principles of Napoleonic military art. Nevertheless, in the wars of 1866 and 1870, military operations already revealed their new character: they were spread out along a front, dispersed into the depth, and developed organically from the entire deployment, that is, they acquired those fundamental characteristics which defined the concept of the operation.

Wars of the second half of the nineteenth century were the historical starting point in the emergence of the operation and marked the beginning of the evolution of its character.

III. THE EVOLUTION OF OPERATIONAL ART DURING THE WORLD WAR

The era of imperialism provided a wide field for further growth of the basic characteristics of the operation, that is, its expansion along the front and dissemination into the depth.

The economics of imperialism, with its struggle for markets, sources of raw materials, and application of capital, made war for a redivision of the world an inevitable result of the politics of the ruling classes, having caused colossal growth in armaments and the size of armies.

This process of broadening the entire military system conditioned the further evolution of military art at the turn of the twentieth century, but, in turn, resulted from its demands as well.

From the experience of the War of 1870, Prussian military doctrine concluded that, in the presence of increasing fire power, a frontal attack could not hope to be a solution.

Schlichting concluded on the basis of the experience of 1870, "Attempts at a purely tactical penetration in the future are almost unrealizable."

The results of the battle at Gravelotte and Saint Privat – the first example of an attack on a reinforced fiery front, an attack in its savage, unfettered form – led to this conclusion. At this time it was already clear that fire destruction means were stronger in the defense than in the offense.

Unprecedented losses, unsuccessful attacks, and the fall of the defensive line from one appearance of an insignificant group of forces on its flank forced immediate rejection of the frontal offensive.

It was recognized as impossible, because, in general, it was not considered necessary.

There still remained much free area for maneuver, and any position could be outflanked. In Moltke's time this was still very poorly understood. Schlieffen writes:

> And only late in the evening the division, guided more by happenstance than by plan, appeared on the flank and in the rear of the enemy, and unwittingly taught the assembled chiefs how, since the time of Leonid, it has been necessary to capture strong positions.

The entire evolution of military art after the War of 1870 proceeded under the guise of shifting the decision from the front to the flanks. Schlieffen conducts the entire thread of his teaching from this position, on which he premised military art of the age of imperialism.

Therefore, linear strategy strived even more toward a widening of the front.

Schlieffen writes:

> Basically the solution is a wide front, which makes it possible to envelope and, naturally, assumes a more powerful and numerically larger army . . . Modern battle is reduced to a struggle for the flanks . . . And in this struggle, he whose reserves are located not behind the center but on the extreme flank will be victorious.

The entire evolution of military art had set off along this path at the threshold of the twentieth century. The attempt to lengthen one's flank and widen one's front required an increase in the size of armies and, in the best way possible, provided for their growth in the age of imperialism. In 1914 the Germans set out with an army numbering two million, four times larger than their 1870 army.

All competition between the military systems of capitalist countries before the 1914 war essentially consisted of the greatest possible expansion of their front to gain an enveloping position.

Linear strategy reached its highest development.

Together with this process, the technical evolution of combat means also continued. New quality in fire weapons attached incomparably greater intensity to combat.

Already in Moltke's time fire means had reached the point where they were able to strike the enemy as soon as he became visible.

In essence, the range of fire underwent an insignificant evolution in the period from 1870–1914. It increased from 1,200 meters to 2,000–2,500 meters for infantry weapons, remaining, however, at its former level, practically speaking. It increased from 3.5 kilometers to five to six kilometers for light field artillery, which did not introduce fundamental changes. As for heavy field artillery, it acquired, in truth, a range of up to 11 kilometers; however, being quantitatively poorly represented, it was not able to influence substantively an increase in range of combat distances.

At the threshold of the twentieth century, the evolution of fire means of combat proceeded mainly along the lines of increasing their rate of fire. Enormous results were achieved in this area. The number of shots per minute are shown in the following chart:

	1870	1914
Rifle	5	12/10
Machine gun	0	500/250
Cannon	2	20/12

Note: The numerator shows the theoretical rate, the denominator – the actual rate.

At the same time, a continuous linear front turned into a front of enormously powerful continuous fire. This was the era of fire destruction in full bloom, which had already begun in the second half of the nineteenth century with the introduction of rifled weapons.

Of course, all these factors in the development of military affairs had to lead to the further evolution of the nature of armed struggle.

It became apparent that events of the greatest scope and intensity were forthcoming, fundamentally changing all conditions of armed struggle.

Engels wrote at that time:

> A complete revolution in the entire military system, caused by the inclusion of everything capable of military service in armies numbering millions, and by the introduction of fire weapons of unprecedented power, decisively formed a boundary to the Bonaparte period of war, having made any other kind of war impossible except for a world war, unheard of in its severity, with an outcome that was not at all subject to calculation.

The next events of the age of imperialism immediately confirmed this and resulted in an increased scale of combat.

During the Russo-Japanese War, the Battle of Mukden took place on a 150-kilometer front and lasted three weeks.

The basic feature of the operation – the expansion of its combat efforts in space and time – grew to the extreme, with respect to its quantitative indicators.

In 1914, German armies deployed against France on a 340-kilometer front. They went over to the offensive with such a broad line of marshalled corps, and fought the Battle of the Marne on a 250-kilometer front. Here, the nature of the front was substantially different from the broken chain of points, spread out in space, of Moltke's time. In 1914 this was a continuous front, merged into one line of points.

Therefore, the nature of the operation's expansion along a front completed its evolution; Napoleon's point broke up into Moltke's number of points, and in the twentieth century the number of points merged into one uninterrupted line.

Now the question was only what limit would the expansion of the entire front line reach.

In addition, a concentric maneuver from various directions, which presupposed a definite freedom of maneuver in space, was not well suited to the sluggish twentieth century front, which occupied the entire space in the sector of one's operations. The wheeling maneuver along external lines along the entire expanse of the front, which became characteristic for the coming era, replaced it.

Concentric maneuver from various directions could be implemented only in separate particular theaters of war which retained sufficient freedom of maneuver. This found its place in East Prussia in the initial period of the 1914 war.

The continuous front in space also entailed further evolution of the second feature of an operation, that is, its fragmentation into the depth.

The matter did not consist of increasing the extent of the operational line, which in 1914, during the offensive on the Marne, had a length of 400 kilometers, which campaigns of earlier centuries had reached.

The qualitative difference was that in 1914 a single chain of combat events, united by an overall operational plan, was played out to an entire depth of 400 kilometers. This was a series of stages in a single operation, or a number of associated successive operations, each flowing out of the preceding and giving birth to the following one.

Thus, operational depth in the 1914 war acquired a new qualitative character as a single chain of a series of associated combat events.

It is true that this chain was still not continuous into the depth. Battles embraced far from the entire depth, and were played out along separate lines in the depth.

Combat events took up only 23 per cent of the time of the entire Marne march-maneuver. This indicator was even less in the Eastern Theater of War. Here, on average, war took up 20.7 per cent of the time in August 1914, and

5.5 per cent in September. Thus, operational saturation of the depth with combat matters was still limited, having the nature of an interrupted series of battles.

However, the fact that this interrupted series comprised a single operational chain was qualitatively new in this phenomenon.

Thus, at the beginning of the twentieth century the operation was formed *as a chain of combat efforts, continuous along a front, uniform with respect to depth, and united by an overall plan for defeating the enemy or opposing him.*

The primary mission of operational art as the study of conducting an operation was the unification of separate combat efforts, not directly connected tactically, in space along a front, in time, and in depth to achieve an overall assigned aim, that is, bringing an entire chain of combat events into an active system, coordinated along a front and in the depth, which purposefully and successively leads to the defeat of an enemy.

Broadening this mission placed before operational art a new, complex problem of leading armies which were formed in a single line along a continuous front.

It could be foreseen earlier that under conditions of an imperialist war, when both warring coalitions similarly pursue aggressive, expansionist aims, armed struggle would adopt a fierce, exhausting character and, with certain economic equilibrium on both sides, would congeal in indirect forms of attrition.

A whole series of objective preconditions – the enormous numerical size of armies, and the colossal fire power under conditions of imperialist war aims alien and hostile to the struggling masses – led along various lines to such a perspective in the developing course of events.

In 1887, Engels wrote the following about future war:

> This would be a universal war of unprecedented scope and unprecedented power. From eight to nine million soldiers will strangle one another and consume all Europe to such a complete degree as clouds of locusts have never done. Devastation occasioned by a 30-year war but compressed to 3–4 years and spread out over the entire Continent, hunger, epidemics, both troops and national masses running wild, caused by sharp need, hopeless confusion of our man-made mechanism in trade, industry, and credit – all this will end with universal bankruptcy; the failure of old states and their routine state wisdom, a failure of such magnitude that by the dozens crowns will be dragged along roadways, and no one will be found to raise these crowns. The absolute impossibility of foreseeing how all this will end and who will emerge the victor from the struggle – only one result is absolutely certain: general exhaustion and the creation of conditions for the decisive victory of the working class.

These general words of Engels 30 years ago foresaw the entire nature of imperialist armed struggle.

Final resolution of the question of the war's outcome by some method or another for conducting operations generally could not be reached within the framework of imperialist war.

But when operational art of the imperialist era, implemented by representatives of the old dying class, turned out to be incapable of rising to the level of the new requirements of its time, relying on conservative military theory basically harking back to the Napoleonic era, the course of armed struggle revealed its contradictions sooner and more clearly, having demonstrated its complete powerlessness to reach just an operational solution, even within those limits in which this was objectively possible.

In no way were all new factors in the evolution of the nature of operations clarified. It is substantively important that this be brought to light in order to structure a contemporary system of operational art.

In Moltke's time, when armies still did not occupy a continuous front, their deviation to the right or left, convergence toward one axis or, conversely, distribution on various axes, and, finally, the turning of the entire bulk in another direction were still ensured by sufficient freedom of maneuver.

Under these conditions, Moltke the strategist had a wide field of operational activity, which required dynamic operational leadership in the course of events.

When, however, deployed armies formed a continuous line and occupied their entire deployment sector, maneuver by *fronts* in space acquired a new qualitative difference through a change of axes.

A high art of control was required in order that energetic operational leadership use each concrete situation to achieve an actual enemy defeat. This could be achieved only by leading armies on strong reins, by holding back some and advancing others for the purpose of gaining the flanks and the rear.

Schlieffen also had this in mind when he said that it was necessary to lead modern armies like battalions.

The age of linear strategy on a continuous front in no way excluded operational maneuver from its limits. A broken front emerging in the course of events provided abundant opportunities for this.

But it turned out that the operational art of command was incapable of rising to the level of new demands. It was still basically nourished by principles of the Napoleonic school, and in the twentieth century of continuous fronts of deployment, it continued to assume that conducting battle did not constitute a sphere of its competence, and when battle had commenced it could rest. With such an approach to operational art nothing remained but to limit its activities to the grouping of forces and to target them along specific axes.

The entire evolution of the nature of the operation, having already demonstrated in 1870 that march-maneuver had organically developed into battle, and that each battle, under new conditions of a continuous operational front, contains within itself preconditions for the subsequent operation, remained quite unclear. Hence, it was also not understood that under new conditions operational art required effective, continuous leadership during the entire course of the operation, including the battle.

This reflected the colossal conservatism of military theory, frozen in such an enormous question of control at the level of Napoleonic times.

The entire conduct of a 1914 operation was reduced to determining and directing groupings. From the start armies received their remote reference points and strove toward them along specific axes.

Even before the war Bernhardi assumed this, saying that modern armies had to be arrows which had been shot.

But as is known, having been shot, arrows are no longer subject to control, and this is what happened with the German armies in 1914.

Army formations were riveted to specific axes and directed to their remote reference points without any consideration of the possible situation, which, arising on the paths of the axis, might require a completely different solution.

Operational art, which failed to comprehend new conditions for conducting an operation, gave birth during the World War to remote sight strategy, whose fundamental distinction was the complete disregard of the given immediate situation.

The creation of this situation at the beginning of battle, and its use and exploitation at the battle's end were not a subject of operational concern at each given stage of the development of events.

Moltke thought:

> Each battle is a kind of springboard for new strategic decisions . . . Material and moral consequences of battle are so enormous that a new situation is always created dependent on its outcome. Much that was in mind earlier becomes unrealizable and, conversely, much that could not have been even considered before becomes possible.

This indisputable principle was forgotten.

Armies moved along their specific axes independent of the outcome of the battle, independent even of where it was forthcoming.

Events were played out in objective development, without any influence on them whatsoever by the main command, which already knew *ex post facto* about the outcome of the battle, which by this time had already managed to lead to further consequences.

Operational art eliminated itself from dynamic guidance of the course of events, having left them to their own development along the targeted axis.

The operation became uncontrollable, and in this lay the enormous contradiction of operational art, which in 1914 did not, in general, find a place for itself in the overall system of conducting military operations. Having excluded battle, according to the Napoleonic school, from the sphere of its competency, operational art remained, in general, out of the picture and actually "rested" during the entire period of the Marne march-maneuver.

Having found for itself neither place nor application, German General Headquarters hid deeply in the rear; had operational art not existed at all in 1914, little would have changed in the historical course of events.

As a result, a whole series of favorable operational situations, which would have provided success in hand, slipped by. Thus, 5th French Army, already squeezed between Cambrai and the Maas, escaped certain death in a border engagement.[4]

German General Headquarters did not trouble itself with an operational analysis of the outcome of the border engagement, and wrote in its directive on 27 August 1914 with complete lack of concern toward the situation which had arisen: "The German armies are ordered to advance toward Paris."

This movement turned into an offensive, in general, a remote sight offensive which disregarded the given concrete situation, jumped over it and, therefore, was conducted indiscriminately and to no purpose, with respect to the enemy grouping.

The matter was reduced to a simple mechanical transfer of an unaltered grouping to the depth of the expanse from the Rhine to the Marne.

It was considered adequate to bring one's operational efforts forward, as if this comprised the entire sense of the operation. Its actual aim – the rout of enemy personnel – was lost in this operational perspective.

Operational art was least of all concerned with the concrete resolution of the issue of where and how to beat the enemy; it replaced this with the issue of where and when to arrive.

Thus, the concept of annihilation and destruction, which comprised the fundamental idea of linear strategy when it was born in the second half of the nineteenth century, was emasculated from it.

And this became the first sign of its degeneration, having discovered the complete powerlessness of operational art in the age of imperialism to rise to the level of new requirements for leading armies in the twentieth century.

Subsequently, the conservative influence of false methods of operational leadership turned out to be so rooted that the offensive of the arrow which had been shot was repeated under completely different conditions of revolutionary-class war.

In an operational context, our 1920 march to the Vistula, which still reproduced the phenomenon of linear strategy on a wide scale, was, with respect to its operational leadership, completely analogous to the German march to the Marne.

Once again armies were unalterably riveted by their grouping to a single axis at a huge depth of 600 kilometers; once again remote reference points were given and a complete disregard of the given immediate situation was permitted; once again a sweeping, straight-line advance was conducted without regard to the given situation as it was unfolding; and once again operational leadership was excluded from the course of the battle, "resting" far in the deep rear.

As a result, once again there were a number of brilliant missed possibilities. III Cavalry Corps and 4th Army occupied a position far forward on the Neman, Narev, and Vkra Rivers. But instead of turning to the enemy flank and rear, making use of the given immediate situation, where an ample operational harvest awaited them, each time they were directed straight forward, like an arrow which had been shot, to remote reference points past the Poles' naked flanks.

In sum, there was a mechanical transfer of an unaltered grouping from the Dvina to the Vistula, and a clearly expressed sweeping "general" offensive, about which Comrade Stalin said, "Sweeping forward movement is death for an offensive."[5]

The death sentence was pronounced over linear strategy from the moment it degenerated into the simple emphasis of a continuous wall, before whose front a withdrawing enemy could freely group to deliver a counterstroke.

And then it turned out that the forward advance of this wall was as possible as its withdrawal, and its fall from one simple thrust into the flank was unavoidable.

This reflected the entire enormous contradiction of operational efforts which had become fixed in their own grouping on a single unalterable axis. When this happened, operational art, not having mastered the operational sense of events which had taken place, fell into complete confusion.

After all, changes in a grouping of armies engaged in battle along their entire operational front could be achieved only by a change in the correlation of forces on separate axes.

But the supply of the front from the depth and the presence of deep reserves were necessary for this. However, since linear strategy was linear it had no operational reserves, nor did it recognize any.

In the spirit of the Napoleonic era, battle was still viewed as a one-act effort which required simultaneous commitment of all available forces.

Clausewitz was still cited as an authority, writing that "all efforts which were allotted and available to fulfill the strategic aim should be used simultaneously; their use will be more complete and absolute the more they are compressed into a single moment." But what the great thinker established as truth according to the experience of the Napoleonic wars turned out to be untrue in the twentieth century, when the operation became a multi-act phenomenon and spread out in a series of successive operational efforts into the depth.

And when on the Marne and Vistula an insignificant number of reserves were, in essence, required to parry the strike delivered by the enemy, it transpired that there was not a single division at the disposal of the operational leadership.

It was this point in the development of events that essentially put an end to linear strategy, for, if operational art had placed itself in a position in which it was, in general, powerless to do anything, this meant that death was imminent.

And then, of course, old lessons were recalled, and the ghost of Schlieffen was summoned for help. It was necessary to search for a solution on the flanks; he whose flanks were longer would be successful – in this they thought to find salvation, and began a feverish race to the sea.

Here, however, they did not take into account that the enemy could do the same, and that lengthening the flanks, in essence, would only increase an already mired front.

And here, during the World War, operational art encountered even greater unsolvable contradictions.

Already at the dawn of the twentieth century, in the presence of a colossal increase of armed forces, it could be foreseen that the growth in numerical size of armies would outdistance the expanse of the fronts which contained them, these having an inherent limit set by nature. With the competition of both sides, striving for the greatest possible expansion of one's flanks in space had to lead inevitably to their natural limits.

This happened in the second month of war on the Western Front in 1914. Spread out in space on an expanse of 700 kilometers, the Western Front flanks found their natural boundary in the north on the sea-shore, and in the south in neutral Switzerland.

There was nowhere to spread out further. The distribution of combat efforts along the front – this first feature of an operation – completed its evolution during the World War and reached its natural geographic limit, beyond which it obviously could not grow, unless the sea dried up.

At the same time, linear strategy arrived at its antithesis. After all, its purport consisted of widening the front to achieve an envelopment in order to avert a frontal attack.

This possibility had now disappeared: freedom of maneuver along a front was lost, which meant that linear strategy lost the basic meaning which had given birth to it.

It carried in its evolution all the factors of its own self-negation. Schlieffen, its ideologist, did not foresee this. His study on the greatest possible intensification and expansion of an enveloping flank, expressed in the idea of "Cannae" as the highest form of linear strategy, appeared when the days of this strategy had essentially already been reckoned, and all characteristics of its antithesis had already hidden in the objective course of events. Schlieffen's "Cannae" was undoubtedly written too late, and its eminent author had lived too early.

When front stood against front, linear strategy essentially came to an end.

Nothing else remained but to turn to the penetration.

What was accepted as impossible after the War of 1870 became necessary during the World War. A random division which appeared on the flank no longer could teach how from the time of Leonid it was necessary to capture strong positions, for there was no such flank.

And then it was necessary to turn to the 1870 battle at Gravelotte–Saint Privat, and turn a wild, unbridled attack into a planned penetration of a reinforced sector. Thus, the evolutionary circle was closed. It led to the great frontal battles of 1918, and created a new stage in the development of armed struggle. It became apparent that the age of linear strategy had come to an end, and that the solution to the problem of penetration had to be sought on new evolutionary paths of operational art.

At this time, the imperialist war had fully revealed its protracted, exhausting nature.

The task of overcoming a fiery front seemed overwhelming. In its tactical content it was elevated to an end in itself, and operational art was put in service as the organizer and supporter of a frontal attack.

The problem undoubtedly required that superiority of offensive means over defensive means be achieved.

This was an enormous technical problem which became pressing with the coming of the age of fire destruction. The superiority of defensive over offensive means undoubtedly occurred before the World War. This precondition was the point of departure for shifting the center of gravity to the flanks. Nevertheless, Schlieffen was much concerned with giving the German Army strong offensive means. He concretely expressed this in his plan for formation of heavy artillery for a field army. The problem was completely new and unusual. It is interesting to note that a perplexing inscription was made in one of Schlieffen's lecture notes: "Does the Chief of the General Staff not wish to turn heavy artillery into artillery for the troops?" Schlieffen laconically answered, "Absolutely."

The German Army was the first to introduce heavy artillery into the armaments of field forces. But it turned out to be completely impossible to resolve the problem of correlating defensive and offensive means in favor of the latter using these assets.

Nowhere did the entire offensive to the Marne overcome the fiery front; it was only capable of moving it back. The annihilation operation turned into an operation of reverse movement, and this was one of the factors for the degeneration of linear strategy.

When the continuous front found its limit, competition between defensive assets and offensive means was the basic axis on which the evolution of the technical means of struggle to our time began to turn.

In the military-technical context, the entire sense of events of the World War from the end of 1914 was reduced to a struggle between offensive and defensive means.

For the first time, the competition was unquestionably decided in favor of the latter.

The primary fire destruction means, the machine gun, was much easier, cheaper, and more quickly accessible for mass production than artillery ordnance, as the primary asset for suppressing this means of fire destruction. If the number of machine guns in a division increased over the four years of the World War an average of 20 times, division artillery increased barely twofold. Fire superiority was preserved on the side of defense. This required an enormous concentration of artillery for suppression.

The average norm was established as 60 guns per kilometer of front. In fact, however, this was surpassed considerably, amounting to up to 100 and more guns per kilometer of front.

However, such a massing of artillery suppression means could not, in the final reckoning, resolve the problem of overcoming the fiery front. Only the forward field of defense was, in reality, overcome; its entire depth remained, for the most part, untouched. Offensive artillery was incapable of shifting its fire power to the entire tactical depth of the defense, because it had not kept up with the advance of attacking infantry.

The problem rested not on the power of suppression fire, but on its mobility, which encountered insurmountable obstacles in the battlefield terrain, which was inaccessible for animal or wheeled traction.

The entire tragedy of attacking infantry was that after 3–4 hours of successful attack from 100 guns supporting it, only a paltry number continued their fire. Then the attack fizzled and died.

It became obvious that the problem had to be solved not only along the line of quantitatively increasing certain means of suppression, but also along the line of finding new means. It was necessary to create a means for suppressing fire means which, in the first place, would be protected against them, that is, these means would receive armor against machine guns; and, in the second place, would be mobile on any terrain in order to enter the depth of the defense and directly suppress and shoot fire means of destruction point blank.

This idea, evoked by the requirements of the situation, was implemented in the construction of the tank as a combination of internal combustion engine, tracked movement, armor, and fire means. The very fact of the tank's appearance had enormous significance for resolving the problem of the superiority of offensive over defensive means.

The requirement for suppressing the entire tactical depth of the defense brought forth other combat means as well: the combat airplane as a trans-porter of fire by air, and poisonous gases appeared; their use was not limited by trajectory and they immediately achieved spatial envelopment.

Colossal technical progress during the World War, caused by new positional fighting conditions and supported by a high level of industrial development, directed the solution of the problem of defensive and offensive means along the path of the latter's gaining superiority.

This, however, was mostly noted theoretically. In practice, the attack with tanks did not succeed at first. The reason was the inability to employ them tactically and their low level of combat use. The tank did not immediately resolve the problem of overcoming the fire front. The first tactical solution was achieved in 1918 by the Germans, even without it. And only at the end of the war did new offensive means demonstrate their ability to break through the fire front.

But this occurred under conditions where, on the German side, the imperialist war had already grown into a civil war, and the masses had turned their weapons against the ruling classes. At that time, the question of defensive strength was to acquire a different political value.

Nevertheless, all data for the tactical solution of the problem of overcoming a fire front were available in the final period of the World War.

At this time, however, operational art turned out to be completely power-less.

Having concerned itself exclusively with the tactical organization and material support of the penetration, it essentially eliminated itself as the art of conducting an operation.

The tenet that it was necessary to place tactics above strategy itself speaks of operational art's loss of the missions of its content.

Having juxtaposed tactics against itself, operational art permitted a com-pletely absurd contradiction, for tactics and operational art are phenomena of a single order, only with different degrees of scale and dynamics. They not only coexist in the process of military operations, but also organically develop from one into the other.

If a tactical effort does not develop into an operational achievement, it becomes, in essence, pointless.

A tactical effort is only a step toward achieving an aim; it can never be an end in itself.

But this is what happened in the events of 1918, and is often understood this way even in our time.

Even today Colonel Duffeur speaks about the experience of 1918 as follows: "A continuous and fortified front ceased to be a simple wall, behind which strategic maneuver could develop in all its fullness; *it became the main goal of this maneuver.*"[6]

The entire problem of penetration was reduced to a tactical penetration of the front.

The entire problem was resolved only on a tactical scale. There was no question whatsoever of crowning tactical efforts with an operational achievement.

General Dubenet wrote, "The characteristic feature of penetrations in 1918 was the fact that only the first phase – the penetration of the front – was envisioned; development of the operation was not taken into consideration."

Operational art did not support the development of tactical efforts of the penetration of a front into a complete operational penetration and rout, and this is what comprised its failure in the imperialist war.

Unification of tactical efforts along a front as the primary feature of the conduct of an operation remained unresolved.

Combat efforts without any system or association were dispersed in space, without any prospects for their unification to achieve a common aim.

The attacker, locked in mortal combat, was thrown first on one, then on another sector of the front, and in the best case hammered away in the name in each of them. This form of action, conscious of its own doom and, therefore, not counted on to achieve decisive aims, was even elevated into a system of battles of attrition with a limited aim, and even today is often presented as a historical necessity in our time and the most complete theory for the penetration of a fortified front.

Under conditions of the imperialist war, there was, of course, a whole series of political and economic preconditions for such a system.

In the situation in 1918, the outcome of the war in general was not decided, in the final analysis, by one or another possible conduct of a penetration operation, although it undoubtedly affected the political, economic, and military situation of the contending sides. The solution matured along other lines.

The political fate of combat operations still does not, however, presuppose their operational foolishness.

Operational art consists not only of taking into consideration objective conditions, but also, having taken them into consideration, of overcoming them within the limits of objective possibility.

The system of battles of attrition, in general, was unable operationally to resolve the problem of penetrating a positional front and was, therefore, pointless. As for exhausting the enemy, this system exhausted the attacker before the defender: this was a self-exhausting system, which is evident from a comparison of expended forces and means on the part of the offense and defense in all the penetrations of 1916–18.

Employment of this system brought to light all the powerlessness of operational art, which had found itself in a blind alley, and it was essentially turned into a pointless system for hammering in nails.

But no wall is brought down by hammering nails into it.

In order to knock down a wall, it is necessary to hew its foundations, that is, to brace up under it through fissures which have been formed.

But here, operational art turned out to be even more powerless. Prospects for operational development of tactical efforts into the depth were hardly envisioned.

There were no operational echelons to develop the penetration, and this reflected the entire indirect influence of already obsolete linear strategy.

When a fracture in a positional front had actually been opened, as in the March 1918 German penetration, there was no one among the attackers to prolong the attack through the formed breach into the depth, so that the tactical breakthrough of the front could turn into an operational penetration and rout. All grandiose efforts of tactical organization of the penetration, all technical progress in arms, all the enormous concentration of forces and means of suppression – all these turned out to be, essentially, in vain, if tactical success was powerless to develop into operational achievement.

It is senseless to break down a door if there is no one to go through it.

But this is just what happened with all the 1918 penetrations.   The imperialist war did not resolve the problem of the penetration: it ended without having demonstrated the ability to implement this on an operational scale.

If, in the final analysis, the German front fell, this event came about beyond the limits of resolving the problem using factors of a military-technical order. The German front collapsed in 1918 not so much from without, but more from within, under the influence of general economic desolation and the powerful process of the revolution of the masses, which led not only to the downfall of the front, but also to the overthrow of the monarchy.

Of course, the colossal economic superiority of the Entente in forces and means had an enormous influence on this process. But here it was not a matter of operational art. And even after the German front fell because the stability of its defense could not hold, the Allies still wasted four months in 1918 to push back deployed German forces a total of only 100 kilometers.

Even here Foch did not intend to resolve the outcome of the war in 1918, and was preparing a general offensive for the following year. But before the decisive attack had begun, the Germans threw down their weapons on the battlefield, and a solution was reached. And after this, Kuhlman had the audacity to announce: "In the course of the last four months of the war, the French command demonstrated how a penetration should be conducted in a modern war, and to which results it leads."[7]

This meaningless boasting sounds like cruel irony in view of the prostration with which General Staffs of imperialist countries were seized in the final period of the World War.

Operational art of this era turned out to be powerless to resolve new problems advanced by the new nature of armed struggle.

It was frozen at the level of linear strategy and became impotent when this strategy reached its antithesis.

Thus, the problem of operationally overcoming a fire front remained unresolved.

We approach today with such an operational result.

Under new political conditions of a different nature of war, with a new army and on a new material-technical base, our operational art must resolve a problem which was not, and could not have been resolved under conditions of an imperialist war.

Linear strategy began with brilliant solutions in an era of national wars in the second half of the nineteenth century.

In the era of the world imperialist war (1914–18), it arrived at its self-negation.

And now, at the dawn of an era of revolutionary-class wars, a new solution must be found. This is the enormous mission of our operational art.

NOTES

1. G. Isserson, "Evolyutsiya operativnogo iskusstva" [The evolution of operational art], *Voyna i revolyutsiya* [War and revolution], 5–6 (1932), pp. 25–52.
2. Marx and Engels, Vol. VIII, pp. 491–3.
3. Lenin, *O programme mira 25 marta 1916 g.* [On a program of peace, 25 March 1916].
4. This issue is broadly illuminated by Groener in his works *Schlieffen's Testament* and *Military Commander against his Will.*
5. Stalin, *Politicheskiy otchet TsK XVI s"yezdu VKP(b)* [Political report to the Central Committee of the XVI Communist Party Congress], p. 50.
6. Emphasis is Isserson's.
7. Kuhlman, *Strategy* (Biblioteka inostrannoy voyennoy literatury), p. 64.

Operational Prospects for the Future[1]

G. ISSERSON[2]

Deep battle and the deep operation, as new forms of employing modern combat means, have turned their cutting edge against the fire front. Their basic task consists of breaking and destroying this front to the entire depth.

Regardless of whether a front is encountered on a march-maneuver, or if it is juxtaposed to an envelopment maneuver, or if it is formed by the enemy immediately upon going over to the defense, overcoming and destroying any resistance are the primary missions which new forms of combat are called upon to resolve, and which have emerged at the contemporary stage.

The basic and decisive condition for overcoming and destroying any kind of resistance is the *penetrating force of the attack*, which is characterized by deep forms of struggle.[3]

It would be a mistake, however, to presume that new forms of combat, with respect to some of their internal properties, directly determine the ability to overcome any resistance, or that they carry in themselves the ability to resolve this mission under any conditions.

Modern combat means possess great offensive capabilities; they encompass unarguable prerequisites for penetrating force. In and of themselves, however, without massive consolidated use on the bases of concentrating overwhelming superiority along selected attack axes, they do not guarantee immediate penetration capability.

Without clear and decisive superiority on the main attack axis, not a single offensive mission will be resolved.

The greater the force of fire and defensive capability – and the growth of these factors is natural for modern conditions of armed struggle – the greater the significance of the strength and superiority of the main attack.

The problem of the main attack and shock groupings had never acquired such great significance for the fate of offensive operations as under modern conditions. Whether offensive operations achieve deep development or are tied down to an immobile front depends entirely on their resolution.

It can obviously be foreseen that any operation begun and conducted with inadequate forces and means will swiftly lead to stagnation. And each bogged-down offensive is a step toward the establishment of a positional combat front.

Therefore, any discussions about the possibility of thinning out fronts, decreasing the density of concentration, or greater expediency of conducting operations by means of separate combined attacks along various axes are detached from modern conditions of fighting.

If the reasons for such discussions are the power of modern combat means, then this seems to be the least correct and most dangerous assessment of their role and significance.

Modern technical means of struggle increase the attack's potential, that is, provide a new quality to its penetrative force into the depth; however, in no way do they condition the attack potential on a wider front.

As for a combination of separate attacks delivered along different axes, this is more a question of deployment density, and in such an alluring situation it is, at the very least, an historic anachronism.

The conduct of operations in a theater of military operations by separate groups on different axes was possible in Moltke's era.

Now, of course, in separate theaters, where continuous deployment is impossible, a combination of such operations will be unavoidable. The massing of an attack along specific axes acquires all the more significance for each of them.

However, in the main theaters, armies will apparently be deployed along a continuous front. A combination of separate operations under these conditions may be possible only during their development into the depth.

From the staging area, operations in a theater of military operations will inevitably take on the character of an advance of a closed operational phalanx having its shock groupings on selected axes. If this phalanx does not have powerful shock groupings on specific main axes capable of overcoming and thwarting any encountered resistance, then the offensive will inevitably come to a standstill in the impotence of separate attacks which can resolve nothing.

He who wishes operations in modern war to support deep offensive development must, above all, be concerned with concentrating an overwhelming superiority of forces and means for the attack. The make-up of these forces and means can never be considered sufficient.

For just this reason, secondary axes should not be activated by allocating them forces and means that are inadequate for an offensive, but at the same time are too powerful for the defense. They will be missed on the main attack axis. But they will not be able to resolve anything on the secondary axis.

Any new formation employed on the main attack axis is a factor of victory; however, if it remains on a secondary axis it is often the reason for defeat.

Shock groups have their own great instructive history and underwent particularly sharp changes during the World War of 1914–18.

The German shock grouping during deployment on the Western Front in 1914 included two-thirds of the entire force deployed against France (26 corps and nine cavalry divisions from an overall number of 35 corps and 10 cavalry divisions). The enveloping right shock flank, consisting of 37 infantry and six cavalry divisions, was deployed on a front of 80 kilometers, that is, one infantry division for every 2.1 kilometers.

The more the resistance force grew, the stronger and denser the shock groupings became.

The subsequent years of the World War saw an enormous growth of shock groupings in density of concentration. Whereas in 1914 there were 37 infantry and six cavalry divisions with 1,572 guns and 180 airplanes on an 80-kilometer front, in 1918 this increased to 75 infantry divisions with 6,800 guns and 1,000 airplanes. Such was the history of the question.

No one could say that such a colossal concentration would not be required in the future as well.

If inadequate support of the penetrative force of the attack or development of new defensive capabilities had led the offensive operation to stagnation, the historical course of events would have required even greater concentration of forces and means.

However, the essence of the problem was that such a concentration was possible only in an immobile situation of front against front, and impossible under conditions of offensive operational movement. It was impossible to put simultaneously a mass of 75 infantry divisions on an 80-kilometer front in free forward march motion. There simply was neither enough area nor roads.

The composition of modern shock groupings must proceed from the possibility of continuous forward advance of one's efforts and continuous provisioning of the entire shock grouping with all types of supplies in the process of developing the operation. This condition, equally with the requirements of the penetrative force of the attack, must determine the composition of forces and means in each individual case.

Two factors – mobility and penetrative force of the attack – can, under specific conditions, lead to a contradiction. And unavoidable friction results from resolving this cardinal problem. Obviously one cannot immediately manage to put in motion a mass of forces and means which may be required at a specific stage in the development of the operation for the penetrative force of the attack. And this once again brings us back to the problem of deep echelonment of operational efforts intensifying the attack from the depth by means of an influx of new forces and means.

The presence of a large mass of reserves, including tank and artillery, and deep echelonment of efforts are, to a certain degree, the foundation of deep strategy.

The penetrative force of the attack solves [the problem].

It is the primary factor which determines the capabilities of a deep operation and the prospects for its offensive development to the entire depth of the theater of military operations. Overcoming this depth inevitably requires enormous intensity.

It is completely obvious that, with the modern scope of armed conflict, a single operation, even with the most decisive outcome, still does not resolve the aims of an armed conflict. The enemy cannot be defeated in one or two operations to such a degree that he is forced to cease fighting.

Future war with its decisive aims will force each side to exhaust all its forces and capabilities to the end.

The struggle will not be resolved with a single lightning blow. Frunze indicated this very soberly. He said, ". . . when the matter comes to a serious encounter, then it can hardly be concluded in a short interval of time by the delivery of a single annihilating blow."

In inflicting one blow after another, it will be necessary to pass through a series of intensified stages of fighting before the ultimate aim of the overall defeat of the enemy is achieved. This intense path to ultimate victory is fraught with many problems which have not yet been investigated.

Revealing the nature of the development of the gigantic struggle to the entire depth is a complex task for strategic research. In the past this task was never resolved correctly.

It is even more complex and grandiose now.

Under the burden of the immense problems of future war, Kuhlman even wrote, "It will be necessary to wage future war in the manner possible, rather than in the manner desired." However, the clarity and purposefulness of struggle has no patience with the issue posed in such a way.

The grandiose, world-historical significance of any war which involves us demands that it be waged as the great aims of our politics require. Therefore, the enormous task of a thorough investigation of the nature of future war stands before our strategic studies.

One basic question stands in the center of this research: What will be the nature of operations in modern war in the theater of military operations, with respect to their maneuver development, until the achievement of the ultimate aim?

The deep operation carries within it annihilating maneuver projected into the depth. But will it be able to support maneuver development of the struggle to the entire depth of the theater of military operations in one, all-suppressing offensive movement? Will it not, in the final analysis, lead to stagnation, as happened in the World War of 1914–18?

Positional forms of war are spoken of with repugnance and fear. They are avowed to be a kind of "military plague." War will be or should be one of maneuver. This is the prediction or desire which is considered a condition that is not subject to change.

But to say that war will be maneuverable means to say nothing, for this does not depend on our desires. Dogma on the maneuver nature of future war alone can resolve nothing in this grandiose problem; rather, it will sooner lead to a positional war.

If the struggling sides in the World War of 1914–18 were fixed for long years on an expanse of many hundreds of kilometers in indirect forms of trench warfare, then it is difficult to ignore this fact.

Positional fighting was a grandiose and fierce manifestation of the forms of a world war. This phenomenon was not a chance one; it was conditioned by a whole series of factors, as it should be.

We are inclined now to examine just this circumstance as one which has lost its significance at the contemporary stage. And this constitutes an absence of a sober, critical approach to an evaluation of the conditions of modern conflict.

The increased numerical size of modern armies, borders fortified on a great expanse, and great defensive potentials cannot exclude the creation of a continuous fortified front; in many cases the contrary is so, that is, they predetermine its emergence. Preconditions for the emergence of a continuous fortified front under modern conditions have in no way disappeared; rather, they have even increased.

There will be fronts, and it will be necessary to penetrate them. But does this mean that the positional nature of future war is predetermined, and that maneuver war is impossible?

In no way; not in any degree.

In posing the question of maneuver war, great dialectical errors are often made.

If all conditions of armed conflict changed, then the content of its maneuver nature changed as well. The essence of maneuver operations naturally are modified in accordance with changing conditions of conflict.

No phenomenon can be examined in stasis, with immutability of its forms.

Maneuverability under modern conditions cannot be what it was in 1914. It is now conditioned by a different material base and developing in a different operational context.

In posing the question of the maneuver nature of war today, it is impossible and incorrect to proceed from indications of empty space and freedom of maneuver, since there will obviously not be any significant empty spaces in future theaters of military operations. This means that there will not be conditions for free development of prolonged maneuver in its 1914 forms.

The maneuver nature of war cannot now present itself as the development of free maneuver in an unoccupied expanse in a single, uninterrupted enveloping movement from the Rhine to the Marne or from the Dvina to the Vistula.

Such operational development, in the course of which first a border engagement is played out, and then armies relatively freely cover an enormous distance of 400–600 kilometers, is hardly possible under modern conditions.

Today it is necessary to fight and overcome an enemy to the entire depth of offensive movement.

If it is assumed that "in future battles maneuver will be possible only when there are breaks in unfriendly lines, through which maneuvering units will be able to pass," then the possibility of maneuver in the future must, in general, be subjected to serious questioning, since obviously such natural breaks in unfriendly lines will not be found; it will be necessary to break through them by force, and then to change the frontal strike into free maneuver into the depth.

Therefore, juxtaposition of the concepts of frontality and maneuverability as mutually exclusive is incorrect in our time.

Under modern conditions, maneuver development of an operation in a theater of military operations will be possible only if enemy resistance to the entire depth is thwarted and destroyed every time and in every case.

Often this resistance will be a continuous fortified front. However, *positional struggle basically depends not on the capabilities of an opposing fortified defensive front, since its emergence at a specific stage of development of events, possibly even at their very outset, is always probable; it basically depends on the capabilities and prospects of an offensive blow.* If an offensive blow each time is able to overcome any encountered resistance, operations in general acquire uninterrupted offensive forward movement and take on a maneuver character in the given theater of military operations.

A front can even be continuous, leaving no free space for envelopment and maneuver; however, if the attack force is able to overcome opposing resistance, then the front will begin to break, enter into motion, and lead to a maneuver war. On the contrary, a front can be broken, permitting envelopments and broad maneuver; however, if the attack is powerless to overcome resistance countering the maneuver, then before long the front will be drawn out as a continuous wall and remain in stasis, as was the case during the 1914–18 war.

Therefore, *the penetrative force of a deep attack acquires decisive significance for the development of modern operations.*

The potential for maneuver development of operations depends now not so much on rapidity of the attack, but on the force of the attack.

This, of course, does not mean that the course of operations will consciously slow down or that attempts to accelerate their development will be given up.

Rapidity is a sign of the technical age we face and it results not so much from conscious decision as from the speed of modern battle means.

The faster acting the weapon, the more impelling is its prompt and rapid employment. If an airplane can cover 400 kilometers in an hour, then why not quickly subject a target located at that distance from the border to an air attack? If a fast-moving tank can cover 100 kilometers in a day, then why not dispatch a mechanized formation such a distance? And since each of these fears a more rapid appearance of the enemy, competition for speed commences, which finally turns into feverish haste.

At the beginning of a war, we undoubtedly will be witnesses to such a race for speed.

When fast-operating combat means did not exist, and it was not necessary to fear the possibility of a sudden and swift attack, there were no preconditions for such competition. At that time, speed was measured by the normal daily infantry march. There was no basis for forcing events. All the same, wars ended relatively soon and this meant that one did not have to hurry. And an encounter with the enemy postponed a day or more in no way changed its significance or its character.

Such were the conditions in the past century. They even prompted Moltke in 1870 to bring the concentration of 2d Prussian Army back six marches toward the Rhine because of one harassment against its forward position. From the viewpoint of modern conditions, such a decision would simply be inconceivable. But at that time there was no reason for Moltke to hurry, for those battles which stood before him in no way changed their significance or nature just because they were waged six days later.

Modern conditions result in completely different consequences.

It is precisely because war today is prolonged and everyone fears this prospect that the rapidity of conducting military operations, which are reckoned to achieve the goal sooner, acquires especially great significance. A delay of an attack for even one day can, under modern conditions, completely change the significance and nature of forthcoming combat operations, for today, if the enemy is only in the process of assembling, then tomorrow he will already have created a defensive system, and the day after he will have erected a fortified front.

All this fundamentally changes battle conditions and, as never before, requires haste so as not to lose a favorable prospect. And the speed of modern combat means assist this better than ever.

Therefore, above all, *the struggle to exploit all capabilities* lies at the basis of conducting modern military operations. And this means *speed*.

Thus, speed will become a property organically inherent to the nature of modern operations.

But will operations, in turn, themselves become faster and more decisive because of this? At times it is assumed that the mobility of modern types of forces will necessarily lead to an increase in tempos of developing operations. But under modern conditions, operational tempos and mobility of types of forces are hardly in direct proportion. When the theater of military operations was relatively empty, as in the nineteenth century, such a correlation was correct. But at that time elements for increasing mobility in the form of modern mechanization and motorization did not exist. Mobility technology appeared when fronts became continuous and empty areas for free maneuver in a theater of military operations, as a rule, disappeared. Of course, where free maneuver was possible – and this was in no way exceptional – mobility of types of forces could fully justify itself and lead to increased tempos in the development of operations.

But where a continuous front is encountered, which will be most normal under modern conditions, a limit will be placed on speed, and it will have to yield to force.

One should not attach exaggerated significance to aviation speed for resolving problems of operational tempos.

Aviation speed has its own significance for the instantaneous employment of this type of weapon in an operation. But this significance is hardly felt in accelerating tempos of operations themselves. One can even suggest the contrary. An offensive operation, the expression of which is open offensive movement of large masses of forces and means, hardly encounters its main resistance from aviation. And if the attacker is not guaranteed air superiority, then his enormous masses are threatened with being pinned down to the ground, unable to continue their forward movement. In this case, resolution of the problem of operational tempos does not promise too enviable prospects. Aviation is the most offensive type of weapon. But, at the same time, it personifies the greatest resistance to the offensive and tempos for its development.

The speed of modern combat means can result in completely reverse consequences, and, under modern conditions, in no way causes speed in the development of operational tempos.

One cannot help but acknowledge the opinion of General Dubenet, who had his own ideas for the future, when he wrote:

> It is necessary to protect minds from the fetishism of speed, which is unintentionally elicited by the too general term, "motorization" . . . We will experience even worse and bloodier disappointments if we enter a new war with the mystique of speed.

In any case, this problem should be understood with complete clarity by advancing the significance of the problem of force.

Increased mobility will retain its full significance in the period of concentration, the approach to the combat front, and for abundant delivery of ammunition. It will again reflect all its speed properties during the period of developing the attack into the depth.

But for the solution itself of the problem of overcoming a fire front, the penetrative force of the attack will acquire principal significance.

Therefore, the force of the attack, which lies at the basis of deep forms of struggle, is the principal factor.

The essence of the issue rests in the fact that, in breaking any opposing resistance, the deep operation carries its efforts into the depth and here, delivering annihilating blows, actually promises to develop maneuver operations, the likes of which the history of past warfare has never known.

Thus, if operations of the World War at first developed a picture of a large enveloping maneuver and then a positional front, which it was hopeless to think of completely overcoming, then deep operations of a modern war will evidently develop along the line of first overcoming opposing resistance, and then developing wide maneuver operations into the depth.

Thus, the course of armed conflict is changing in comparison with 1914 in reverse order of its successive development.

This, however, should not be conceived of in too simplified a form.

Overcoming a single opposing front and developing maneuver operations into the depth cannot immediately resolve the outcome of the armed conflict. Efforts carried into the depth will, before long, encounter new resistance in the form of a meeting counterstroke or a new front organized in the depth.

Moreover, the initial period of war provides unquestionable opportunities for maneuver operations. Thus, it conditions a maneuver prologue to the development of the armed conflict.

This prologue cannot, however, be too prolonged. And dispersal of operations of fast-moving formations (mechanized forces, cavalry, and motorized forces) also will evidently not be too great.

Maneuver actions from the staging area will, obviously, soon run into an occupied front, and then speed will have to yield to force.

Finally, despite the complete restrictiveness of conditions in space, it is impossible to exclude the prospect for enveloping maneuver movement; this cannot be lost sight of under any circumstances whatsoever – in no way can it be rejected.

Each of these possibilities must be exhausted with all the completeness and decisiveness that conditions will allow.

Renunciation of developing maneuver operations at the beginning of the conflict, when deployment conditions allow them, would be doctrinal neglect of those potentials which historical conditions have still preserved.

The essence of this question rests, however, in the fact that sooner or later – sooner, under modern conditions – an enveloping maneuver will encounter frontally opposing resistance which must be broken and annihilated, to acquire once again the potential for maneuver. Thus, in this case as well the course of events will lead to some general channel for their development in a theater of military operations.

One can roughly imagine the following sequence for the course of these events:

- maneuver operations of invasion during the initial period of war;
- overcoming of opposing resistance;
- development of maneuver operations into the depth;
- meeting new resistance in the depth;
- overcoming again of opposing resistance; and
- resumption of a new round of operations, including alternation of these stages, etc., to the entire depth of the offensive, until the ultimate aim is achieved.

Of course, at each stage of operational development, individual formations will sometimes have great maneuver potential within specific limits. However, in the entire operational scale, the course of events in a theater of military operations will obviously, with some deviation or other, be subordinated to conform with general natural laws of their development into the depth.

Indeed, one must view such operational development in the maneuver nature of modern war.

Modern maneuver develops on the basis of frontality.

This comprises the principal difference from past maneuverability.

Modern maneuver principally lies not before the front (as it was in time and space in the World War), *but behind the front and in its depth.*

Thus, the contours of possible operational development in future wars are sketched through a veiled curtain.

And it becomes obvious that only on the basis of the penetrative force of a deep attack do these operations acquire a new maneuver nature of their offensive advance, right up to achieving the ultimate aim.

Problems of future operations find their basic resolution in deep forms of struggle.

If these forms are not possible, then there are no other methods at the disposal of military art or conditions permitting it in the immediate period with which to overcome the lack of prospects for operational development, to provide operations with a maneuver character (in the modern sense), or to crown them with a really decisive, annihilating result.

Therefore, where the achievement of decisive aims will be sought in modern war, we should see enormous masses of forces and means echeloned in the depth, while simultaneously extending one's own overwhelming attack into the entire depth of opposing resistance, breaking through the front by means of a sweeping, penetrating onslaught, and then bursting into the maneuver space of the enemy's operational depth.

Forces and means must be enormous for such an operation.

Powerful, long-range heavy aviation, airborne infantry, and super-long-range artillery – this is what must immediately spread an overwhelming attack in the entire enemy depth.

Powerful combined-arms infantry formations, numerous tanks from the smallest to the largest ground forces armored carriers, powerful artillery of varied caliber up to the heaviest and longest-range, and numerous light combat airplanes assaulting the target on the battlefield – this is what must break through an opposing front by means of a penetrative onslaught.

Powerful, fast-moving, independent mechanized formations, modernized cavalry and motorized infantry supported by this mass of combat airplanes – this is what must explode into the enemy's operational depth.

And finally, numerous motor vehicle columns, transports, and trains loaded with abundant materiel reserves – this is what must continuously feed the voracious future front.

Such, in general, is the picture of a grandiose deep operation as a form of struggle which will be characteristic and typical for this era.

This, however, does not mean that this form of operation will be implemented in all cases and everywhere.

Each era in military art is a combination of many varied methods of struggle, for the conditions in which it proceeds in various theaters of war and in various sectors of each of them cannot be identical.

Lenin wrote:

> An era is, therefore, called a era in that it embraces the sum of various phenomena and wars, both typical and atypical, both great and small, characteristic of both the leading countries and those countries which lag behind.[4]

Together with the typical form of the deep operation, modern war will inevitably abound in a number of other forms of struggle, in which a deep nature will be considerably less expressed, in some cases almost lacking.

The deep operation is, above all, an operation of an enormous mass of tanks, artillery, and aviation.

It is completely obvious that only where this mass of technical combat means is concentrated in the necessary quantity will the deep operation attain its developed execution.

And this is possible only on specific main axes.

On the enormous expanse of those fronts where, at the given time, a major solution is not being sought and where, therefore, there will be a different concentration of combat means, military operations will inevitably retain a character close to the linear forms of the past.

Therefore, it would be completely incorrect to gloss over the concept of deep forms of struggle while considering that all military operations will now bear a deep nature and that other forms will be of no use.

Tanks, heavy artillery, and aviation will obviously take part in modern operations in all theaters and fronts, even the hindmost and secondary ones.

It is difficult to conceive of any sector of struggle where these technical means would not be employed.

However, this still does not mean that their employment will take place in deep forms of struggle.

In order that new technical means give rise to new quality in forms of struggle, it is necessary that quantity reach a specific level of saturation.

Only where technical saturation steps beyond the specific limit of a quantitative norm will the struggle be able to acquire the new qualitative content of deep forms.

We say only *"will be able to acquire,"* because new forms of struggle, even in the presence of everything mentioned, are not born spontaneously; they often come into being in torturous births, passing through severe, prolonged trials.

Here, a clear representation of the nature of new conditions of struggle and the natural regularities of their development is the indispensable condition for new forms of struggle to triumph.

In future war, in the presence of the tempestuous development of modern military equipment, methods for conducting battle and operations will obviously have to change and be improved more than once.

It must be kept in mind that in a grandiose, prolonged war, forms of struggle cannot develop along a single line.

Struggle as a fierce encounter between two forces inevitably gives birth to new conditions and new forms.

In the stormy process of armed struggle, which compels warring sides to manifest the highest intensity of which they are capable, phenomena are rather subjected to changes and arrive at their self-negation, demonstrating the indisputable truth of historical development, in which "there is not a single phenomenon which, under certain conditions, could not be turned into its own antithesis."[5]

Thus, in the era of the World War (1914–18), linear strategy arrived at its antithesis. Deep strategy, in the process of its future development, cannot be an exception in this respect.

Therefore, it is necessary to be sufficiently far-sighted, so that in the course of events all new conditions are quickly revealed, and one proceeds boldly along the line of the subsequent development and changes of forms of conducting military operations, when the changing situation demands it.

We still cannot foresee what these changes will be, but we can state, without any miraculous prophecy, but on the basis of understanding the natural laws of historical development alone, that modern battle and the modern operation will develop on the basis of deep forms of struggle with some degree of fullness in their implementation, for *at the contemporary stage, forms of deep battle and deep operation are historically natural and, therefore, necessary and inevitable.*

An understanding of the process of historical development is an indispensable condition for the understanding of all phenomena.

The study of the majority of unsuccessful operations of past wars demonstrates that the greatest command errors often occurred not because of poor understanding of military affairs, but because of lack of familiarity with the overall course of historical development of military art and, as a consequence of this, employment of obsolete methods and forms of armed struggle.

Where new combat means are represented fully in their necessary quantity, linear forms of operations have become obsolete; the greatest errors will be unavoidable when there are attempts to resurrect them under the completely changed historical conditions of the modern era.

NOTES

1. Editor's note: in investigating the density of *fronts*, the nature of operations, and operational forms, it is necessary to proceed from concrete theaters of military actions and the probable enemy. Here, the principle stated by Engels on battle and operations, which has not lost its significance even at the present time, should be constantly taken into account: "Armaments, composition, organization, tactics, and strategy are directly dependent on the given degree of development of production and means of communication. It is not the 'free creativity of the mind' of great military commanders which brings about a revolution in this field, but the acquisition of better weapons and changes in the composition of armies . . ."
2. G. Isserson, "Operativnyye perspektivy budushchego" [Operational perspectives of the future], *Voyennaya mysl'* [Military thought], 8 (1938), pp. 14–26.
3. Translator's note: unless otherwise indicated, all emphasis is the author's original.
4. Lenin, Vol. XIX, p. 202.
5. Ibid.

CHAPTER TWO

The Test of War, 1941–45

While theoretical concepts of operational art dominated the attention of the Soviet military establishment in the interwar years, operational realities and practices plagued Soviet military planners after 1938 and understandably preoccupied the Soviet military after 22 June 1941. The chief motivating force for the Soviet military was at first its defense and then its survival and the survival of the state.

Dismal Soviet military performance during the crises and wars which preceded the German invasion of the Soviet Union (Czech crisis, the invasion of eastern Poland, and the Finnish War) and the catastrophic course of the initial period of war from June until December 1941 vividly demonstrated Soviet lack of mastery of the operational realm, an especially devastating fact given acute Soviet appreciation of the threat they faced. Despite sound theoretical concepts, no Soviet commanders at any level could implement them in the field. The ensuing disasters were strategic in scale and consequence.

Retrospective Soviet analysis concluded:

> Commanders and staffs were not fully familiar with all the theories of conducting deep battle, and there were shortcomings in the material base that hindered its realization. Thus, during the war it was necessary to reassess and clarify some aspects of preparing and conducting offensive operations and decide anew many questions on the conduct of defensive operations on a strategic and operational scale.[1]

These questions were addressed anew under the immense pressure of combat conditions and as a part of a quest for survival. The German attack of June 1941 achieved strategic, operational, and tactical surprise, and encountered only a partially prepared Soviet strategic defense. Soviet command and control was inept, Soviet *front* and army commanders being unable to establish coherent defenses and displaying an alarming propensity for launching counterattacks predestined to failure. Disaster after disaster finally drove the Soviet High Command to seek practical remedies to these problems. The imperative of an ongoing war dictated the need for practical, rather than theoretical, solutions. For four years of war, battlefield practice preceded theory as the Red Army relearned how to operate at the strategic, operational, and tactical levels of war. For this reason, while theoretical writings on operational art dwindled in number, practical works on the conduct of war at all levels blossomed (much of it of classified nature).

In November 1942, the Soviet High Command and General Staff established a mechanism for systematically collecting and processing war experiences, primarily from *front* and army command level. This elaborate and effective system ultimately produced 26 volumes of secret or top secret analysis of operational techniques and countless other classified series on tactical issues compiled by *front* command and branches of forces. This analysis provided the basis for a whole series of new regulations, orders, directives, and instructions for the wartime employment of all types of forces. The resulting volumes educated the Red Army in the techniques of modern warfare and made possible the transformation of the Red Army from a force barely able to survive in 1941 into the victorious army of 1945. These documents, and subsequent ones on wartime experience prepared after the war, reflect the practical rebirth of operational art and the fulfillment of those theoretical writings of the 1920s and 1930s. In fact, the Red Army during wartime finally realized its theory of "the deep operation."

The three selections contained in this chapter illustrate Soviet approaches to operational art just before June 1941 and at the end of war. The first expresses the hope of the General Staff that reforms carried out in 1940 and 1941 had placed the Red Army on an adequate wartime footing. The second illustrates acute Soviet appreciation of what was occurring in 1941, while the third surveys Soviet wartime lessons learned.

S. K. Timoshenko, a close associate of Stalin and Voroshilov and a Marshal of the Soviet Union, was Minister of Defense in December 1940 when he gave his closing speech to a controversial military conference in Moscow. Although by this time the purges had done their work and discredited the theorists of the 1930s, it is remarkable how much of the intellectual legacy of operational art and the deep operation retained importance in his speech. The speech resembles a mini-*ustav* (regulation) on the conduct of operations. Timoshenko, by this time, had the task of reforming the Red Army after its poor performance in Poland and the Russo-Finnish War. Despite the remnants of original thought in Timoshenko's speech, Red Army performances in 1941 showed the parlous state into which the Red Army had fallen.

Brigade Commander P. D. Korkodinov's article from *Voyennaya mysl'* (Military thought) typifies an entire series of 1940 and 1941 articles which surveyed the Polish-German War and the beginning of the Second World War in Western Europe. This, and its companion articles are striking in their acute appreciation of what was occurring. Tragically, the Red Army was unable to convert this appreciation into sound military practice.

Major General N. Talenskiy was a preeminent Soviet wartime and postwar writer on issues of military strategy and operational art. His numerous articles are noteworthy for their high-quality contents and for the fact that he was able to write openly despite the looming presence of Stalin, who, even in wartime, tended to stifle creative thought and claim credit for all military innovation, however slight. Talenskiy's article surveys the state of operational art in 1945, cites those few of the prewar theorists who had not been discredited, and resurrects the concept of the deep operation (without resurrecting the memories of its creators). He correctly ends with the statement that, "Our operational art has amassed the richest experience, which has permitted in theory and, of necessity, in practice further steps in the development of that most important branch of military art."[2] Talenskiy's subsequent enjoinder that the nature of war was ever-changing and that further study of wartime experiences was essential to a mastery of operational art in the future set the tone for the subsequent Soviet approach to operational art in the first postwar period.

NOTES

1. V.G. Kulakov, "Operativnoye iskusstvo" [Operational art], *SVE*, 1978, Vol. 6, p. 53.
2. N. Talenskiy, "Razvitiye operativnogo iskusstva po opytu poslednikh voyn" [The development of operational art according to the experience of recent warfare], *Voyennaya mysl'* [Military thought], No. 6–7 (June–July 1945), 30.

Closing Speech of the People's Commissar of Defense of the USSR, Hero and Marshal of the Soviet Union S. K. Timoshenko at a Military Conference held on 31 December 1940[1]

OPENING REMARKS

A Brief Assessment of the Significance and Results of the Conference

1. With respect to its content and significance, the present conference held by the Main Military Council is a new, important stage in the Red Army's life.

2. The results of the conference are enormous. They are so enormous that at present it is impossible to sum them up fully.

3. The conference results demonstrate, above all, that we are beginning to create new foundations and new conditions for the further growth of our Red Army, that we are deepening and broadening restructuring in the Red Army which was begun six months ago according to Comrade Stalin's directive.

The conference results will assist us in planning the further path of this restructuring and simultaneously adopting a correct orientation on questions of combat training and army indoctrination on the basis of considering recent military experience.

4. New topical and problematic issues of military art were discussed at this conference.

The content of our conference work demonstrated that we found a new base for the rapid growth of our higher command level, and that we are striving to elevate the leadership of the great armed forces of our country to the required height.

5. A discussion of the great problematic questions of military art opened for us the path of bold individual and collective creative activity, which is the foundation of military science and military art.

In discussions conducted here, we laid the foundation for an objective and healthy look, provided by the past, at the experience of military history.

We have boldly and innovatively begun to approach the experience of modern military art.

We have found a source of military thought, from which it will spill forth over all the pores of our military organism.

We have begun to fulfill Comrade Stalin's instructions on elevating the military-ideological level of command cadres, and have laid the foundation for the creation of our own military ideology.

6. Finally, the conference laid the foundations for current military psychology in the indoctrination of our command cadres.

From here they will spread to the fighting man as well.

This will guarantee the high moral indoctrination of our forces, without which modern war cannot be waged.

These, in short, are the results and significance of our conference.

I shift now to the findings with respect to individual questions discussed at the conference.

I will begin with operational issues.

PART I: ON THE NATURE OF MODERN OPERATIONS

I. Extractions from the Experience of Past Wars

1. The experience of past wars, especially the Western European War of 1939–40, demonstrates that great shifts are occurring in the field of military art, conditioned by the employment of new combat means of armed struggle and the improvement of certain others.

2. In the sense of strategic creativity, the experience of the war in Europe has, perhaps, provided nothing new. But enormous changes have occurred in the field of operational art, that is, in the field of *front* and army operations.

Above all, it is important to note that mass use of such means as tanks and dive bombers in combination with motorized and motorcycle forces, cooperating with parachute and air assaults and mass aviation, apart from other reasons, has provided the high tempo and force of the modern operational offensive.

Offensive operations during the 1914–18 war bogged down only because the tempos of the offensive and the tempos of the approach of defensive operational reserves were the same. During a penetration, the defender always managed to organize new resistance in the depth.

German tank divisions in 1939–40 forestalled the bringing up of these reserves. And the specific point is that they were the first to surge forward, that they themselves created passages in the enemy's defensive sectors, and that they themselves developed the penetration.

It is not coincidental that the Germans employed a new formation for the penetration, with tank divisions forward. The unreliability of penetration attempts during the 1914–18 war forced them to this. They correctly reckoned that the force and success of a modern offensive lie in its high tempo and continuity.

3. As the experience of modern operations shows, the base of an infantry mass remains as broad and powerful, but the role of infantry in an attack has changed. It has changed from an attack means into the foundation of an armored shock wedge, which cuts into the depth of the enemy's territory using the spike of tank divisions.

Operational independence of high-speed mobile groups consisting of various types of formations (tank, mechanized, motorized, motorcycle) was conditioned by the organizational structure.

4. Operations in the West have made it clear that the deep attack, based on a system of interaction between aviation, high-speed motor-mechanized formations, and an army's main infantry mass, has one dangerous link, that is, the possibility of an interruption between operations by aviation and high-speed formations. This question was effectively resolved by using air assaults, which filled in the interval between the aviation attack and the approach of high-speed formations.

5. It is also important to note that if formerly military operations usually began with a meeting offensive, now this is not always possible.

Today the borders of large states, especially on important axes, are girded by reinforced concrete fortified sectors.

Despite this, it is also possible today to go around these fortifications.

Thus, for example, the German Army was not dissuaded from attacking and penetrating the Maginot Line. Not relying on a successful penetration, it preferred enveloping the French Maginot Line, ignoring Holland's and Belgium's neutrality.

However, there may be cases when envelopment of permanent fortified concrete sectors will not be possible, and it will be necessary to begin the war with the penetration of a modern permanent fortified sector.

This was so on the Karelian Isthmus in 1939–40, when the Red Army, for the first time in the history of warfare, successfully penetrated a modern reinforced concrete sector, strongly developed into the depth, thereby demonstrating the sole modern example of penetrating a modern defense; on the basis of this, it is necessary to study the complex art of penetrating fortified regions.

Proceeding from this, the Red Army and our higher command must be prepared for both operations under maneuver conditions and the penetration of modern reinforced concrete defensive sectors from the very beginning of a war, so as to develop this penetration relatively swiftly, arrive in maneuver space, and fully exploit the advantages of mobile formations in maneuver war.

The Red Army has at its disposal all necessary combat means for this.

Experience demonstrated that to penetrate a modern defense such as the Maginot Line, the following are necessary:

(a) skillful control, special training, and correct indoctrination of forces, combined with heroism and bravery of soldiers and commanders;
(b) a two–threefold superiority of forces on the main axis, especially in suppression means;
(c) mass use of artillery, tanks, and aviation on the battlefield, and their precise interaction;
(d) development of the tactical penetration into an operational-strategic penetration by introducing large mobile formations into the penetration and landing airborne forces.

The penetration of the Mannerheim Line should be mainly examined as an act of the greatest heroism and self-sacrifice on the Red Army's part, and as the sum of achievements of military equipment and military art in our country.

Here all the newest and most powerful artillery weapons systems were used, possessing enormous shock force and capable of destroying concrete fire points made of special concrete, and armored cupolas made of special steels.

The most modern types of tanks with thickened armor were also used here, operating in close cooperation with the infantry.

In the process of penetrating the Mannerheim Line, all combat arms were supported by powerful heavy artillery and bomber aviation. The entire Mannerheim Line was isolated from the rear by air force operations.

The offensive was conducted methodically, continuously, and with un-diminished power. Specially trained forces were sent into the attack. Flame-throwing tanks attacked underground shelters directly and directed a stream of burning liquid into embrasures. Combat engineers, included in the composition of shock detachments, directly followed the flame-throwing tanks and implemented mechanical destruction.

6. Careful preparation of theaters of forthcoming military actions and operations had enormous significance in the successes of the German Army in the war of 1939–40, including development of motor vehicle and rail routes; creation of an airfield network on their own territory and agent support of it on enemy territory; mass placement of agents in the zone of forthcoming operations to create panic among the population and to receive rapidly information about force groupings or important movements; preparation of forward material-technical support bases; and accumulation of assets for regenerating means of communication.

7. The morale factor played a great role in the success of offensive operations in the West, to include solid discipline, great initiative and

dynamism on the part of commanders of all ranks, and readiness of troops for self-sacrifice.

Briefly, these are the first conclusions drawn from the experience of recent wars:

(a) A high operational tempo is a decisive condition for operational success.
(b) A high operational tempo is provided by mass employment of motor-mechanized and aviation formations, used to deliver the first attack and develop it continuously into the depth.
(c) A decisive effect of aviation is achieved not by raids into the distant rear, but by united force operations on the battlefield in the division and army region.

II. Brief Assessment of our Operational Views

1. The Red Army has at its disposal excellent personnel and all the latest means for armed struggle; *questions of our operational and tactical leadership of forces should correspond to all modern demands.*

When studying an army and *front* operation, it is necessary for us to take into account continually the current materiel base, with a prognosis for the future, in connection with our country's economic growth.

2. All reports and presentations at this conference demonstrated an almost convergent and basically correct understanding of all fundamental operational and tactical forms of troop combat action.

Everyone without exception, to a greater or lesser degree, soberly considered the experience of recent wars.

Views on the operation are completely modern.

The offensive is understood as the mass employment of modern attack means, which strike the enemy's entire operational depth and operate in the deep operational formation.

The defense is considered possible only as an antitank defense capable of subduing the attack of large mobile groupings, and countering artillery and aviation actions, that is, the defense is both tactically and operationally deep.

One principal error made by many who gave presentations here at the conference should be noted. It consists of a gap in the assessment of the capabilities of modern combat means and methods for their employment, which leads, in the final analysis, to their limited employment.

3. After this brief assessment of our operational thought, I will turn to an examination of our views on separate types of operations.

Before examining *front* and army offensive operations, it is necessary to see what the modern defense involves.

III. The Nature of the Modern Defensive Operation and Defensive Battle

1. All presentations on the army defense and on defensive battle demonstrate a basically correct understanding of the essence of modern defense.

However, many of the principles presented here require more precise definition and substantive correction.

2. Above all, we must speak about the right of the defense to exist, in connection with its unsuccessful experience in recent wars.

A series of successfully executed penetrations in the West in the 1939–40 war gave birth among some researchers to the idea of a crisis in modern defense.

Such a conclusion is not justified.

It cannot be made, because neither on the Polish nor on the French front did the Germans encounter the necessary resistance which could have been rendered against them with appropriate enemy use of existing defense means (mechanization of defensive work, a varied arsenal of engineer means, powerful antitank fire means).

The Weygand Defensive Line, for example, was slapdash and not at all outfitted with modern equipment; in addition, as a tactical defensive sector, it completely lacked prepared operational depth. All the same, despite their multifold superiority, the Germans took more than a week to overcome by force this obstacle alone.

3. War experience demonstrates that modern defense cannot be limited to a single tactical zone of resistance, but against new deep penetration methods a second and even third operational defense echelon is needed, consisting of operational reserves, special antitank units, and other assets, based on anti-tank defensive regions or lines prepared in the rear.

Under these conditions, defense once again attains its stability and retains all "rights of citizenship" in the future.

4. I shift to a discussion of the essence of the defense and an examination of conditions for conducting it in a modern situation.

We will understand "defense" ("defensive operation," "defensive battle") as the totality of combat operational methods of military formations or units employed to counter an enemy offensive by holding an occupied line or region, based on the use of a prearranged system of fire, prepared terrain, and troop counterstrokes.

5. The defense is not a decisive operational method for defeating the enemy: the latter is achieved only by an offensive. One resorts to the defense when there are insufficient forces for an offensive, or when it is advantageous in the existing situation to prepare an offensive.

6. The primary reason for using the defense as an operational mode is to create large masses for an attack on a decisive axis by economizing forces through defensive actions in secondary sectors.

Under modern conditions, there may be instances when it will be necessary to resort to the defense even on the main axes.

For example:

– when it is necessary to gain time to prepare an offensive operation until all designated forces are assembled;
– when it is necessary to await the outcome of operations on other axes, fronts, or theaters;
– when it is convenient first to throw the enemy into disorder or exhaust him, for the purpose of subsequently going over to the offense;
– when the defense is, in a word, a component part of planned operational maneuver.

The defense is especially advantageous only in the case where it is planned as a method for organizing an offensive, and not as an end unto itself.

7. The defense itself should embrace the notion of maneuver.

In all cases, the defense should pursue the aim of forcing an attacking enemy to fight under disadvantageous conditions, in order to inflict on him the greatest losses and frustrate his offensive, thereby preparing conditions for one's own transition to the offense, all this being accomplished by using terrain selected and prepared beforehand, and an organized system of all types of fire. If to this is added the absence of a constant pattern in the structure and conduct of the defense, and an attempt each time to find new procedures and methods for fighting, then this will, in essence, encompass the idea of maneuver in the defense.

8. The principal enemy of modern defense, which relies on critical fortified points, is artillery. The experience of penetrating the Mannerheim Line demonstrated this a number of times.

A second enemy is the tank with good armor used on a mass scale.

The scope of a possible modern mass tank attack on the main axes, where the enemy is searching for a solution, is characterized by the following indicators, taken from the experience of the last war.

In the offensive against the Belgian, British, and French armies in June 1940, and in the offensive against the French on the Somme, German tank divisions (around 400–450 tanks) on attack axes attacked on a front of 3–4 kilometers, although the Germans did not encounter a serious defensive line in these sectors.

This resulted in a density of the tank attack on decisive sectors equal to 100–150 tanks per kilometer of front.

A third enemy of the modern defense was short-range aircraft – bombers, ground-attack aircraft, and fighters – also used with great effectiveness to demolish defensive structures, continuously accompany the attack, and suppress the depth of the defense.

Only the combination and concentration of operations of all these three types of weapons could ensure the penetration of a modern defensive line like the Mannerheim or Maginot Lines.

Soviet forces are the only ones which successfully realized the experience of such a penetration on the Karelian Isthmus.

German forces did not penetrate, but rather bypassed the Maginot Line from the north.

He who wishes to study the matter of the penetration of a modern fortified defensive line should study our operations on the Karelian Isthmus.

9. Methods of modern attack are also employed on the basis of all these means of suppression.

According to German views, which were reflected in the latest events in the West, the attack itself is conceived as the mass use of aviation and parachute units to paralyze the operational depth of the defense; as the mass use of artillery and aviation on the battlefield for the purpose of supporting the suppression of the entire depth of the tactical defense; and as the mass use of mechanized formations, which, with the support of aviation and artillery, lay the path for the main infantry forces and independently develop success.

But this all relates to the penetration of such weak defensive lines as the Weygand Line.

Such methods of attack used by the Germans made it possible to penetrate the Weygand Line, structured in a slapdash fashion, and develop success at a higher tempo than in the First World War.

The defender was in a serious situation in the sense of the impossibility of countermaneuvering against the noted success of the penetration, in view of the lack of reserves and mobile force repulsion groups.

These were the new conditions of the situation to which the modern defense had to respond.

10. With what could the defense respond to these conditions? What requirements had to be placed at the foundation of the organization of a defense?

The organization of a defense had to respond to the following conditions:

(a) The defense had to be, above all, anti-artillery, counted on to protect personnel and fire means against destruction by mass artillery fire, especially during the first artillery strike, characterized by careful preparation beforehand.

(b) The defense had to be antitank, counted on to repel a mass tank attack in decisive sectors, on the order of 100–150 tanks per kilometer of front.

(c) The defense had to be antiaircraft, capable of countering the attacker's strong aviation power. Here what is in mind is not only active antiaircraft defense, but also, above all, defense with the help of mass fighter aviation and a whole series of measures relying on the special nature of the construction and outfitting of defensive structures and on their careful camouflage.

(d) The defense had to be multi-echeloned, multi-sectored, and deep, with intensified resistance in the depth.

Inasmuch as with modern methods of attack maneuver and all movement on the battlefield becomes difficult for the defender, thanks to the speed of development of such an attack, which is accompanied by a mass of airplanes and artillery bursts, the defense must be organized into its combat formation beforehand, and it must carry out during the preparatory period all measures to guarantee its survivability and stability.

In all instances the defense should be persistent and dynamic, constantly ready to shift from the defense to the offense. The pledge of victory for the defense is the greatest persistence, dynamism, and decisiveness of actions, consisting of a constant attempt of forces not only to repel the attacker, but also to deliver a crushing blow against him.

11. The conduct of a modern defense against powerful offensive strike means has developed beyond the framework of tactics, and has become a matter of operational scale, the matter of armies and *fronts*. The fullest expression of the nature of modern defense is found within the framework of an army defensive operation.

Until now, we have subdivided the defense, depending on missions, forces, and means, into a persistent defense and a mobile defense. Such terminology is not accurate, since any defense must be persistent.

If a defense has the purpose of holding specific terrain prepared for a defense, then this will essentially be a *positional* defense.

If a defense, in the presence of inadequate forces and means to create a positional defense, is structured on principles of mobile troop actions and attempts to weaken the enemy while protecting its own forces, sometimes not even taking into account spatial losses, then this will be a *mobile* defense.

In the former case, it is necessary to create and develop a defensive sector and protect it with all means; in the latter case, the defense is structured on rapid and sudden counterstrokes or on a timely withdrawal to a new line. In the latter, the defender's mobility has great significance.

At the conference, all presenters adhered to roughly the same views as to how to structure and how to create a defense on an operational scale.

With a positional defense on the operational scale, a developed army defensive region (as shown in Sketch 1) will include the following:

(a) first operational obstacle zone;

(b) tactical defensive zone;

(c) operational defensive zone.

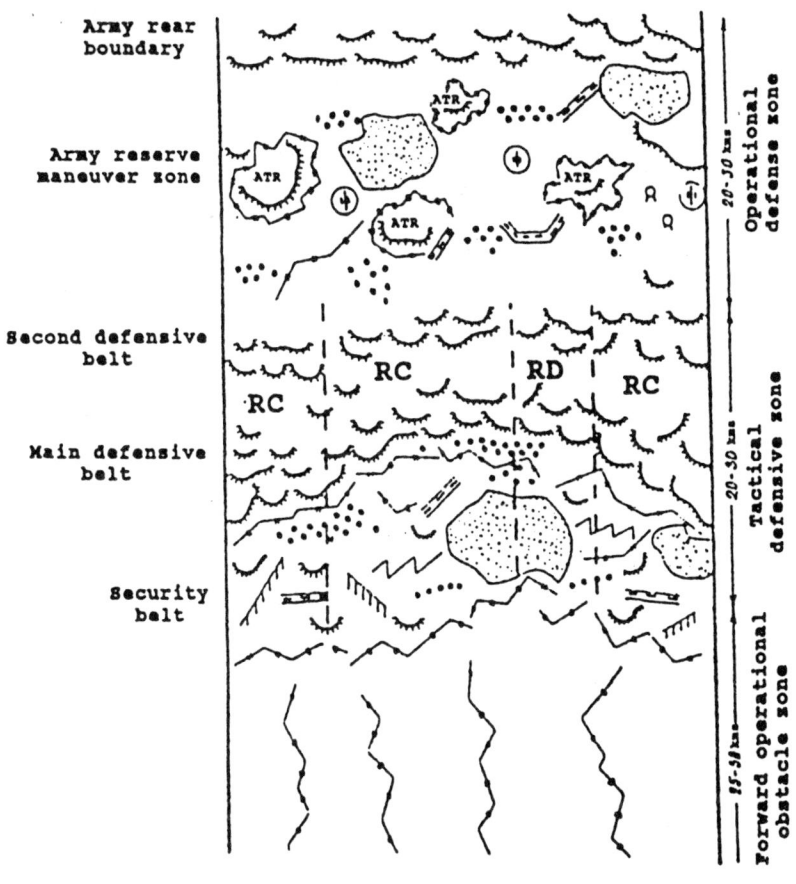

Sketch 1.
Army defensive region (one variant)

12. *The forward operational obstacle zone* is a large operational under-taking, the implementation of which is possible in full measure only in peacetime.

We saw such a zone with the White Finns on the Karelian Isthmus, where it had an overall depth of 30–50 kilometers.

Forces which will have to operate in the forward operational zone, regardless of whether they will be allocated directly to the *front* command or will be part of a defending army, should have, as a consequence of their isolation from the primary defense forces and with respect to the nature of the tasks standing before them, not only tactical independence, but also sufficient mobility.

13. *The tactical defense zone* (Sketch 2) is the main zone of resistance, where the principal defense forces should be concentrated, and where the enemy offensive must be broken.

It includes the following:

(a) the *security belt* with a depth of 10–15 kilometers, created to stop and exhaust the advancing enemy, and gain time to prepare the defensive zone. The security belt is outfitted with obstacles; reconnaissance units and forward detachments operate in it;

(b) the *main belt of resistance* with a depth of eight to ten kilometers, assigned to stop and disrupt the enemy attack; the principal defense forces are deployed in it;

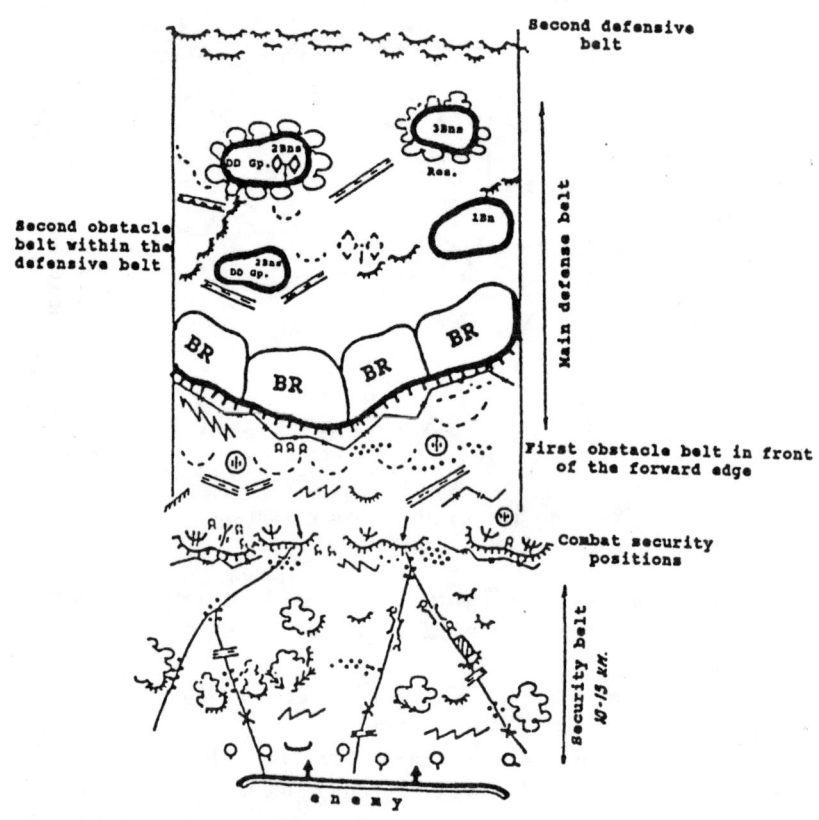

Sketch 2.
Main (basic) defense sector (one variant)

(c) the *second defensive belt*, where corps reserves are deployed; it must obstruct access into the depth by penetrating mobile enemy units, and serve as the staging line for counterattacks from the depth.

Recently the issue has been debated: how to protect forces densely occupying the forward edge of the main belt of resistance from organized enemy artillery fire during the artillery preparation.

There is the opinion that during this period forces should be brought back into shelters in the depth of the defense. It is hardly possible to do this under modern conditions, if one takes into consideration the tempos of a tank attack and its aviation accompaniment.

There is also a second suggestion, which in my opinion fully answers the demands of modern defense. It speaks to the necessity of creating two belts of resistance in the main defensive belt (Sketch 3): a *forward belt* with a

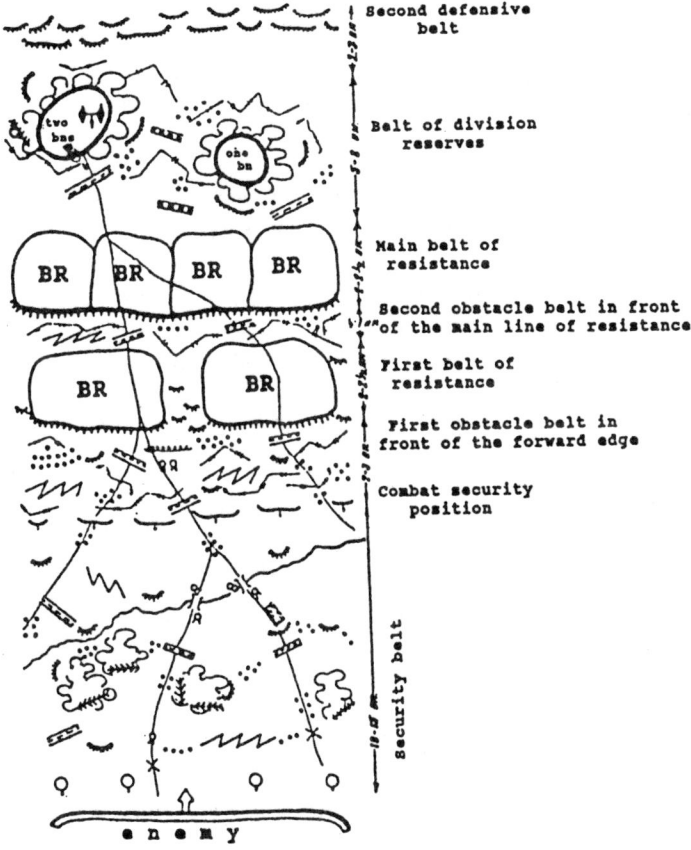

Sketch 3.
Force defensive zone in an army defensive region (one variant)

depth of two to two and a half kilometers, and a *main belt* with a depth of two to two and a half kilometers as well. In the former would be one-quarter to one-third of the defense forces, while the main defense forces would be deployed in the second, that is, the main belt of resistance.

The principal assignment of the forward belt would be to cover and camouflage the main belt of resistance.

The *forward belt of resistance*, having before it a zone of continuous obstacles, must stop the enemy offensive. In the presence of a significant superiority of offensive forces, the defense in the forward belt of resistance must attempt to inflict the greatest losses on enemy tanks and separate them from their infantry.

On secondary axes, with a limited number of forces, and on broken terrain, the forward belt may be substituted by reinforced combat security.

The *main belt of resistance* also has obstacles in front of it, and its forward edge is developed as the *main line of defense*, which must be most strongly supported by fire and engineer antitank defense means.

The main infantry forces and main fire means are deployed here.

The *belt of division reserves* follows behind the main belt; on the most threatened axes this is supported by antitank and interdictory positions created by division reserves.

The latter are formed either from a division (one–two rifle battalions) or from machine gun-artillery units of the Reserve of the High Command (RGK), attached to the division.

The *second defensive belt* is outfitted similarly to the first.

Such is the development of the defense and deployment of forces in the main belt of resistance which we must introduce into our practice as one of the variants of the defensive formation.

It is necessary to conduct a series of experimental exercises to refine several issues associated with a similar type of defense.

In essence, we saw such a defensive formation in 1918, at the end of the World War, exemplified by 4th French Army's defense east of Reims, and 17th German Army southeast of Arras.

In both cases the defense concluded with complete success.

14. The *operational defensive zone* is created in the depth of an army defensive region to fight against large mechanized forces which have penetrated into the operational depth of the defense. In light of recent combat experience, this is acquiring exceptional dynamism.

This zone is filled with antitank obstacles, antitank regions, and isolated lines.

Army reserves reinforced by RGK antitank assets are deployed and operate in it.

The composition of the reserve should include, to the degree possible, tank units or formations.

The operational defensive zone should be maximally unburdened by any type of rear units or establishments, so as to provide reserves with freedom of maneuver within it.

15. The overall depth of an army defensive region, excluding the operational obstacle zone, will be 50–60 kilometers.

The norms indicated here of 100–120 kilometers are unarguably unrealistic, and lead to dispersal of forces.

16. The following should be considered as possible frontages under positional defense conditions:

– for a rifle division: 6–8–10 kilometers (12–16 kilometers on secondary axes);
– for a rifle corps (three rifle divisions): 20–25 kilometers;
– for an army (10–12 rifle divisions): 80–100 kilometers.

17. Allocation of reserves must not take place to the detriment of troop defense capabilities in the belt of main resistance.

The deployment of reserves must not be tactically or operationally isolated from those sectors of the defense with which they are assigned to cooperate.

18. When organizing counterattacks in the defense, it should be kept in mind that defensive infantry reserves can effectively operate against attacking infantry, and defensive antitank reserves (mainly tanks, aviation, and infantry reinforced by antitank means) can effectively operate against attacking tanks.

19. The composition of a defending army depends on many circumstances. With respect to the number of divisions, this will fluctuate within the framework of the average norms indicated above.

A defending army usually needs reinforcement by mobile RGK antitank means, supplementary artillery (up to three mortar battalions), tanks (one to two tank brigades), aviation (up to one air division), and chemical units (one to two technical brigades).

IV. The Offensive Operation

A. General Principles of a Front Operation

1. The modern operation develops most fully on a *front* scale.

It is conducted by the efforts of several armies cooperating with mobile groups of forces, large short-range air forces, and, in individual cases, with naval forces.

2. In reports and presentations at the conference, there was sometimes a hint of an attempt to shift, without necessary analysis and serious criticism, the models of Western European *front* operations to the conditions of our Western Theater. Such attempts are wrong.

Our Western Theater has features with respect to both the nature of the terrain and the development of the road network, which will particularly affect the nature of *front* operations.

Moreover, we have several theaters of possible war in addition to the Western Theater, that is, Near Eastern, Middle Eastern, Far Eastern, and Balto-Scandinavian, and in each of these forces operations in tactical and operational context will have their own particular distinguishing features. Accordingly, our theory on operational-tactical questions, in addition to general principles, must include particulars concerning troop operations in various theaters and under different geographical conditions.

3. With the development of modern aviation and military equipment, and with the creation of large, fast-moving formations requiring especially precise organization of cooperation, the *front* cannot be viewed only as a strategic organization which implements general planning of army operations on a given strategic axis and distributes forces among armies. The *front* has turned into an operational-strategic organization, *whose functions include the planning of army combat efforts and direct guidance of them in the process of the development of operations* (establishing cooperation between the air forces and ground forces, guiding mobile formations, conducting combined operations).

4. In modern times, in large-scale armed conflict, immediate achievement of the ultimate military aim (the aim of the war or campaign) is rarely attained by means of a single decisive operation. The achievement of this ultimate strategic aim for the most part must proceed by achieving a series of intermediate aims, of which each can turn out to be so significant that it will be the content of a special *front* operation – the content of an entire strategic stage.

In turn, each *front* operation breaks down into a series of stages. Separate, intermediate missions for the given operation will be resolved in each of these stages. Within the framework of each such stage, it is necessary to assign partial missions to armies and organize operational cooperation among them.

5. The possible scale of *front* operations depends on the totality of the entire series of data: correlation of opposing forces, quality of forces and commands, technical outfitting of the forces, characteristics of the theater of military operations, degree of its operational-engineer preparation, development of means of communication, presence of reserves and rapidity of their approach to the front, etc.

The experience of modern wars demonstrates that the scope of large *front* operations is rather varied and was expressed by the following indicators: width of the offensive sector – 80–150–300 kilometers; depth of a single operation – 60–250 kilometers (and that of a number of successive operations was significantly greater); tempo of the offensive in operations reached 10–15 and more kilometers per day.

6. The duration of *front* operations also depends on the above-mentioned conditions. In addition to the enumerated conditions, the time necessary to prepare a *front* operation affects its duration.

The preparation of a *front* operation in a new strategic stage requires dozens of days, even months. The preparation of a successive operation within the framework of a single stage can be counted in days, weeks at the maximum.

7. With respect to its scheme, a *front* operation in its internal and external expression is exceptionally diverse. *Stereotypical patterns are absolutely unacceptable.*

In view of manpower and technical outfitting of *fronts*, the penetration is the primary type of offensive operation.

8. The experience of twentieth century wars fully disclosed three typical forms of operational penetration.

The first is when, on a *front* scale, a single blow by the concentrated forces of several armies against one comparatively narrow sector of front can be used with the mission of creating a breach and then broadly exploiting it, as shown in Sketch 4 (an example of which is the March penetration in 1918 by three German armies on a front of up to 70 kilometers).

This form of penetration makes it possible to deliver a powerful, annihilating blow using concentrated *front* forces. It supports the arrival of large mechanized cavalry formations in the enemy rear.

At the same time, masking the preparation of such a strike in a limited zone is difficult; difficulties also arise in supplying the *front* shock group forces, especially in theaters with a poorly developed communications network. A particularly negative aspect of this form of penetration is the fact that countermaneuver by defensive reserves is most simple and, as experience has demonstrated, such operations quickly get bogged down. An attack in a narrow sector, although conducted against the entire depth of the operational defense, involves a very insignificant portion of enemy forces.

Another form of penetration is when several shock armies formed on a wide attack front smash the enemy defense on the entire offensive front, as shown in Sketch 5 (an example of which is the German offensive on the Somme in June 1940 – an attack of several shock armies on a 200-kilometer front).

This form of penetration is modern and very effective, but the necessary condition for its implementation is good development of routes and means of communications in the theater. Without this, such an operation will not be materially supported.

The third form envisions delivery of several mutually coordinated attacks and the formation of separate army penetrations on several operational axes, as shown in Sketch 6 (the prototype for this form of penetration is the

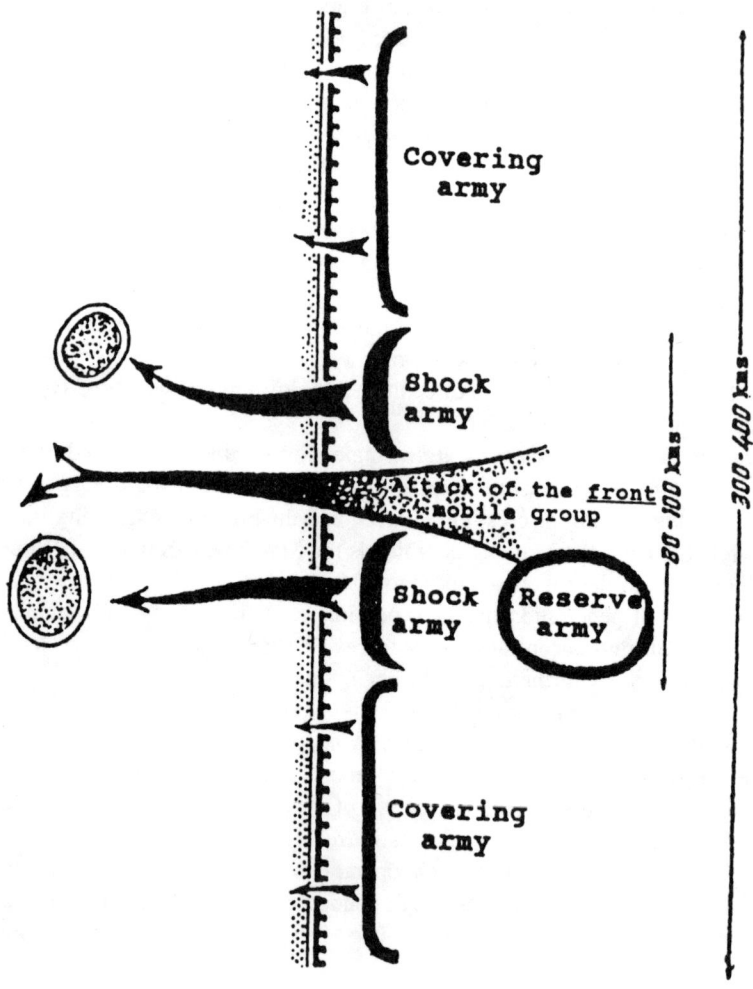

Sketch 4.
Front offensive operation (variant: attack on a narrow front)

Brusilov Offensive in 1916; the Germans also used it in their offensive in Poland).

This form of penetration is also completely modern. It is used in the presence of relatively large forces and means sufficient to guarantee the creation of each of the operational penetrations at the necessary scale.

This form of penetration corresponds more to theaters with a relatively poorly developed communications network. It facilitates covertness of preparation and reduces regroupings; the offensive develops on a wide front, with-

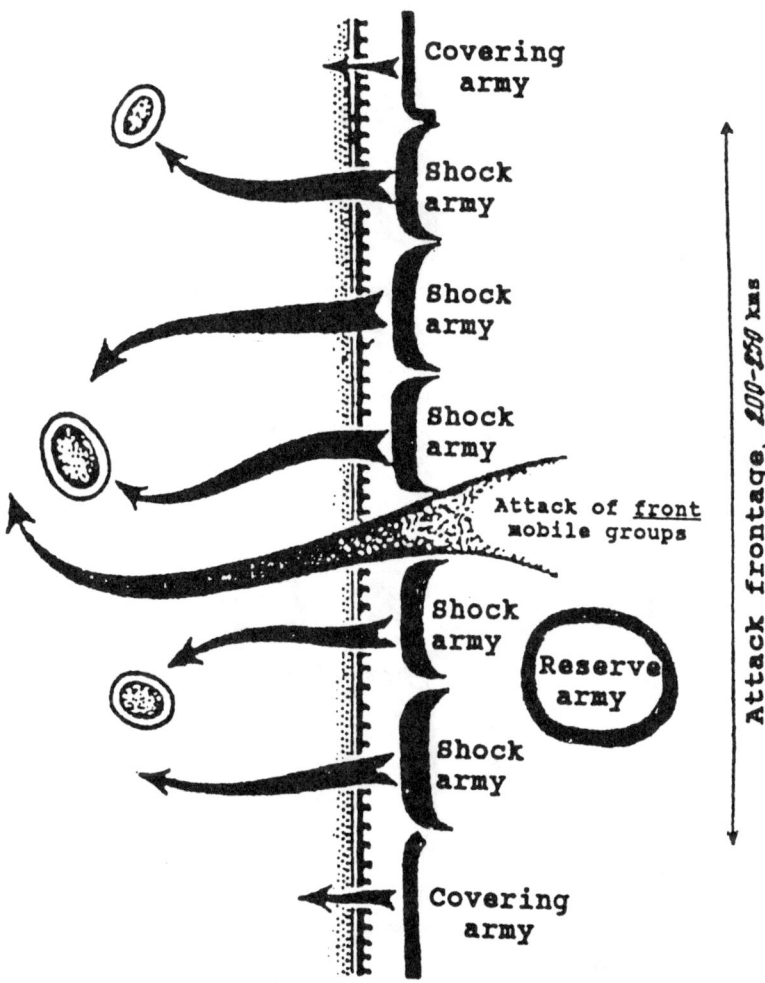

Sketch 5.
Front offensive operation (variant: attack on a broad front or operations by
adjacent *fronts*)

in whose framework the enemy will be jolted and pinned down and his
reserves routed, and it facilitates the conduct of a concentrated strike conducive to encircling the enemy.

The possibility of simultaneously conducting two and even three offensive
operations of different *fronts* in a theater of war for the purpose of strategically jolting the enemy's entire defensive capability as widely as possible
should also be kept in mind.

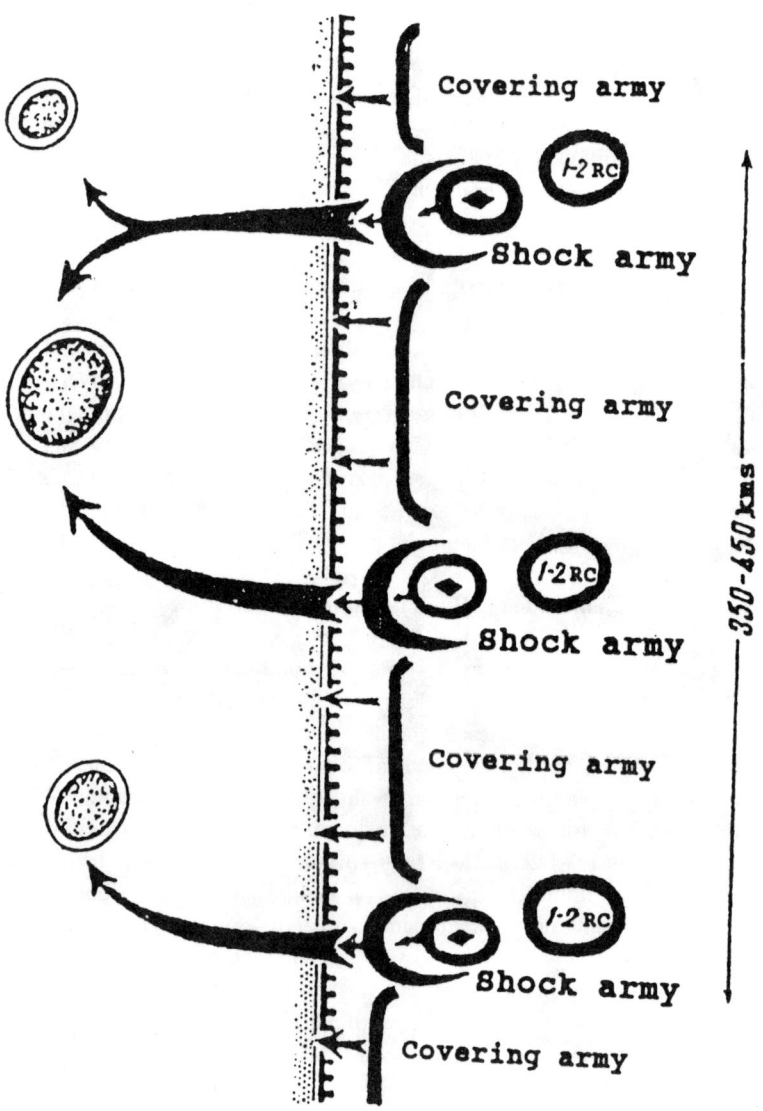

Sketch 6.
Front offensive operation (variant: several army penetrations along various operational axes)

Sketch 7.
Army formation in an offensive operation (one variant)

9. The question arises: how best to penetrate operationally and in which combat formations to direct forces? Taking into account the structure of the defense and offensive means, this is a valid contemporary question.

Proceeding from the composition of modern shock armies, a penetration can usually be implemented according to the following variants.

In the first variant, rifle formations supported by a powerful echelon of infantry support tanks, after a powerful artillery preparation, and under cover of a fire barrage and mass short-range aviation penetrate the enemy's tactical defense and create conditions for moving mobile formations into the rear (Sketch 7). This variant is employed under conditions of a strongly developed enemy defense, and when the defense line passes along terrain which is inaccessible for tanks.

The danger of this variant is the same as it was for penetrations during the First World War: they jam up, since attack tempos do not exceed concentration tempos of defensive operational reserves.

The second variant is used under conditions opposite those of the first. It consists of mobile mechanized formations not being held in reserve in the initial stage of the operation; they are moved forward and, supported by powerful artillery and aviation fire, destroy the enemy defense on a wide front (Sketch 8).

We saw this form of penetration on the Belgian border and on the Somme in 1940.

This form of penetration is very effective operationally speaking; it responds to the nature of modern arms.

10. An issue which also has great significance and which came up at the conference several times is that of the composition of *front* forces.

We understand that this depends on many circumstances.

In France in 1940, during the operation on the Somme River, the Germans deployed two army groups on a front of up to 350 kilometers (Abbeville–Montmedie); these groups had an overall composition of 95–120 infantry divisions and 8–10 tank divisions, which meant more than a twofold balance of forces in the Germans' favor.

Our operational calculations on the composition of *front* forces should proceed from the creation of the following density on shock axes:

force density – 1 rifle division per two to two and a half kilometers;
artillery density – 50–100 guns per kilometer;
tank density – 50–100 tanks per kilometer;

and this is in the presence of powerful mobile reserve groups in *fronts* and armies. Air force reinforcement of the *front* can fluctuate from 15 to 30 aviation divisions.

In short, there should be approximately a twofold balance of forces in favor of the attacker.

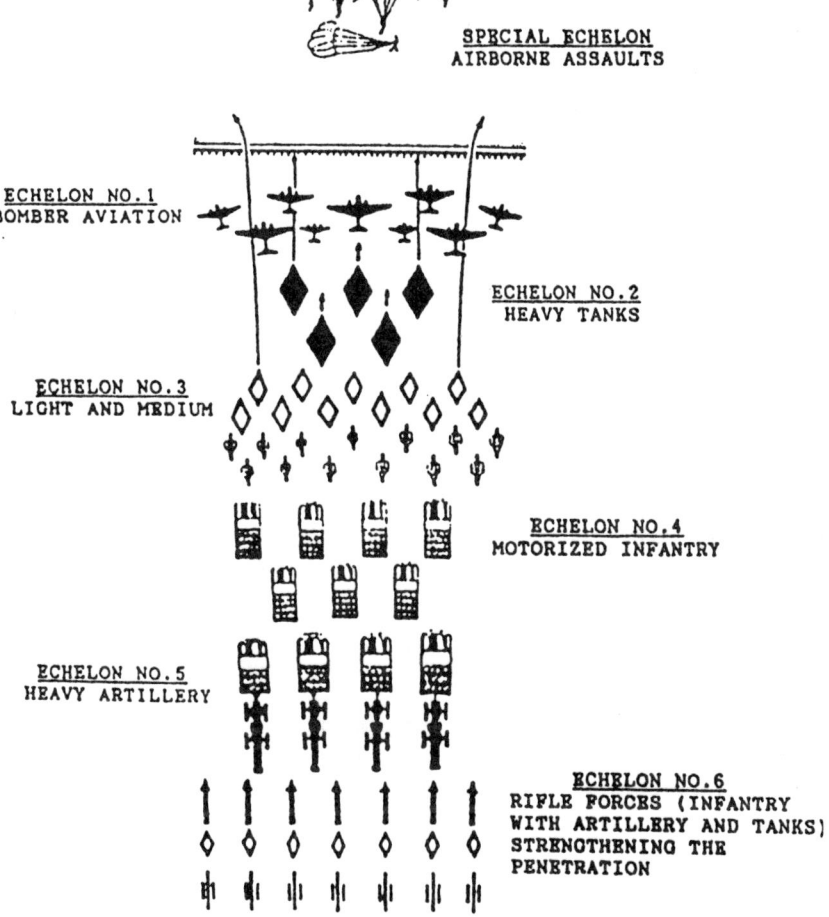

Sketch 8.
Formation of a mobile shock group of forces for the penetration (one of the possible variants)

11. Motor-mechanized forces and aviation are elements which modernize the modern *front* offensive operation. On the whole, they are subdivided into two parts: one directly supports army forces, the other forms a mobile group at the disposal of the *front*.

12. In a *front* offensive operation, a *mobile group* is enlisted to resolve the task of creating conditions which support the development of tactical success into operational (and sometimes operational-strategic) success. It resolves

this task together with aviation, in cooperation with other *front* armies. With respect to its composition, the mobile group should be capable of not only delivering brief attacks, but also capturing an operational region and holding it so as to split the enemy front into pieces, creating conditions favorable for encircling and completely destroying him.

13. The depth of the mobile group attack is measured by the depth of the enemy's operational defense (up to 100–120 kilometers), the duration of operations, and the state and quality of materiel and repair means.

14. The order for using mobile groups in a modern operation was addressed above. They can be introduced into openings made for them, or they themselves can form a breach in the defense.

Under some conditions one or two mobile groups can be created from mobile *front* formations; these will also be introduced into a penetration by order of the *front*.

Under other conditions it will be preferable to create strong shock army mobile groups.

The choice of a particular variant for using mobile formations depends on the structure of the *front* operation, the nature of the theater of military operations (mountainous region, ravine), the development of means of communication, the quality of the enemy, the degree of operational support of operations by mobile formations, and the quality of materiel.

In all cases, the order for introducing mobile formations into a penetration should be regulated by the authority introducing the mobile group into the penetration.

15. Shifting to an examination of the question of the *role of air forces in modern operations*, it is necessary to emphasize that, taking into account the massiveness of aviation and coordination with infantry actions, the struggle for air superiority must be implemented within the framework of a *front* and army operation.

The struggle for air superiority begins in peacetime. Its success is the result of cadre preparation, the quantity and quality of materiel, and the presence of a rich network of airfields. It is organized on the basis of instructions from the *front* and high command.

The use of air forces in *front* and army operations will proceed in the sequence of successive execution of the following tasks:

(a) Suppression of the air enemy, material and moral exhaustion of his ground forces, simultaneously with covering our own forces and rear from the air.

(b) Direct assistance to forces in penetrating the enemy's tactical defense, simultaneously with operations against immediate operational reserves and further suppression of enemy aviation.

(c) Assistance to ground forces during pursuit and destruction of the withdrawing enemy, simultaneously with a continuation of the struggle against enemy air forces and support of airborne landings and operations.

16. With respect to the use of air forces in operations, we have great accumulated experience; however, as was noted at the conference, up to now this experience has not been generalized or studied. Moreover – and this, perhaps, is especially fraught with serious consequences – our air force leadership personnel do not have uniform views regarding such issues as the structure and planning of operations, assessment of the enemy, method for conducting an air war and imposing one's will on the enemy, target selection, etc.

It is necessary to bring order into this area, and the sooner the better.

17. A very important problem in questions concerning the use of air forces in modern operations is achieving the necessary operational-tactical results even in the absence of numerical superiority in aviation.

It is necessary to work continually on this problem.

B. The Offensive Army Operation

1. Recent war experience demonstrated that under conditions of continuous *fronts*, outfitted with modern means of armed struggle, an army loses its meaning as a self-contained operational entity. Even the shock army with maximum combat composition has lost its independence in achieving large operational objectives, and more so with respect to strategic objectives. An army is a part of a *front*, and only within the framework of a *front* operation, in cooperation with other armies, does it carry out its operational activity with maximum effectiveness.

Logically connected with this is the proposition that in a number of cases it is more advantageous to use in a more extended fashion such means as aviation, airborne forces, and mobile formations in a *front* deployment than to distribute them by armies.

2. Under conditions of non-continuous *fronts*, in theaters where, by dint of geographic and topographic terrain conditions, force operations will proceed along separate operational axes, and army's operational independence will be fully maintained. Its outfitting with aviation and mobile formations is related to this principle.

3. The following are decisive elements in modern army operations:

(a) experienced and bold leadership;
(b) tempered cadres;
(c) roads, road structures, and materiel-technical supply of the army.

An operation which is brilliant in plan can turn into a catastrophe if, for example, there is not enough fuel; on the contrary, even a surplus of materiel-technical supplies and the presence of excellent roads cannot save an operation from failure if the operation's leaders do not satisfy correct leadership requirements, if, among the cadres, dull-witted and weak-willed people, impractical men, and windbags predominate.

4. A *shock army*, with its powerful modern means of destruction and suppression, is capable of penetrating any enemy tactical defense zone and arriving to fight in his operational depth. Developing success at this depth (turning it into a complete operational penetration and achieving a strategic effect) remains, even at present, a very serious problem. The presence on one's front of an enemy who has not lost his head, one who is capable of resisting and who is capable of bringing up a large number of antitank and antiaircraft means to the threatened axis and creating a new defensive belt, can place in doubt success which has been achieved if the attacker does not take necessary measures promptly.

It is this which determines the necessity of a broader offensive front (several armies) and a deeper army and *front* formation on the whole. Reserve divisions and corps, reserve armies and mobile formations, and uninterrupted replenishment of aviation losses – only these will assure the desired scope of the operation and its completion. The quantity of reserves in relation to first-echelon forces will be determined every time by the situation.

5. Several armies of varied composition participate in a *front* offensive operation. Armies which are most powerful and best equipped technically, that is, so-called shock armies, are grouped on axes of the main *front* attack.

Armies which are not as powerful, that is, conventional armies, operate on auxiliary axes.

A shock army should have at its disposal powerful suppression means which will provide it with the potential to penetrate the enemy defense with sufficient breadth (up to 20–30 kilometers) and overcome the entire operational depth of enemy resistance.

6. The calculation of forces and means for an army operational penetration will depend each time on the concrete conditions of the situation in which the penetration is being executed. Fluctuations in the composition of shock armies operating on a particular axis can be very considerable.

Proceeding from these densities on attack axes, already cited above in calculating the composition of *front* forces, it can be stated that for conditions of our Western Theater the composition of shock armies on the average will include up to 14–18 rifle divisions, up to 10–12 RGK artillery regiments, up to six to eight tank brigades, up to two to three aviation divisions, and a powerful mobile group.

Front assets and reserves do not enter into this calculation; this can sometimes considerably raise the average operational density on a particular operational axis.

Superiority in forces should not be calculated only by the number of rifle divisions; technical outfitting of forces today serves as a most important indicator in this respect.

In some cases, a shock army may not include large mobile formations. This depends on both the form of the *front* operation (for example, the presence of a mobile *front* group developing the penetration at the juncture of two armies) and local conditions unfavorable for using mobile formations for developing the penetration along a given axis. In these cases, penetration on an army scale will be developed using reinforced rifle formations and aviation.

8. The scope of an army operation and its developmental tempo should be orientationally mapped out in its plan.

The scope of offensive operations, that is, the width and depth of sectors captured by them, depends on the totality of an entire series of political, operational, and materiel-technical factors.

One of the criteria for the scale of a modern army offensive operation with respect to depth can be the depth of the modern operational defense (up to 75–100 kilometers).

9. The developmental tempo of an operation also depends on many conditions. The political-moral condition of forces, their training and stubbornness, the quality of control, the degree of force superiority, the power of suppression means, the mobility of forces and rear areas, etc. – all this affects operational tempos.

The latest historical experience and theoretical research demonstrate that the *average speed* of a modern shock army advance is around 10–15 kilometers per day (it can be as much as 40–50 kilometers).

10. The forms which an army operation can take are varied (as shown in Sketch 9).

The following must be considered the most often encountered forms: an attack either against the center or on one of the flanks of an army. With such an operational plan, there are both shock and holding forces in the army's combat formation.

In the presence of modern troop saturation of *fronts* and allocation of narrow army offensive sectors (up to 50 kilometers), an army formation where all its corps will be shock corps should be anticipated. Such a form of operation is also shown in Sketch 9.

11. One of the variants of army combat formation for a penetration operation is shown in Sketch 7. In this case, the penetration is implemented by infantry, supported by a strong anti-personnel tank echelon and aviation; the mobile force group is introduced into the penetration already made by the infantry.

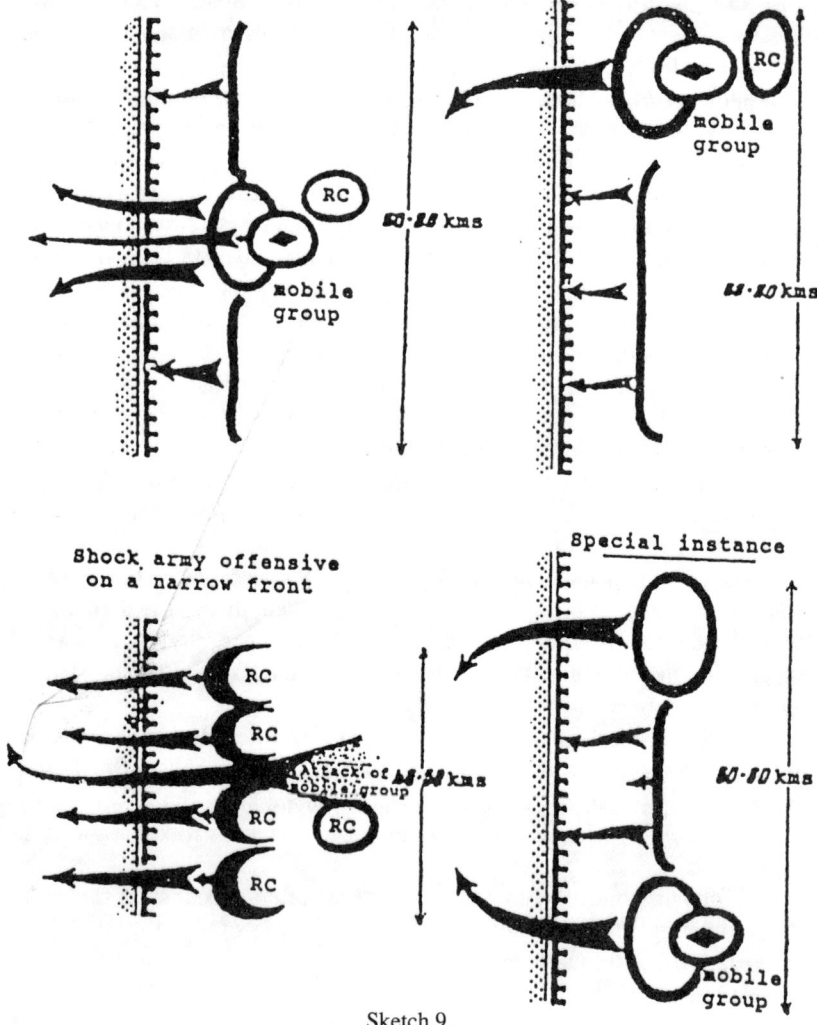

Sketch 9.
Different variants of an army offensive against a defending enemy

C. Control

Touching briefly on the issue of control, the following basic questions must be noted:

1. A most important task of army and *front* commands and staffs is creating an overwhelming force superiority on the main axis, organizing their cooperation, and providing it in the course of the battle and operation by means of maneuvering the mass of artillery fire, tanks, and aviation;

promptly introducing reserves; and coordinating efforts among neighboring units in the interests of the main attack.

In no way is it permissible to take apart a shock grouping.

2. Operations of modern armies fully outfitted with artillery, tanks, aviation, and other technical means of fighting have lost their linearity and tenacity. They have become complex and dynamic, characterized by encounters of large mobile formations and considerable masses of aviation in a sharply changing situation.

In the course of a *front* operation there may develop a meeting engagement on one axis, a penetration on another, and on a third there may be a shift to the defense. *The fight will take place in various forms, on a wide front, and at great depth. It will require great intensity, mobility, capable and flexible control, and mainly a high degree of preparedness and solid practical skills on the part of high command personnel and staffs.*

The art of control of a modern operation consists of the ability of higher command personnel and staffs to anticipate the course of the operation, its forms, and conflicts, so as always to have an overwhelming superiority of forces and means on the axis of the main strike, and to organize their cooperation.

V. Separate Questions

A. Mobile Formations: Trends for Their Use and Development

1. Recently, in connection with some growth in the independence and defensive capability of tanks, views have appeared on granting still greater independence to tank forces and, in particular, attempting to avoid tying down an infantry support tank group to the tempos of the infantry advance.

It will be more correct to confine ourselves to the viewpoint that independent mobile groups of *front* and army order, equipped with powerful tanks with a large radius of action and well-supported by motorized infantry (on motor vehicles and motorcycles), mobile artillery, aviation, and other combat support assets, will receive increasingly greater independence on an operational and even strategic scale, inasmuch as they will be dealing with an enemy's poorly fortified defense (a defensive line which is not as fortified as were the Mannerheim or Maginot Lines).

Infantry support tanks must move with the infantry, clear a path for it, and directly support it.

2. Inasmuch as recently there has been an attempt to increase the caliber of antitank artillery assets, there has also been and will be an augmentation and increase in the weight of tank systems by thickening their armor.

3. With respect to the organization of our motor-mechanized arms, we are on the right path: it is necessary to create mixed mobile formations with a greater radius of action, and RGK formations for immediate support of rifle

forces, which must have powerful armor, strong armaments, and high cross-country capability.

4. It should not be thought that today's tank is the last word in the area of forms of all-terrain combat vehicles or general vehicles for penetrating the modern defense.

B. The Air Forces: Their Use and Developmental Trend

1. Recent experience in the West has confirmed the necessity of the presence of an air force element, that is, army and *front* aviation used, with respect to the situation, to support forces and operate independently; also necessary is RGK aviation.

2. Developmental trends are as follows, with respect to types of airplanes:

– fighter: single-seaters, single-motor, armored, fast, with cannons; two-seaters, dual-motor, long-range for accompanying long-range bombers;
– bombers: short-range - dive bombers; long-range – fast, well-armed;
– ground attack aircraft: single-seaters, armored, with cannons, fast;
– reconnaissance aircraft: two-seaters, fast, well-armed.

3. Developmental trends with respect to bombs are as follows: small incendiary bombs; high-explosive bombs with different weights up to two tons; supplementary acceleration bombs; rocket-propelled bombs/shells; special bombs (chemical, etc.).

C. Preparation of Theaters of Military Operations

The preparation of theaters of military operations has exceptional significance for conducting modern operations. This consists of the following measures:

– preparation of rail and motor vehicle routes;
– set up of bases for materiel-technical supply and creation of a mechanical repair base;
– development of an airfield network;
– development of a communications network;
– creation of a medical-veterinary base;
– publication of good theater maps;
– preparation of troop quarters;
– preparation of the theater with agents on enemy territory;
– study of the theater by staffs and command personnel;
– engineer preparation of the theater;
– development of an air defense system.

D. Features in the Nature of Operations in Poorly Developed Theaters

1. In such theaters as the Middle Eastern, Far Eastern, and Near Eastern,

operations will proceed along separate operational axes; therefore, an army there maintains its independence. Sometimes corps and even divisions will be independent.

2. The development of rail routes and motor vehicle transport creates the possibility of outfitting individual operational axes in poorly developed theaters with forces and technical means for fighting at almost the same norms as those in fronts of Western theaters (experience of Khalkhin-Gol, Abyssinia, and China).

3. The primary problem of an operation in poorly developed theaters, taking into account the modern structure and nature of armaments, is routes and methods of communication.

The insufficiency of a local work force in these theaters requires that the troops be taught road construction.

The basic type of transport on all theaters is motor vehicle transport.

Transport using pack animals maintains its significance in the army link during actions in regions without roads.

A tractor may be used under any conditions at all levels.

NOTE

1. S. K. Timoshenko, *Zaklyuchitel'naya rech' narodonogo komissara oborony Soyuza SSR, Geroya i Marshala Sovetskogo Soyuza S. K. Timoshenko na voyennom soveshchannii 31 dekabrya 1940 g.* (Moscow: Voyennoye izdatel'stvo, 1941), pp. 3–44.

The Nature of Modern Battles

BRIGADE COMMANDER P. D. KORKODINOV[1]

THE DEVELOPMENT OF NEW COMBAT MEANS AND THE THEORY OF THEIR COMBAT USE

Special methods and forms of conducting war, engagements, and battles are inherent to every historical epoch.

In his article, "The Engagement," and in Chapter III of Part 2 of his work *Anti-Duering*, Engels gave a very clear and precise description of methods for conducting engagements and their forms in different historical epochs, from ancient Greece to the end of the nineteenth century inclusive. Here he demonstrated "how the introduction of technical improvements each time almost by force brought about changes and even revolutions in the method of waging war, often against the will of the military leadership."

The history of twentieth century warfare confirms Engels' position.

The most important technical innovations which most affected the form of battle at the beginning of the twentieth century were the magazine rifle and, especially, the machine gun, which began to predominate, literally, on the battlefield, pressing everything living to the ground. In combination with the trench and wire obstacles, the machine gun in the First World War attached almost insurmountable strength to the defense. A quantitative increase in howitzer and heavy artillery and its qualitative improvement were required to fight against the machine gun. The machine gun brought into being new means for fighting, including the tank.

Both sides "dug in" to produce the necessary quantity of artillery and other assets required to overcome the strength of the defense (which for general staffs had unexpectedly become so strong), and the war took adopted positional forms.

From 1915, two most important tasks arose before warring armies: (a) to penetrate the enemy's positional front; (b) to develop this penetration into decisive success beyond the limits of fortified belts.

The first task was resolved several times in the course of the first imperialist world war; the second task could not be resolved on the fields of Western Europe until the end of the war, since an offensive with the aim of a penetration developed so slowly that the defender managed, sooner or later, to concentrate his reserves at the penetration location and, having counter-balanced forces, stopped the offensive. The defense usually used railroads and motor vehicle transport to concentrate reserves.

It became obvious that, to convert tactical success into operational success, it was necessary, in the first place, to increase offensive tempos as much as possible and, in the second place, have mobile force formations, which would be capable of swiftly entering into the established penetration and develop its annihilating operations into the depth of the enemy's operational formation.

Many methods and forms for increasing offensive tempos were already established in 1917–18; these were repeated and have provided positive results in today's world war.

The following are the methods and forms:

1. Short but powerful artillery preparation, counting mainly on suppression of the enemy.
2. Accompaniment of attacking infantry with artillery fire (fire barrage or successive concentrated fire) and wheels of separate batteries, and then as rapid as possible a shift (together with all remaining artillery) behind the infantry.
3. Accompaniment of the infantry attack with newly fielded combat means (tanks).
4. Use of combat aviation on the battlefield to suppress enemy fire means, in particular his antitank guns and artillery, and – at the very end of the war – to attack enemy reserves approaching the battlefield.
5. Complete outfitting of infantry itself with heavy high-trajectory fire weapons (for example, mortars) capable of hitting the enemy behind cover. These weapons make it possible for the infantry to resolve combat missions independently in the period when help for it on the part of other combat arms is weak or has even ceased altogether.
6. Operational flexibility and skillful exploitation of each breach in the defense is required of infantry.

All these operational methods had already provided very notable results in engagements at the end of 1917 and 1918, with respect to increasing offensive tempos. Thus, for example, in the March 1918 offensive, 18th German Army for the first two days of battle – 21 and 22 March – advanced 10–12 kilometers, having completely overcome the entire British defensive system on the main attack axis; only from 28 March, when, as a result of the arrival of French reserves, the forces began to become balanced, did the offensive gradually expire. High tempos of advance were also attained during the May offensive, reaching 15 and even 17 kilometers on the first day – 27 May – for 7th Army.

The Germans conducted both these engagements, as is known, without tanks. Here, increased offensive tempos on the battlefield were achieved for the following reasons: (a) thanks to great artillery density, amounting to up to 100–110 guns per kilometer of front in March, and up to 120–130 guns per kilometer of front in May; (b) thanks to new methods of using artillery, which assured surprise of attack and support of infantry by artillery fire in the depth of the defensive position.

Aviation was employed on the battlefield, but it still did not have notable influence.

The British resolved the problem of increasing offensive tempos mainly by using tanks.

In the battle at Cambrai on 20 November 1917, when for the first time tanks were used in a significant quantity (378 tanks), and on favorable terrain, the British, having attacked the strong Siegfried position without artillery preparation, advanced to a depth of 8–10 kilometers and in one day penetrated the enemy front. Here the British infantry registered an offensive tempo of 1.5 kilometers per hour.

The British achieved even greater success on 8 August 1918 at Amiens, with the help of 415 tanks. Here the British advanced to a depth of 11 kilometers in one day, defeating eight of ten German divisions located in this front sector.

Thus, in all the aforementioned engagements, penetrations were realized, but they did not develop into operational penetrations. Everywhere these penetrations were delayed by approaching defense reserves, and achieved only a "pressing in" of the operational front.

It became clear that the development of success by infantry formations, the tempo of whose advance under the best circumstances could not exceed the speed of someone on foot, would not lead to great results.

The Germans had no mobile forces at all on the Western Front; British attempts to introduce cavalry into the penetration at Cambrai and Amiens were not successful.

According to Martel's testimony, the question of creating fast-moving tanks with a great operational radius for a semi-maneuver war beyond the main trench system was raised at the headquarters of the British tank corps after the battle at Cambrai. In July 1918 the overall specifications for such a tank were compiled. The following requirements were demanded: speed under good ground conditions – no less than 32 kilometers per hour; operational radius – 320 kilometers; capability to cross wide trenches easily.

British tank corps headquarters planned to send into the enemy's rear sub-units of such fast-moving tanks under cover of night or a smoke screen; this was contemplated for attacking enemy division, corps, and army headquarters, as well as for attacking his railroad stations and supply centers, and for destroying lines of communication at the moment when slower tanks, together with infantry, were attacking enemy positions. However, the state of technology at this time did not allow for creating such a fast-moving tank.

Only in 1925 did the British construct fast-moving tanks of more or less satisfactory quality. After this they constructed many models of this vehicle type and, beginning in 1927, conducted experiments on the use of independent mechanized formations.

At the same time, aviation was also developing. In comparison with 1918, the speed of airplanes increased approximately threefold, the operational radius eightfold, and the load capacity of bombers tenfold.

All this made it possible to use new methods of combat operations.

The Germans drew correct conclusions from the combat experience of the first imperialist world war, taking into account the development of military technology; they also exploited experiments with new combat means being conducted in all countries.

French General Brossait in the article "Tactical Forms of Modern Battle," appearing in a newspaper on 19 May 1940, was basically correct in noting that the Germans had borrowed the idea of an armored division from the British; in Spain they studied flights at low altitudes, used dive bombers on the basis of experiments conducted in the US, and prepared several thousand bomber pilots.

On the same day the *New York Times* openly wrote that "the idea of parachute assault forces capturing airfields, with landed assault forces using them, is a page torn from the book of the Red Army, which was the first to demonstrate these methods on a wide scale . . ."

And the Germans placed all this in the service of increasing offensive tempos.

They focused exceptional attention on the creation of armored divisions and the development of their tactical actions. Here they considered that armored divisions could not only be used to carry out operational missions in the depth of the enemy deployment after his front had been penetrated, but also that they themselves could independently penetrate an insufficiently strong enemy defense, similarly to how this was done, for example, by our cavalry in the Civil War, which did not wait until the gate was opened for it, but penetrated the enemy front and swiftly made its way into his rear.

From the experience of the war in Spain, the Germans drew two important conclusions:

1. Aviation acquired enormous significance in modern war; its dynamic actions could thwart an operation, even if the operation were supported by an overwhelming superiority in forces, as was seen in Guadalajara, where an Italian motorized corps was essentially destroyed by republican aviation.

2. With insufficient or no artillery, aviation (bomber and ground attack)

could carry out the preparation of the attack and its support, thus support-ing the attack of armored divisions.[2]

In accordance with these conclusions, the Germans increased significantly the numerical size of their air forces. By the beginning of active operations in the West in 1940, their air fleet numbered as many as 9,000 airplanes.

It cannot be said that the French did not consider the experience of the first imperialist world war; after its termination they drew correct conclusions, in general, but without sufficient prognosis for the future with regard to the development of technology. They were conservative in this respect, and remained so until the beginning of the second imperialist world war. In a report to the war minister, in which the *1937 Manual for Use of Large Military Formations* was presented for approval, the editorial commission wrote that "technical progress was not reflected essentially in the tactical area in earlier established regulations." It is true that further on the commis-sion noted that "in less than 15 years new and important material assets were created and developed in all armies, after which there followed inventions designed to neutralize the results of their actions."

Of these new means the commission placed in the foreground fortified regions, whose system, created to cover the territory of the state, in its opinion "makes it possible at present to mobilize under strong cover . . ."

With respect to the use of tanks, the report stated the following: "It is necessary to emphasize most decisively that today antitank weapons are as threatening to the tank as was the machine gun to the infantry during the last war . . ."

And this circumstance, in the opinion of the commission, "leads to the necessity of foreseeing the use of tanks in the offensive only under cover and with support of powerful artillery."

The commission considered that "tank operations in the depth of an enemy position are possible only after the preliminary breakdown of his defensive system, in particular with the exploitation of success . . ."

The French Army had only light mechanized divisions, which were designated to carry out the same missions as cavalry: long-range reconnais-sance, support service, attack of the enemy's system of lines of communica-tion after penetration of the enemy front, and pursuit; in the defense they were to close the penetration or counterattack.

By May 1940 the French Air Force consisted of only 3,000 combat air-planes in all, not counting tourist, postal, or transport planes.

The Polish, Belgian, and Dutch Armies took even less account of the level of modern development of military-technical means. As for Britain, its ground forces, having participated in combat operations in Western Europe, were too few in number to affect noticeably the nature of engagements there.

Thus, engagements in 1939 and 1940 occurred between enemies having different military doctrines and outfitted with different combat equipment, and with aviation and tank forces that had been trained differently.

NEW METHODS AND MEANS OF CONDUCTING BATTLE IN OPERATIONS

We still do not have at our disposal sufficiently complete materials on the course of the German–Polish war in September 1939 or the military actions in the West in 1940, especially data on how separate engagements and battles proceeded. However, there is sufficient information to draw general conclusions on the nature of battle and on the most important new methods for its conduct.

THE GERMAN–POLISH WAR

The following conditions of the overall situation had a strong effect on the nature of battles:

1. Correlation of forces. There were approximately equivalent numbers of infantry divisions on both sides;[3] however, the Germans had considerable superiority in artillery: twice as much heavy and one and a half times as much light artillery.

    The Germans had particularly great superiority in aviation (more than twice as much: 2,500 airplanes versus 1,200), including enormous qualitative superiority. The Germans also had great superiority in mobile combat arms. There were five armored divisions, four light divisions, six motorized divisions, and one cavalry division making up the German Army deployed against Poland. The Poles had all of one motor-mechanized brigade and nine cavalry brigades. The Germans had three to four times as many tanks as the Poles.

    The large German superiority in aviation, tanks, and artillery predetermined the necessity of defensive operations for the Polish Army.

2. Extent of the border. The border between Germany and Poland, calculating in a straight line from Grodno to the region of Poznan and from there to the upper San River, extended more than 1,000 kilometers. If all Polish infantry divisions had been moved into the first line, then each would have been responsible for 25 kilometers.

    Therefore, the Poles had to deploy their army in groups with considerable intervals between; it was necessary to defend on a wide front on many sectors and outside of these intervals.

    This made it possible for the Germans to penetrate the extended Polish front on many axes using tank and motorized divisions, and to send light divisions immediately into the rear of the Polish armies through the intervals.

3. The Poles were continually preparing for war against the USSR, and not against Germany. When war against Germany became probable, they counted on Germany deploying its main forces in the West, giving Poland the possibility of operating offensively. Therefore, the Poles did not even have prepared field-type fortifications on which they could rely in a defense situation.

OVERALL PICTURE OF COMBAT ACTIONS

On 1 September at 0545, German armed forces invaded what was then Poland. Aviation bombarded Polish airfields and major railroad lines, providing German aviation with immediate air superiority. At the same time, Polish railroad transport was paralyzed.

Part of German aviation assisted ground forces, mainly tank divisions. The quantity of this aviation gradually increased as it was freed from carrying out operational and strategic missions.

Tank divisions advanced in the first echelon of the majority of German armies, and behind them advanced motorized divisions. In the majority of cases they independently penetrated the weakly defended enemy front, enveloped his flanks, and penetrated into gaps and into the deep rear, without stopping to clear the territory and destroy remaining centers of enemy resistance – this was all to be done by infantry formations following behind.

In those cases where tank formations encountered strong resistance which they were unable to overcome either independently or with the help of motorized divisions, the advance temporarily halted, and the tank divisions awaited the approach of infantry formations and assisted them in the attack. This was the case on 2 September at Czestochowa.

The main mass of combined arms infantry formations advanced in the second echelon of the German armies; these entered combat against the main enemy mass when the latter was already being attacked from the rear by armored divisions and other mobile formations.

Already by 8 September German armed forces operations on the ground and in the air had broken the Polish Army into a number of groups which had no communications between one another; several of these groups were either in encirclement or semi-encirclement.

On 10 September, three large Polish groups were completely encircled: the Poznan Group (up to nine infantry divisions) in the region of Kutno, a large group in Warsaw, and three–four infantry divisions in the region of Radom. One rather large grouping (two infantry divisions and one cavalry brigade) had already been destroyed in the Danzig Corridor.

The ultimate liquidation of these centers of resistance was completely transferred to infantry divisions; with their approach, armored and motorized units began a wide enveloping maneuver to completely encircle the remnants of the Polish Army from the west to the Western Bug River. Guderian's group was advancing from the north, and Hoth's group from the south. On 16 September they closed the pincers at Wlodawa.

Nevertheless, the encircled groups of Polish forces continued to resist.[4] In the region of Kutno the Poles went over to a counteroffensive several times to penetrate to Warsaw. Despite this, however, the Germans continued to advance the front of their infantry formations.

Offensive tempos were quite varied. Where the Germans encountered considerable resistance (for example, in the regions of Czestochowa, Mlawa, and Prasnysza) they managed to advance an average of 10–15 kilometers per day; in the majority of cases the front line advanced 25–30 kilometers per day.

The average daily speed of advancing units amounted to around 40 kilometers; the maximum speed of advance reached 110 kilometers.

MILITARY ACTIONS IN THE WEST IN 1940

By the commencement of active operations, the Germans had deployed 125–130 divisions in the West, and had around 40 divisions in the center of the country.

Allied forces were as follows: 85–120 French divisions, around 15 British divisions, 21 Belgian divisions, and 10–12 Dutch divisions; in all, the Western European Allies had 130–170 divisions.

The Germans deployed 90 divisions on the right flank, that is, on the border with Holland and Belgium. Against these forces the Allies had the Dutch and Belgian armies, amounting to 31 divisions, and 40–45 French and British divisions in the north of France.

In general, ground forces were almost equal. The Germans were superior to the Allies in forces by a maximum of 20–25 per cent.

The advantages of the German armies consisted of the following:

1. Coalition forces were operating against them, and each Allied army was striving more to defend the interests of its own country than to operate cooperatively with other Allied armies.
2. Allied forces on the northern flank were deployed in two echelons: in the first were the Dutch and Belgian Armies on the eastern borders of their countries, 150–200 kilometers behind the Belgian Army; the Anglo-French forces were on the Franco-Belgian border.
3. The Germans had superiority in aviation and a great superiority in armored units.

4. The Germans had numerous parachute units, the Allies had none.

5. Finally, the Germans had the advantage of surprise and initiative.

If not all, then the majority of these advantages in the Germans' favor were taken into account by the Allied command; however, it counted on reducing all these advantages to naught by a system of fortifications erected in France, Belgium, and Holland. The Allied plan consisted of swiftly advancing Anglo-French forces from the northern departments of France to the main lines of Belgian and Dutch fortifications with the commencement of the German offensive against Belgium and Holland.

The German command took all measures to penetrate these fortifications before the Anglo-French forces approached them.

The German command exploited the weak links of the entire system of Allied fortifications in order to penetrate it. The weakest link was the Dutch border fortifications, built hastily and defended by weak forces (with an average density of no less than 30 kilometers – and more probably around 50 – per division). These forces had the mission of only delaying the enemy offensive for two to three days, the time necessary to open locks and flood the center of the country.

However, German parachutists prevented the flooding system being put into operation, and German motor-mechanized formations swiftly penetrated the Dutch border fortifications. On 13 May, the fourth day of the offensive, units of these formations had already advanced to the region of Rotterdam, and on 15 May the Dutch Army surrendered.

Having penetrated the Dutch fortifications, the Germans bypassed from the north the main defensive sector of the Belgian system of fortifications – the "Devez Line." They attacked only the extreme northern fortification of this line – Fort Eben-Emael, and on 12 May captured it. On this same day they broke through the field-type position on the Albert Canal.

In battles in Holland and Belgium, dive bombers, ground attack aviation, and parachutists participated particularly dynamically. Parachutists helped in the capture of Fort Eben-Emael and the forcing of the Albert Canal, and captured two bridges across the Maas River.

Anglo-French armies, which had begun to advance to Belgium, were under pressure from German aviation. Only on 14 May did their motor-mechanized forces encounter German tank divisions northeast of Namur. There was a large tank engagement, in which, according to the foreign press, more than 2,000 tanks from both sides took part. German tank operations were supported by dive bombers and ground attack aviation. The Anglo-French forces retreated.

Moreover, in southern Belgium on 14 May, German mobile formations, having swiftly broken through Belgian border fortifications, which had also been weakly occupied (apparently with a density of no more than one infantry division per 25 kilometers of front), had already arrived at the Maas River from Namur to the region of Sedan, and on 15 May had forced the Maas River on its entire front.

Thus, already by 15 May the Germans had penetrated not only the principal Belgian defensive lines, but also the French lines – in the weakest link – in the so-called "Ardennes obstacle sector," the defense of which was based on earlier prepared strong obstacles, but for the defense of which only field-type positions were built.

Approaching Anglo-French forces, together with the Belgian Army, succeeded in hastily organizing a defense on the line of the Dyle River, but German mobile formations, swiftly heading from the region of Dinant, Sedan to St. Quentin and further to the coast of the English Channel, had already bypassed this position from the south.

The Allies attempted to obstruct the path of the Germans by using their motor-mechanized forces, as a result of which there was another large engagement on 13 May on the front of Avene, Landresse, Guise, Vervins, in which a large number of tanks took part. German armored units were once again supported by dive bombers and ground attack aviation, and were again victorious.

On 22 May, German motor-mechanized forces reached the coast of the English Channel; soon, following behind them, infantry divisions moved in as well. The Allied front was split.

After this, the Germans began the tactical encirclement and destruction of separate Allied army units cut off in Belgium from the remaining forces.

Counterattacks by 9th French Army from the region of Rethel and Reims concluded with its defeat, and several attempts by Allied motor-mechanized forces to counterattack from the regions of Arras and Valanciene toward Cambrai were unsuccessful.

However, main Allied forces continued to resist stubbornly on the line of the Ghent fortified region, Upper Schelde. The many fierce attacks by German infantry with strong artillery support were unsuccessful. Only on 25 May did the Allied right flank, in connection with its envelopment by German mobile forces, withdraw to the Lys River, where the defense continued until 28 May.

From 30 May through 4 June, stubborn battles – defensive on the part of the Allies and offensive on the part of the Germans – continued on the approaches to Dunkirk, from where British and French forces were being evacuated. The English were forced to send their entire fighter aviation to cover the evacuation.

While these events were taking place, the French hastily created a defensive front on the line of the Somme and En Rivers, the so-called Weygand Line.

Large-scale defensive work on the Weygand Line commenced on 22 May. The French focused special attention on antitank defense. By 5 June the Weygand Line was a field-type fortified position, consisting of a system of strongpoints and centers of resistance, echeloned to a depth of 15–20 kilometers.

The French deployed 55–60 divisions (counting reserves) between the left flank of the Maginot Line and the mouth of the Somme River. Thus, one division was responsible for around five kilometers of front, which made it possible to organize the defense on a normal front and have a relatively small number of divisions in reserve. According to all data, the French had few tanks, since the majority of Allied mechanized forces perished in Belgium and northern France.

The Germans deployed two army groups against the Weygand Line, each consisting of three armies: on the right flank, from the coast of the English Channel to Laon, on a front of around 160 kilometers, was General Bock's group; on the left flank, from Laon to the Maginot Line, on a front of around 150 kilometers, was General von Rundstedt's group.

These two groups totalled 130–135 divisions, of which eight to ten were tank divisions consisting of around 4,500–5,000 tanks.

Thus, here the Germans had at least a twofold superiority in forces over the enemy; in numbers of tanks and aviation they had an approximate fourfold superiority over the French.

However, in view of the French forces having an organized defense, albeit relying on field-type fortifications, the Germans changed their tactics. They attacked the Weygand Line after a powerful artillery and aviation preparation, using infantry formations with only tank support on the main attack axes; only after penetrating the enemy's defensive system did they introduce their mechanized and motorized forces to develop success.

General Bock's army group began the attack on 5 June. For a little more then three days his infantry formations fought stubborn battles in the enemy defensive zone (offensive tempo – 6–7 kilometers per day), and only on 9 June did General Hoth's motor-mechanized group enter the penetration, developing success in the direction of Rouen.

On the same day, that is, 9 June, General von Rundstedt's army group began its offensive. His infantry divisions needed two days to penetrate the French defense zone (offensive tempo – around 10 kilometers per day).

On 11 June General Guderian's motor-mechanized group, standing ready, was introduced into the penetration on the axis toward Troyes and Saint Dizier.

By 12–13 June, the French command had already exhausted all its reserves, and the high offensive tempos of the German motor-mechanized forces, behind which the infantry divisions advanced swiftly, made it impossible for the French to organize a defense on rear lines. The Germans shattered the French Army into separate groups, the majority of which were then encircled and forced to capitulate.

THE ROLE OF COMBAT ARMS IN OPERATIONS AND BATTLE

The air force has two principal missions:

1. To provide dominance in the air, thereby creating a favorable air situation for one's own forces. This mission is so important, that in September 1939 and May 1940 the Germans at first committed all or almost all of their air forces to achieve their aims. In May 1940 they began air operations two days earlier than the ground forces offensive, even risking relinquishing the advantage of surprise in ground forces operations.
2. To assist ground forces operations both on the battlefield by attacking enemy fire means and personnel, and in the theater of military operations by attacking operational reserves, especially those approaching the battlefield, destroying lines of communication, disrupting the enemy's rear area, etc.

When supporting tank division operations, aviation essentially replaces artillery, conducting an aviation attack against the enemy instead of an artillery preparation before the tank attack, and supporting their operations during the attack by suppressing the enemy's antitank defense and personnel.[5]

Tanks are not dispersed along the entire front, but are employed en masse on main attack axes.

Their principal purpose is to penetrate into the enemy's rear as swiftly as possible, and, using wide maneuver operations and powerful attacks with help from combat aviation, to defeat enemy reserves before they arrive in the first echelon of the operational formation, which is being attacked at this time by infantry divisions, or before they are able to organize a defensive front in the rear area.

Depending on the situation, one of the tank formation units (or all of them) at a certain moment attacks the flank and rear of the first echelon of the enemy's operational formation, thereby directly contributing to the success of infantry formations attacking it.

During an enemy withdrawal, the primary mission of tank and other mobile forces is to prevent him from organizing a defense on one of the rear lines, and to obstruct the path of his withdrawal.

Tank formations serve as a kind of peak of a wedge, which splits the enemy front and thrusts into his deployment. Motorized divisions follow, and then come infantry formations.

If tank divisions encounter resistance they cannot overcome, either independently or with the help of requested aviation, and if there is very strong resistance, then they wait for the approach of infantry divisions and help the latter destroy the enemy.

In the presence of a sufficiently strong enemy defense, tank formations assist infantry and artillery in penetrating it and then rush into the rear area.

Air forces and tanks, however, can in no way supplant or replace infantry and artillery. At the same time, they are assigned a series of new missions for both cooperating with and organizing air defense and antitank defense.

Infantry formations with artillery in no way play a lesser role in a modern engagement than previously. On the contrary, their purpose has become more varied and their missions more complex.

On the main attack axis, infantry follows as swiftly as possible behind mobile combat arms, clears the enemy from the terrain, and reinforces it or initially (usually with the help of tanks) penetrates the enemy front and supports the commitment of mobile forces into the penetration, afterwards following swiftly behind them.

On secondary axes infantry resolves offensive missions usually without tanks, or defends until the operation has been resolved on the main axes.

In general, in a modern, large, combined arms engagement, infantry, artillery, tanks, and combat aviation operate in close cooperation.

Cavalry, completely outfitted with tanks and other mechanization and motorized means, as well as with air defense and antitank defense means and supported by aviation, will play a significant role; depending on the situation, it will carry out those missions which were carried out by light and motorized divisions in the German Army, or even missions which resemble those assigned to tank divisions.

Parachutists are principally assigned to capture important points in the enemy rear and hold them until the approach of the tank divisions, or to disorganize enemy troop control and materiel support in his rear area by means of bold operations, thereby assisting the operation's success.

TYPES OF BATTLES AND THEIR NATURE

The following types of battles figured in 1939 and 1940 operations: (a) offensive against defensive positions of different strength; (b) defense of positions both on a normal and on a wide front; (c) meeting battles; (d) pursuit; (e) complex battles for encirclement and in encirclement, with attempts to break out of it; (f) street battles in large towns, etc.

THE OFFENSIVE

An attempt to increase tempos of a penetration and its development in the enemy's operational depth was seen in two types of offensives: (1) An independent penetration of the enemy defense by tank divisions for their swifter arrival in the rear; and (2) An attack on the enemy defense by infantry divisions, usually supported by tanks, to penetrate the front and support the commitment of tank divisions and other mobile formations into the penetration. The exploitation of success was realized by these same infantry divisions.

As we have seen, the Germans undertook the *penetration of an enemy defense by tank divisions* in all instances where the enemy defense was weak – when enemy divisions were defending on a wide front, for example, in Holland and at border positions in Belgium – or when the enemy had hastily organized the defense.

Such attacks were based on surprise, ensured by the high operational and tactical mobility of armored formations. They swiftly concentrated at the designated sector, and conducted the preparation and attack itself.

Dive bombers and light bombers, which supported tank operations during the entire battle, began the attack. If artillery concentration did not cause a delay in the preparation for the attack, then it took part in such battles.

According to General Guderian's description, the attack by tank divisions took place in the following way:

> From a staging area selected sufficiently distant from the enemy, tank units moved into the attack in precombat formations – subunits in columns, in order more easily to make use of roads, overcome ravines, and freely outdistance motorized infantry units located ahead, already deployed into combat formation. Immediately before the encounter, tank units reformed into combat formation. All movement in the enemy's observation zone took place with maximum speed, covered behind camouflage available in the given region.

A simultaneous surprise invasion of an enemy position on a wide front, with a deep formation, took place in this way:

> Usually the first echelon, formed in several lines, immediately penetrated into the depth of the enemy deployment and attacked his artillery, headquarters, and reserves. The second echelon, also in deep formation, attacked the enemy's antitank defense system. The third echelon suppressed machine-gun fire and supported the incursion of its own infantry against the enemy position.
>
> Depending on the situation, infantry followed behind tanks, either dismounted or on their own vehicles. Their duties included the capture and reinforcement of terrain on which the enemy had been suppressed by tank operations. Then followed infantry divisions, which freed the motorized infantry of tank divisions to follow behind their own tank brigades.

An attack on the enemy defense by infantry divisions takes place in those cases where an enemy defense is sufficiently strong (as, for example, on the Weygand Line) on secondary axes (the attack of the Allied defense on the Upper Schelde, on the Lys River, etc.).

Many of these attacks took place without tanks, by methods approximating those of 1918. In those cases where tanks participated in such attacks (on the Weygand Line), they also had a deep formation and immediately suppressed the enemy to the entire depth of his tactical deployment.

During an attack with tanks, the artillery preparation was, as a rule, brief, so as to achieve surprise, and so as not to turn the terrain into a continuous field of insurmountable craters.

With the commencement of the attack, the Germans foresaw using artillery to hem from the flanks and the rear sectors attacked by tanks, and to suppress the enemy at those terrain points which could not be attacked by tanks – groves, ravines, villages, etc.

Tank operations in the depth are supported by artillery moving behind them on mechanical traction, dive bombers, and ground attack aviation.

As a rule, infantry always advanced in readiness to break enemy resistance using its own forces, penetrate into any breach which had been formed in the enemy's defense system, and develop this success by means of operations on the flank and rear of units of his combat formation.

THE DEFENSE

All armies attached great significance to the defense before the current world war. This included the Germans, who spent enormous forces and assets on the creation of the Siegfried Line and the "Western Rampart." They also seriously fortified the eastern border, especially East Prussia.

The difference between the German and French arrangements was that the French placed their main hopes on passive defense means and least developed their active modern defense means – antitank defense and air defense means. For example, there were 72 antitank guns and 81 antitank rifles in a German division, while a French division had only 62 antitank guns.

Considerably more powerful air defense means had also been developed in the German Army. Already by the beginning of the war against Poland the German Army numbered more than 100 antiaircraft artillery regiments. In addition, each German infantry division had 16 20 mm guns.

Instead, the French command had developed means in its army for fortifying positions. The formation of a large number of fortified parks with cement mixers and cement reserves, reinforced steel, etc. was envisioned still in peacetime in the French Army. Each such park was reckoned to hastily outfit a division defense sector on a front of 5–6 kilometers in the course of seven days.

The French command counted on the fact that new positions would be built in the rear with the help of these parks while the enemy was penetrating the first defensive belts.

We know that the German Army offensive broke the defense in Poland, Holland, Belgium and Northern France in the Sedan region in a short time. However, it must be taken into account that there were no fortifications in Poland, while in Holland, Belgium, and the Sedan region defensive structures were occupied by weak forces. The Germans had gone around the Maginot Line and already attacked part of its fortifications at the moment when the French garrisons had to think more about withdrawing from encirclement than about a stubborn defense, since there was already no purpose to such a defense.

The Weygand Line, which the French had created hastily in two weeks, was, to a certain degree, adapted to the forms and methods of attack which the Germans were already using. According to data from foreign military observers, here the French command was attempting to use new tactics of fighting against German armored units. The French let them through, and then attempted to close the penetration, cutting off the tanks from infantry. French tanks were to have taken on the fight against tanks which had penetrated to the rear, but the French did not have sufficient forces.

In any event, in the attack on the Weygand Line the Germans were unable to develop high offensive tempos: their average daily advance did not exceed 10–12 kilometers, that is, it did not exceed the offensive tempos of a number of battles in 1918. Had the French had reserves of sufficient strength and quality (tank formations), they would have had the ability to concentrate them promptly at the penetration sectors. But in this period the French force was already small, and, in addition, the small number of reserves were pinned down by German aviation attacks.

On the basis of battle experience on the Ghent, Upper Schelde Line, on the approaches to Dunkirk, and on the Weygand Line, the conclusion can be drawn that an appropriately organized defense has sufficient resistance to provide the command with time necessary to bring up available reserves.

A number of conclusions on the organization of the defense can also be drawn:

1. Inasmuch as the modern offensive attempts to increase tempos, the defense should take all measures to retard these tempos. Above all, it is necessary to slow down in every way possible the enemy's approach to the defensive sector and his preparations for attacking it. The most important methods for achieving this aim are the following: (a) creation of a forward ground which is efficiently equipped and defended by small forces; (b) exhaustion of the enemy who is approaching the defense position by means of aviation attacks and surprise artillery fire raids;

(c) counterpreparation, that is, a sudden and powerful fire attack by artillery and aviation against the main enemy grouping at the moment it occupies its staging area for the offensive.

2. The modern defense should be deep, antitank and antiair to its entire depth.

3. In the modern defense exceptional attention must be focused on air defense to the entire depth, for covering both reserves and fire forces, especially artillery and antitank gun fire positions.

4. Reserves designated for counterattacks should be completely outfitted with tanks; it is necessary to have powerful armored formations in the composition of the operational reserves, and they must all be protected against air attacks.

A new type of meeting battle has appeared – between tanks and antitank formations. The side which wins this battle acquires an enormous advantage – the ability to force its way into the operational formation of enemy infantry formations by using mechanized forces, and split it, thereby providing favorable battle conditions for its own infantry formations.

Tank divisions have acquired a major role in *pursuit*; they make their way into withdrawing enemy columns, force them off the roads, and, firing on the march, overtake them. Thus, a new type of parallel pursuit has appeared, formerly rarely successful, but which had always been sought, since it is most effective.

Battles for encirclement and in encirclement, which have the most varied forms, were practiced on a very wide scale.

Street battles also occupied a significant place in the military actions of 1939–40. It must be noted that even large towns are subject to attack by tank divisions. It is true that it was unsuccessful in Warsaw, but Boulogne was taken by a tank division.

CONCLUSIONS

Here basically are those conclusions which can be drawn about the nature of modern battles on the basis of the experience of the German–Polish war and operations in the West in 1940.

Lenin wrote: "An epoch encompasses the sum of various phenomena and wars, both typical and atypical, both large and small, for both progressive and backward countries."[6]

One can still speak about the "partial" typicalness of the German–Polish War, inasmuch as it took place between economically powerful Germany and economically backward Poland, whose population was two-and-a-half times smaller than that of Germany, was extremely varied with respect to nationalities, and was poorly held together by the imprudent policies of the *Szlachta* (Polish gentry).

The war of Germany against the Allies is unarguably typical for the given epoch of large wars. But this war too, as any other, had its own specific features which could not help being reflected in the nature of its engagements and battles.

The first of these, already mentioned above, is that the Germans, in accordance with the combat experience of past wars and the development of military equipment, put into practice a number of modern methods of conducting war and battles at a time when their enemies wanted to fight using 1918 methods, only slightly modernized. Naturally, this placed its imprint on the course of all combat operations. It must be assumed that without this advantage for one side, battles and operations would have taken on a fiercer nature and would not have led to such swift results as they did in the West in 1940.

However, this does not diminish the significance of those basic forms of battles and methods of combat operations which the Germans employed; they may become more complex, and a number of new methods and means will appear. One can even propose a general trend in the development of tactics and equipment under such conditions – the struggle between airplanes and air defense, between tanks and antitank defense.

The second feature is that the current world war is taking place between capitalist states. A revolutionary-class war will, of course, have its own characteristic features, and their influence will be reflected, to a great degree, on the nature of the war as a whole and, albeit to a lesser degree, on the forms and methods of battles.

A third feature is the geographic conditions, theater of military operations, and army rear communications. Geographic conditions in Western Europe have their peculiarities which are considerably different from other theaters of military operations.

The war against the White Finns demonstrates just how sharply geographic conditions affect the nature of military operations. The wide expanse between Lake Ladoga and the North Arctic Ocean, with its extremely poorly developed road network, inaccessibility of terrain, and severe winter climate, created conditions which, in combination with the fortified Mannerheim Line, severely restricted the Red Army's employment of mobile combat arms. Aviation operations were limited to the extreme by climatic conditions. Therefore, the offensive developed very slowly.

Red Army command personnel, who must be ready to protect the sacred borders of the socialist Fatherland on the most varied theaters of war and against probable enemies with armies of varied qualities, must assimilate the following words from Comrade Stalin particularly solidly:

The skillful conduct of war under modern conditions consists of mastering all forms of warfare and all the achievements of science in this field, astutely using them, and capably combining them or employing one or another of these forms in a timely fashion, depending on the situation.[7]

NOTES

1. P. D. Korkodinov, "Kharakter sovremennykh boyev," *Voyennaya mysl'* [Military thought], 2 (1941), pp. 72–86.
2. Editor's note: aviation could not replace artillery. The experience of the war in Spain made it possible to conclude that it was necessary to support a tank attack not only by artillery, but also by aviation.
3. Editor's note: according to data from the foreign press, the Germans sent up to 60 infantry divisions against Poland, while the Poles had only 30 infantry divisions, since German aviation prevented them mobilizing secondary divisions.
4. They surrendered as follows: Radom Group (60,000 men) – on 13 September; Kutno Group (170,000 men) – on 18 September; Gdynia Group (13,000) – on 14 September; Warsaw Group – on 27 September.
5. Editor's note: this is an incorrect assertion. Aviation cannot replace artillery, and it did not replace it in the war in the West.
6. V. I. Lenin, *Sochineniya* [Works], Vol. XIX, p. 202.
7. I. Stalin, *O strategii i taktike russkikh kommunistov* [On strategy and tactics of Russian communists].

The Development of Operational Art According to the Experience of Recent Warfare

MAJOR GENERAL N. TALENSKIY[1]

The operation in its modern understanding – an organized totality of actions of large troop formations joined by an overall plan and directed toward the execution of a particular aim of a campaign or war – was born at the turn of the twentieth century. Wars of the latter third of the nineteenth century, in particular the Franco-Prussian War (1870–71) and especially the Russo-Japanese War (1904–05), brought to light quite clearly new features of military art such as the increase in a combat front, its subdivision into a series of centers of struggle tactically dissociated from one another, the breaking up of combat efforts into the depth, etc., which could not be placed within the framework of accepted concepts of strategy and tactics.

Life required theoretical development of this new phenomenon and, together with an overall theory of war (strategy) and theory of battle (tactics), the creation of a theory of conducting an operation, or operational art. However, military theory before the First World War lagged behind, even in the developmental work of its most prominent spokesmen. The non-dialectic perception of historical experience prevented bourgeois military theorists from seeing the new features of military art engendered by changing economic and political conditions and by the rapid development of technology. War experience, which had receded into the distant past, had a preeminent and determining significance for the development of military doctrines.

Theorists and practicians of military affairs, and the general staffs of the majority of countries on the eve of the First World War saw the highest achievement of military art in reproducing models of Napoleon's and Moltke's military leadership creativity. Theory idealized models of nineteenth century military art, separated by time gaps of 30–40 years, even by a whole century. More recent war experience was, to a significant degree, ignored. Respected "academic military theory" passed by new phenomena which had arisen on the battlefield, but which had not been fit within the framework of existing concepts.

These new phenomena, which did not correspond to existing concepts, were viewed as exceptions, as chance occurrences resulting from either the peculiarities of the theater of war (the Anglo-Boer, Russo-Japanese, and Balkan Wars – the latter in 1912–13 – were, in reality, conducted on unique theaters of war), or by the poor preparation of forces and erroneous actions on the part of military leaders.[2]

The more dynamic scientific young people expressed very valuable ideas on the printed page, evoked by war experience, but they did not possess the scientific authority to introduce radical changes into the theory of military art. And it should be noted that one could hardly cite a keener example of the distance between theory and reality than what happened in the First World War in the field of conducting operations.

German operational doctrine was defined by the strategic idea of the sequential defeat of its enemies in ground theaters by decisive attacks during a short war. "Having begun in spring, the war must be concluded with a complete victory over the enemy by the time the leaves fall in autumn" – thus did Schlieffen, one of the principal creators of German military doctrine, express the idea of a short war. Operational art of the German Army had to find a path to realize this strategic concept.

Future war (the First World War) was described to the German General Staff as a war on at least two fronts. Consequently, it could be waged only along internal strategic axes. Historical experience attested that under such conditions it was necessary to rout completely the enemy against whom the main effort was being directed, and that under such conditions one could not count on victory by achieving only limited successes. Napoleon's concentrated frontal blow could no longer be used to achieve victory. The possibility of a successful frontal offensive was rejected by many authoritative German theorists, in light of the enormous growth of the fire power of armies. Schlichting, for example, considered that in the future an attempt to penetrate the front was almost unrealizable.

German military doctrine rejected the frontal blow for other reasons as well. In the article, "Modern War," Schlieffen wrote:

> The Russo-Japanese War demonstrated that a simple offensive against an enemy front can, despite all difficulties, succeed admirably. But the result achieved by such an offensive is only very limited under the most favorable conditions. It is true that the enemy is driven back, but some time late in another place he reconstitutes the resistance he temporarily halted, and the campaign bogs down.[3]

And Schlieffen, the author of the plan for a short war who envisioned defeating the enemy in an annihilating engagement, could not be reconciled to getting bogged down. He advanced the maneuver executed by Hannibal at Cannae in 216 BC as the ideal for modern manuever, writing:

Annihilating battle can be given even today according to Hannibal's plan, compiled in ancient times. The enemy front is not the object of the main attack. Essentially, it is not the concentration of main forces and reserves against the enemy front, but pressure on the flanks. The flank attack should not only be directed against a single extreme point of the front, but should also capture the entire depth of the enemy deployment. Annihilation is conclusive only after attacking the enemy rear.[4]

He went on to write, "The modern engagement, to a greater degree than formerly, reduces to a struggle for the flanks . . . He whose reserves are located not behind the center, but on the extreme flank will be victorious in this fight for the flanks."[5]

Thus, a characteristic feature of German operational doctrine in the period preceding the First World War was the attempt at a decisive annihilating engagement, the basis of which was an enveloping maneuver on the flanks to encircle the enemy. The German General Staff and command cadre of the German Army were nourished on these ideas.

By the beginning of the war, the flank maneuver was, to a considerable degree, schematized in the German Army. It must be stressed, however, that the General Staff was able to provide some technical prerequisites for its successful implementation. It was at the request of the General Staff, Schlieffen in particular, that heavy field artillery was introduced into corps; this made it possible to overcome the enemy defense relatively swiftly.

A clearly declared offensive spirit formally permeated French military doctrine. As with the Germans, the French saw the achievement of strategic aims in the annihilation of enemy forces in an offensive engagement. Official manuals on commanding large formations considered that "military operations have the aim of annihilating organized enemy forces." "The importance of introducing large forces, the difficulty in supplying them, and the disruption of the social and economic life of the country – all this awakens the search for all means for the most rapid resolution." "Decisive battle brought up to full intensity, which destroys an enemy army, is the single means of breaking the enemy's will." "Only an offensive leads to positive results, taking the initiative into one's own hands, and creates a situation instead of being subordinated to it." "Defense leads to true defeat; it is necessary to reject it completely." And the French, in reality, almost completely banned defense in the military preparation of their forces. According to Lucas, the word "defense" so grated on the ears that it was not allowed to be mentioned in exercises on maps or in maneuver problems in the field. He who was very interested in defensive questions risked ruining his service reputation. "The theory of the offensive in the French officer corps was brought to an unhealthy state. In the most dire straits the offensive was to rescue the troops in all cases."[6] The clearest expression of offensive doctrine was Colonel Grandmaison, who propagandized the idea of the offensive "no matter what, under any circumstances whatsoever."

The flank maneuver was not made into a fetish in French operational doctrine, although in general great significance was attached to maneuver. The *Regulations* for commanding large formations stated, "It is necessary to destroy a combat formation by force to achieve victory." And in resolving this problem, great significance was attached to fire. However, there was an enormous gap between French theory and practice. The French war plan had an expressly passive "wait-and-see" character.

Strategic deployment schematically reproduced Napoleonic ideas. There was a hint of the fear of an enterprising enemy who was well prepared for war – as was the German Army – and who was deployed on the Western European theater of war in this deployment and in the fundamental operational-tactical plans of the French command. This dissonance of operational-tactical doctrine and strategic concept could in no way be associated with the strong aspects of the French Army of 1914. Its operational doctrine was not reinforced by the necessary combat equipment. French corps and divisions had as armaments only light field guns; an excellent gun in the defense and for actions against open targets, it was powerless against an entrenched or sheltered enemy. It is natural under such conditions that the offensive "no matter what, under any circumstances whatsoever" turned into an empty declaration. Afterwards Foch had to admit that French "military doctrine was too paltry, since for all it was restricted to the splendid, but too exclusive, form of the offensive."[7]

By the beginning of the First World War, the army of tsarist Russia did not have a fully formed operational doctrine. The Russian higher command was influenced considerably by the ideas of the German and French schools. Only the best representatives of Russian military thought turned their attention to the military legacy of the great Russian military leaders, Suvorov in particular. Regulations and military-scientific works were permeated by the ideas of a short war and the offensive form of combat operations. These ideas were not, however, based on necessary materiel-technical prerequisites. Large formations were distinguished by inadequate mobility. Operational leadership was characterized by slowness. It easily ceded to the enemy the struggle for operational initiative, and often shifted to countering him instead of imposing its will on him. Ideas of operational and tactical maneuver were sufficiently reflected in regulations and leading military literature, but military formations and army operational leadership were not in the necessary condition to realize them.

The armies of the remaining war participants appeared on the battlefield without their own clearly formulated operational doctrines and, to some degree, adopted the ideas of the German and French schools.

How were these operational doctrines implemented on the battlefields? To what degree were they confirmed by combat experience, and to what degree did operations conducted on the basis of these doctrines resolve those strategic missions assigned to them?

Armies of the primary war participants professed the ideas of the enveloping maneuver, and almost all operations of the maneuver period of war were permeated by the concept of operations against the flanks.

The offensive operations of 1st and 2d Russian Armies and 8th German Army in East Prussia in August 1914 were executed in the form of an enveloping maneuver. The plan for offensive operations of the Russian Army in Galicia called for a wide flank envelopment. We encounter forms of the shallow and wide envelopment and concentric offensive to encircle an enemy in the Lodz operation (November 1914), in the Sarykamysh operation (December 1914), in operations in 1915 in the Eastern European theater of war and on the Serbian front, and in operations against Romania in 1916. In the Western European theater, the German enveloping maneuver took the form of a gigantic wheel around the right flank, consisting of five armies. If in operations in the Eastern European and Balkan theaters of war the concentric maneuver had as its prerequisite favorable border profiles for an appropriate force deployment, then the movement of German armies in the Western European theater of war gave rise to a new form of maneuver resulting from the features of deployment on a continuous wide front.

Until the stabilization of the front, both sides attempted envelopment and encirclement maneuver. Nevertheless, with extremely rare exceptions (the defeat of 2d Russian Army in August 1914 and the encirclement of 20th Corps in February 1915), not a single enveloping maneuver succeeded. In some instances, forces which had executed an envelopment themselves fell into a difficult position and suffered a severe defeat, as was the case with General Scheffer's group in the Lodz operation, and with Turkish forces in the Sarykamysh operation.

Not a single warring army succeeded in achieving the ultimate aim of an enveloping maneuver – an annihilating engagement – nor were those strategic aims achieved which were assigned in the initial operations.

In the form into which it had developed by the beginning of the 1914–18 war, operational art was powerless to execute the missions which strategy assigned it. It could not manage to carry out the most decisive form of maneuver for an annihilating engagement. What was the reason for this? Was the experience of the maneuver period of the First World War a negation of the significance of the enveloping maneuver as the most decisive form of operation?

Such a conclusion would have been incorrect, for, despite all failures, the experience of the maneuver period of the war quite clearly illuminated the fact that a flank strike which resulted in the encirclement of the enemy was the most powerful form of operational maneuver, and if it was unsuccessful then the reason, in any case, was not in the essence of this maneuver. The primary reason for lack of success of an encirclement operation in the campaigns of 1914 and 1915 was insufficient superiority in attacking forces and the absence of those mobile combat means which would have made it possible to execute an encirclement maneuver, while overcoming possible resistance, earlier than the enemy could organize countermeasures. At this time the only mobile combat arm, the cavalry, did not have appropriate armaments for the requirements of such a maneuver, was poorly prepared to execute this on a wide scale, operationally was used incorrectly, and was often poorly led.

Thus, the encirclement maneuver in the First World War was not up to strength for operational art, and this operational form remained a matter of chance in military art, a rarity which succeeded not so much because a modern Hannibal implemented it, but rather because on the opposing side there was a modern Terentius Varro, as happened in the August 1914 operation in East Prussia.

The maneuver period of war in 1914 yielded a series of new phenomena in the field of operational art. The latter encountered significantly growing combat fronts and an increase in the scope of operation and combat intensity. In a number of cases, 40–50 per cent of the overall duration of an operation fell to the engagement. The imperfection of the old system of operational-strategic leadership, which had been structured on the design of headquarters [*stavka*]-army, was clearly brought to light. The number of armies operating on a front increased. The necessity for cooperation among them became quite clear, and their consolidation by means of a special *front* command (army group command) was required. During the 1914 campaign, the *front* operation was clearly formed. It should be mentioned that these new phenomena in the field of operational art were established and formed first in the Russian Army.

Having failed to resolve the missions which strategy assigned, operational art at the turn of the year 1914–15 in the West, and at the end of 1915 in the East encountered a completely new phenomenon in the form of a continuous positional front. Flank maneuver became impossible, since there were no flanks. There remained a single form of maneuver – the frontal blow for penetration, that is, the form which had inadequately attracted the attention of theory in the period preceding the war. To speak to the point, there were quite convincing prognosticators of positional forms of battle even before the First World War, particularly in the Russo-Japanese War and the Chataldjin Battles of the Balkan War of 1912–13. However, this experience was not properly taken into account or theoretically understood.

Protracted attempts to resolve the problem of overcoming a positional front commenced. This was understood in a rather simplified way. Joffre, in planning offensive operations for the summer campaign of 1915, considered that the main task properly came to a tactical penetration; it was only necessary to penetrate the front in one of the sectors for it to completely burst, like a soap bubble, and the war would once again take on maneuver forms. However, reality turned out to be different, and for almost two years tactics were powerless to resolve the issue of penetrating a front. In the long competition between offense and defense, the latter continued to demonstrate its strength. Its development proceeded at first along the line of reinforcement of fire power, fortification structures, and an increase of the tactical and operational depth of the defense, and then, as the power of the attack increased, by tactical maneuver of fire means and maneuver of operational and strategic reserves.

As the defense developed, the penetration operation changed. Operational maneuver over the period of the entire war had a simplified form. In the majority of cases this was a straight-line attack, sometimes developed along converging axes if the situation permitted. Its primary and predominating stage, which determined the entire essence of the offensive operation, was the penetration of the tactical defense belt, which did not succeed on the Western Front until the end of 1917.

The problem of developing tactical success into operational, and then strategic success, in this period did not attract much attention and was not resolved, since neither side had succeeded in achieving a tactical penetration of the front. The development of the offensive operation proceeded along the line of increasing forces and means assigned to execute the penetration. All attention was directed toward tactics, toward the development of the combined arms battle.

At the end of 1917, at the Battle of Cambrai, the problem of the tactical penetration of the front was resolved. The solution was found by the mass employment of a new combat means – the tank – and on the basis of well-organized battlefield cooperation of four combat arms – infantry, artillery, tanks, and aviation. However, operational art turned out to be incapable of using the tactical penetration of the front and developing it into an operational penetration, mainly because there were no mobile means at its disposal for developing the penetration, the maneuver of which would have forestalled maneuver of reserves from the depth of the defense. Combat potentials of tanks, in the sense of developing the blow into the depth, were not extended beyond the framework of tactical scales. Cavalry was weak for developing an attack into the depth, and aviation still did not possess sufficient numerical size and did not have the necessary fire power to retard maneuver by defensive operational reserves or to prevent the enemy from reestablishing a defensive front in the rear of the penetration sector. In the

1918 campaign, the Germans achieved a large-scale tactical penetration of the front three times, but not one of them was developed into an operational penetration; nor were large-scale operational results achieved in offensive operations conducted by the Allies in this campaign.

Assessing the development of operational art in the period of the First World War in the Western European theater, we must mention that, having encountered a phenomenon which had clearly not been sufficiently studied before the war, that is, positional struggles, neither Allied nor German operational art found a solution to the problem of operational penetration of a front and shift to decisive maneuver forms of combat operations. It was capable only of executing a tactical penetration of the front by mass employment of new, more powerful combat means, significant improvement of forms of combined arms battle, and cooperation of all combat arms. Western military thought did not find a solution to the problem of overcoming a positional front in either operational art or strategy.

A positional front was overcome twice in the Eastern European theater. The first time was during the "Gorlice Breakthrough" by German forces in May 1915. This operation is not particularly instructive from the point of view of resolving the problem of penetrating a positional front, for the breakthrough was achieved by the clearly overwhelming superiority of German artillery (40 times superior in numbers of heavy guns) over tsarist Russia's poorly armed artillery. That it was chance and not the correctness of the methods of this operation was confirmed by the employment of similar procedures on other fronts in later campaigns not bringing success to the Germans.

The solution to the problem of overcoming a positional front, as found by the prominent Russian military leader, General Brusilov, in the 1916 offensive, had a completely different character. Despite the clearly unfavorable conditions of the strategic situation, Brusilov found a successful solution to the problem of penetrating specifically in the area of operational art, in the *front* operation, by employing such forms of operational maneuver as a simultaneous attack against several front sectors to penetrate it on a wide expanse. Only the extreme technical backwardness of the Russian Army in the tsarist period, the conservatism and lack of leadership talent in tsarist general headquarters, and the absence of strategic cooperation among the Allied armies made it impossible to develop the great success achieved by General Brusilov into a decisive victory. Nevertheless, Russian military art gave birth to a new form of operational maneuver, which corresponded to the conditions of modern war. This form of operational maneuver did not receive its ultimate development in the 1914–18 war, but only in the Red Army's military art during the Great Patriotic War, and in this respect it can be rightly associated with a number of national forms of Russian military art.

What, then, was new in the experience of conducting operations in the First World War?

Above all, there was an increase in the scope and exertion of operations and the rich experience of executing the frontal attack to penetrate the front. Although these attacks were not crowned with a complete resolution of the problem of penetrating the front, they did, nevertheless, come close to its solution. The increase in the scope of the struggle and employment of enormous masses of forces and combat equipment in a theater of military operations decisively changed the significance not only of tactical, but also large operational troop formations. The division ceased to be the configuration in which combined arms battle was concluded; the full development and completion of combined arms battle shifted to the corps and, to a significant degree, the army. The enlistment of several armies operationally cooperating with one another was required to resolve strategic missions. A *front* or army group received full recognition as the most important operational configuration, but the *front* came out of the First World War as a configuration which organized army cooperation in a rather simplified form. All problems of tactical cooperation and cooperation among combat arms were completely resolved within the framework of armies, whose combat might at this time increased greatly, mainly by the introduction of tanks, artillery, aviation, and other technical means into their composition for the period of the operation.

With respect to scope and duration of developed armed struggle, the Civil War in Russia was one of the most important military events after the First World War, having substantial influence on the development of operational art. This war took place under specific conditions, characterized by weak operational density, as a consequence of combat events unwinding on gigantic expanses of fronts. Armies were poorly outfitted with equipment, especially heavy reinforcement means. The socio-political nature of the Civil War advanced extraordinarily decisive aims for strategy. All this could not help being reflected in operational art.

Operations acquired a highly maneuverable character. If the positional period of the First World War, when operational art encountered new combat conditions (under positional conditions), was filled with errors, the essence of which came to attempts to resolve operational missions by means of fighting under maneuver conditions, then in the Civil War we encounter the reverse phenomenon. Despite combat conditions sharply changing in comparison with the positional period of the First World War, traditions of positional forms of struggle still dominated for a rather long time over the operational art inherited from the old army. A bold and decisive turn was necessary in order to bring operational art into accord with general conditions of struggle, and in this respect a decisive role belongs to Comrade Stalin, who in the period of the Civil War laid the first foundations of Soviet operational art. In Comrade Stalin's works, as well as those of his associates and pupils, the operation acquired a clearly expressed decisive character. Maneuver was revitalized with new force and, to a certain degree, on a new basis, since a mobile operational group was created in the form of 1st Cavalry Army, which made operational maneuver a primary factor.

During the Civil War, the Red Army conducted a series of outstanding operations with respect to expertise and form, the latter going further than the experience of the maneuver period of the First World War. Once again flanking maneuver acquired greater significance. The brilliant flank attack executed on the Eastern Front in spring 1919 by M. V. Frunze, a prominent representative of Stalin's school of military art, led to great strategic results, forcing the enemy into a deep withdrawal along the entire expanse of the Eastern Front. During the subsequent struggle, the Red Army employed the flanking maneuver with new success and great strategic results in the Kiev Operation (1920), conducted according to Comrade Stalin's plan. This attack led to a sharp change in the strategic situation on the Southwestern Front, and forced the enemy to withdraw deeply to the west with enormous losses. The flanking maneuver also played a great role in operations for the liberation of northern Tavriya. Although it did not receive full development in the form of an encirclement of the enemy, it nevertheless disclosed its strong aspects and solidly confirmed its position as the most decisive form of operational maneuver.

Together with successful use of such an old form of operational maneuver as the flanking maneuver, the Red Army's operational art found a new, original form of operational, or more precisely operational-strategic, maneuver in the form of the cleaving strike, employed by Comrade Stalin in the defeat of Denikin's Army in 1919. Elements of frontal penetration and the flanking operational maneuver with a swift cleaving blow delivered to a great depth were combined in this maneuver of enormous scale.

Of course, all these operations were conducted under the specific conditions of the Civil War. From the point of view of numerical size of participating forces, combat equipment, and operational and tactical density, they were far from modern operations; nevertheless, features of the operational art of a new type of army were clearly outlined in them, and the military genius of the creator of the Red Army's military art, Comrade Stalin, was disclosed. As one can already see the expertise of his brilliant canvases in the sketches of a great artist, so in Stalin's military leadership activity during the Civil War one could clearly follow the basic trends along which his creative genius unfolded during the Great Patriotic War.

Foreign military thought in the first years after the First World War found itself directly influenced by the experience of military operations in the Western European theater. This was a completely natural phenomenon, since the materiel-technical base had still not changed in comparison with the First

World War. Tens of thousands of 1917–18-model guns and tanks piled up in arsenals still dominated the further development of operational art.

However, new trends in the development of operational art were already quite clearly contemplated in this period. Above all, they were characterized by an attempt to find an escape from the positional dead end created in the second half of the war, an aspiration to work out problems of maneuver war. Two paths were mapped out in this respect. Supporters of the first, which was most fully reflected in French military thought, considered that the key to maneuver forms of operations were found namely in the course of the concluding general offensive of the Entente armies, and that future war would have such unique forms of maneuver as were employed in September–November 1918. There were many authors who interpreted this latter period of the war as a maneuver period. However, it was already clear then, and it is completely obvious now, that there was not the shadow of operational maneuver in these offensive operations. The essence of 1918 operations was reduced to Allied forces delivering successive attacks similar to the blows of a gigantic hammer on various front sectors. Resulting penetrations of the front were not developed operationally, but were completed within a tactical framework. But the continuous alternation of these attacks and the multitude of tactical penetrations forced the Germans to move back their entire strategic front successively. The Allies employed a colossal quantity of materiel-technical combat means in these operations. All this led to an exhaustion of forces and heavy losses, but the Allies did not once succeed in achieving an operational conclusion to the penetration, and the entire Allied advance during an offensive lasting a month and a half did not exceed 80 kilometers. It is true that Foch planned a deep attack to the Rhine on 14 November 1918, but the war concluded before then.

Of course, such operational forms were far from maneuver, although the solution reached in these operations to the problem of the tactical penetration of a front provided a basis for counting on the fact that as such means as tanks and aviation, mobile and capable of operating at a great depth, developed, the problem of operational development of the penetration could be resolved in the future. With no solution to this problem, one could not speak of maneuver forms of war. And at this time these means had not developed much in comparison with 1918, so that possibilities for developing maneuver operations were viewed only as a matter for the future.

Another direction of military thought saw the reason for positional stagnation in the ponderous masses of armed forces, numbering millions, which exceeded the "normal" operational capacity of European theaters of war. And since the arming of these masses represented a serious danger to the ruling bourgeois class, there soon arose in theory a unique attempt to get away from the "nightmare" of mass armies by means of using small armies, whose equipment was highly improved and whose personnel were highly professional.

The theories of "mechanized" "professional" armies, which turned out to be impractical, played a certain role in working out individual problems of employing combat equipment in war. However, not one of these theories provided a polished explication of the modern operation. Nevertheless, military equipment increased and was improved, and this was inevitably reflected in the development of operational art. Especially rapid growth, beginning in the 1930s, resulted in very intensive work on the theory of the modern operation. Soviet military thought occupied a prominent place in this respect.

Soviet operational doctrine proceeded from an assessment of future war as maneuver war. This not only issued from its socio-political essence, but was also based on the extremely intensive development of attack means such as tanks, artillery and aviation making it possible to resolve the mission of not only a tactical penetration of the front, but also of its development into an operational penetration, despite the fact that, according to all calculations, the operational density of theaters of future war might exceed corresponding norms for the First World War.

These possibilities, which were opened wide by the use of mass aviation and motor-mechanized forces to counter maneuver by defensive reserves in the operational depth, provided the basis for counting on the operational development of a penetration being executed at tempos considerably higher than the tempo of countermeasures on the part of the defensive reserves. There were no particular misgivings about being able to achieve a tactical penetration of the front, since the development of breakthrough means after the First World War proceeded at greater tempos than the development of defensive means. Mechanized techniques of fortification work and the use of prepared materials for defensive structures and rapidly hardening concrete did not occur so fast that it would make it impossible to penetrate a front.

In the 1930s, our theory of the offensive operation, at the base of which was the idea of the deep operation, was finally formed. The primary characteristics of Soviet operational doctrine were reduced to the following. An operation is conducted with the decisive aim of routing enemy armed forces. The most important means, which imparts to an operation a decisive nature, is powerful action against the entire tactical and operational depth of the enemy defense, and operational maneuver of a predominantly enveloping nature, completing the encirclement of the main enemy force grouping. In the majority of cases, the offensive operation begins with a penetration of the enemy's defensive front. This penetration is achieved by an attack of superior infantry forces supported, on the basis of tactical and operational cooperation, by mass tank, artillery, and aviation operations, to influence simultaneously not only the entire tactical depth, but also the operational depth of the enemy's defensive formation. Penetration of the front, achieved by forces of the first operational echelon (combined arms formations reinforced by tactically cooperating artillery and tanks, and supported by air strikes in the enemy's tactical defense zone), is developed operationally by means of a special operational force echelon which consists of mobile motor-mechanized formations, reinforced by cavalry formations, and supported by mass aviation operations in the operational depth of the enemy positions. Widespread, decisive maneuver is understood as the basis for operations of the echelon for the operational development of the penetration.

The problem of overcoming a defensive front occupied, as before, a predominant position in theoretical works, and was worked out with adequate completeness. The problem of operational development and maneuver in the operational depth was not worked out so fully.

Soon the Red Army's operational thought had the opportunity to be tested in practice. The operation on the Khalkhin-Gol River confirmed with exceptional persuasiveness the enormous potentials, hidden in modern combat means, for conducting an annihilating battle on the basis of the enveloping maneuver. Some time later, theoretical development of the frontal penetration operation was also tested in combat. The experience of penetrating the Mannerheim Line in the 1939–40 Soviet–Finnish War, having confirmed the correctness of the principal tenets of our theory of a frontal penetration operation, provided a number of valuable conclusions with respect to both the role of new combat arms and the significance of such an "old" combat arm as artillery.

If French operational doctrine was bogged down in the experience of the First World War, then the German General Staff widely borrowed progressive operational ideas from Soviet military doctrine. The Germans took from Red Army experience modern ideas of maneuver operations with a decisive purpose and with deep pressure on the enemy's defensive system, and adapted them to strategic "blitzkrieg" plans. New operational forms of struggle played a large role in their successes in Western Europe. The experience of struggles which unfolded there demonstrated that forms of deep operation met the demands of modern war. This verification of new forms was, however, far from fully valuable, since the features of the political and strategic situation in Western Europe did not make it possible to judge how effective these forms of operational art employed by the Germans were, since in Western Europe there was no appropriate counteraction to them. Only the Great Patriotic War subjected these operational forms to a general test, and the experience provides extremely instructive results.

It is completely understandable that operational forms of struggle, however perfected they might be, cannot in and of themselves predetermine victory in war. They are a powerful asset in the hands of a military leader to achieve victory by force of arms, but they should be in complete harmonic combination with the political and economic situation of the struggle, and in full organic combination with strategy; the latter must also fully meet the requirements of modern war.

Deep forms of operation, despite the Germans using them widely in the initial period of the Great Patriotic War, did not provide them with the results on which they were counting. They did not succeed in routing our armed forces or disrupting the Soviet economy to such a degree as to deprive us of the ability to wage war. Modern operational forms, borrowed by the German General Staff from the Red Army, were an asset in the hands of a strategy which was basically defective, and so naturally they could not provide the required effect. At the same time, these operational forms of struggle, which required a highly creative approach on the part of the executor, were transferred into the German Army, a medium alien to them. Here they very soon turned into stereotypical patterns at all levels, beginning with the large strategic operation and ending with operations of automatic weapons groups [combat groups – *kampfgruppen*]. The transformation of new operational forms into stereotypes meant their death.

We observe another picture in the operational ingenuity of the Red Army. New forms of struggle, both operational and tactical, were knitted together organically with the nature and spirit of the Red Army and our command cadres. They fully corresponded to Soviet strategy, the missions of which they were to resolve. All this led to our operational forms of struggle, whose roots were joined with national Russian military art, taking into account the experience of world military art, and associated organically with the features of the Red Army as an army of a socialist state, receiving not only their confirmation in the Great Patriotic War, but also an unprecedented high degree of development and absolute and harmonious completion.

The Great Patriotic War had a clearly expressed maneuver nature. In the second half of the war, the German command unsuccessfully attempted to shift it to positional forms. And the fact that the Great Patriotic War proceeded in maneuver forms until the end was a consequence of the high quality of Soviet military art and the technical might of the Red Army.

Positional forms in the First World War were conditioned by a number of factors. M. V. Frunze wrote:

> A positional nature is created on the basis of the inability of the sides in contact with one another to find a solution by a direct mass strike. On the other hand, objective conditions in the form of limited territory and a rich technology made it possible for each side to go over to the defense at immobile positions after having rejected a speedy solution.[8]

In light of this principle, it is not without interest to examine the situation in the autumn of 1942. The German command had declared a transition to the defense for the purpose of holding captured territory. This meant acknowledgement of the inability to "find a solution by a direct mass attack." The Soviet Supreme High Command fully retained these capabilities, and the annihilating blow at Stalingrad and other sectors of the front was a clear confirmation of this.

It cannot be said that the Germans in the autumn of 1942 did not have the necessary equipment to make it possible for them to resolve defensive missions as in 1914–15. The front was, of course, larger than in 1915, but German forces on the Eastern Front in the autumn of 1942 were at least two-and-a-half times greater than in 1915, in a period of front stabilization. If the features of the struggle on our Karelian Front are taken into account, then it can be said that, with respect to the expanse of the front and the forces, the situation in the autumn of 1942 was barely different from that of 1915, when front stabilization had been achieved. At that time, the Germans also attempted in the course of subsequent campaigns to shift the war to positional forms in narrower sectors, using such powerful defensive lines as the Dnepr, Western Dvina, Dnestr, Vistula, and Oder; nevertheless, they suffered a permanent defeat. The failure of attempts to shift the war to positional forms was determined by the fact that the Red Army was strong, and positional forms of struggle could not be implemented against it.

The strategy of the Soviet Supreme High Command, which relied on the high level of defensive capabilities of the socialist state, was able to use the armed forces with such consequence as to provide for the capability of conducting offensive operations of enormous scope in a period when the enemy had already lost these capabilities. Furthermore, the Red Army had at its disposal such materiel-technical means for fighting, as to make it possible to overcome successfully the enemy's powerful, technically equipped defense. And finally, operational and tactical forms of struggle made it possible for the Red Army to resolve successfully not only the mission of an operational penetration of a positional front, but also the conduct of operations with a decisive aim – encirclement and destruction of the enemy's main groupings. The harmonious combination of strategy, operational art and tactics, multiplied by the might of combat equipment, was the foundation of being able reliably to overcome a positional front during the Great Patriotic War. This will retain its effectiveness fully in future wars as well.

The primary feature of Red Army offensive operations was their decisive character. This emerged fully from the social nature of war and the essence of our politics and strategy. The enemy, having insidiously attacked our country in order to destroy the socio-economic and political foundations of the Soviet state and our national independence in an attempt to enslave our people, had to be destroyed. This mission could be executed only by means of large-scale offensive operations conducted with a decisive aim. The encirclement operation responded most fully to this demand. That is why this form of operation was used so much in Red Army offensive operations.

Beginning with the operation at Stalingrad and in the course of the entire subsequent development of the Great Patriotic War, maneuver for the purpose of encirclement on operational and tactical scales acquired predominant significance in Red Army operations. The main achievement of Soviet operational art lies in the fact that for the first time in history it fully disclosed the entire substance of an encirclement operation; secondly, it demonstrated the possibility of executing an encirclement operation under any conditions; thirdly, it completely refuted the thesis of the extreme rarity, almost chance occurrence, of surrounding an enemy, a thesis which had been unshakable for a long time in military theory.

Thorough development of the theory of the encirclement operation was still to come, but, based on the experience of such outstanding operations as Stalingrad, Korsun–Shevchenkovskiy, Vitebsk, Bobruisk, Iassi–Kishinev, and others, the fundamental elements of an encirclement operation, namely the decisive penetration of the enemy defense along two or more axes; swift maneuver of powerful mobile groupings leading to the encirclement of the main forces of an enemy grouping, and the liquidation of the encircled enemy had already been brought to light. In addition, an inseparable element of the encirclement operation is its operational support, determined by various methods, depending on the operational-strategic situation.

Military theory in the past considered that favorable conditions of a situation such as an advantageous front profile and a grouping of forces which successfully developed in connection with this, albeit only in basic features, were necessary for a successful encirclement. Our operational art clearly demonstrated that it was capable of resolving the mission of encirclement under any conditions of the situation. The Red Army executed maneuver to encircle an advancing enemy; it encircled enemy forces which had taken up a stable defense; it executed encirclement during maneuver after the penetration of the front and during pursuit of the enemy. This was also a new achievement in the field of conducting operations.

In the past, as historical experience demonstrates (and theory cannot be distant from it), the successful execution of encirclement operations was, to a significant degree, a result of a favorable confluence of circumstances and, to a significant degree, a chance occurrence. Schlieffen had to admit in the conclusion of his work *Cannae* that

> a complete embodiment of the battle at Cannae is encountered only very rarely in military history, because for this what is necessary is, on the one hand, a Hannibal, and, on the other a Terentius Varro, both of whom in their own way contributed to the achievement of a great goal.[9]

General Ehrfurt, another representative of the German General Staff who had continued to investigate the annihilating engagement, considered that possibilities for conducting such an engagement had increased; nevertheless, in 1939 he had to admit that a plan for an engagement similar to Cannae "would be a rarely achieved ideal even in future wars."[10] These illustrations were especially revealing of representatives of the German General Staff, who laid claim to a monopoly in the art of conducting similar operations. And this was only three years before the Battle of Stalingrad.

In the recent past, a military leader still did not have at his disposal the necessary combat means and scientifically developed operational methods to execute an encirclement operation reliably by subordinating the will of the enemy to his will, decisively creating preconditions for successful implementation of the encirclement operation, and conducting it on the basis of these preconditions. Forces and equipment capable of reliably penetrating the enemy defense in a short period of time were necessary for a successful encirclement. And mobile strike means were necessary for this, making it possible to complete the encirclement in the shortest time, despite enemy counteraction. And there had to be methods and means for this which would make it possible to counter dynamically all enemy attempts to liquidate the established encirclement.

The Red Army disposed all this in full measure, and this made its operational art the brilliant bearer of the most decisive and complex form of operations.

The frontal attack as a form of operational maneuver experienced great development during the Great Patriotic War. As is known, the frontal attack in the First World War was never once brought to full operational, let alone strategic, completion. Consequently, all those plans associated with the subsequent development of a frontal attack, as, for example, the concentric maneuver after penetrating the front, were not properly developed. Basically the development proceeded along the line of quantitative changes: an increase in the number of forces and technical means being used to execute the attack, and an increase in the width of the offensive front. Qualitative achievements were not great. They did not break out of the framework of the achievement of organized tactical cooperation of combat arms and resolution of the problem of the tactical penetration of the front.

We observe a different picture in the Red Army's operational art in the Great Patriotic War. As with the encirclement operation, the frontal attack saw full expression in its operational form. In the overwhelming majority of cases, the Red Army's frontal attack unfailingly led to a penetration of the enemy front, then experienced wide operational development, and in the final analysis led to the achievement of the assigned strategic aims. If the frontal attack to penetrate the front was fully developed within the context of a single operation in one sector of the front, then, at the same time, it acquired tremendous significance as a new form of operational maneuver in the form of a number of frontal attacks completed in operational cooperation in several sectors of the front. And if in Brusilov's genius in 1916 one could see only the conception of the idea of operational maneuver, then in the Red Army's genius it acquired the character of a fully completed, highly perfected operational form of struggle. In gigantic offensive operations the Red Army simultaneously delivered powerful frontal attacks which led to operational penetration of the front. Then, after the penetration, rather complex maneuver was executed, which led to the encirclement of large enemy groupings and the complete rout of his forces, both in the main defensive sector and in the operational zone. The enemy front was chopped to pieces, and in the final analysis the large operational, and often even the strategic link was torn out of his defensive system. Almost all the Red Army's largest operations associated with the achievement of decisive successes were conducted in the style of attacks which splintered the front; this was especially so in its most developed form, that is, in the 1944 rout of German Central Army Group forces in Belorussia.

In addition, a variation of the frontal attack, the cleaving attack, came fully to light. Its essence consisted of a swift cleavage of the enemy defense to great depth. The cleaving attack, which was not a decisive form of operation, nevertheless created favorable preconditions for subsequent maneuver against the enemy's deeply exposed flanks and rear. Such an attack often acquired very important significance by creating exceptionally favorable conditions for subsequent offensive operations. The attack of Central Front forces from the sector Sevsk and Ryl'sk to Konotop, Bakhmach, and Kiev (September 1943), the blow of 1st Ukrainian Front forces along the southern edge of Poles'ye to Kovel' in winter 1943/44, and especially the attack of 1st Belorussian Front forces from the Vistula to the Oder on the Berlin axis (January 1945) are the clearest examples of the cleaving attack. Their success created the greatest advantages for our subsequent operations. There is no doubt that this new variety of frontal attack has a great future and requires serious theoretical development.

In the Red Army's frontal attack, as with the encirclement operation, we see its sufficiently full, completed forms. During the First World War, and then in theoretical works based on its experience, the offensive operation to penetrate a front was usually divided into two stages: tactical penetration of the front and its operational development. Main attention and the principal center of gravity usually fell to the first task, that is, tactical penetration. Regarding operational development of the penetration, necessary practical experience had not been obtained. This stage of the operation was not sufficiently theoretically developed, and remained in the form of a simplified scheme.

The Great Patriotic War provided rich experience for the operational development of the penetration and, in our opinion, demonstrated quite precisely that now, after the penetration of the front, a stage should follow including operational maneuver to destroy the main enemy grouping, against which the operation is directed. In modern complex operations conducted with a decisive aim, the mission of routing large enemy forces in the operational zone requires independent and complex maneuver, which goes beyond the limits of what we formerly understood as the stage for the development of success. The latter usually came down to a swift penetration into the operational depth by mobile groupings to fight against approaching reserves and pursue a withdrawing enemy. Now the development of success on a wide operational scale begins after the main enemy forces are routed in the tactical and operational zones, and is a complete stage of an operation, having the purpose of pursuing and destroying remnants of enemy forces which have escaped the attack, impeding maneuver of approaching strategic reserves, destroying them, disrupting the creation of a new defensive front, deeply penetrating into enemy territory, and providing a favorable situation for subsequent operations. In general, an all-round and fuller exploitation of success takes place in the interests of strategy.

What factors, then, determined such a rapid and full development of the modern operation in the Red Army's combat practice?

Undoubtedly, the development of combat equipment and, especially, mobile combat means – tanks and aviation – played an enormous role. Large tank formations, supported by the penetrating power of mobile artillery and mass aviation, made it possible to conduct decisive maneuver, three and sometimes four times the tempo of maneuver of combined arms formations. Motorization of combined arms formations also permitted development of maneuver capabilities. The presence of large masses of aviation had a paralyzing effect on operations by enemy operational reserves and, thus, facilitated, to a large degree, offensive maneuver capabilities. However, the role of new technical assets would have been significantly less if such an "old" combat arm as artillery had not acquired new significance in the modern operation. In comparison with the First World War, artillery was not only a powerful means which paved the way for infantry and tanks, but also an extremely mobile and highly maneuverable asset, whose mobility must be understood not only in the sense of wheeled movement, but also in its more rapid readiness to resolve assigned missions. Improvement of fire methods and wide-scale introduction of direct fire made it possible for artillery to resolve many very complex missions with relatively fewer shells than during the First World War.

The system of indoctrinating and preparing our cadres, and the significant improvement of the operational troop control system also played an incontrovertible role in the matter of providing broad maneuverability for our operations. The outstanding operational expertise of modern mass armies is unthinkable without indoctrination and preparation of a considerable number of operational experts – *front* and army commanders and their staffs. The power of Stalin's military school rests in the development of military art and simultaneous maturation of military leaders capable of implementing all that Stalin's military science creates being combined harmoniously.

The Great Patriotic War led to a complication of operations, and resulted in new enormous development in operational art. This was the direct consequence of the growth in the scope and intensity of war and the complexity of those strategic aims and tasks which operational art had to resolve, an increase in the numerical size of forces and combat fronts, and an enormous quantitative and qualitative growth in technical combat means. All this increased the scope of the modern operation, its duration, and its intensity, and considerably complicated it.

Before the First World War it was usually thought that a partial strategic aim could be achieved by a single operation. Practical experience demonstrated, however, that usually one operation was insufficient to achieve a strategic aim when fighting strong enemies. The idea of successive operations appeared after the First World War. Triandafillov wrote, "Ideally one should plan one's armed forces operations so that, by means of a series of annihilating attacks leading to an end, they would result in the full defeat of an enemy and his full capitulation."[11]

However, by the commencement of the Great Patriotic War only general features of the theory of successive operations had been worked out; this was more an attempt to look into the future than an elaboration of practical war experience, for the First World War and all subsequent wars did not provide necessary material in this respect. Only the Great Patriotic War provided rich experience in this area of operational art.

The idea of successive operations experienced such great sweep in the Red Army's combat activities and in the practice of the Supreme High Command, that, in our opinion, it went beyond the limits of prewar prognoses. If from the very essence of the term "successive operations" comes the idea of a successive delivery of attacks along a single operational axis or, with their shifting, along a front, then the Great Patriotic War brought a new solution to this question. The solution of a strategic mission assigned to the Red Army in an offensive campaign was executed by a whole series of operations conducted simultaneously in a number of sectors of the combat front, dissociated in operational order with respect to space and time, but joined by the idea of achieving a single strategic aim. It seems to us that this circumstance is an unarguable sign of a new phenomenon in the development of operational art, which could conditionally be called a strategic system of operations. The essence of this phenomenon does not fit within the framework of the concept of the operation, even in such a developed form as the operation of a group of *fronts*; at the same time it cannot be identified with a campaign, which encompasses a much wider circle of phenomena. We must restrict ourselves to only this brief and general posing of the question, with the understanding that it requires even more serious work.

The experience of the Great Patriotic War confirmed the vitality of army and *front* operations, which experienced new development during the war. In addition, it introduced substantive changes into their interdependence. The enormous development of technical combat means and the complexity of the modern operation led to the fact that now full resolution of the most complex operational missions could not be achieved within the framework of an army operation, but required a *front* operation. Now the *front* operation has changed from an operation structured on the operational interaction of individual armies of more or less uniform composition into a complex set of operational interactions of field armies and mass technical combat means in the form of large tank and motor-mechanized formations and large aviation formations. In addition, a new form of operation – the operation of a group of *fronts* – has come into being. This latter form strongly confirmed its position in the Red Army's operational art, and has become a basic means for resolving strategic missions.

Substantive fundamental achievements were also made in questions of controlling modern operations. In studying the course of the Great Patriotic War, one is struck by the exceptional orderliness of operational-strategic cooperation of our *fronts*. This is a most genuine confirmation of the correctness and vitality of the system of strategic and operational leadership adopted in the Red Army. Its basic characteristic features are judicious centralization of troop control, allowing the lower echelons of authority initiative, and the logical approach of higher control organs to the solution of operational and tactical problems. The *stavka* [headquarters] of the Supreme High Command today is not only already working on issues of general planning for war, determining strategic aims and missions, and distributing combat forces and means among the fronts. It is also the organizer of fundamental decisive operations. In turn, the *front* and army command has also come closer to the organization of army operations and battle. Such a control system makes it possible to accelerate tempos of planning and preparing an operation, to achieve an organic correspondence to their general war plans, and to distribute and use correctly combat forces and means.

We have touched upon only some issues in the development of operational art during the Great Patriotic War. The war provided so much rich material in the area of conducting operations that it will be necessary to do much work on this in order to fit the primary conclusions from this experience into an orderly system.

However, one can consider it indisputable that in the Great Patriotic War Soviet operational art achieved all-encompassing development, and has been confirmed in progressive positions of world military art. The Red Army's operational art became a reliable, irrefutable weapon of strategy. It achieved a level of development which provides it with the ability to resolve success-fully all missions assigned by strategy. The experience of the Great Patriotic War attests that our operational art found forms and methods of struggle capable of countering an enemy's mass attack; in addition, it brilliantly resolved the mission of the annihilating defeat of enemy forces, whatever forms and methods of defense they might employ.

Such a decisive form of maneuver as encirclement for the purpose of fully destroying the enemy became a normal method of combat operations in Soviet operational art. Operational art resolved all principal problems of the frontal attack, beginning with the tactical penetration of the front and ending with the development and exploitation of success on a large operational-strategic scale. It was capable of keeping stride with the gigantic scope of armed struggle, and of resolving the most complex problems of operational cooperation on a wide scale.

Our operational art accumulated the richest experience, making it possible to implement in theory – and in practice if necessary – further steps in the development of this most important branch of military art.

It should not be forgotten that operational art – and military art as a whole – does not stand still, but continually develops. In researching operations which have just concluded, we should examine their development, attentive-ly study from where and how new phenomena have arisen in the area of operational art, and capture the further direction of this development, so that in the future Soviet operational art will fully meet the demands of con-temporary times.

NOTES

1. N. Talenskiy, *Razvitiye operativnogo iskusstva po opytu poslednikh voyn, Voyennaya mysl'* [Military thought], 6,7 (June, July 1945), pp. 15–30
2. Colonel F. Kuhlman of the French Army, the author of *Strategy* and *General Tactics*, writes that "until 1914 the history of recent warfare was not studied thoroughly enough." Military journals published entertaining anecdotes more than serious research of recent warfare. "It would be immeasurably more useful to study the Manchurian War, the Balkan Wars, and the war in the U.S., or even to conclude the superior works already begun on wars in the period of the First Empire." See F. Kuhlman, *Strategy* (Voyenizdat, 1939), p. 107.
3. Schlieffen, *Cannae* (Voyenizdat, 1938), p. 364.
4. Ibid., p. 14.
5. Ibid., pp. 292, 293.

6. Lucas, *The Evolution of Tactical Ideas in France and Germany during the War of 1914–1918* (GIZ, 1926), p. 9.
7. F. Foch, *Memoirs* (Voyenizdat, 1939), p. 31.
8. M. V. Frunze, *Izbrannyye proizvedeniya* [Selected works] (Voyenizdat, 1940), p. 48.
9. Schlieffen, *Cannae,* p. 350.
10. W. Ehrfurt, *Victory with Complete Annihilation* (Voyenizdat, 1941), p. 88.
11. V. Triandafillov, *Kharakter sovremennykh operatsiy* [The nature of modern operations] (GVIZ, 1932), p. 129.

CHAPTER THREE

The Stalinist Postwar Years, 1946–53

In the immediate postwar years, Soviet concern for the operational level of war continued to intensify. Stalinist controls over open and detailed discussion of operational matters in written works produced the outward appearance of atrophy in Soviet military science. Most general texts and shorter articles in open journals paid deference to Stalin's role in military science and stressed the universal application of Stalin's permanent operating factors to matters of war.

Expressed as lasting principles which determined the course and outcome of war, these included the following: (a) rear stability; (b) army morale; (c) the quantity and quality of divisions; (d) the armament of the army; (e) the organizing ability of command personnel.

The apparent retrenchment in military art was real and a product of native Stalinist suspicion and censorship. While some of this is also evident in closed source writings, it is also clear that military thought did continue to develop despite Stalin's dominance. As recently released archival materials now demonstrate, candid General Staff and General Staff Academy analysis of wartime operations continued unabated. Soviet military theory and operational art also evolved in logical consequence of Great Patriotic War experiences, and the Soviet armed forces were restructured and reequipped in consonance with evolving requirements of operational art and accelerated postwar technological change. There were, of course, certain topics which military theorists were constrained from addressing. These included the politically sensitive issues of surprise, in particular regarding the circumstances of German success in June 1941; the entire topic of the initial period of war; and weaknesses in Soviet strategic and operational defensive theory, which the events of 1941 and 1942 had made so vividly evident. Also proscribed was serious discussion of the impact of atomic weaponry on future warfare, in part because of Stalin's deliberate belittling of the effects of atomic warfare (which, in part, concealed Stalin's real concern for the subject). Aside from these prohibitions, before 1953 Soviet theorists could and did address most other facets of operational art, albeit while extolling

Stalin's contributions to every positive Red Army wartime achievement. After Stalin's death in 1953, the constraints on writing abated, and significant discussion began on those hitherto proscribed military issues.

The article by Lieutenant General V. Zlobin and Major General L. Vetoshnikov typified postwar Soviet attitudes toward operational art. In a comprehensive approach, it reviewed Stalin's efforts in the Civil War period and credited the Soviet Union with being the first nation to identify the unique operational level of war as opposed to Western experiments with "small strategy" and "grand tactics." The two authors recognized the important theory of deep operations of the 1930s (without mentioning the theorists who developed it) and even alluded to the factor of surprise in June 1941. They, however, underscored the superiority of Soviet operational art, which enabled the Soviet Union ultimately to absorb the German blow and to emerge victoriously (according to the authors largely because of Stalin's enlightened leadership). The authors' detailed examination of Red Army operational techniques, particularly from 1943 to 1954, demonstrated the postwar dominance of those wartime experiences.

The additional subsequent articles by Zlobin and Vetoshnikov further developed the thrust of their combined article with greater emphasis on the nature of contemporary and future war, with due deference to Stalin's role as preeminent military theorist and practitioner.

Concerning Soviet Army Operational Art

LIEUTENANT GENERAL V. ZLOBIN AND MAJOR
GENERAL A. VETOSHNIKOV[1]

Operational art was formed relatively recently as an independent scientific discipline.

Military art in wars during the era of feudalism and absolutism did not yet have the earmarks of an operation. But during the Napoleonic Wars some traits of the operation had already emerged, notably exhibited, for example, in the operations of Kutuzov's Army in 1812–13.

In the second half of the nineteenth century, conditions determining the development of military art radically changed in comparison with the Napoleonic era. A number of new factors emerged, engendered by the flowering of industrial capitalism and the rapid growth of associated productive forces and technology. The introduction of universal military conscription led to the creation of mass armies. The appearance of the railroad reduced the time for concentrating forces, and they began to deploy on broader fronts. The scope of armed struggle increased. Instead of a single "general" engagement, which had formerly decided the outcome of a war, a series of large and small engagements usually occurred. Under these conditions, the military leader was required to join skillfully the dissociated efforts of military masses to achieve an overall war aim. Thus, by the end of the nineteenth century, military operations had acquired new characteristic traits peculiar in some degree or other to the principal indicators in the modern understanding of the operation. A number of new phenomena in military art remained outside the sphere of strategy, nor did they have at that time a direct relationship to the sphere of tactics. However, theoretical military thought at that time was incapable of dialectically interpreting historical experience and detecting these new phenomena. Bourgeois military theory continued to idealize nineteenth-century models of military art. Such a situation could not help but affect the nature of armed struggle in the initial period of the 1914–18 World War, when theory had diverged so sharply from reality.

The initial operations of the war, occurring on a completely different material base from nineteenth-century wars, to a considerable degree refuted all calculations and all basic tenets of the military doctrines of the main warring powers. The theory of a short-term war was compromised. The massiveness of armed forces naturally required broad fronts for troop deployment. In such a situation, it was impossible to conclude the war by means of a single blow. Emerging continuous fronts and some depth of force operational formations, which became possible as a result of the subsequent deployment of increasingly newer formations, led to the planned attack, given the development of combat operations into the depth, being naturally broken up into a series of battles and engagements, dissociated with respect to space but united by an overall plan. Thus, the new phenomenon in military art (the operation), whose birth we associate with the era of the Napoleonic Wars, now received clear expression and a considerably more complete content.

Conduct of the operation became a matter for an army, which had formerly resolved strategic missions. In addition, the growth in the number of such formations required the creation of large operational-strategic forma- tions to coordinate their actions – in the West, in the form of army groups, and in the Russian Army, *fronts* (the creation of *front* directorates in the Russian Army was planned before the war).[2] Leadership of separate opera- tions became the function of army or *front* (army group) command, and the operation was a single associated and purposeful chain of combat events which developed on a specific axis in a theater of military operations.

In addition, the material base of armed struggle, conditioned by the unprecedented scale of war, continued to develop rapidly, both qualitatively and quantitatively, resulting in further change in the nature of military operations. During the war itself, combat means were continuously renewed and modified, and new types of weapons and combat equipment were created. Infantry fire power increased two-and-a-half to three times in com- parison with the beginning of the war. The quantity of artillery increased. Tanks and aviation appeared, which by the end of the war had, in fact, turned into independent combat arms. At the same time, the qualitative and quanti- tative change in weaponry and equipment affected the importance of "old" combat arms: the role of artillery grew while the significance of cavalry fell; the specific weight of infantry fell somewhat, but, despite this and despite the appearance of new combat arms, infantry remained, as before, the main combat arm, and its combat quality and actions determined the outcome of battles and operations. The mass appearance of new technical combat means literally changed the overall look of the battlefield and brought about new methods and forms of conducting the operation.

The maneuver character which the war adopted in its initial period con- tinued for several months; then positional forms of battle began to dominate. Defense was stronger than offense during the greater part of the war. Above all, this was the result of new types of weapons being more suitable for defensive than offensive operations. Tanks and aviation had not yet experienced necessary qualitative or quantitative development. By using basic combat means with great success, the defense in subsequent years assumed a deep character, with high tactical density of force saturation. Therefore, both warring sides attempted to find those forms and methods of using forces which would make it possible to overcome a defensive front, which had continued to increase its durability and fire power. The formation of a strongly extended, continuous, reinforced front and the increase in defensive depth imparted to the offensive operation and its forms a completely different character from that conceived before the war, even in comparison with what had taken place during its initial period.

The following were used as forms of operational maneuver in the First World War: enveloping maneuver of one or two flanks; penetration on a narrow front; and frontal attack with penetration of a positional defense along several axes. The form of the enveloping maneuver of one or two flanks was very effective if supported by appropriate forces and means having the necessary mobility. However, with few exceptions, under conditions of the First World War, it did not lead to decisive results. The most typical form of maneuver in the positional period of the war was the frontal attack with penetration of the defense on a narrow or wide front. Employment of this form of operational maneuver did not, however, extend beyond the limit of the penetration of a tactical defense, and this (tactical) penetration did not turn into an operational penetration. In the operation's preparatory period, the attacking side created considerable superiority in forces and means, but in the penetration of a defense on a relatively narrow front and with low tempos of operational development, the defender was always able to regroup his forces to the region of the penetration, thus equalizing the correlation of forces. As a result, the frontal attack pressed in the enemy front without achieving even small operational successes.

Further evolution of the art of penetrating a positional defense proceeded along the line of widening the penetration sector in a frontal attack, massing artillery with a simultaneous reduction in time allocated for the artillery preparation, and creating more deeply echeloned force combat formations in the form of consecutive waves. These measures did not, however, succeed in resolving the problem of an operational penetration. Offensive tempos were still considerably lower than maneuver tempos of defensive reserves. Operations developed slowly; therefore, the enemy easily deduced the offensive plan and succeeded in taking measures to counter the transformation of tactical success into operational-strategic success.

General Brusilov achieved somewhat different results in 1916, having organized a broad frontal offensive with a penetration of the defense along several axes. The employment of this form of penetration limited the freedom of maneuver of the defender's reserves. Brusilov's operation could have led to broader operational-strategic results if there had been powerful mobile means to develop operational maneuver, and if the attack's force had been intensified by using additional reserves.

The problem of the operational penetration was not successfully resolved during the First World War. Warring armies still did not have means which would have made it possible to penetrate the tactical defense with fewer losses and at a higher tempo. Tanks as a means for overcoming defensive infantry fire (above all, machine guns) appeared only at the war's concluding stage. Artillery was the only strike force; however, it could not support rapid and continuous infantry advance into the depth of the defense. There were no long-range means, which would have made it possible to suppress the tactical defense to its entire depth. Tanks, which had limited mobility, could be used only as a means for immediate infantry support. Cavalry did not have the necessary technical equipment to fulfill missions for developing tactical success into operational success when penetrating a fortified front. Aviation was basically capable only of carrying out reconnaissance missions. All this made it impossible to execute an operational penetration.

The First World War was a definite stage in the development of operational art. It did not, however, resolve the problem of the operational penetration and did not provide a single model of a fully executed offensive operation. Nevertheless, this war provided initial data to develop a theory of offensive and defensive operations in the years preceding the Second World War.

Our country's Civil War of 1918–20, a significant stage in the development of the theory of the operation, laid the foundation for the formation of Soviet operational art.

The Soviet Army, formed on principally different socio-political foundations than the armies of capitalist countries, creatively exploited the experience of the previous war and, at the same time, created and successfully employed methods and forms of armed struggle which sharply differed from First World War positional forms. Operations were conducted with a decisive aim, that is, the destruction of the enemy.

The principal burden of direct guidance of the Soviet Army's combat operations fell to Comrade Stalin, who was not only the inspiration for the most important strategic plans, which guaranteed victory over the counter-revolutionary and interventionist armed forces, but was also the direct organizer of the most important operations in 1918–20. Comrade Stalin, the founder of Soviet operational art, brilliantly exploited the specific conditions of the Civil War and achieved decisive strategic aims in the large-scale operations he conducted. The operations Comrade Stalin organized were mobile, conducted with a high tempo of development, and had a clearly expressed maneuver character. Large masses of cavalry were widely used at Comrade Stalin's initiative in Civil War operations.

The principal forms of Soviet Army operational maneuver were deep and decisive attacks which developed, as a rule, until the complete defeat of the enemy, with the use of deep and shallow envelopment maneuver during the operation. Deep and decisive attacks were executed by conducting a series of successive operations.

Kolchak's defeat in 1919 was accomplished by a series of successive and continuous operations united by a single plan. The Buguruslan, Belebey and Ufa operations are models of the employment of the flank maneuver from one or both flanks, executed under conditions where the enemy had force superiority.

In 1919, Southern Front forces, which were carrying out Stalin's plan for defeating Denikin's Army, widely employed flank attacks. This form of operational maneuver was also used in the operation to defeat Wrangel's forces in North Tavriya. In operations against Denikin, First Cavalry Army was a *front* means for developing the attack into the depth. Thanks to this, Stalin's plan for defeating Denikin's Army can be viewed as the beginning of the birth of the modern deep operation. The operation to defeat Wrangel is characterized by a combination of flank attacks against enemy rear areas and a frontal offensive, made possible by the front configuration and conditions in the theater of military operations. A double enveloping attack with the cavalry's simultaneous penetration of the front and arrival in the rear of the principal enemy grouping was used to defeat the White Poles' Kiev grouping in 1920. In their totality, shock group operations led to the operational encirclement of the White Poles' 3d Army.

Thus, the Civil War of 1918–20, with its maneuver and goal-oriented decisive offensive operations, was a significant stage in the development of military art. At the same time, here, on the Civil War battlefields, especially in operations organized and conducted by Comrade Stalin, Soviet operational art was, practically speaking, born and formulated; it then developed into a well-composed scientific theory.

Only in Soviet military art did operational art achieve the right to exist as an independent part of military theory, occupying an intermediate position between strategy and tactics. Only our military science, based on the most progressive study – Marxism-Leninism – and the scientific method (inherent to it alone) of cognition of social and, consequently, military phenomena, was able to interpret historical military experience dialectically, clarify new phenomena and new traits in military art which appeared at the turn of the twentieth century, and, in accordance with the overall development of military affairs, create a new scientific discipline – the theory of operational art.

In the armies of capitalist countries, even now operational art has not been formulated as an independent scientific discipline. It is true that in some countries, especially Britain and the United States, attempts were made to separate the theory and art of conducting operations from general strategy and tactics, naming this "minor strategy," or "grand tactics," or "tactics of a theater of military operations," but this issue was not fully resolved. Thus, Soviet military thought in the very first years of its creative development occupied a leading position in relation to bourgeois military science.

Having absorbed the entire experience of recent wars, Soviet military thought in its scientific constructs proceeded from an assessment of future war as a predominantly mobile war, but extremely intense and prolonged, and not resolved by a single annihilating blow. The maneuver nature of future war was predetermined by the inevitable growth of new and powerful offensive means, especially artillery, tanks, and aviation. In the 1930s, the theory of the deep offensive operation was formulated in Soviet operational art. Recognition of the tenet that operations in future war, as distinct from operations of the First World War, could and would bear a dynamic nature, pursue decisive aims, and be accompanied by annihilating blows to the entire operational depth of the defense lay at the foundation of this theory. It was considered that, despite the anticipated increase in the operational density of *fronts* and intensification of defensive fire and engineer power, the presence of new mobile offensive means would make it possible, after penetrating the defensive belts, to arrive at maneuver space and conduct decisive offensive engagements to destroy the enemy.

The principal prerequisites for formation of the theory of the deep operation were a correct analysis of the reasons which limited offensive operations in the First World War, and a correct determination of necessary conditions for overcoming and annihilating a defensive fire front and for deeply exploiting an offensive. By dialectically analyzing the experience of the First World War, Soviet military thought determined conditions necessary for providing operational success associated with penetrating a positional front. Such conditions were: the presence of means for suppressing the entire tactical depth of the defense (tanks, artillery), simultaneity in striking the tactical defense to its entire depth in order to deprive the enemy of the ability to re-establish it using tactical reserves (long-range tanks, artillery, aviation), the presence of means for the operational exploitation of the penetration (an echelon for exploiting the penetration of fast-moving motor-mechanized formations), and the presence of means for isolating the front penetration region from deep operational defensive reserves (aviation).

These requirements were also at the basis for the formation of the theory of the modern operation, which was thought of as an operation calculated to hit the entire depth of the defense's operational formation. Its essence reduced to resolving two principal tasks: penetrating the defensive front to its entire tactical depth by one or several simultaneous attacks; and turning achieved tactical success into operational success by rapid introduction of a mobile force echelon and isolation by aviation means of the penetration region from an influx of defensive reserves from the depth. In such a form the operation occurred in several stages, consisting of a series of engagements which could develop simultaneously or successively at a great depth, requiring continuous, intensified operational efforts as the planned aim was approached, to break enemy resistance to the entire depth of his deployment. Therefore, in structuring such an operation, it was necessary to distribute forces and means not only along the front (linearly), but also in the depth, by creating operational echeloning.

Deep penetration of the tactical defense, executed by an attack echelon, was considered the initial stage of an offensive operation. This penetration was achieved by a frontal attack of superior infantry forces supported by mass tank, artillery, and aviation operations. An echelon for exploiting the penetration was subsequently introduced, which shattered defensive resistance to its entire operational depth. The enemy's entire tactical and operational depth was subjected to simultaneous pressure by the organized interaction of all combat arms and echelons of the operational formation. In its development the frontal attack turned into maneuver to envelope, encircle, and destroy the enemy.

Soviet military thought subsequently adhered to the principle that combat operations in future war and the operational forms employed would be very complex, varied, and changeable. Depending on the concrete situation, various forms of operational maneuver would be employed during the war. Our operational thought never juxtaposed certain operational forms against others. In addition, focusing on the growth of the Soviet Army's technical equipment, we gave clear preference to decisive, offensive operational methods. Offensive operations were understood as the mass employment of modern shock forces and means concentrated on the most important axes, with holding or even defensive operations on other, secondary axes.

Forms of operational maneuver in offensive operations had to be determined by the concrete conditions of the situation, and could be most varied; stereotypical patterns were forbidden here. Three possible forms were considered most typical for a *front* operation:

– an attack by concentrated forces on a single, comparatively narrow front sector, with the mission of creating a breach in the defense and then widely expanding it to the flanks and exploiting it into the depth by means of mobile formations;
– an offensive of several shock armies on a broad front; this form was considered very effective, but required large forces, and was executed mainly in an operation being carried out by two adjacent *fronts*;
– the delivery of several interrelated attacks on adjacent operational axes,

subsequently employing concentric maneuver to encircle separate enemy groupings.

Under conditions of an army operation, other forms of maneuver were also examined: an attack on the center, an attack on one of the army's flanks, an attack by all corps (with a narrow offensive front and adjoining flanks), and, as a special case, an attack against both flanks (concentric).

The operational formations of forces for a penetration and the methods of executing it were considered possible in two basic variants. In the first, rifle formations supported by a strong echelon of direct infantry support tanks, after a powerful artillery preparation under cover of a fire barrage and mass, short-range aviation, penetrated the enemy's tactical defense and created conditions to commit mobile formations into the rear. This variant was considered applicable under conditions of penetrating a strongly developed enemy defense, and when his defense line ran along terrain inaccessible for tanks. In penetrating a permanent defense, a "methodical" penetration on the basis of a carefully prepared infantry attack using shock detachments, with the subsequent capture of the defense line and exploitation of success frequently by infantry formations, was considered a version of this variant. In the second variant, the penetration was completed and exploited independently by large tank and mechanized formations supported by powerful artillery fire and aviation; combined-arms formations attacked behind mobile forces and, liquidating remaining centers of defense, together with the mobile group encircled the principal enemy force grouping. This penetration method was considered possible under conditions opposite to the first variant.

Our official views in all instances emphasized that operational forms and inclusive methods of action always had to be selected in strict accordance with the situation and a sober consideration of the actual correlation of forces and nature of anticipated resistance. Mobile forces – independent motor-mechanized and cavalry-mechanized formations – were viewed as a primary element which modernized the operation, giving it great scope and depth. The depth of a possible mobile group attack was changed by the depth of the enemy defensive operational formation (up to 100–120 kilometers).

With respect to the role of the air forces, our military doctrine mainly adhered to the principle of using aviation for direct support on the battlefield. The struggle for air superiority as a most important prerequisite for the successful conduct of an operation by ground forces was of no little significance.

We viewed the defense as a method of action employed on secondary axes in cases where it was necessary to allot forces and means to a decisive axis. It was permitted to resort to the defense on the main axes when it was necessary to gain time to prepare an offensive operation, or when it was

advantageous first to disrupt or exhaust an advancing enemy for subsequently going over to the offense. The defense was not an end unto itself,
but a means of organizing an offensive. The requirement for stubbornness,
dynamism, and decisiveness of actions, and preparedness at any moment to
go over to a counteroffensive was included in methods of conducting a
defensive operation. Our regulations envisioned two basic types of defensive
actions: positional defense, associated with holding some specific terrain
(line) no matter what; and maneuver defense, structured on the principle of
mobile operations and use of maneuver.

The Great Patriotic War confirmed the viability of our prewar operational
doctrine's basic tenets, and, at the same time, conditioned its further development, logically flowing out of the changing conditions for conducting armed
struggle.

In the development of the armed forces and their technical outfitting, we
were guided by Stalin's profoundly scientific position, which stated:

> The forms for organizing the army, combat arms, and services are
> usually tailored to the forms and methods of waging war. The former
> change along with changes in the latter ... The mission of military art
> consists of supporting all combat arms, leading them to perfection, and
> skillfully combining their actions.[3]

Soviet military doctrine was liberated from various one-sided theories which
made a preconceived assessment of the role and significance of any separate
combat arm or type of weapon. Stalin's military art provided harmonious
development of all combat arms and types of weapons.

During the Great Patriotic War, Soviet operational art covered an enormous
path of further development. This development, directed by Stalin's genius
for military leadership, unswervingly proceeded along ascending lines, and
was one of the factors which provided for our historical victory of worldwide significance over the most powerful imperialistic military system – the
armed forces of fascist Germany.

The first period of the Great Patriotic War, which concluded with the
Soviet Army's winter offensive in 1941/42, occupies a special place in the
development of our operational art. The struggle during this period was conducted under conditions sharply different from all subsequent stages of the
war. The situation was exceptionally tense for us. The Soviet Army was
forced to conduct a one-on-one struggle against the German–Fascist
Army, which had been well trained beforehand. The enemy had numerical
superiority in forces and especially in combat equipment, a superiority he
succeeded in maintaining during the first period of war. The German Army
had another advantage as well, which arose from the surprise of its attack.

Nevertheless, even under these difficult conditions the Soviet Army was able not only to stop the advance of German forces, but also to inflict heavy losses on them. At the beginning of the war the strategic content of the Soviet Army's actions consisted of a dynamic defense combined with a forced withdrawal into the depth of the country, which made it possible to gain time to deploy its principal forces, and wear out, exhaust, and bleed the enemy dry in defensive operations, so as to change the correlation of forces to its advantage and, finally, create favorable conditions to go over to a strategic counteroffensive on a specific line. The situation which had unfolded naturally placed its imprint as well on the operational art of this period of the war.

The primary features characterizing our defensive operations in this period were most clearly exhibited in our forces' defensive operations on the Moscow strategic axis, where the German–Fascist Army delivered its main attack. The operational defense on this axis bore a clearly expressed maneuver character with wide use of dynamic counteractions. The defense was organized to a significant depth, supported by the creation beforehand of a number of operational defensive lines consisting of two to three belts. The army's combat formation in this case was one of two echelons; the second echelon consisted of the army reserve. The depth of force deployment on the main axes increased as a result of *front* reserves. The tactical defense was intermittent.

Artillery was the principal and decisive force for fighting against the attacker's tanks; as the accumulation of experience and strengthening of artillery increased, its actions became more and more effective. If at first there was an attempt to cover many of the likely tank approaches with limited assets, thereby rendering artillery incapable of countering a massive tank attack on individual axes, subsequently they began to replace the uniform distribution of artillery with the development of an antitank defense in the depth, massing artillery means on the most important axes. Antitank artillery strongpoints were created on likely tank approaches. Tank forces operated in small groups, with tactical goals in close cooperation with infantry and cavalry. They were a means for reinforcing infantry, and were used in ambushes, to hold lines temporarily, and in counterstrokes and counterattacks. Aviation struggled for air superiority during the entire defensive operation, giving greater stability to the defending forces. Already in the Moscow defensive operation an attempt was made not to dissipate aviation efforts, but to use aviation for massive strikes against objectives on the battlefield and in the immediate operational depth.

In general, during our forces' defensive operations on the Moscow strategic axis, the following traits were exhibited, also characteristic of other defensive operations of that period (Leningrad, Odessa, Rostov-on-the-Don): the exceptional staunchness of our forces, who stubbornly contained the powerful onslaught of the enemy, despite his superiority in forces, especially tanks, and their ability to inflict enormous losses on the attacker; high dynamism, expressed in the organization and conduct of counterattacks and, under favorable conditions, counterstrokes, which thwarted enemy plans and exhausted and bled his forces dry; the use of artillery as a decisive means for fighting against enemy tanks, which also led to the swift weakening of his shock forces; and the attempt to organize a deep defense by means of preparing defensive lines beforehand in the operational depth.

Affecting the transition from defense and withdrawal to offensive operations was always a most difficult and complex type of combat activity. The counteroffensive is a special type of offensive operation, different from the usual offensive, which under modern conditions is, as a rule, organized during a stable situation for both sides. The defender prepares the counteroffensive during the enemy offensive, which, although successfully developed for the enemy, has not, however, produced decisive results. The defender, exhausting and bleeding enemy forces dry and leading his offensive to ruin, gathers forces under these difficult conditions and then goes over to the counteroffensive, inflicting a decisive defeat on the enemy. And although this form of operation was known even earlier, it was rarely used successfully because of its complexity. Under modern conditions, only Stalin's operational art was up to the task. The Moscow offensive operation, organized under the direct leadership of Comrade Stalin, was the first brilliant example of a well-organized counteroffensive in the Second World War. The success of this operation was guaranteed, above all, thanks to our command's correct calculation of the favorable moment for seizing the initiative, determination of the time to go over to the offensive, correct selection of the main attack axes, and skillful grouping and commitment of operational reserves. All this made it possible to achieve decisive success on the main strategic axes.

The Moscow offensive operation was conducted by Western Front forces in cooperation with the Southwestern and Kalinin Fronts and lasted 58 days. The scope of the operation in the depth during the first stage (6–25 December) amounted to 80–200 kilometers, with an average offensive tempo of 4–15 kilometers per day; in the second stage, after overcoming the Lama, Nara, and Oka River line, the advance into the depth amounted to 30–100 kilometers. The operation concluded with a success of great strategic significance: the German Army's main shock grouping was routed, a decisive turning point was created in our favor, the enemy lost the strategic initiative, his strategic plan was thwarted, and Soviet forces drove the enemy away from our Motherland's capital and developed a successful offensive on a number of other axes.

The mode of operational maneuver for the entire Western Front took the form of two powerful attacks undertaken on both flanks, separated by

200–250 kilometers. These attacks led to the defeat of both enemy flank groupings, which had attempted to capture Moscow from the north and south and which had most deeply penetrated to the east.

The experience of the Moscow offensive operation, especially its first stage, demonstrated that operational maneuver could yield success only in the case where the basic principle of the offensive – the creation of over-whelming superiority of forces and means on the decisive axis – was strictly observed. This principle always was and remains unshakable for Stalin's strategy and operational art. However, in a number of instances our tactics, and partly our operational art as well, inclined toward linear forms and uniform distribution of forces on a wide front. During exploitation of the operation, our Supreme High Command gave instructions to *fronts* and armies to reject the practice of operations by separate divisions deployed in a line, since this did not provide a preponderance of forces in the penetration sector, and to go over to shock group operations along decisive axes. This achieved the necessary preponderance of forces and means in the penetration sector.

New methods for employing the principal strike force – artillery – and its cooperation with infantry and tanks can be observed in this operation. In offensive battles during the first stages, the main artillery efforts were used to conduct the artillery preparation; this was done simultaneously against the entire front, with uniform distribution of artillery means. In January 1942, Comrade Stalin issued instructions to restructure fundamentally methods for using artillery, stressing its decisive significance both in the penetration of the defense and in development of the offensive. These instructions began a new stage in the development of artillery tactics and its cooperation with other combat arms. Comrade Stalin advanced a more effective method for the combat use of artillery – the artillery offensive – and provided clear and rational instructions for its organization. Three main conditions were speci-fied in Stalin's instructions, upon which the success of the artillery offensive depended: artillery continuously supports infantry and tanks until it has over-come defensive resistance to its entire depth; infantry advances together with artillery, under cover and with the support of its fire; the principal mass of artillery means is concentrated and operates along the axis of the army/*front* main attack. Subsequent experience of the Great Patriotic War confirmed the viability of new methods for employing artillery.

Tank forces, in view of their relatively small numbers, were employed in small groups in 1941–42 offensive operations, and were used as a means of direct infantry support. Soviet aviation, thanks to the artfulness of its maneuver, maintained superiority over enemy aviation for the entire duration of the operation; enemy aviation was forced into defensive operations. Air force missions were the following: to destroy enemy personnel and equip-ment, to hinder railroad and highway transport of his reserves to the front, to disrupt communications and control, to destroy lines of communication in the rear of the German forces; and to cover its own forces against enemy aviation. Up to 80 per cent of all of our aviation flights were made to support ground forces operations.

Exploitation of the penetration was implemented by both combined arms formations and mobile groups consisting of cavalry formations reinforced by tanks. This mobile group composition naturally left its imprint on the nature of the development of operations.

The second important stage in the development of Soviet operational art during the Great Patriotic War was the period of organizing and conducting the Stalingrad operation. With respect to operational maneuver forms and achieved results, this operation is a classical model of Soviet operational art.

Above all, it should be noted that this operation was possible thanks to the Soviet system of national economy, the organizing role of the Bolshevik party, and the wise leadership of Comrade Stalin providing for rapidly deploying military industry and setting in motion enterprises evacuated to the east, leading to a significant increase in the supply level of tanks, airplanes, antitank assets, and other types of combat equipment for the Soviet Army. Operations of the second winter campaign already demonstrated significant changes in the correlation of Soviet and German–Fascist forces' combat equipment. Our army now had at its disposal incomparably more powerful weaponry than a year earlier; its shock and fire forces had grown. In addition, the operational-tactical preparation of our forces, based on assimilating the experience of the first year of the war, increased immeasurably; they had mastered more perfected combat procedures. Our tactics became more flexible and mobile, linear forms having been rejected.

All these new conditions made the growth of our operational art possible, which was so clearly exhibited in the Battle of Stalingrad.

The defense of Stalingrad was structured, as was the defense of Moscow, on the basis of several defensive lines created on the distant and close approaches to the city. The degree of completeness of engineer preparation was different for each line; defensive lines were completed by the forces of military units occupying them. The defense on the Stalingrad axis, including the defensive system of the town itself, was most developed into the depth.

The defensive operation on the approaches to Stalingrad was characterized, above all, by extremely purposeful actions. One of the basic principles of conducting offensive operations – massing forces and strike means on the decisive axis – received more clearly expressed practical employment in this operation. Our forces, occupying intermediate lines and alternative positions beforehand, and relying on them, guaranteed defensive success by a series of continuous counterattacks which increased in force, executed with the use of tanks. This created greater defensive resiliency, which exhausted and bled the enemy dry, and provided time to create large operational reserves and powerful groupings for the subsequent counter-offensive. Counterattacks became increasingly more frequent in our forces' combat operations as the enemy and our reserves moved closer to Stalingrad. However, forces were still sometimes introduced into battle piecemeal, at different times and without sufficient reinforcing means. The structure of combat formations of counterattacking units and subunits did not always correspond to the basic principle of offensive battle, that is, immediately committing sufficient forces to break enemy resistance. Despite all this, forces defending Stalingrad were able to wear down the enemy and bleed him dry, stop his offensive, and, by their strong defense, which continued for a long time, provide our command with the capability and time to con-centrate large reserves and organize a strategic counteroffensive.

Artillery was the principal and decisive means for engaging tanks, just as it was in operations during the first period of the war. However, army large formations and force formations were now reinforced with tank-destroying units. A characteristic feature of artillery actions at Stalingrad was extensive maneuver by fire and movement on axes of the enemy tank offensive. By using massed fire with a great mass of guns on the main axes, artillery pre-determined the defensive battle's success.

A greater number of tanks took part in the defensive operation on the approaches to Stalingrad than in the Moscow operation. They were used dynamically in counterattacks together with infantry and antitank units. However, tank units were still introduced into battle without sufficient reinforcing means or artillery support. They were often diverted from executing their primary mission – destruction of enemy personnel – directing their efforts instead toward enemy tanks and artillery. The experience of defensive battles on the Don and at Stalingrad resulted in certain instructions from the Supreme High Command on methods for the combat use of tank and mechanized units and formations in a defensive operation. Censuring the practice of allotting independent defensive sectors to tank and mechanized formations, it was emphasized that these formations were to be the principal means for executing counterstrokes against an enemy who had penetrated into defensive positions. These instructions were fully implemented in sub-sequent Soviet Army operations, and their correctness was completely con-firmed by combat experience.

In addition, the Stalingrad defensive operation was a clear manifestation of the high level of excellence of Stalin's art of military leadership. This was the second, albeit more instructive, example in this war of organizing and executing a counteroffensive which produced enormous strategic success. The genius and surprising simplicity of the plan of this outstanding operation was manifested, above all, in selection of the main attack axis and determina-tion of the time for going over to the offensive. Stalin's well-known principle that the main mission of strategy consisted of organizing a decisive blow "on the axis on which an attack would most quickly provide maximum results" was brilliantly implemented here. The Supreme High Command selected attack axes that ran along the weakest link in the enemy's defensive operational formation, and that could also lead more swiftly to the attainment of the operational aim.

The experience of delivering several attacks on a broad front had already taken place during the Moscow operation. Such an operational maneuver form was also used, albeit on a wider scale, in the November operation at Stalingrad, where seven attacks were planned and executed on a very extensive front. It was just this that deprived the German command of the capability of wide maneuver of its own reserves. The width of gaps between individual penetration sectors varied from 15–20 kilometers, which fully supported operational cooperation between neighboring shock groups. A similar form of offensive along several axes was also employed in the Southwestern Front's December operation. In this case, shock groupings attacked from sectors separated from one another by 120 kilometers; nevertheless, the adopted operational form was completely appropriate for the situation, since the shock groupings possessed great penetrative power and, with a concentric form of maneuver, the attacks swiftly amalgamated into a single overall offensive on a broad front.

The Stalingrad offensive operation, conducted with three *fronts* participating, was structured on the basis of flank blows delivered by two *fronts* along converging axes to envelope and encircle the main enemy grouping. The third *front* – the Don Front – delivered a frontal attack to penetrate the front in a narrow sector and subsequently widen it by means of attacks along divergent axes. The operation was planned for a depth of up to 150 kilometers. Operational maneuver, bold in concept, brilliantly thought out by our Supreme High Command, and dazzlingly executed, led to decisive results – the encirclement and then complete liquidation of the enemy grouping, numbering more than 300,000 men and much equipment. Comrade Stalin, who in the very difficult situation at the end of 1942 planned and executed such an operation, made a great contribution to military science and enriched operational art with a classical model of a modern offensive operation crowned with the achievement of a decisive strategic aim.

The December operation at Stalingrad envisioned operational cooperation of the Voronezh, Southwestern, and Stalingrad Fronts. The basic aim was to rout the enemy's newly created Tormosin and Kotel'nikovskii groupings, 8th Italian Army, and remnants of 3d Romanian Army, and to deprive all these forces of the possibility of penetrating to the main enemy grouping, surrounded at Stalingrad. Southwestern Front was given the main mission of routing 3d Romanian Army, 8th Italian Army, and the Tormosin grouping. Southwestern Front's plan of operation was built around the concentric envelopment of the primary enemy grouping, simultaneously chopping up the front so as to liquidate this grouping unit by unit. The plan called for defeating the enemy's Tormosin grouping by means of flank attacks. The planned operational depth was 220 kilometers, and a leading role in it was accorded to tank and mechanized formations, which also made it possible to execute the planned maneuver successfully. Use of the adopted operational form was also supported by the possibility of achieving considerable force and equipment superiority on attack axes and high tempos of operational development. The success of the Southwestern Front operation, despite the cited conditions, was also provided by close operational cooperation with the Voronezh and Stalingrad Fronts: the latter at first, by means of a dynamic defense, tied down Manstein's Kotel'nikovskii group, and then defeated it by going over to a counteroffensive.

In offensive operations at Stalingrad, thanks to skillful maneuver by reserves and their maintenance until the decisive moment, our command was able to ensure the achievement of decisive force superiority on the main axes. In comparison with the Moscow operation, the norm for supplying the offensive front with artillery and tanks on main axes increased several times. This was a consequence, above all, of the increase in the degree of technical outfitting of the Soviet Army, and of the decisive maneuver of forces and means on the most important axes. During both the November and December operations, a leading role was assigned to tank and mechanized formations. Their average offensive tempo under winter conditions amounted to 20–30 kilometers, which ensured swift penetration of the enemy defense to its entire tactical and operational depth, and the piecemeal defeat of his reserves, depriving them of the capability of organizing counterstrokes. The offensive tempo of rifle units amounted to 15–20 kilometers per day. With the penetration of the tactical defense, the tempo of advance reached six kilometers per day. The overall tempo of the development of the operation and its depth increased significantly in comparison with the Moscow operation.

Several changes in the structure of troop combat formations could also be noted in these operations. The combat formation of large operational formations became far deeper. A strong second echelon was created on the main axis, which consisted not only of mechanized and tank formations designated to develop success into the depth, but also rifle formations. Such a formation provided the capability of continuously maintaining the strength of the attack by building up its force from the depth, and developing and consolidating success achieved on the main attack axes. The command of the large operational formation was able continually to maintain superiority in forces and retain the initiative until the end of the operation. Large *front* reserves had still not been created in these operations, but their origin could be observed already in the form of tank and mechanized corps deployed at the beginning of the operation in the army's second echelon; subsequently, as the operation developed, their guidance was concentrated at *front* level.

Far greater attention than previously was focused on questions of supporting the operation. This was achieved, above all, by covering the flanks of *front* shock groupings to deprive the enemy of the ability to conduct counter-strokes on the basis of the penetration. Operational support was structured as well on the skillful use of the element of surprise, which was ensured by careful observation of *maskirovka* discipline. Covert concentration and regrouping of forces, in combination with dynamic operations on secondary axes, disoriented the enemy.

Artillery was massed more decisively on the main attack axes. Its inter-action with infantry and tanks became more organized. Special attention was focused on planning the artillery offensive.

The Stalingrad operation was the first in the Great Patriotic War in which large tank and mechanized formations participated as an echelon for exploiting success. It was these formations which had a leading role in carrying out the basic operational plan. In exploiting success of combined arms formations which had penetrated the enemy defense on his flanks, they closed the ring of encirclement around the main German grouping by developing success into the depth. Part of the tank forces were used for direct infantry support.

Materiel-technical support of forces and planning rear area operations had an especially important place in the preparation and conduct of the offensive operation.

The Stalingrad offensive operation bore clear witness to the rapid growth of the Soviet Army's operational art. Speaking about the results of the Stalingrad operation in his order of 23 February 1943, Comrade Stalin pointed out:

> The fact that the Red Army command not only liberated Soviet land from the enemy, but also did not allow the enemy to leave our land alive by executing decisive operations to encircle and liquidate the enemy's armies, operations which serve as a model of military art cannot be considered accidental. Undoubtedly this is a sign of the maturity of our commanders.

The 1943 campaign was a turning point in the course of the Great Patriotic War in favor of the Soviet Army. This turning point, clearly appearing as a result of our victory at Stalingrad, was decisively consolidated by the 1943 operations, above all the Soviet Army's great victory at Kursk, where the Germans undertook their third strategic offensive. The operations at the beginning of the year at Velikie Luki, at Leningrad, in the Demiansk, Rzhev, and Viaz'ma regions, and then in the summer on the Kursk sector of the front, then developed into our forces' great summer-autumn offensive along the Smolensk and Kiev axes and in the Donbass, concluding in October with the Battle for the Dnepr.

Newly created large tank and artillery formations, designated to resolve missions of penetrating the defense, mass antitank artillery, and aviation of increased quantity and quality participated as part of our forces in the 1943 operations. Employment of large quantities of the newest equipment accorded the operations an intensified character, at the same time providing the ability to conduct the operations using deeper and more decisive forms.

The most characteristic features of our operational art in this campaign were exhibited in operations in the Belgorod, Kursk, and Orel regions.

The operational defense in the Kursk sector of the front was organized and conducted with consideration of previous campaign experiences. This operation is a model of a modern defense with a subsequent shift to a counter-offensive. In this case, a peculiarity of the defense was the fact that it was prepared beforehand to support the defending forces' shift to a strategic counteroffensive.

Attempting to cut off the front salient formed in the Kursk region and encircle our forces defending there, the Germans delivered blows along converging axes, intending to penetrate the front in narrow sectors, having formed for this purpose two powerful groupings from infantry and tank divisions. These groupings included a large number of new heavy tanks and self-propelled guns. This was an attack of enormous force, but our defense was stronger than the German offensive. The purpose of this defensive engagement was to defeat the principal German groupings and ensure the creation of favorable conditions for a counteroffensive. This plan determined the forms and methods for conducting a defensive operation.

A series of defensive lines echeloned at great depth were equipped to create the most stable defense capable of countering mass attacks by large enemy tank groupings. The depth of first-echelon division defenses amounted to five to six kilometers. Second army defensive belts were, as a rule, occupied beforehand by troops. Rear army defensive belts were occupied by forces only on operationally significant axes. *Front* defensive positions were situated 40–75 kilometers from the main defensive belt. The presence of such a deep and articulated defense system made it possible to organize a flexible and stubborn defense and maneuver extensively in any direction. The principle of massing forces and combat means on the decisive axis, as well as selecting the operational form based on a correct assessment of the situation and correlation of forces, was most clearly exhibited in this operation. An enormous mass of artillery, brought together in large artillery formations, was included in the composition of large *front* formations. Newly formed large tank formations and self-propelled artillery units were also part of large *front* formations. By the commencement of the operation, *fronts* had strong reserves in the form of tank and mechanized formations.

Our aviation, having gained air superiority, provided greater freedom of action for the ground forces.

The stubbornness of the defense was achieved due to its deep formation, the presence of massed forces and means on decisive axes, and the troops' high moral-political condition. The defense bore an extremely dynamic character, which was achieved by extensive maneuver of reserves and conduct of powerful counterstrokes by tank groupings against enemy formations which had penetrated into defensive positions. In comparison with the Stalingrad operation, maneuver of reserves and conduct of counterstrokes this time received wider employment. Army second echelons and mobile *front* reserves, as well as *front* reserve formations, were basically used. The skillful employment of counterstrokes during the defensive engagement made defensive stability possible to a considerable degree, and prepared a complete turn-around in our favor in the development of the engagement.

A number of peculiarities can also be noted in the use of combat arms in this operation. Artillery means massed fire power on the main axes to a maximum. This was achieved by both appropriate deployment and extensive maneuver of artillery means. The echeloned structure of the antitank defense, using all antitank means, artillery of all calibers, and antiaircraft guns to engage tanks, had special significance in the organization of the fire system. Mobile antitank reserves were a primary means of *front* and army commanders to counter enemy mass tank attacks. The creation of powerful artillery formations made extensive maneuver of artillery means possible. Large tank formations were used primarily to deliver counterstrokes. Tank and mechanized forces also operated within infantry combat formations, comprising a defensive "tank barrier," by which defensive stability and fire power increased, and employment of tank ambushes increased the survivability of the defense. Our ground attack and bomber aviation delivered concentrated strikes by large forces against objectives on the battlefield, while almost completely abandoning operations against enemy airfields and rear objectives. Aviation directed its greatest efforts toward destroying enemy shock groupings which had penetrated into the depth of the defense, executing missions in cooperation with artillery and tanks.

As a result of our forces' stubborn and dynamic defense, the German summer offensive on the Kursk axis suffered complete defeat in the very short period of 10–12 days. The enemy succeeded in wedging into our defense at a total depth of 10–35 kilometers, at the cost of enormous losses. Our forces exhausted and bled dry select German divisions in fierce battles.

The defensive operation at Kursk prepared favorable conditions for a decisive counteroffensive.

Offensive operations on the Orel–Kursk and Belgorod–Khar'kov axes were a direct continuation of the defensive engagement, without operational pauses. The circumstances were similar in the Moscow and Stalingrad operations, but this time the unity of defense and offense to achieve the complete rout of the enemy was more striking.

Our army gained experience in organizing and executing coordinated attacks along several axes in operations at Moscow and Stalingrad. The advantages of this operational form were once again confirmed in the 1943 offensive operations. Three concentric attacks (against Orel) by forces of three *fronts* were delivered on the Orel axis. The destruction of the enemy's Belgorod–Khar'kov grouping was conducted in the form of frontal attacks delivered by the forces of two *fronts*.

On a *front* scale, the operation assumed the form of an attack along a single axis with subsequent widening of the penetration in the direction of the flanks, or several frontal attacks delivered along various axes. Western Front delivered one blow, Briansk Front two enveloping blows to envelop Orel from the north and southeast, and Central Front also one blow. All these attacks were purposeful and mutually connected. *Fronts* and armies extensively employed encirclement maneuver in developing the offensive operation.

The composition of large *front* and army formations was reinforced by penetration artillery, direct infantry support tank units, and large mobile formations. Shock groupings were supported by a quantity of forces and means which made it possible for them not only to penetrate the tactical defense, but also to exploit success to a great depth. Operational density, in comparison with the Stalingrad operation, increased considerably. Massive use of large forces and powerful equipment ensured an enormous shock force on the main axes. The deep formation of shock groupings (two to three echelons), the presence of large mobile formations in the *front* second echelon, and powerful aviation support provided shock groupings with great penetrative power and the ability to intensify forces during the operation. This ensured rapid offensive tempos, averaging 15–20 kilometers per day. The enemy's tactical defense was overcome, in the majority of cases, on the first day of the offensive, which was not observed in previous operations, although the durability of the German defense increased as a result of their extensive use of trench systems.

The method of the artillery offensive had already been firmly included in the system of planning offensive operations. Massing artillery means on attack axes and their accompaniment by infantry and tanks, and then mobile groupings, in the depth of the defense were done in a very organized fashion. Tank and mechanized formations were used to exploit the success of combined arms formations by introducing them into the penetration for operations in the operational depth. In 1943 summer offensive operations, air forces already fully used the methodology of the aviation offensive. Aviation efforts swiftly shifted from one axis to another. Control of fighter and ground attack aircraft actions was carried out directly on the battlefield. Cooperation between the air forces, combat arms formations, and tank formations was organized more carefully than before. In contrast to previous operations, aviation achieved continuity in its operations above the battlefield, massing forces on narrow sectors of the front and against a limited number of important objectives, which significantly increased its striking force and provided more effective support for ground forces.

A characteristic feature of 1943 summer offensive operations is that forces overcame many river obstacles, which were usually forced from the march; this ensured the maintenance of a high overall offensive tempo and retention of initiative. In this way the Desna, Sozh, and Dnepr were forced. Forces of 1st, 2d, and 3d Ukrainian Fronts created operational bridgeheads (within the confines of the Ukraine) on the opposite shore of the Dnepr, where forces and means for subsequent offensive operations were concentrated.

The 1943 summer offensive was also characterized by decisiveness of actions and employed operational forms. Well-organized cooperation among all combat arms was combined in these operations with bold and skillful battlefield maneuver. The deeply echeloned force formation on the main axes ensured an intensification of force from the depth and the possibility for continuous and deep development of the operation.

In operations conducted by the Soviet Army in 1944–45, new distinct features of our operational art appeared, attesting to its further development – increased scope of operations and their decisive character. This development was a result of the increased technical base of our armed forces, and was based on the universal study of war experience. The rapid growth of the war industry made it possible to increase the number of military formations and equip the Soviet Army with a large quantity of first-class artillery, tanks, aviation, and other technical combat means. All this served as a base for the development of offensive operations which were enormous in their scope, and ensured the Soviet Army's decisive victories. As a result of ten successive and annihilating blows carried out by the Soviet Army in 1944, the entire eastern German front, extending 3,000 kilometers, was broken, and German forces were driven out of the confines of the Soviet Union. In 1945 a further change in the correlation of forces made it possible to shift from successive blows to a simultaneous offensive on a front of almost 2,000 kilometers. As a result of the January, April, and May 1945 operations, the enemy's armed forces were conclusively defeated and fascist Germany capitulated.

The principal feature of all Soviet Army offensive operations at this stage of the war was their decisive nature: they ended with the defeat and destruction of large enemy strategic and operational groupings. Thanks to the genius of the leadership of Comrade Stalin's Supreme High Command, by 1944 the

Soviet Army was so strong and had at its disposal such a large quantity of reserves that it was able in just one year to carry out ten large offensive operations. Here our command invariably provided decisive superiority in forces over the enemy on Soviet forces' attack axes.

The decisiveness of missions assigned to the Soviet Army conditioned the forms of the operations being conducted. Operations to encircle and destroy primary enemy groupings became the principal form of Soviet Army offensive operations.

Decisiveness of offensive operational aims reckoning on the destruction of the main enemy strategic and operational groupings imparted them with unprecedented scope in respect to front, depth, and quantity of forces employed in the operation.

The 1944–45 operations were characterized by attacks on a wide front, executed by forces of several *fronts* cooperating with one another. The swift and decisive rout of large enemy groupings on a series of axes led to the creation of enormous breaches in the enemy front, which made it possible for large numbers of our forces to advance rapidly into the depth. And this resulted in the enemy defense being swiftly disorganized, and he suffered a series of successive strategic defeats. An offensive of several *fronts* was usually conducted on a series of important axes, and as it developed into the depth it turned into a general offensive of our forces across an extended front. Following the advance of the shock groupings into the penetration sectors came forces deployed on the flanks, which "knocked the wind out" of the enemy defense, widening the front of the offensive. *Front* cooperation and expert use of strategic reserves provided for an intensification of forces and depth of the attack, and high operational tempos.

In the 1944–45 campaigns, as in the previous war years, our Supreme High Command brilliantly resolved extremely difficult problems of strategic and operational leadership, coordinated the operations of several *fronts* participating in an offensive operation, and provided new outstanding models for strategic cooperation between *fronts*. It should be kept in mind that it was necessary to solve this problem under very complex conditions of combat operations, which had developed on an enormous front and at a very high tempo. Only thanks to strict centralization of leadership and a high level of expertise for controlling the operations of several *fronts* solving a single strategic mission did cooperation among them not fall apart; this, in turn, ensured the operations a full resolution of the assigned tasks.

A feature of Soviet operational art in these campaigns was the bold and wide employment of maneuver at all stages of the operation, in the majority of cases directed toward the encirclement and destruction of the principal enemy groupings. Here it should be noted that in selecting the form of maneuver there was no stereotypical pattern, no plans which had been worked out once and for all and become petrified. The 1944–45 operations are characteristic: the delivery of powerful deep blows which hewed the enemy defense at such high tempos that he was deprived of the ability to withdraw to previously prepared lines; swift closing of converging *front* and army attacks in the operational depth, which led to the encirclement of large enemy groupings and simultaneous pursuit of remaining opposing forces; and the establishment of cooperation between formations, armies and *fronts* and combat arms, which had been well-coordinated during the entire operation.

Under 1944–45 conditions, the most typical offensive form was the frontal strike to penetrate the defense, inevitable in all operations of this period. The maneuver nature of operations did not exclude positional forms of struggle. The German command attempted to shift combat operations into positional forms whenever the situation was suitable, since it still had considerable forces and equipment. It is true that all these attempts invariably failed under the annihilating blows of the Soviet Army, but, nevertheless, they confronted the attacker with the necessity of penetrating the defensive front. The frontal attack as a form of operational maneuver was developed logically in harmonious combination with other forms of maneuver. In addition, the model where a penetration was carried out on a wide front in the form of a series of frontal attacks conducted in operational cooperation along several axes was widely disseminated in 1944–45 operations. The penetration operation based on delivering several operationally related attacks, simultaneously or successively, had enormous advantages in comparison with a penetration in a single sector, and was more appropriate for modern fighting conditions. A simultaneous attack on a number of axes made it possible to burst the enemy's defensive front at several isolated centers, which subsequently facilitated maneuver for the encirclement of each such isolated grouping.

Beginning with the Stalingrad operation, maneuver for the purpose of encirclement, undertaken at the operational and tactical levels, gradually acquired predominant significance in Soviet Army operations. First, 1944–45 operations demonstrated developed and varied forms of this maneuver and disclosed fully its entire content; second, they showed that our operational art was capable of resolving the problem of encirclement under any conditions: against an attacking enemy, against an enemy who occupied a stable defense, as a result of maneuver following the penetration of a front, and in the process of pursuit.

Finally, 1944–45 operations provided the richest experience in the operational exploitation of a penetration. In the past, when there was still no experience in the operational exploitation of success, this stage of the operation was in the form of a rather simplified scheme. Soviet Army operational experience clearly demonstrated that now, after penetrating the front, a stage should follow which included operational maneuver to destroy the main enemy grouping, against which the operation was directed. In modern complex operations conducted with a decisive aim, the mission of routing large enemy forces in the operational zone requires independent and complex maneuver, the purpose of which is to pursue and destroy remnants of enemy forces which have slipped out from under the attack, to prevent maneuver allowing operational reserves to be brought up from the depth and to destroy them, to prevent the creation of a new defensive front, and, finally, to create a favorable situation for subsequent operations.

As a rule, a large army formation penetrated the front on one narrow sector, with subsequent linear movement into the depth or widening of the penetration in the direction of the flank, using the procedure of "knocking the wind out" of the enemy's combat formations. An attack was delivered: with a narrow offensive sector – on the entire army front; with a wider sector – in the center or on one of the flanks. A large *front* formation used two primary forms of maneuver in the penetration: penetration in one sector by means of a powerful attack by a strong grouping, with subsequent exploitation into the depth and in the direction of one or both flanks; penetration in two (sometimes more) sectors with subsequent maneuver along converging axes to envelope and encircle an enemy grouping located between the attack axes. Penetration along two or several axes to split apart the enemy front, dismember his forces and destroy them piecemeal, with the execution of an encirclement maneuver in the operational depth of the defense, was usually employed on the scale of a group of *fronts*. The operational form of maneuver was always selected with consideration of the concrete situation, that is, the primary operational aim, the configuration of the front, and the presence of forces and means.

The operation to defeat the enemy's main forces on the right bank of the Ukraine (March 1944), from the point of view of the form of maneuver on the scale of the group of participating *fronts*, consisted of three primary deep blows to cut the entire German southern strategic grouping into isolated units and create conditions to envelop them.

The Belorussian operation to defeat German Army Group Center's main forces (June–July 1944) was executed with close cooperation among four *fronts*, and had as its purpose chopping the enemy front into pieces and encircling and destroying him piecemeal. The operational concept envisioned delivering the main attacks against both flanks: in the north to rout the Vitebsk–Orsha–Lepel' grouping, and in the south to rout the enemy's Bobruysk grouping. In the center, 2d Belorussian Front was to conduct a secondary offensive on the Mogilev axis. During the first stage of the offensive the intention was to penetrate the enemy defense on a front of around 600 kilometers along six axes, and to encircle his groupings on the flanks. The plan for the second stage was to exploit success, pursue the enemy along the entire front, and encircle and destroy his grouping by having our flanks overwhelm his grouping located in the center along the Mogilev–Minsk axis. The most important task during the third stage of the operation was unyielding pursuit of the remnants of the enemy's beaten forces.

The first stage of the offensive operation lasted six days, during which the enemy defense was penetrated and the German Vitebsk and Bobruysk groupings encircled and destroyed. During the second stage of the operation (29 June–4 July) Minsk was liberated and the German grouping to the east, numbering around 100,000 men, was encircled and destroyed. As a result of the first two stages of the operation, the German strategic front was shattered, and a wide breach of around 400 kilometers formed in its center on the most important strategic axis leading to Berlin. As a result of the third stage of the operation and subsequent operations, the Soviet Army reached the borders of East Prussia and arrived at the Narev River. The Belorussian operation, with respect to its operational scope, quantity of participating forces and means, and expertise of execution, is one of the classic modern operations. It employed and skillfully executed all basic forms of operational maneuver, with extensive use of the most complex form – encirclement with full annihilation of large enemy groupings.

The Iassy–Kishinev Operation, conducted by the forces of two *fronts* in August–September 1944, was planned, from the point of view of form of operational maneuver, as two powerful converging frontal blows with the immediate aim of encircling and destroying the main forces of German and Romanian Army Group Southern Ukraine in Bessarabia. The attacks were delivered from sectors separated from one another by several hundred kilometers. This operation was distinguished by exceptional purposefulness and decisiveness; it led to the encirclement of a large grouping, numbering more than 22 divisions (only German), and created conditions for developing a deep strategic thrust across southeastern Europe to the southern borders of Germany.

From the point of view of the form of operational maneuver employed on the scale of two *fronts*, the East Prussian operation, in January 1945, consisted of two blows delivered by the external flanks of 3d and 2d Belorussian Fronts. 3d Belorussian Front delivered a deep frontal attack on the Königsberg axis and supporting attacks against Tilsit and Darkehmen. 2d Belorussian Front forces executed an enveloping maneuver along the southern border of East Prussia, south of the Mazurian lakes, to cut off the enemy's entire East Prussian grouping from the west. The two *fronts'* coordinated attacks aimed at isolating the East Prussian grouping, pressing it to the sea, and destroying it. The plan was successfully implemented, and the defeat of German forces in East Prussia created favorable conditions for an offensive on the Berlin strategic axis.

The Vistula–Oder Operation of 1st Belorussian Front was executed in the form of a deep frontal blow, from bridgeheads occupied beforehand by our forces on the western shore of the Vistula, in the general direction of Poznan. This attack, together with attacks by 2d Belorussian and 1st Ukrainian Fronts, led to the shattering of the enemy's strategic front, the defeat of his central grouping, and the arrival of our forces at the Oder River. During the first stage of the operation, the form of 1st Belorussian Front's operational maneuver consisted of a series of frontal attacks, broadening them in the direction of the flanks to "knock the wind out" of the enemy front; subsequently, the *front* offensive took the form of a single frontal attack, whose effectiveness increased, thanks to simultaneous attacks by 2d Belorussian and 1st Ukrainian Fronts. The operation concluded with a complete rout of the enemy's Central Army Group and the arrival of our forces at the Oder River.

The Silesian operation of 1st Ukrainian Front, conducted in January 1945, was executed in the form of a single powerful frontal blow, delivered from the Sandomierz bridgehead in the general direction of Radomsko, Czestochowa, and, subsequently, Breslau. As the operation developed, the penetration front widened in the direction of the right flank, for cooperation with 1st Belorussian Front. Operations of the main grouping were supported from the south by an offensive by part of the *front* forces along the Vistula River in the general direction of Krakow. The Silesian operation assumed enormous scope and produced dazzling results.

The principle of massing forces and attack means on decisive axes was strictly observed in all these offensive operations. Skillfully amassing forces and means from secondary axes, sometimes transferring them from other *fronts*, and concentrating them in the main attack sector, was a basic condition for ensuring success. Maneuver of large tank and artillery formations was used extensively. In comparison with previous operations, the width of the penetration front for large operational formations was practically unchanged, but the artillery and tank density on the main attack axes increased, providing destructiveness and rapid tempos of the operation. In 1945 operations, operational density was greater than for those in 1943–44. The increase in artillery density was conditioned by the necessity to suppress in a short time the forces and means of the main defensive belt, with its broadly developed system of trenches and communications trenches.

As experience demonstrated, the strength and nature of the enemy defense, its depth, and the stubbornness of the defenders always predetermined the operational and combat formation of forces in offensive operations. In offensive operations of this period, the operational force grouping was, as a rule, three-echeloned. This formation ensured an overwhelming superiority of forces on the main attack axes and its maintenance during the operation; the development and widening of the penetration by the second echelon and mobile group; and intensification of efforts from the depth by introducing reserves and the second and third *front* echelons. The first echelon usually consisted of combined arms armies reinforced by artillery units and formations, direct infantry support tanks, engineer forces, and air defense assets. This echelon penetrated the defense, destroyed its first operational echelon forces, and then continued the offensive jointly with mobile formations. The army second echelon consisted of combined arms and tank formations; in *fronts* – large combined arms, tank, and mechanized formations. The second echelon's mission was to widen the penetration and exploit success in the operational depth. The third echelon, made up of the *front* reserve, consisted of combined arms formations, antitank artillery units, and engineer forces. Its mission was to intensify efforts throughout the entire depth of the operation and repel counterstrokes.

The increased scope of operations was a consequence of large *front* formations having in their composition large mobile groups capable of advancing swiftly into the operational depth of the enemy deployment, shattering his front, and, together with combined arms formations, destroying groups of his cut off forces. The tempo of advance of combined arms armies, which during the first two to three days of the operation was comparatively slow (six to eight kilometers), subsequently reached 25–30 kilometers per day, and in individual operations was no lower than the tempo of advance of mobile formations.

In 1944–45 operations, large artillery densities were created in penetration sectors, and these continually increased. Such a situation made it possible to shift to shorter periods of artillery preparation, employing the method of suppression by mass fire. An artillery grouping was created so that during the period of artillery preparation all artillery was operating according to the army plan, and, from the commencement of the attack, each combined arms commander had an artillery group at his disposal. There was also an apportionment of artillery into artillery groups in 1943 operations, but now this acquired more decisive and precise form. As in previous operations, mobile antitank artillery reserves were widely used. The high density of artillery concentration on the main attack axis required centralized planning of an artillery offensive on a *front* scale. Extensive artillery maneuver was employed during the offensive, which provided a favorable correlation in suppression means at all stages of the operation. Artillery maneuver was executed not only within the framework of large *front* and army formations, but also outside their limits.

Operations in 1944–45 are characterized by high offensive tempos. As a rule, deeply echeloned fortified positions were penetrated and mobile groups reached the operational depth in one and half to two days. This was achieved by precise organization and purposeful use of tank and mechanized forces. The presence of powerful direct infantry support tank groups to penetrate the tactical defense increased the infantry's shock force and created more favorable conditions for the introduction and operations of mobile groups in the operational depth of the enemy defense (Belorussian and Iassy–Kishinev operations). During the Berlin operation, where it was necessary to overcome a continuous fortified belt (the Oder to Berlin), mobile formations were used to penetrate the defensive line on the first day of the operation, attacking jointly with combined arms formations. Maintaining the shock force of mobile groups for operations in the operational depth of the defense made it possible to achieve high operational tempos. Thus, in the Belorussian operation mobile formations covered up to 500 kilometers in 20 days; in the Iassy–Kishinev operation mobile formations covered 350–380 kilometers in 10–13 days.

As for the use of air forces during 1944–45 operations, the following basic features should be mentioned: a favorable correlation of forces for our aviation, both qualitative and quantitative, guaranteed its absolute air superiority; there was more massing of aviation efforts on main attack axes of their ground forces in narrower sectors (and against a limited number of objectives) than in 1943 operations; aviation formations rapidly switched from support of combined arms armies to support of the introduction of mobile groups into a penetration; airfield maneuver was widely employed in connection with the rapid offensive tempos of ground forces. Our aviation's complete air superiority from the beginning to the end of the operation provided ground forces with a high penetration tempo of the main defense belt and of intermediate lines; it also provided for exploitation of the offensive into the depth of the defense. Principal *front* aviation efforts were directed toward supporting the ground forces offensive. During the first stage of the operation, aviation was distributed among combined arms armies to assist in penetrating the defense. With the introduction of mobile groups into the penetration, ground attack aircraft switched to supporting them and were transferred into operational subordination to these groups.

Soviet forces went over to the defense during 1944–45 operations in those instances where an operational pause was created in the offensive to prepare a new offensive operation, or when the enemy, attempting a counteroffensive using large forces, achieved temporary superiority in forces in some sector (the Balaton operation). In the first case, the defense was basically characterized by the same features we mentioned during the examination of the Battle of Kursk. In the second case, the defense was built under enemy pressure, usually from his mobile forces. Under these conditions, a deep defense was achieved by both extensive maneuver by first-echelon forces and concentration of operational reserves from the depth at the region of the enemy's main attack. In this respect, the Balaton defensive operation is instructive.

The first stage of the Balaton operation was characterized by our forces going over to the defense during the offensive. By means of skillful maneuver of reserves and conduct of individual counterattacks, our command was able to gain time to organize defensive lines in the immediate rear. The second stage of the operation was characterized by successful defensive operations, which employed dynamic maneuver of forces to mass them on the decisive axis and deliver counterstrokes to reestablish the lost position. Counterstrokes were successfully executed, and the enemy was thrown back to the initial position. The third stage of the operation was characterized by defensive battles under conditions of a deeply developed and prepared defense, with the presence of strong second and third echelons and reserves. The organization of the defense was based on an attempt to exhaust the enemy and create conditions to go over to a decisive counteroffensive. Deep forms of defense were achieved not only in an engineer respect, but also by echeloning forces and means. Tank and mechanized formations were used as a means to reinforce infantry, operating in its combat formations, by means of defensive battle.

The great scale of 1944–45 operations, under rapidly changing conditions and supply difficulties (great distance from bases) required of commanders at all levels a high degree of control efficiency, which made it possible to maintain high offensive tempos. The organization and conduct of an operation was conditioned by strict centralization of control, especially when organizing the penetration, when it was necessary to provide especially reliable cooperation. The use of fast-moving communications means provided control flexibility. *Front* commanders' operational groups played a large role in controlling operations. Communications with rear areas remained a bottleneck, because of their great distances.

Periods of the preparatory stage of the operation were directly dependent on operational pauses; in comparison with previous campaigns, these were significantly reduced in 1945 operations. Measures were carried out during these periods to equip and reestablish the road network, equip staging areas (bridgeheads) for the offensive, prepare airfields and landing areas, prepare and equip command and observation posts, make supply deliveries, and conduct command-staff games in accordance with the actual situation and plan of the operation. In addition, combat preparation of forces was carried out, taking into account missions of the forthcoming battle; staff reconnaissance of all combat arms was also conducted. Concentration of forces and combat equipment on the attack axis was so significant that it required considerable engineer preparation to deploy forces in the offensive staging area. The primary missions of rear organs were reduced to amassing reserves for the commencement of the operation, as established by the command, at field depots and among the forces, and organizing deliveries both during preparation of the operation and while it was being executed. Primary attention was focused on delivering ammunition and fuel.

In general, the Soviet Army's operational art clearly developed further during 1944–45 operations. The conduct of operations was based on Comrade Stalin's fundamental instructions, in which he demanded the following: maintenance of the purposefulness of actions, originating from missions of the given stage of war; use of objective analysis of all situational data, and sober consideration of one's own and the enemy's combat capabilities; skillful exploitation of the enemy's weak points and, most basic, avoidance of any stereotypical patterns in methods of conducting operations; timely concentration of maximum forces and means on the most important axes; constant availability of operational reserves to strengthen forces and means from the depth during an operation, thereby creating conditions for relentless pursuit of the enemy and his defeat; and careful preparation and support of the operation.

Soviet operational art covered an enormous developmental path during the Great Patriotic War. Guided by Stalin's military genius, this development unswervingly followed ascending lines, having achieved its quintessence during the last stage of the war.

The principles of organizing and conducting offensive and defensive operations, as developed by Comrade Stalin, received further development in Great Patriotic War operations. Included among these are decisiveness of aims and forms of operations based on a correct assessment of the situation; conduct of large-scale operations by means of coordinated blows on several axes; correct choice of the main attack axis, and surprise in delivering it; massing of forces and shock means on decisive axes; deep forms of conducting operations at high tempos, to prevent the enemy forestalling the attacker by maneuvering his own reserves; full and careful support of the operation in all respects; and centralization of control, based on purposeful unity of the plan of the operation and its conduct.

Decisiveness of aims and operational forms were the basis of our offensive operations at all stages of the Great Patriotic War. They were all characterized by delivery of attacks along several axes on a wide front simultaneously to tie down maximum enemy forces and inflict upon him the greatest possible losses in personnel and equipment. War experience demonstrates that operations conducted by the simultaneous delivery of a number of attacks, executed in operational cooperation between several *fronts*, chopped the enemy front into pieces and created the most favorable conditions for destroying him piecemeal.

The correct choice of the main attack axis had decisive significance for operational success, and was a most important aspect of decision-making, determining the form of operational maneuver as well. The main attack axis was chosen, taking into account the defeat of the enemy's main grouping.

Soviet Army operations executed by *fronts* or a group of *fronts* provided different models of forms of operational maneuver, employed in accordance with the existing situation. Successful employment of different forms of maneuver was guaranteed by the achievement of surprise in the attack, massing of forces and shock means on decisive axes, swiftness in developing maneuver, and reliable operational support of the attack. The width of the offensive sector directly depended on the assigned mission, the presence of forces and means, the nature of the enemy's defense, supply and evacuation routes, and the quality of control assets. Beginning with the 1942–43 Winter Campaign, a large portion of combined arms formations, almost all tank and mechanized formations, more than 60 per cent of artillery, and an absolute majority of aviation forces were allotted to a large *front* formation to launch the main attack against a decisive sector. War experience also demonstrated that superiority in forces and means on the decisive axis was usually created in such a way that the attacker had a favorable correlation of forces at all stages of the operation, which also ensured continuity in exploiting the operation to great depth, and its high tempo. The scale of Soviet Army operations grew in a direct relationship to its ability to increase the operational density of forces while penetrating the tactical defense belt, to its degree of superiority, and to the strengthening of the power of mobile groups on decisive axes, above all with shock means.

In the past war the defense was mobile or positional, depending on missions and forces and means. The purpose of a mobile defense was to gain time at the expense of space, inflict maximum losses on the enemy, maintain one's own forces, and then, with a change in the situation, deliver annihilating counterstrokes against him and create conditions for going over to a decisive counteroffensive. Positional defense was the principal and strongest type of defense. Its mission was to stubbornly hold an operational line, strike the enemy, and ensure conditions for a counteroffensive. Defense during all stages of the war was a temporary, forced type of combat action. It was employed in those instances where an operational pause was created during an offensive to prepare a new offensive operation, and it was necessary to reinforce captured lines and gain time to concentrate forces and means designated for the offensive; when in the course of an offensive the enemy went over to a counteroffensive, using large tank masses, significantly superior in shock force to the attacking forces, and when it was expedient to shift temporarily to the defense; and when it was necessary to create overwhelming superiority in forces on a decisive axis, while on secondary axes forces were temporarily restricted to defensive actions. During the Great Patriotic War, the basic feature of our forces' defense at all its developmental stages was its deep structure and stubborn and dynamic nature.

The experience of the Great Patriotic War demonstrated that defense must be antitank, anti-artillery, anti-air, and deeply echeloned, which assures its survivability and staunchness; it must be stubborn and dynamic, capable of quickly exhausting the enemy and bleeding him dry; it must be constantly ready not only to repel an attack, but also to deliver an annihilating attack against him.

All Soviet Army operations were conducted according to a single aim and plan, worked out under the leadership of the Headquarters of the Supreme High Command. This purposeful unity of operational aim and its plan was introduced at all levels of command, within the limits of what was possible and necessary for the chain of command. Centralization of control and precise execution by subordinate levels at all stages of operational development was an important condition for its success. This does not mean that creative initiative at all levels of our command, especially in the process of developing the operation, was not encouraged. Centralization of control was a result of the necessity for organizing cooperation among large formations and formations, and of the purposefulness and unity of operational plans.

In conclusion, we will attempt to formulate some general theoretical principles concerning the nature of modern operations and their organization.

An operation is not an isolated phenomenon; it is conducted in the interests of resolving a strategic mission. Its objectives may be the principal enemy grouping, against which the main efforts of a specific large operational formation is directed; an important political, economic, and/or military center or region, or an operational line, the capture of which is the mission of a given large operational formation. As a rule, the rout of the main enemy grouping leads to the capture of a point, line, or region, whose seizure is the mission of a large operational formation.

With respect to their aims and missions, modern *front* and army operations are divided into two primary types: offensive and defensive. Both can be combined with one another, that is, there can be offensive and defensive operations simultaneously in a *front* sector, and sometimes an army. The counteroffensive is a type of offensive operation. The offensive operation is the fundamental and decisive type of action, since only a decisive offensive which concludes with the encirclement and pursuit of the enemy leads to his complete defeat. The overall aim of each offensive operation is the complete defeat of the enemy grouping opposing a given large operational formation. As a rule, under modern conditions the achievement of an operational or strategic aim is related to the defeat of large groupings split apart in the depth; therefore, this cannot be accomplished as a result of a single attack. The execution of a series of successive attacks to resolve intermediate missions, each of which will be executed by its own special method and under changing conditions of the situation, is required to achieve the ultimate operational aim.

With modern continuous and reinforced *fronts*, in the majority of cases the offensive operation begins with the penetration of a defense by a frontal attack, which in its development turns into an attack against internal lines to envelope, encircle, and destroy the enemy. Hence, the initial stage of the operation is penetration of the entire tactical defense and the creation of conditions for the development of the operation. The mission of the initial stage of an offensive operation is always the rout of opposing enemy forces, which also creates conditions for favorable development of the operation. The subsequent stage of the operation and its second mission is the use of the existing tactical penetration to exploit success into the depth and in the direction of the flanks to penetrate the entire defensive operational formation, and maneuver in the operational depth to destroy the principal enemy forces. In order to accomplish the mission of developing the penetration, it is necessary to prevent the link-up of the immediate defensive operational reserves with the remnants of its first-echelon forces, and to support the commitment of one's own mobile forces for development of the penetration into the depth and its widening in the direction of the flanks. With the further development of the operation, the attacker strikes the deep defensive reserves or, in an extreme case, ties them down, thereby depriving them of the ability to conduct a counterstroke. In other words, it is necessary to isolate the operational region from an influx of deep reserves so as to maintain superiority for the attacker in forces and means until the achievement of the planned aim.

Defense is a temporary and forced type of combat action. Under specific conditions of a situation, it may take the form of intentional maneuver. Operational defense has the task of delaying, exhausting and bleeding the enemy dry by using the terrain, engineer assets, and modern fire power; it should wreck the enemy's offensive, gain time, and create conditions necessary for going over to a counteroffensive to ultimately defeat the enemy. The principal defensive requirements are unity of operational plan, force grouping, and engineer support. The defense cannot be strong everywhere; however, it is necessary to concentrate its efforts on the most important axes, where the main enemy attack is most probable. Defensive dynamism is expressed in counterattacks and counterstrokes. The counterattack is a function of units and formations which comprise the tactical defense echelon. As a rule, a counterstroke is organized at the instruction of the army or *front* commander to strike a large enemy shock grouping which has penetrated into the defense, and to reestablish and improve a lost operational position. The counteroffensive is a special type of offensive operation; depending on the situation, it may be a continuation and natural development of a counterstroke.

Combat operations to achieve an operational aim take the form of an engagement [*srazheniye*] – the most important and decisive part of an operation – which consists of the totality of battles [*boy* – tactical actions], dispersed in space (along the front and into the depth) and in time.

A most important factor in changing the nature of operations is combat equipment and its mass employment, which has sharply increased the shock force and mobility of modern armies. Mass outfitting of armies with technical means has made it possible to impart to operations a mobile, extremely decisive, deep, and maneuverable character, and to execute complex forms of operational maneuver. This very factor, and the massiveness of modern armies have led to a broadening of the theater of military operations and an increase in the scope of an operation (depth, width of the offensive sector, duration, quantity of forces and means taking part in the operation).

As a rule, modern operations unfold in several sectors of a strategic front by simultaneous or successive attacks, coordinated by a single operational plan. Such simultaneous or successive attacks then merge into a single powerful offensive along an enormous front (with respect to its extent), which deprives the enemy of freedom of maneuver and the possibility of mass use of his operational reserves. The width of the offensive operational sector for each large operational formation can be most varied; it is determined by the operational plan, the importance and capacity of the axis on which the large formation is operating, and its forces and means. Operational tempo and depth are determined, in the first order, by the degree of superiority in forces and, especially, mobile means. Further augmentation in equipping large operational formations with technical combat means provides a basis for assuming that the duration and tempos of the operation can increase in comparison with the past war. A high operational tempo gains time, ensures initiative to the attacker, and deprives the enemy of the ability to take measures which would stop the development of the offensive. Operational tempo is determined with respect to the primary operational axis along which the main attack is developing.

Forms of operational maneuver correspond to the aim and plan of the operation. Modern operations are extremely varied with respect to their plan and methods and forms of their execution, but the principal forms of maneuver are those which would be directed toward encircling and destroying the principal enemy groupings. Maneuver for encirclement should be used under any conditions of the situation, both in the course of the operation after penetration of the front, and during pursuit. The following are the basic forms of operational maneuver in an offensive operation:

– the frontal attack on a narrow front, with subsequent widening of the penetration in the direction of the flanks. In the presence of operations in the direction of the flanks, this form of maneuver makes it possible to "take the wind out" of an enemy front, forcing it to withdraw or place itself under threat of encirclement and defeat. It is more suitable for large *front* and army formations;

– penetration of the front along several axes. In modern operations this is the most decisive form of maneuver, and is used for operations of a large *front* formation or, most often, a group of *fronts*. When delivering powerful attacks along several axes, the enemy defense is broken on a wide front, which deprives him of or limits his ability to countermaneuver. On the scale of a large *front* formation, the delivery of attacks along several axes should be done simultaneously or with extremely limited interruptions. In its development this form of operational maneuver creates favorable conditions for employing such forms as the shallow and deeper envelopment to encircle isolated enemy groups;

– maneuver along converging axes (concentric attack) by two shock groupings to encircle and destroy an enemy grouping located between the two attacks. This form of maneuver is extremely decisive, since it always counts on encircling the enemy, and is employed by a large *front* formation or a group of *fronts*.

Our Soviet military science, enriched by the experience of the Great Patriotic War, views modern engagements and battle above all as co-operation between all basic combat arms – infantry, artillery, tanks, and aviation.

With respect to its authorized organizational structure, technical outfitting, and motorization of the rear service, infantry has become stronger and more mobile in battles and operations. Its shock force and combat stability have increased significantly. However, without assistance from other combat arms, mainly artillery and tanks, infantry alone cannot achieve success in a modern operation. Aviation, tanks, and artillery can deliver an annihilating blow against the enemy, destroy his defensive structures, and destroy and suppress his fire system and personnel, but only infantry can ultimately capture terrain and hold it. The primary burden of battle falls to the infantry. Only the steadfastness of infantry in the defense and its decisive advance in the offense makes it possible for forces of other combat arms to carry out their missions successfully.

With respect to its technical capabilities and the missions it carries out, modern artillery plays a decisive role in an operation. It is the primary fire shock means for penetrating the defense. Maneuver capabilities of modern artillery have turned it into an operationally significant factor. It paves the way for infantry and tanks in the fight for the tactical defense belt, and accompanies them in the operational depth, using the artillery offensive. The established artillery organization facilitates maneuver of artillery assets and their massing on decisive axes.

Modern offensive operations require the presence of means which would be capable not only of penetrating the enemy's tactical defense, but also of developing tactical success into operational success to a depth which would result in a sharp change in the operational-strategic situation. Tank and mechanized forces are such means. Tanks, comprising the direct infantry support echelon, together with infantry and artillery, penetrate the tactical defense. Mechanized formations and mobile groups are means for the exploitation of operational success, and are used both independently and in cooperation with combined arms formations, artillery, and aviation.

Great creativity and skill in supporting defensive and offensive actions of all combat arms is required of engineer forces, which have grown significantly in number and are equipped with various technical means. The development and extensive employment of mobile forces and massive use of artillery and aviation in a new way have posed problems associated with the organization, preparation, and employment of engineer forces. In modern war they have begun not only to support combat operations, but also to participate in them as a dynamic combat force. In addition, the modern operation, both offensive and defensive, requires a high level of military-engineer preparation of infantry, artillery, and tank forces.

Past war experience confirmed that air forces are one of the decisive combat arms. While rendering combat assistance to ground forces in executing tactical and operational missions, they became capable of executing missions of strategic significance independently. Modern aviation takes part in all ground forces operations. Therefore, its operations are planned, organized, and supported on the scale of a *front* operation by instructions from the *front* commander, and sometimes by instructions from the High Command.

Airborne forces are extensively employed in modern operations. An airborne operation is often part of a general operation. Its operational-tactical success depends on cooperation with ground forces and systematic support from aviation, which is supporting the operations of ground and assault forces. The depth to which airborne forces are sent is determined by the possibility of the timely arrival of the ground forces' shock grouping at the airborne forces' area of operation for the purpose of joint destruction of the enemy grouping.

Growth in the role of mechanized and tank forces does not exclude the possibility of using cavalry. Cavalry-mechanized formations are a *front* command means. They are equipped with tanks, artillery, and other combat means, and can be used as a decisive means for exploiting success in an offensive operation, in pursuit, and also in counterstrokes. They can carry out their missions in cooperation with combined arms, tank and mechanized formations, and aviation.

During the past war, influenced by unprecedented growth in the quantity of deployed forces and combat means, and the more decisive, mobile, and extremely intense nature of combat operations, requiring tough and centralized leadership, large *front* formations were broken up, mainly with respect to territory they occupied, but not with respect to quantity of forces and combat equipment. Moreover, the large operational *front* formation lost its strategic independence and became more a higher operational formation than a strategic formation. In the majority of cases, a *front* operation is now a part of a strategic operation, although in some cases and in separate theaters of military operations a large *front* formation can independently resolve a strategic mission. The modern *front* operates, as a rule, on one to two operational axes, and very rarely on one strategic axis. The latter is possible when the capacity of a given strategic axis cannot accommodate or does not require armed forces larger than one modern large *front* formation. The role of *front* command in the leadership of operations has also changed somewhat. The *front* commander now is not only the organizer of his armies' operations, but also must resolve even tactical problems when organizing the penetration of a defense.

In our opinion, the army is the principal large operational formation. As a rule, the army operation is an integral part of the *front* operation. Only in individual cases, along separate operational-strategic axes, does the army conduct an operation independently. The modern army is made up of approximately the same number of formations as the First World War army; however, the quantity and quality of combat equipment have sharply increased, which has improved the army's maneuverability. The army possesses great shock force and a high degree of mobility. It exhibits most fully its operational capabilities in an offensive in cooperation with several armies. This is explained by the fact that an isolated attack by a single army in the presence of a deeply echeloned defense can be quickly liquidated by enemy counterstrokes, and preventing an enemy counterstroke is possible only if several attacks are delivered on a wide front in close cooperation with several contiguously operating armies; a single army is not capable of defeating a large enemy grouping by encircling and destroying his principal forces; for this, the coordinated efforts of several armies are required. The principal mission of a large army formation, operating in the first echelon along an attack axis in a *front* operation, is to penetrate the defense to its operational depth.

The maneuver nature of modern operations presents great demands for its organization and leadership. The art of conducting operations is based on consideration of the correlation of forces and combat means, the moral condition of one's own forces and those of the enemy, the organizational abilities of command personnel, and the degree of materiel-technical support of the operation. Conditions of conducting modern operations make it necessary to possess decisive superiority in forces and means on main attack axes. The operational formation of forces must correspond to the principles of a deep attack, which necessitates the creation of one or two powerful groupings to penetrate the tactical and operational defense, create a strong mobile force group to exploit the attack into the depth, allocate sufficient reserves to intensify the attack during its exploitation in the depth of the enemy's operational formation, and concentrate aviation forces for powerful air strikes, so as to deprive the enemy of the ability to maneuver reserves and conduct operational regroupings. In addition, the operational formation of forces should envision achieving surprise in the operation, which may require the conduct of dynamic operations with a limited aim along auxiliary axes to widen the attack front and pin down enemy reserves on those axes. Massing forces and means on the main attack axes in offensive operations and on probable axes of the enemy's primary efforts in defensive operations predetermines a deep, echeloned (two to three echelons) operational formation of forces.

Further development of our operational art should proceed along the path of interpreting the lessons and conclusions of the last war in light of new potentials for the operational use of forces, created by the development of combat means and the organized formation of armed forces improved on this basis.

NOTES

1. V. Zlobin and L. Vetoshnikov, "Ob operativnom iskusstve Sovetskoy Armii", *Voyennaya mysl'* [Military thought], 3 (1947), pp. 3–15, and 4 (1947), pp. 3–18.
2. Translator's note: for the sake of consistency, the Russian terms *soyedineniye* and *ob"yedineniye* will be translated as "formation" and "large formation" respectively unless otherwise noted.
3. I. Stalin, "K voprosu o strategii i taktike russkikh kommunistov" [On the strategy and tactics of Russian communists].

Operational Art and its Place in Soviet Military Art

MAJOR GENERAL L. VETOSHNIKOV[1]

The requirement for creating a scientific theory of operational art and the necessity for allocating questions of organizing and conducting operations to a special category of military art already began to appear in the nineteenth century, and matured particularly sharply after the First World War (1914–18) and the Civil War (1918–20) as a result of radical changes in methods and forms of conducting armed struggle.

War in the imperialist era, in the presence of mass armies with numerous and varied equipment, became a more complex phenomenon than previously. As is apparent from the experience of recent wars, it was necessary to conduct several long military campaigns, which, in turn, consisted of a number of simultaneous and successive operations in different sectors of the combat front, in order to achieve the aims of the war under such conditions. An operation with the participation of mass armies of millions of men in a period of mechanized methods for conducting war became a distinctive phenomenon.

These new features of conducting armed struggle were reflected in both world wars of the twentieth century, although they differed in form. The imperialist war of 1914–18 proceeded mainly under the guise of positional forms of struggle. The drawn-out nature of combat operations and the succession of efforts to achieve strategic and operational aims, reflected by the war's subdivision into a series of campaigns and operations, were inevitable. The Great Patriotic War, as a result of mass introduction of motorization in all areas of military affairs, and continued mechanization of combat methods, also bore an extremely intense, mobile and maneuver character. Although the war was characterized by the extreme dynamism of events and rapid changes in the situation of the opposing sides, on the whole it was protracted and also required a succession of efforts to achieve the war's aims. In the Great Patriotic War, the characteristic features of the modern mechanized method of conducting war were delineated especially precisely. Naturally, this placed its imprint on the nature and forms of operations, which, in the course of the war, changed, depending on the growth of army mechanization. The Great Patriotic War provides the richest,

most exhaustive material for determining the essence and nature of modern operations, demonstrating the great significance of the special study of questions concerning their organization and conduct.

Despite the completely obvious necessity for special study of the operation as a new and large field in the theory of military art, a necessity which had already appeared at the end of the nineteenth century, before and throughout the First World War not a single army focused necessary attention on this question, and it was not scientifically developed. Bourgeois military leaders and theorists were unable to comprehend and resolve scientifically the urgent problem of creating and scientifically developing a new branch of military art – operational art. Even the experience of two world wars did not lead them to a radical solution of this problem.

The strategy of lightning war was the dominant principle in the military art of imperialist armies in the wars of our century. This was especially clearly expressed in the fallacious military doctrine of German imperialism, before which many imperialist armies kowtowed. Germany's military ideologists, who adopted uncritically Clausewitz's reactionary–idealist teaching, representing the manufacturing period of war, took positions of adventurism and stereotypical patterning. As is known, Clausewitz rejected the significance of scientific theory in strategy, acknowledging it to some degree only in tactics. He wrote: "It is absolutely impossible to supply military art with supporting props in the form of a positive scientific system which would provide in all cases an external support to the military figure."[2] Basing itself on this, German military thought attached special significance to talent and genius, which would seemingly operate on the battlefields "outside of law and theory."

Similar views on the significance of theory in military art, an idealistic assessment of the moral factor in war, and under-appreciation of the capabilities of probable enemies naturally gave birth to adventurism and stereotypical plans for organizing and conducting both war on the whole and separate operations.

It should be mentioned that in bourgeois armies, if one discounts individual published statements by military authors, official military doctrine, as reflected in their regulations and instructions, even now continues to divide military art into only two parts: strategy and tactics.

According to the definition of the American military press, strategy in its military understanding is the art of concentrating superior forces in a theater of military operations at the necessary moment in time and under such conditions which will be conducive to attacking or completely destroying the enemy's armed forces on the battlefield. Tactics, according to their definition, is the art of movement to battle (engagements) and using forces in battle. The British also adhere to the same point of view.

Thus, we see that Anglo-American views on military art continue to be based on the positions of the reactionary-idealistic teachings of Clausewitz and his followers.

The practical experience of the latest wars required development of a theory of conducting operations (operational art), representing the comprehensive totality of combat operations of large military formations (army, army group, *front*).[3] Nevertheless, in neither the American nor British Armies did military thought allocate the issues of conducting operations to a special category of military art. Besides this, one can observe, for example, in the American Army field regulations a series of contradictory definitions concerning the purpose of tactical formations and large strategic formations. Thus, in one section of the field regulations, where operations of an army group, army, and corps are being elucidated, these large formations are associated with "strategy," while in another place in the regulations corps operations are defined as "tactical," and an army is an "administrative-tactical unit with administrative, territorial, and tactical functions." Finally, in a third place, an army group is declared a "large tactical formation."

All this points once again to the fact that the military art of the American Army does not have a strict system of scientific theory. Moreover, in the American Army old, already bankrupt idealistic theories on the disappearance of mass armies continue to be expostulated – as do the possibility of determining the outcome of a war by means of air forces alone (General Arnold), "small wars" (General Kenny), atomic war in which all combat arms will disappear and atomic energy alone will remain and the "polar concept of air strategy," etc. continue to be expostulated.

Finally, in the foreign press, together with the propaganda of the German blitzkrieg theory, other judgements are stated concerning future war as a drawn-out war, whose conduct requires further army mechanization and motorization, increase of automatic weapons, strengthening of artillery, expansion of air forces, and force procurement for mass armies from future "allies" (the Truman Doctrine and Marshall Plan). Judgements in the American military press concerning the question of conducting future wars envision two stages. The first stage of war must bear, to a certain degree, a protracted character, counting on exhausting enemy forces by aviation, the naval, and ground army operations; the second stage is the rapid defeat of the weakened enemy by army ground forces in cooperation with air and naval forces.

These are some American views on the nature of future war, which appeared as a result of the postwar aggressive policy of American imperialism.

As for the essence of the British Army's military doctrine, it is now basically influenced by American military thought.

Thus, as is obvious from the above statements, military thought of imperialist countries, in attempting to find a solution to the basic problems of military art, is proceeding along the path of searching for victory "recipes," manifesting, in addition, an inability to interpret uncritically past war experience or provide a complete theoretical formulation to the problems of military art and, in particular, the problem of operational art. Only our Soviet military science was able to solve this problem.

One of the clear manifestations of the progressive nature of Soviet military science, the creator of which is the great Stalin, consists of the theoretical development of problems of operational art which emerge from the changed nature of war. Soviet military science, based on Marxist-Leninist study, was able to interpret dialectically historical experience and disclose new phenomena and new features in military art. Having created a progressive scientific theory of military art, our military science assigned a significant place to problems in the theory of conducting operations.

Proceeding from the experience of recent wars, Soviet military art considers that the operation, as a new phenomenon in conducting combat actions, acquired a precise and clear expression in these wars. In its contemporary understanding, the operation is the organized totality of combat actions of large military formations (armies, *fronts*, and that which corresponds to them) conducted along a specific axis and joined by a unified plan to achieve a single overall aim.

Operational art under modern conditions not only presents a single creative solution to practical issues of organizing and conducting operations, but also has its own scientific theory, which substantiates methods and means of leading forces in an operation; therefore, it is one of the most important branches of military art.

Thus, as a theory operational art is the study of the use of large military formations (armies, *fronts*) in a theater of military operations to resolve specific operational or strategic missions; methods and forms of organizing, preparing, and conducting operations; methods of leading forces in an operation; and organization of cooperation among different combat arms, formations, and large formations participating in the operations.

In a more concrete definition, operational art's subject and content are the theory and practice of preparing and conducting operations by army and *front* forces. Here, the most important tasks of operational art are, in accordance with the aims assigned to large operational formations by military strategy, the following: developing a plan of operations; determining forms and methods of employing and leading large operational formations in an operation; determining methods and means of cooperation among different combat arms within the framework of an operation; determining the nature and sequence of cooperation among large operational formations participating in the operation; implementing all prepared measures for organizing the operation and its support; and executing the operation and leading forces during the operation.

All this once again confirms that the subject of operational art has broadened so much, that it has ceased to be an attendant issue of military theory. The subject of operational art has turned into a large scientific field with its own theory, laws, problems, and methodology. Therefore, in the Soviet Army operational art is viewed as a large, special, and most important category of modern military art, as a scientific discipline, and as a practical field of leading large operational formations. Operational art, being one of the main categories of Soviet military art, is also organically associated with strategy and tactics. Moreover, the essence of operational art can be expressed only through its relation to strategy and tactics. Operational art occupies, as it were, a middle position between strategy and tactics.

Strategy, being the highest branch of military art, deals with problems of war as a whole, and the conduct of large-scale military operations (campaigns and operations of a group of *fronts*), encompasses the sphere of the highest military leadership, and, on the basis of instructions from the political leadership, is responsible for using the armed forces to achieve victory in war.

Operational art is the second important branch of the theory of military art, occupying a certain subordinate position with respect to strategy. It serves, as it were, as a means for strategy to achieve strategic war aims, which are resolved by a series of operations. Dealing with issues of conducting operations using basic large operational formations, that is, armies or *fronts*, operational art is guided by instructions, aims, and missions which strategy places before specific large troop formations in accordance with the overall plan of the campaign or the war as a whole.

In modern wars, the operation unites tactical force actions by a unified plan, and attaches to them a specific purposefulness. It uses tactical means and tactical force actions to resolve missions of operational and strategic significance. Thus, tactical actions, to some degree or another, are subordinate to the interests of an operation, and tactics are a means for resolving operational missions.

This middle position which operational art occupies in relation to strategy and tactics fully corresponds to the nature of our military science and to those requirements which modern conditions of waging war present to the development of the armed forces, their technical outfitting, and methods for using them under combat conditions. We are guided in this question by Stalin's thoroughly scientific principle that

> the forms of organizing armies, combat arms, and services are usually adjusted to forms and methods for waging war. The former changes with a change in the latter . . . The task of military art consists of supporting all combat arms, leading them to perfection, and capably bringing their actions into concord.

The correct assessment of the nature of modern war as predominantly an intense maneuver war unresolved by a single annihilating blow predetermined the inevitable growth of new, powerful means of suppression. And this was a most important factor, which changed the nature of operations and increased the shock force and mobility of modern armies. Mass saturation of armies with technical means made it possible to impart a maneuverable, extremely decisive, deep, and mobile character to operations, and to execute complex forms of maneuver in the context of the growing scope of the operations themselves, the decisive act of which became the engagement [*srazheniye*]. Our military science views the latter, which included the totality of battles [*boy* – tactical actions] concentrated in space and time, as organized combat efforts of all combat arms, directed toward the achievement of a single aim. It is natural that the engagement, consisting of a series of battles, goes beyond the framework of tactical actions, while, however, not going as far as directly resolving missions on a strategic scale. Operational art is also called upon to include problems associated with the successful organization and conduct of a series of combined arms battles and engagements which pursue a specific operational aim. This is a completely natural condition for conducting modern wars. Soviet military science, having created a complete theory of operational art, thereby provided a thoroughly scientific solution to the most important problem of military art, which emerged from the experience of modern wars.

Soviet military art developed along its own independent path and, having created a complete and harmonious theory based on delimiting of methods of waging war, operations, and battle among three mutually connected disciplines – strategy, operational art, and tactics – occupied a leading position with respect to so-called "progressive" bourgeois military theories.

The primary direction of development of our theory of operational art was already predetermined in the Civil War (1918–20). The operational art of the then still-young Soviet Army, taking into account historical experience and based on political and moral factors conditioned by the Soviet system, created new methods and forms of armed struggle, characteristic for the First World War. Even with the absence of numerical and technical superiority over the enemy, Soviet Army operations were conducted with the decisive purpose of defeating the enemy. This resulted from the fact that our army, the army of the Soviet state, had and has principal features which distinguish it from all other armies of the world. Unity of the aim of the war which confronted the Soviet republic combined organically in the struggle with unity of the army's and people's will to achieve this aim. Hence, the struggle against interventionists and White Guards bore a clearly expressed, decisive character, which reflected the invincible will of our nation to defend the world's first socialist state.

Comrade Stalin, as the founder of Soviet operational art, brilliantly used the characteristic conditions of the Civil War, conditioned by its socio-political nature, and achieved a complete rout of enemy forces in operations which the Soviet Army conducted under his direct leadership.

Civil War combat operations developed on broad fronts extending 600–1,000 and more kilometers. The relatively small numerical size of operating armies on both sides led to the conduct of operations on thinned-out fronts with weak operational density. It was characteristic that in the majority of cases the Soviet Army conducted offensive operations with either an insignificant superiority or equivalency in forces. All large operations were conducted in the form of coordinated attacks along several axes (the operations to rout Denikin and the White Poles at Kiev, etc.). Annihilating deep attacks were executed using various forms of operational maneuver and employing large masses of mobile forces (at that time cavalry armies, created on Comrade Stalin's initiative).

The Civil War contributed much that was new to the theory of military art, especially related to Soviet Army operations conducted under the direct guidance of Comrade Stalin. For example, Stalin's plan to rout Denikin's armies, which provides initial data for both strategy and operational art concerning the selection of the main attack axis, has enormous theoretical and practical significance for Soviet military art. The Civil War also enriched military theory with several conclusions concerning successive operations, the counteroffensive, and the role and significance of reserves and partisan forces under modern combat conditions. A characteristic feature of Soviet operational art in the Civil War was the great attention focused on all questions of operational support. Stalin's genius, under conditions of waging war characteristic for that time, brilliantly anticipated fundamental features of future operations and provided us not only with very important starting points, but also a series of models for conducting modern operations, which also provided the foundation for further development of the theory of operational art. The theory of operational art, as a new integral component of military art, took shape in our military science soon after the Civil War.

After the Civil War and the defeat of foreign military intervention, Soviet operational art covered a large path of development. Stalin's five-year plan for developing the Soviet Union's national economy outfitted our army with improved combat equipment, and created a materiel base for intensive work on the part of Soviet military thought on the theory of modern operations. Having critically assimilated First World War and Civil War experience, Soviet operational art, in contrast to bourgeois military art, which invented different theories of "modernizing war," created its own completely contemporary, progressive, and scientific theory – the theory of the deep offensive operation. In this respect, Soviet military thought far outdistanced the military thought of bourgeois armies.

Soviet operational art reached its heyday during the Great Patriotic War, when our armed forces, inspired and directed by Comrade Stalin's military leadership genius, provided numerous and unsurpassed models of organizing and conducting modern operations.

Great Patriotic War engagements of enormous scope and great intensity, in which all combat arms actively participated, resolved the most important problems of modern operational art practically and successfully. Among those problems were, for example, organizing and conducting a defense powerful enough to counter a massive attack by large numbers of tanks and powerful aviation, and capable of creating conditions necessary for shifting to a decisive counteroffensive; finding new forms and methods of conducting offensive operations, under new combat conditions, suited to the resolution of the two principal offensive tasks – penetrating a continuous, strongly fortified defense developed to great depth, and exploiting the penetration in such a way as to paralyze enemy resistance to his entire defensive depth; organizing command of large troop masses and using a large quantity of various technical means on decisive axes; and organizing operational co-operation of large masses of different forces and means participating in the operation.

Only Soviet military cadres, indoctrinated by Comrade Stalin and the Bolshevik Party, were capable of resolving these and similar types of complex problems assigned to operational art. Under the difficult combat conditions, Soviet Army generals and officers, armed with the principles of Stalin's military science, assimilated war experience in the briefest period of time and engaged the enemy with a creatively developed art for conducting modern operations.

The Soviet High Command's strategy in the Great Patriotic War was distinguished by operations of enormous scope, exceptional purposefulness, and an ability to find new combat forms and methods, which most fully corresponded to the operational aims and the existing situation; as a rule, the enemy did not anticipate them.

Under conditions of unprecedented scope and intensity of combat operations, during the Great Patriotic War Soviet strategy and operational art successfully resolved all fundamental problems of leading large troop masses in operations, operationally penetrating a deep enemy defense under new conditions, and exploiting it to great depth at unprecedented high tempos. Soviet military art provided models for organizing and conducting complex types of operations such as encirclement of large enemy groupings. Soviet forces encircled the enemy in any situation, both under conditions of a penetration and in the process of exploiting an operation.

Neither the German, nor French, nor British, nor American Armies pro-vided any outstanding operational models for the encirclement of large groupings in either the First or Second World Wars. As is known, in July–August 1944 the Anglo-American command at Normandy attempted to tighten the "noose" of the Falaise "sack" in the Argentan region, but, despite the absence of strong enemy resistance, they failed and were unable to conduct an operation to encircle 7th German Army, even with overwhelming superiority in forces and means. 3d American Army approached the decisive stage of the operation with scattered forces on a broad front: army units were operating indecisively and were pushed back from Argentan. The Germans, having taken advantage of the 20-kilometer outlet from the Falaise "sack," withdrew their 7th Army beyond the Seine and avoided encirclement. Only the Soviet Army was the bearer of a highly mobile operational art, which placed at the forefront the development and conduct of operations for encirclement with the most decisive aims.

The most important principles of Stalin's military art concerning methods for organizing and conducting an offensive under modern conditions, close cooperation of all forces participating in an operation, and use of combat equipment in battle and operations were developed and implemented during the Great Patriotic War. The experience of the Great Patriotic War demonstrated that our military art provided a clear and exhaustive solution to the fundamental questions of offensive and defensive operations, and also provided a new solution to the problem of cooperation of all combat arms in battle and operations on the basis of their mass employment.

Problems of organizing and conducting offensive operations in the Great Patriotic War were more complex than problems of defense, since successful resolution of offensive operational missions depended, to a great degree, on creation of an appropriate materiel-technical base for conducting large wartime operations. In addition, if defensive experience in past wars left some substantive lessons, in the area of large-scale offensive operations we had to rely mainly on Civil War experience. But that war took place under conditions which sharply differed from conditions during the Great Patriotic War. Because of this, the process of developing the art of conducting offensive operations was more complex than development of the defense.

The theory of the deep operation, worked out·by us before the war, predetermined the principal direction of developing the art of organizing and conducting offensive operations; the principles of this theory were already laid out, as already mentioned, in Civil War operations. The development of offensive operations during the Great Patriotic War proceeded along the line of increasingly greater introduction and use of principles for organizing and executing the deep operation, expressed in an increase in the scope and scale of conducted operations. At the same time, operational forms and methods, right up to the extensive employment of such a decisive form as encircling the enemy, were improved and became increasingly varied.

The attempt to resolve the problem of offensive operations by means of deep, decisive, and annihilating blows also predetermined the path for

searching for operational forms and methods. This was manifested in the area of strategy, above all, by a shift to conducting large offensive operations by coordinated attacks along several axes, which deprived the enemy of freedom of maneuver of reserves, and supported the achievement of surprise. The ten annihilating blows delivered by the Soviet Army against the enemy in 1944, when our Armed Forces were tasked with the great mission of liberating all Soviet territory from the enemy and shifting the war to his territory, are an unprecedented model of such offensive operations. Soviet strategy and operational art superbly resolved this mission by conducting operations which grew in power, continuously followed one another, and developed along the most important axes of the entire combat front, from the Baltic to the Danube. The Soviet Army conducted operations, depending on the situation, by penetrating the enemy front along several axes simultaneously or, having penetrated the front along a single axis, by following this with an attack or series of attacks along other axes. Under these conditions the enemy was forced to disperse his reserves, and they were not at the necessary location on time. As a result, it was possible for our forces to exploit the penetration successfully and carry out an operation to encircle large enemy groupings.

Within the framework of a *front* operation, in a number of cases the principle of splintering the enemy's defensive front by means of attacks along several axes was employed. For example, the Western Front counteroffensive of 1941/42 during the Battle of Moscow commenced with counterstrokes north and south of Moscow, which developed into a counteroffensive along these axes; this was followed by counterstrokes on the central sector of the front. The Southwestern Front November–December 1942 offensive at Stalingrad also developed in the form of several attacks. Several other Soviet Army *front* operations during the later campaigns of the Great Patriotic War were structured similarly.

During the war, when organizing offensive operations, the quantity of forces and means and the density and depth of shock groupings subsequently increased, which provided increasing shock force when developing the penetration. Execution of the penetration took the form of coordinated infantry, artillery, tank, and aviation blows, with the attainment of great superiority of forces and means over the enemy in the penetration sector. During the penetration and its development, simultaneous suppression to the depth of the enemy rear area (mainly by means of aviation) was achieved in order to prevent the enemy maneuvering reserves to the region of the penetration. Various flexible and complex forms of operational maneuver were used to develop the penetration, with encirclement of the main enemy grouping.

The resolution of these problems of operational art depended on the resolution of such problems as providing for the overall growth of our armed forces during wartime; changing their organizational structure to adapt to new conditions of conducting war, operations, and battle; creating new equipment; and continuously increasing the combat expertise of forces, etc. These tasks, as we know, were brilliantly resolved thanks to the foresight and wise leadership of Comrade Stalin. The tasks of successfully conducting offensive operations were executed because weapons and equipment were in the hands of Soviet military cadres capable of putting them in motion and squeezing out of them all they could.

Our defense at all stages of the Great Patriotic War had a deep formation and was stubborn and extremely dynamic. The defense on the approaches to Moscow, characterized by dynamic force operations and an increase in density and depth of its development as combat operations moved closer to Moscow, provided a turning point in our favor, and made it possible not only to stop the enemy offensive, but also to create favorable conditions for going over to the counteroffensive. More improved forms of conducting defensive operations were employed in the Battle of Stalingrad, where, as a result of the successful defense, conditions were also created to develop decisive, large-scale offensive operations.

Forms and methods of conducting defensive operations received their greatest development during the Battle of Kursk in 1943, and at Lake Balaton in 1945. Here it should be noted that the Kursk defensive operation was prepared beforehand and proceeded under conditions of preparation of a large counteroffensive along this axis, while the defensive operation at Lake Balaton was conducted under conditions of enemy force superiority on his attack axes, and had the characteristic feature of the defense being structured and developed subsequently during the engagement against advancing large enemy mobile force groupings. During the Battle of Kursk, an attempt to exhaust the enemy, relying on a deep defensive system, and create conditions for going over to a decisive counteroffensive lay at the basis of the defensive organization. This was achieved by a deeply echeloned combat formation of forces, the outfitting of a series of defensive lines, the creation of a powerful antitank defense also echeloned in the depth, extensive maneuver of reserves for massed use of forces and means to localize and liquidate the enemy penetration, and dynamism and readiness to execute counterstrokes and shift to a counteroffensive.

The experience of the Great Patriotic War demonstrated the clear superiority of Soviet operational art over the German Army's operational thought and art of conducting operations. Soviet operational art rightly occupied the foremost place in the development of the operational art of modern armies. It is a powerful means of Soviet strategy, and demonstrated its ability to resolve great and complex problems in the modern mechanized period of war. New forms and methods of conducting struggle, which Soviet operational art discovered, provided the Soviet Army with the ability to resolve the most important problems of modern military operations, which not a single imperialist army was able to resolve in full.

The reasons which conditioned the rapid development of Soviet operational art and made it unattainable for the armies of imperialist states lay, above all, in the historical advantages of our socialist system over the capitalist system, and in the special class nature of the Soviet Army as a new type of army, created to defend the fundamental interests of the workers and relying on the insuperable power of the Soviet social and state system. The socialist economy of our country and national support provide our army with a powerful materiel foundation, on which it grows and develops. The Soviet Army also has at its disposal the most progressive military science in the world, based solely on the scientific foundation of Marxism-Leninism and completely appropriate for the modern mechanized period of war.

Comrade Stalin teaches us that military affairs develop continuously and present increasingly newer demands on military cadres. The further development of combat equipment and new phenomena in the development of combat arms and services of the armed forces confront operational art with a series of new and complex problems. The very rich experience of the Great Patriotic War and the creative nature of our military thought will help to find correct answers to new questions which arise on organizing and conducting operations, and to choose the true path for the solution of all fundamental problems of operational art.

NOTES

1. L. Vetoshnikov, "Operativnoye iskusstvo i yego mesto v sovetskom voyennom iskusstve," *Voyennaya mysl'* [Military thought], 11 (1949), pp. 3–12.
2. Clausewitz, *O voyne* [On war], Vol. I (Voyenizdat, 1937), p. 130.
3. Translator's note: for the sake of consistency, unless otherwise noted the Russian terms *soyedineniye* and *ob"yedineniye* will be translated as "formation" and "large formation" respectively.

The Triumph of Soviet Operational Art in the Great Patriotic War

LIEUTENANT GENERAL V. ZLOBIN[1]

The Soviet Armed Forces' epoch-making victory over Hitler's legions in the Great Patriotic War was won, no matter how the military ideologists of the Anglo-American imperialists try to conceal, misinterpret, and falsify this fact, in the gravest and bloodiest engagements, the likes of which were unknown to military history. Neither the "miracles" which seemed to take place on the Volga and on the Russian plains, nor the Russian winters, nor the Russian expanse, nor the notorious "American aid," nor the operations of the so-called "Allies" in Africa, Italy and Western Europe were the reason for the defeat of Hitler's militarists. The socialist state's economic and spiritual might prevailed; the Soviet people, the Soviet soldier, Soviet equipment, and the art of Soviet military leaders prevailed; the genius of Stalin's leadership of the armed forces prevailed. Hitler's army and Hitler's military leaders were defeated head on by the Soviet Army in grave battles, one on one, and this – and this alone – forced the German–Fascist command into complete capitulation. The entire chain of brilliantly conducted operations and engagements crown the victorious path of the Soviet Armed Forces in their titanic struggle against the fascist hordes of all Europe.

The military victories, which were invariably gained by Soviet forces in all decisive operations of the Great Patriotic War, signal a genuine triumph for Soviet operational art, created by Stalin's genius, and are clear evidence of its complete triumph over the Western military school, which has been praised at all times. The great battles and operations at Moscow, Stalingrad, and Kursk, brilliantly executed under conditions of a military situation which at that time was exceptionally difficult for us, and operations in the decisive 1944 and 1945 campaigns, grandiose in scale and consequences, are unprecedented models of Stalin's strategic and operational inventiveness. Hitler's command was not capable of similar operations, and the ill-starred Anglo-American "military leaders" could not, and in the future would not be able to even dream about such operations.

Even before the Great Patriotic War, Soviet operational art had created a completely modern, progressive, scientific theory of conducting operations. Dialectically interpreting the experience of past wars and all the latest achievements of military-technological progress, and creatively making use of the best traditions of Russian national military art and everything progressive in military affairs, Soviet operational theory even before the war, had found, in contrast to the endless vacillations of bourgeois military science, the uniquely correct paths for resolving problems of conducting operations under new conditions of the mechanized period of war. The Great Patriotic War not only confirmed the viability and correctness of this theory, but also conditioned its further development, which naturally proceeded from the continually changing conditions of conducting armed struggle. Led by Stalin's genius, Soviet operational art during the Great Patriotic War achieved unprecedented heights and a flowering not seen until then, and rightly occupied the position of the most perfect and progressive operational art in the world.

The greatness and triumph of Soviet operational art in the Great Patriotic War find their clearest expression in the continuously new and original resolution of all fundamental problems of conducting modern operations under any conditions. Operational problems do not belong to the number of problems which can be resolved once and for all according to an operational pattern. Stereotypical patterning is tolerated least of all in operational creativity. The nature and methods of resolving problems associated with organizing and conducting operations constantly change, depending on changes in the situation and combat conditions, determined by war aims, development of combat means, evolving correlation of forces, and the enemies' economic might and political state. Each time a new situation places new problems before operational art, it requires a solution which takes into account all conditions of this situation. It is this which also determines the continuous developmental process of operational art. And only that operational art which develops continuously and constantly searches for and finds new methods of resolving tasks set before it, envisioning beforehand all possible changes in combat methods and means, can be at the apex of its position. Such a progressive character is inherent only to Soviet operational art, which is based solely on a scientific theory of knowledge – Marxist-Leninist methodology; this ensured its utter triumph in the Great Patriotic War over the German–Fascist school's "new" operational methods, touted in Western Europe, and over the stagnant, obsolete procedures of Anglo-American operational "methodologists."

Soviet Armed Forces' operational art during the Great Patriotic War covered an enormous and glorious developmental path. This development, guided directly by Comrade Stalin's military leadership genius, unswervingly proceeded along an ascending line. And if during the first period of the war the military situation unfolded unfavorably for us, this is explained solely by the surprise and treachery of the enemy attack. The entire subsequent course of events, which provided us an with epoch-making victory over the strongest imperialist war machine, is irrefutable evidence of this.

The clearest landmarks characterizing the continuous growth and constant superiority of Soviet operational art over German–Fascist military art and that of the Anglo-Saxon countries are the events of the first months of the war, which concluded with the rout of Hitler's armies at Moscow, the great Stalingrad epic, the Battle of Kursk, and particularly the brilliant operations of 1944–45, leading to the enemy's ultimate defeat and complete capitulation. At all these stages of Soviet operational art's glorious developmental path, as well as during the entire war, the Soviet Army, under Comrade Stalin's leadership genius, demonstrated unprecedented models of the most complex defensive operations and greatest (in scale and results) offensive operations, extremely varied in form and method of conduct.

It is especially significant that the scales and decisiveness of operational aims during the entire war continuously increased from year to year. With each day, the Soviet soldiers' high moral spirit, combat experience continually accumulated by the Soviet Army during the war, the growth of the Soviet state's war economy, and the ever increasing equipping of active formations and units with new, improved, and modern combat means created for our operational art increasingly greater capabilities for using decisive and bold methods of conducting operations, which counted on a large, ever increasing depth. We can see how our operations continuously grew in scale, and how the most complex and modern methods of conducting deep annihilating operations were increasingly introduced into the Soviet Army's combat practice. Our operations in the last period of the war differ considerably from operations in the initial period, and even from those of 1943. If earlier operations bore, to a certain degree, a limited scale with respect to front, depth, and tempos of development, subsequently they were planned and conducted as mobile, deep operations, which counted on deep penetration of the enemy's entire operational formation on a broad front, and were almost always associated with bold maneuver to encircle and decisively destroy main enemy groupings.

In all Soviet force operations, whatever the situation in which they might be conducted, attention is focused, above all, on a realistic calculation of all factors – political, economic, moral, and military-technical – which affect or can affect the course of military operations. In each operation we see extreme purposefulness of actions, flowing from the missions of the given stage of the war, sober analysis of all conditions, complete consideration of the opposing sides' combat capabilities, correspondence of the operational plan to these capabilities, use of one's advantageous operational position and the enemy's weak points and mistakes, absence of any stereotypical patterning in the organization and methods of conducting combat operations, and, finally, brilliant models of scientific forecasting of the possible development of events. These qualities also ensure that Soviet operational art will success-fully resolve all problems of conducting operations which arise during war.

During the first years of the war, the most outstanding models of the Soviet Armed Forces' operational art were the Battle of Moscow and the Battle of Stalingrad.

The first months of the Great Patriotic War, which concluded with the Soviet Army's 1941–42 winter offensive, occupy a special place in the development of Soviet operational art. This period was the severest test for our operational theory and practice. And, perhaps, it is remarkable that operations during the initial stage of the struggle, a period that was so diffi-cult for us, should so clearly illustrate the superiority of this theory and practice over the celebrated operational doctrine of Hitler's General Staff.

The struggle during this period was conducted under conditions which differed sharply from the conditions characterizing all subsequent stages of the war. The situation was exceptionally unfavorable and tense for us. The Soviet Army was not yet fully mobilized, and stood one-on-one against the strongest, most excellently prepared imperialist army, which had already acquired great experience in conducting modern operations.

The enemy had considerable numerical force superiority, and especially great superiority in combat equipment, which had enormous significance for the conduct of modern operations. During the entire first year of the war, the Soviet Army experienced serious difficulties in this regard. It was forced to conduct operations against Hitler's huge invading hordes, under conditions of strongly pronounced enemy numerical and technical superiority. Moreover, the enemy possessed other strategic and operational advantages as well, arising from the surprise of his perfidious attack and from his temporary seizure of operational initiative.

The situation which thus arose at the beginning of the war confronted the Soviet Army's operational art with especially complex missions, and left its mark on the nature of the resolution of these missions.

The strategic content of this stage of the war for the Soviet Armed Forces was a dynamic strategic defense to gain time to deploy its main forces, wear out and exhaust the enemy, and create a turning point in the situation to our benefit, which would ensure conditions for shifting to an overall strategic offensive. The concrete resolution of this complex task required our operational art to solve a number of very difficult problems. The Soviet forces' operations, which resolved the problem of a dynamic defense against overwhelming enemy forces, bore an exceptionally intense, varied, and maneuver nature, distinguished by frequent changes in the types and forms of combat operations – defense, withdrawal, counterstrokes, and special offensive operations of varied scope. In such a complex situation, great skill in organizing and conducting combat operations was essential for forces to carry out their assigned missions. The operational expertise of our command and forces was at an apex, the mission of conducting a dynamic defense with decisive results against superior enemy forces having been resolved once again according to Stalin's instructions. As a result of the skill, steadfastness, stubbornness, and dynamic operations of our forces in the summer–autumn period of 1941, the enemy suffered heavy losses. The final result of this heroic struggle was the rout of German–Fascist armies at Moscow and the Soviet Army's shift from defense to offense.

The defeat of Hitler's hordes at Moscow was prepared excellently by dynamic defensive operations executed by Soviet forces on all the most important axes of enemy invasion. Soviet skill in conducting an operational defense with few forces on widely extended fronts was higher and stronger than the enemy's offensive skill, and triumphed in fierce contest over the publicized methods of Fascist blitzkrieg; this conditioned his complete downfall.

Victory in the Moscow counteroffensive was won by conducting very complex maneuver operations along two axes, operations which counted on a double operational envelopment of the German–Fascist tank spearheads penetrating toward the capital. In addition, these operations were associated with the resolution of very difficult and complex tasks of operational art – organizing an immediate shift, without any pause, from defense and withdrawal to counteroffensive and offensive operations on a broad scale, to rout the enemy's large offensive forces. It should be stressed here that superiority in equipment remained, all the same, on the enemy's side. For example, at Moscow he had two-and-a-half times as many tanks as we had. Our superiority in personnel and means of suppression was not very great. At Moscow we triumphed not by quantity, but by the skill of our strategic and operational leadership, and the ability to conduct complex and decisive operations with small forces by skillfully using and combining various forms of maneuver. Soviet forces' operations at Moscow are related to those few operations, which are little known in military history. They rise to the pinnacle of operational art and are an indicator of the maturity of the operational art and practice of their armies.

Thus, Soviet operational art already during the first period of the war, despite colossal difficulties in conducting operations arising from our unfavorable military situation at that time, demonstrated its full maturity and superiority over German–Fascist methods of offensive operations, having, under those conditions, successfully resolved very complex operational problems of organizing and executing maneuver defensive and offensive operations, withdrawal operations, and operations associated with shifting from the defense and withdrawal to offensive operations, as well as problems

of creating a dynamic, stable, stubborn, and insurmountable defense along decisive lines.

A second most important event of the first years of the war, which demonstrated continuous development during the difficult struggle, growth, and unarguable superiority of Soviet operational art was the immortal Stalingrad epic. The great Battle of Stalingrad crowned the second significant stage of development of our wartime operational theory and practice. This stage brought new brilliant victories to Soviet arms, and raised the Soviet Army's operational art to a new, higher level.

Operations in 1942 were conducted under significantly changed conditions, in comparison with the situation in which the Battle of Moscow had taken place. The deployment and activation of a powerful war industry in the Urals and Siberia provided the Soviet Armed Forces with a large quantity of equipment: artillery, tanks, airplanes, and small arms. Conditions were created to form new reserve armies and artillery, tank, and mechanized formations. It became possible to conduct large-scale operations of great scope with respect to depth and tempos, and with large operational densities.

The operational-tactical training of Soviet forces, personally directed by Comrade Stalin, increased immeasurably during this period. Forces acquired combat experience, began to maneuver more skillfully, and mastered more improved combat techniques. Skill in organizing cooperation and control improved.

All these new conditions permitted further growth of the Soviet Army's operational art. Soviet forces' operations acquired new quality and content. Above all, the great variety of forms and employed operational techniques in the conduct of operations during this period should be noted. The problem of operational penetration of a fortified front using large masses of artillery, tanks, and aviation was successfully resolved. Methods of deep exploitation of a penetration also changed, thanks to the creation of mobile groups of large tank and mechanized formations. Exploitation of the penetration was conducted to great depth, with more decisive aims, and at increasing tempos. Average operational tempos increased two to threefold. Increased mobility and maneuver, and operational-tactical training of forces made it possible to execute brilliant operations to encircle the enemy. In this period one can observe in our operational art the developed forms of the modern deep maneuver operation, which counted on the encirclement and complete defeat of large enemy groupings.

The Stalingrad operations, astutely thought out and expertly conducted, best attest to the continuing growth of Soviet operational art during the second year of the Great Patriotic War and its superiority over the military art of Hitler's Germany. The Battle of Stalingrad, which concluded with the encirclement and imprisonment of two select Fascist armies of 330,000 men, represents a genuine triumph of Stalin's strategy and operational art. This is a classic example of a modern deep offensive operation, which ended in an unprecedented short period of time with the complete encirclement and subsequent destruction of the large enemy force grouping, an example which will always be a perfect model of an operation about which military leaders can only dream.

The planning of the Stalingrad offensive operations and their brilliant execution are an excellent example of the skill of Stalin's strategic leadership and the operational expertise of our command and forces. Everything in these astutely thought-out and precisely executed operations speaks of the greatness of Soviet strategy and operational art.

Despite the difficult situation in the south during the second half of 1942, the Soviet Army Supreme High Command was able to resolve the problem of massing and maintaining large reserves and materiel-technical means to conduct dynamic offensive operations on the Stalingrad axis. Soviet forces in the south did not have overall superiority in forces, but, thanks to skillful maneuver, our command covertly and in a short time achieved decisive superiority on the main axes by means of strict economy of forces in other sectors. The problem of deploying shock groupings, in the presence of a known equilibrium of forces, is one of the most difficult problems of operational art, and this problem was brilliantly resolved at Stalingrad.

One of the decisive conditions for success of an operation is the skillful selection of main attack axes, leading to the destruction of the main enemy grouping, and determination of the moment for shifting to the offensive, especially if operations are conducted in a situation of a strategic counteroffensive, as was done at Stalingrad. Our command resolved both these problems with surprising expertise in the Stalingrad operation. The main attack axes were planned against the weakest link in the enemy's operational formation, that is, against his weak flanks. The moment for shifting to the offensive was chosen when the enemy least expected it, when all his attention and forces were absorbed by the unprecedented stubbornness of our defense at Stalingrad, and, therefore, when, having weak and unsupported flanks, he was not prepared for serious defense.

The Stalingrad offensive operation was a masterpiece of operational ingenuity. The offensive was conducted by three *fronts* on a 650 kilometer-wide front. The main attacks were delivered along converging axes, counting on the encirclement of the entire enemy grouping operating at Stalingrad. The three-*fronts* offensive simultaneously deprived Hitler's command of freedom of maneuver and the possibility of purposefully using its reserves. They were defeated piecemeal. Bold in plan, complex in execution, and executed at high tempos, the concentric attack of the main offensive groupings – Southwestern and Stalingrad Fronts – led to an unprecedented encirclement and destruction of very large forces. It is noteworthy that, simultaneously with the encirclement of the main enemy grouping, the operation developed into the depth. This is the most absolute principle of conducting modern operations, the employment of which is within the reach of only the most progressive army.

Finally, the offensive of our forces at Stalingrad is noteworthy for the tempos of its execution. The average daily tempo of advance was 30–35 kilometers. Such offensive tempos under difficult winter conditions reflect the high quality and operational-tactical art of the entire chain of command and forces taking part in the operation.

Defensive operations at Stalingrad, which preceded the counteroffensive, are no less illustrative for Soviet operational art.

In defensive operations on the approaches to Stalingrad, Soviet operational art brilliantly resolved the problem of conducting a dynamic and insurmountable defense capable of stopping and exhausting very large enemy shock groupings. At the foundation of the defense lay its deep formation, with the creation of a number of intermediate lines and cut-off positions, concentration of forces and means on decisive axes, maneuver of reserves to threatened axes, and dynamic methods of fighting against the attacking enemy by conducting frequent counterstrokes which increased in might, that is, all those operational methods which subsequently entered into the unfailing practice of our forces and are now fundamental principles of modern defense theory.

The defeat of select German–Fascist forces in the Battle of Stalingrad was a very great victory in the history of warfare, and threw the world into amazement and disbelief.

Western imperialist military theorists, unable to understand the natural logic of the reasons for the events which occurred at Stalingrad and attempting to minimize the significance of the victory there, tried to present it as a matter of chance occurrence. Lovers of historical analogies recalled the "miracle" of the Marne and began to write about the "miracle" on the Volga. If, from the point of view of these theorists, "a miracle had occurred" on the Marne, of course on the Volga there was nothing similar. Here there were no "chance occurrences"; here all was thought out, prepared, and worked out beforehand. The victory was won by the force of Soviet arms and by the art of their employment.

During the first two years of the war, including the Battles of Moscow and Stalingrad, Comrade Stalin's great and fruitful activities in the field of the development of operational art ensured its rapid and uninterrupted growth. Many orders and directives from the great military leader are associated with this period, exposing shortcomings in our forces' combat operations and providing new principles in instructions on the conduct of operations and battle. Comrade Stalin's innovative and creative genius, with profound understanding of all aspects of military affairs, attentively studied the course of combat operations, vigilantly noted and eliminated all errors in organizing Soviet troop operations, and taught them the highest expertise of waging modern war.

As elaborated by Comrade Stalin, the major principle of our military science concerning permanently operating factors, which determine the fate of war, provided direction and specified new paths for further development of Soviet Armed Forces' operational art during the war, achieving unprecedented heights thanks to this. Stalin's operational art, as well as military science and military art on the whole, was based, above all, on correct and dynamic use of permanently operating factors in each operation, and the success of all combat operations. Stalin's operational plans were always an exceptional expression of knowledge, and consideration and expert use of these factors under the concrete conditions of each given instance.

Using the principle of the decisive role in war of permanently operating factors, Stalin's genius developed a genuinely scientific strategic plan for the Soviet Union's national war against Hitler's Germany, based on a combination of a dynamic defense and offense, and brought this plan to a victorious conclusion. Soviet operational art, based on these factors, was able to resolve the most complex operational problems of conducting dynamic defensive and wide offensive operations, ensuring the complete achievement of strategic missions which evolved from the war plan. The continuous growth during the war of the number of divisions, thanks to Comrade Stalin's untiring concern, the increase in their quality, the outfitting of the army with modern weapons and first-class equipment, and the development of organizational capabilities in command personnel, provided Soviet operational art with the ability to organize and conduct classical operations, unprecedented in their decisiveness, scope, and results, even during the first difficult war years. Based on the growth of permanently operating factors, which were a genuine expression of the power and art of modern armies, Soviet forces, under Comrade Stalin's leadership, mastered the most modern and perfected methods for conducting operations. Our operational art improved continuously on this basis, and achieved a high, outstanding level of development.

Comrade Stalin personally directed the improvement of the operational expertise of Soviet forces. Not a single question on troop organization, their operational art, or combat tactics escaped our great leader's attention during these first years of the war. A whole series of detailed instructions from the Supreme Commander-in-Chief, who understood all aspects of our forces' organization and combat practice, made it possible to restructure the Soviet Army in a short time in accordance with new war requirements, to acquire necessary experience, and already in 1941 to inflict powerful attacks against the enemy at Moscow, Rostov, Tikhvin, Kalinin, and Leningrad, and in 1942 to execute an unprecedented encirclement at Stalingrad.

During this period, forces, in particular aviation, artillery, tank, mechanized, and engineer troops, acquired a new organization, corresponding to the war's actual conditions and requirements. Large tank and artillery formations were formed, which supported Stalin's principle of their mass operational employment.

During this time, Comrade Stalin's creative genius introduced a number of new forms and operational methods into the theory and practice of Soviet operational art, which, to the greatest degree, corresponded to the concrete situation and best ensured the defeat of the strong enemy. The Supreme Commander-in-Chief developed the forces and provided them with extensive instructions on the organization and conduct of a modern dynamic and insurmountable defense, which created conditions for going over to a counteroffensive; on methods for organizing and preparing a counteroffensive; on forms for the successful penetration of any enemy defense and its development; on execution of large-scale operations to encircle enemy groupings; on careful organization of cooperation; on employment of the most flexible combat formations in accordance with the situation; and on the use of artillery, aviation, and tanks.

Stalin's wise leadership ensured undeviating growth of the Soviet Army's operational expertise during this most difficult war, the likes of which the history of past military art, covering many centuries, had not known, and which was unattainable for our enemies. This made it possible for the Soviet Armed Forces to execute an annihilating offensive operation, unprecedented in its scale, such as the Stalingrad operation.

Stalingrad became synonymous with the highest class of operational art, but it was not the limit of development of operational theory and practice. In subsequent war years, Soviet operational art continued to develop and improve. Operations during the war's concluding period raised it to new, even greater heights.

The central events of the subsequent war years, characterizing the development, force, and complete triumph of the Soviet Army's operational art, are the Battle of Kursk and, especially, the unparalleled operations of 1944 and 1945.

The Battle of Kursk and subsequent offensive operations of 1943 are at least equal in intensity, significance, and expertise of conduct to the battles of 1942, which lasted many months; for the most part, they even surpass them, especially in variety of equipment and complexity of formation. Never before had the forces of both sides been so richly outfitted with military equipment as in the 1943 summer operations. This placed its imprint on the structure and conduct of operations, and presented new, complex requirements for operational art, especially in the organization of purposeful and effective use of numerous equipment.

A new factor in the 1943 operations, affecting operational art and its development, was the creation of large tank formations, massive antitank artillery, and large artillery units, and the significant growth of aviation. The appearance of large quantities of the newest equipment imparted to operations an even greater intensity, simultaneously ensuring the potential for conducting operations in decisive forms and at great depth.

The unprecedented defeat of German–Fascist forces at Stalingrad, achieved partly because of the fatal miscalculation by Hitler's command of the Soviet Army's forces and capabilities, forced the command to focus great attention on preparation and establishment of powerful and deep defensive lines. Under these conditions, each of our offensive operations inevitably commenced with a penetration of strongly fortified deep defensive belts. New problems of conducting operations, associated with the organization of an operational penetration of a powerful and deeply echeloned defense, arose before operational art. The operational situation became increasingly more complex. This concerned the conduct not only of the offense, but also the defense, which was now forced to counter the deep coordinated attack of large masses of varied equipment, which, following our example, the enemy began to concentrate on axes where he was still conducting offensive operations.

Under these complex conditions of conducting operations, Soviet operational art was still at its apex, and superior to that of its enemies.

In the Battle of Kursk we see, above all, brilliant execution of one of the most important conditions of modern operations – creation of prerequisites during one operation for new operations even broader in scale and united by a single plan, and development of one operation into another without any pauses. The resolution of this most difficult operational problem was possible only on the basis of profound foresight regarding the entire course of development of expected events. The ability to foresee developing operational events was possible only for Soviet military leaders of Stalin's school; the organization of operations on the basis of foresight is a distinguishing characteristic of Soviet operational art and its superiority. During the Battle of Kursk, as always, our command, led by Stalin's genius, was able to discover the enemy's plan, anticipate the development of events, and channel them in a favorable direction.

The Battle of Kursk demonstrated to us new principles, developed by Comrade Stalin, for conducting defensive and offensive operations under conditions where both sides employ massive technical combat means and large military groupings.

Our operational defense at the Kursk salient was a classical example of creating a modern insurmountable defense, which counted on the destruction of powerful advancing enemy shock groupings and the subsequent shift to a counteroffensive. Deep structural forms and dynamic conduct lay at the basis of its organization. The overall depth of the defensive formation, taking into account the prepared state defensive line, amounted to hundreds of kilometers. Conduct of the defense was structured on broad maneuver of reserves and the conduct of powerful counterstrokes by tank groupings against enemy forces which had penetrated our defensive positions.

The first stage of battles demonstrated that the defense, organized in this way, was stronger than the enemy offensive, despite the enormous forces and extensive improved equipment introduced here by the Nazis. For the first time in the history of the Second World War, the defense was so skillful and stubborn that it repelled the main German–Fascist shock group's offensive without loss of territory and with enormous enemy casualties. This was new, clear evidence of our command's and forces' operational superiority over Hitler's hordes.

The counteroffensive on the Orel–Kursk and Belgorod–Khar'kov axes was a direct continuation of the defensive engagement without any pauses. The situation was similar to the Battles of Moscow and Stalingrad, but in the Battle of Kursk our developing operational art was able to combine defense and offense more tightly to achieve the aim of completely routing the enemy. Here the defense, by swiftly shifting to a counteroffensive, directly prepared conditions for the decisive defeat of an enemy who had been worn out in defensive battles. The final offensive operational plan was refined and prepared during the defensive engagement in an extremely short time. Our command's operational inventiveness and organizational capabilities were at their apex and provided a brilliant resolution of one of the most difficult tasks of operational art.

The deep formation of attacking shock groupings was a significant step forward in these operations, even in comparison with the Stalingrad operation. This resolved the problem of ensuring great penetrative force of shock groupings and the ability to increase forces from the depth during the operation, which was a most important condition for continuous and deep conduct of the offensive at high tempos using decisive maneuver. The density of the shock grouping deployment also increased. Great densities on the main axes were created, above all, by skillful maneuver of forces from secondary sectors, which characterized our command's developing operational expertise.

In offensive operations during the Battle of Kursk, we see the employment of the most improved and modern forms and methods of conducting a large-scale operational offensive. In subsequent war years, these forms and methods acquired further and conclusive development, and became the basis of our theory of offensive operations.

The absence of stereotypical patterning in the structure and execution of operations, decisiveness of aim, correct choice of methods based on careful analysis of the situation and consideration of the enemy's strong and weak aspects, unprecedented massing of forces and means on decisive axes, operational coordination of attacks conducted against several sectors, excellently organized cooperation of all combat arms, and, finally, bold and skillful battlefield maneuver are all features at the foundation of the Soviet Army's operational art in operations at Orel, Belgorod, and Khar'kov, which led to brilliant results. Especially noteworthy is the fact that these operations developed directly into an unbroken chain of offensive operations encompassing an enormous front and continuing for four months without interruption to a depth up to the Dnepr River line. During this offensive Soviet operational art brilliantly resolved tasks of operational pursuit, overcoming intermediate lines from the march, and successful forcing of large river lines such as the Dnepr.

The great summer offensive of 1943 demonstrated once again the unarguable superiority of the Soviet Army's operational art over Hitler's, and, in a word, exploded fascist myths that Soviet forces could not conduct successful summer offensive operations.

Soviet skill in conducting operations using large masses of artillery, tanks, and aviation under conditions of continuous, strongly fortified *fronts*, appearing as a result of Nazi attempts to shift the war to positional forms after their disastrous defeats at Stalingrad and Kursk, greatly improved in 1943 operations. But we see the complete triumph of Soviet operational art – the genuine art of the mechanized period of the war – subsequently in 1944 and 1945.

By this time the Soviet Union, led by the great Stalin and the judicious Bolshevik Party, achieved enormous growth in the defense industry. Thanks to the Soviet system's advantages, our country's powerful social, economic, technical, and military progress did not cease during the war either. The Soviet Union created a coordinated, rapidly growing war economy and brilliantly resolved the problem of broadening socialist production in the sphere of defense industry. Our party and our heroic nation, under conditions of unprecedented difficulties, found in themselves gigantic strength not only to maintain the defense industry at the prewar level, but also to increase it several times with respect to quantity and quality of production. The powerful defense industry, created in the depth of the country in the Urals and Siberia, played its historic role in ensuring victory over Fascist Germany.

The rapid growth of the defense industry made it possible, already in 1943 and especially by the beginning of 1944, to increase significantly the development of the armed forces, create a large quantity of new formations, and outfit the Soviet Army with an abundance of first-class artillery, tanks, aviation, and other technical combat means.

Stalin's genius, which raised military science and army organization to even greater heights and prepared and ensured its outfitting with necessary combat equipment, brilliantly resolved during this most difficult war

exceptionally complex problems of dynamic change in the correlation of forces to our advantage, achievement of quantitative and qualitative superiority over the enemy, and creation and accumulation of considerable strategic reserves.

Beginning in 1944, all this served as a foundation for the development of Soviet Army operations, unprecedented in their colossal scope, and ensured decisive success in the struggle against Fascist Germany.

The Soviet Armed Forces' operational art, raised to unknown heights in 1944 and 1945 operations, developed in leaps and bounds under the influence of these factors.

The Soviet Army's decisive successes in 1944 and 1945 were pre-determined by ten of Stalin's blows, delivered against German–Fascist forces and forces of the vassals of Hitler's Germany. With respect to the profundity and boldness of the plan, careful preparation, scope of action, and expertise of execution, all operations conducted with the delivery of these blows are classic examples of modern operational art.

The primary feature characterizing the high degree of development of operational art in the decisive campaigns of 1944–45 is the further increase of decisiveness of aim and the nature of the operations being conducted. Each operation encompassed colossal *fronts* and enormous forces within its orbit, and was conducted, as a rule, to rout and destroy very large strategic and operational enemy groupings. Operations followed one another almost continuously, and were conducted in the winter and summer in different front sectors, sometimes considerably separated from one another, and requiring great skill in the maneuver of forces and means from one axis to another. Operations very often developed simultaneously along several axes. Never during the entire war was Hitler's command able to use such a decisive method of conducting operations, nor, for that matter, were the British or Americans.

In 1944, for example, the Soviet Army, thanks to Comrade Stalin's leadership genius, which ensured the successive intensification of efforts during the war, was so strong and had at its disposal such a large quantity of reserves, that it was able in only one year to conduct ten very large offensive operations of strategic significance and scope. Here, on the axes of attacks delivered by our forces, the art of the Soviet military's operational leadership unalterably ensured decisive superiority over the enemy in forces due to skillful maneuver of reserves and forces from secondary sectors. Each operation bore an annihilating character, and overall they led to the shattering of the enemy's entire eastern front, putting the main forces of the German–Fascist Army out of action. The final operations of 1945 bore an even more decisive character, when our forces shifted from a system of successive attacks to a simultaneous offensive along almost the entire front. Military history has never before encountered an example of where for 18 months continuous operations of a similar scale were conducted. Only Stalin's strategy and operational art could execute such grandiose operations.

Decisiveness of missions confronting the Soviet Armed Forces in the 1944 and 1945 campaigns required of operational art the development of corresponding decisive forms of operations and methods for conducting them. Soviet operational art brilliantly resolved these missions. Comrade Stalin, the Supreme Commander-in-Chief, assisted our forces in the gigantic operations they conducted to employ each time new, unexpected forms of decisive actions, combining in them the force of the attack with flexible and bold maneuver. Operations to encircle the main enemy groupings became the primary form of the Soviet Army's offensive actions. Our operational art led to a high degree of improvement of maneuver for encirclement, executing it under any conditions. Thanks to this, large enemy groupings were destroyed literally in a few days. For example, in the Korsun–Shevchenkovskiy encirclement, 11 German–Fascist divisions were destroyed in 14 days, while in the Minsk encirclement, up to 30 divisions were destroyed in eight days; in the Iassy-Kishinev operation, around 22 divisions were encircled and routed in nine days. And these are not isolated incidents. We observe such decisive actions in other operations of this period. They attest to the high operational expertise of the Soviet Army's command and forces, and the incomparable superiority of Stalin's military art over German strategy and tactics.

Decisiveness of aims and forms of combat actions planned for the destruction of the principal enemy strategic and operational groupings imparted to 1944 and 1945 operations an unprecedented scope in front, depth, and quantity of forces and means employed in an operation. Operational art had never had practice in organizing and conducting operations on such a gigantic scale as in the campaigns of the last years of the war. And in this case Soviet operational art found a brilliant and original solution to the problem of leading enormous groupings equipped with large quantities of the latest combat means.

The 1944–45 operations are characterized by the delivery of attacks on a broad front using fully and closely cooperating forces of several *fronts*. The swift and decisive rout of the enemy on a number of axes led to the creation of enormous breaches in the enemy front, which provided our forces with the ability to attack rapidly into the depth of the defense, using large forces. This resulted in the enemy's defense becoming disorganized rapidly and his suffering a number of defeats on a strategic scale. Cooperation of the attackers on various front axes and expert maneuver of reserves ensured continually intensifying and increasingly deeper attacks, and paralyzed all enemy countermeasures. This made it possible to develop our operations to a great depth, conduct them at high tempos, and prevent them from fading prematurely.

In the 1944 and 1945 campaigns, as in previous years, Stalin's strategy and operational art, despite the increased scale of the struggle, brilliantly coped with the extremely difficult tasks of strategic and operational leadership, and coordination of the actions of several *fronts* simultaneously participating in the offensive operation. It should be kept in mind that this task had to be resolved under very complex conditions of combat actions developed on an enormous front and at swift tempos. Thanks to strict centralization and high expertise of control, cooperation among *fronts* during engagements was not disrupted. And this in turn provided our forces with a full resolution of all tasks before them. Soviet strategy and operational art were at their apex as well in such a difficult and complex situation.

A noteworthy expression and clear illustration of the complete triumph of Soviet operational art during the entire war, especially in 1944 and 1945 operations, is the brilliant resolution, original in all cases, of such complex, difficult, and important problems of conducting modern operations as penetrating a fortified front, exploiting it on an operational scale, and executing bold and extensive maneuver at all stages of the operation, in the majority of cases directed toward encircling and destroying the principal enemy groupings. Here it should be noted that in selecting methods and forms of action, any stereotypical patterning using obsolete models was alien to Soviet operational art; here its progressive and scientific nature was especially expressed.

Under 1944 and 1945 conditions, penetration of a front was the most typical case of the principle of offensive operations. In all operations of this period, penetration of the front was inescapable. The attempt by Hitler's command after the 1943 defeats to shift the war to positional forms, with his still considerable forces and abundant equipment, led in individual periods to the creation of a stable front based on strongly fortified positions. It is true that these attempts to achieve prolonged stabilization of the front inevitably failed under the annihilating blows of Soviet forces, but, nevertheless, they put the attacker into situations which necessitated each operation commencing with penetration of the enemy's strongly fortified defensive front.

The operational penetration of a front in concluding operations of the Great Patriotic War in 1944–45 acquired the most complete and ultimate development in harmonic combination with other types of operations. As is known, in the First World War the problem of the operational penetration of a positional defense was not solved by a single one of the warring armies; deep penetration and its exploitation on an operational scale did not once succeed, and the war, therefore, came to a positional dead end. We observe a new picture in the Soviet Army's operational art in the Great Patriotic War.

We fully developed methods and ultimate forms of operational penetration. In the overwhelming majority of cases, and always in 1944 and 1945 operations, the Soviet offensive against fortified positions unalterably led to decisive penetration of the enemy front, and then acquired deep operational exploitation. A complex maneuver was very often executed after the penetration, leading to the encirclement of large enemy groupings and their complete rout.

It is very important to emphasize as characteristic of the high level of development of Soviet operational art that the type of offensive where the penetration was executed on a wide front in the form of a series of attacks, delivered in operational cooperation along several axes, was widely practiced as a special type of operation in the practical experience of Soviet forces during the Great Patriotic War. Operational penetration, which counted on delivering several operationally coordinated attacks, either simultaneously or consecutively, is an exceptionally complex and difficult operation, but it has enormous superiority in comparison with penetration in a single sector, and corresponds most to modern battle conditions. Penetration along several axes makes it possible to shatter the enemy's defensive front into a number of isolated centers, which subsequently facilitates the rout of each such isolated grouping. The development of the offensive immediately along several axes disorients the opposing command and makes it difficult for them to use their reserves and undertake other measures to parry the attacks. In 1944–45 operations, this most modern and highly improved operational combat form experienced its ultimate development and crowned Soviet operational art with the glory of unprecedented victories.

The Soviet Army's operational art in 1944–45 campaigns was also the brilliant bearer of the most decisive and complex form of operational maneuver – maneuver to encircle. Beginning with Stalingrad, maneuver to encircle on the operational and tactical scales gradually acquired a predominant role in Soviet forces' combat operations. An especially large number of these operations were undertaken during 1944–45.

In the past, military theory considered that, for an encirclement to be possible, special favorable conditions (advantageous front profile, advantageous force groupings, etc.) were necessary, and that successful execution of encirclement was, as a rule, the result of a favorable confluence of circumstances. Our operational art in 1944–45 operations demonstrated that it was able to resolve the problem of encirclement under any conditions. In this period the Soviet Army executed encirclement maneuver against an advancing enemy and an enemy occupying the position of a stable front; finally, it encircled enemy forces during maneuver following the penetration of a front and during pursuit.

Comrade Stalin's creative genius in 1943, 1944, and 1945 enriched our operational art by working out in new and original ways a number of problems of modern operations. Of these, the main ones are organization and conduct of large-scale operations in a system of several cooperating *fronts*;

organization of the penetration of a strongly fortified enemy front simultaneously or successively along several axes; encirclement of large enemy groupings under various conditions and at various stages of an operation; new methods of forcing large water lines – forcing from the march; and swift and decisive maneuver of large operational formations and smaller formations during an operation. Stalin's strategy and operational art also brilliantly solved the problem of employing reserves, having ensured the possibility of conducting a simultaneous offensive with increasing force on an enormous front and at great depth, as took place in January 1945. Finally, during this period problems of organizing cooperation on the basis of strict centralization of control and large operational formations fully equipped with large quantities of artillery, tanks, and aviation used on decisive axes acquired their ultimate development. The creative solution of these most complex problems (each time in a new way, depending on the actual new conditions), together with the use of other tactical and operational modes of action, and the absence of any stereotypical patterning in Stalin's strategic and operational ingenuity, ensured for Soviet military art unsurpassed expertise in organizing and conducting these great operations, the equal of which history had never known.

The Soviet Army's operational art in 1944 and 1945 achieved such a high level of development that it left us models of operations which, in their significance, intensity and scale, the variety of equipment, the art of maneuver, and all remaining indicators, are an example for structuring modern operations, and provide initial data for developing a theory of future operations. The 1944 and 1945 operations crown the triumphant path of development of Stalin's Soviet operational art during the Great Patriotic War.

Soviet operational art, having absorbed many centuries of Russian combat experience, the best traditions of the Russian army's national military art, and all that was good and progressive in the past history of military art, developed along its own independent and distinctive path on the principles of Stalin's progressive military science, inseparably linked with the political and economic conditions of our socialist society. At all stages of its development, Soviet operational art, as a genuinely scientific theory, always moved forward and occupied a leading place with respect to various foreign schools, demonstrating more than once its superiority on the fields of battle.

The Great Patriotic War multiplied, enriched, and raised the theory and practice of our operational art to new and greater heights. It introduced much that was new and original into the field of organizing and conducting operations, and outlined a series of new, concrete forms and modes of action for the successful achievement of great operational results in a modern situation. It demonstrated the exceptional variety of our operational resource-fulness, the inventiveness and richness of our operational combinations, and the ability to find the necessary means for victory in any situation. It demon-strated to the whole world the greatness and superiority of Stalin's Soviet operational art over the metaphysical operational doctrine of Hitler's command and his imitators of today.

The Great Patriotic War and its victorious outcome is an unarguable, worldwide triumph of Soviet operational art, which brought it the renown as the foremost progressive operational theory.

Soviet operational art achieved these results because its creator was the great Stalin.

NOTES

1. V. Zlobin, "Torzhestvo sovetskogo operativnogo iskusstva v Velikoy Otechestvennoy voyne," *Voyennaya mysl'* [Military thought], 5 (1950), pp. 15–30.

CHAPTER FOUR

On the Eve of the Revolution in Military Affairs, 1954–59

Stalin's death and subsequent political changes in the Soviet Union, accompanied by de-Stalinization which gripped the nation after 1958, permitted Soviet military theorists slowly to strip off the veneer of Stalinist principles, which had insulated that theory from intensive examination and prevented more active open discussion of operational questions. It also allowed those theorists to ponder more fully the likelihood and nature of nuclear war. Theoretical debates grew in intensity and culminated in 1960 with full Soviet recognition that a "revolution" had occurred in military affairs. As these articles indicate, however, the roots of that recognition were already apparent well before 1960.

Writing in 1955, two years after Stalin's death, Lieutenant General A. Tsvetkov traced the evolution of operational art and, in particular, the impact of technological change on its content. More important, he assessed the impact of that change on the operational art of all modern types of combat forces. Refreshingly, references to Stalin's role in the development of operational art virtually disappeared.

In 1956, Colonel V. Vasil'yev surveyed anew the place of operational art in the context of strategy and emphasized the need to develop distinct and detailed theories of operational art relating to the various branches and types of forces. He argued for continued updating of the nature of operational art and, in so doing, reemphasized the factor of surprise, which had been so often ignored in the writings of Stalinist times.

Even more importantly, the article by Marshal of Tank Forces P. A. Rotmistrov, illustrious tank army commander and chief of armored and mechanized forces during the Great Patriotic War, evidenced Soviet recognition that atomic weaponry was having a growing influence on operational art. Rotmistrov's transitional article stood astride two periods with one leg in the postwar celebration of wartime operational art and the other hesitatingly probing the nuclear future, with all that it held for future war. Just as he had done with his 1955 article on surprise in war (also published in *Military Thought*), Rotmistrov focused attention on new weaponry of mass destruction, which would preoccupy Soviet theorists for decades to come.

Close analysis of the contents of these initial post-Stalin articles demonstrate that the basic information in them accords well with the details of operational art's evolution contained in articles of the postwar Stalinist period. What had changed was primarily the incessant reference to Stalin's role in that evolution. In addition, the new articles included greater emphasis on the potential impact of technological change on military art and considerably less emphasis on the role and utility of "permanently operating factors" in war.

The Operation, its Essence, and its Significance in Modern Armed Struggle

LIEUTENANT GENERAL A. TSVETKOV[1]

As is generally known, the methods and forms of armed struggle in the course of historical development change under the influence of changes in productive methods. The development of production and, in particular, the growth of military technology result in the emergence of new conditions for armed struggle, which determine the appearance of new natural laws governing it and the disappearance of those natural laws no longer appropriate for these conditions.

The operation first appeared as a phenomenon of armed struggle in nineteenth century wars, with inherent specific regularities that did not fit within the framework of existing military theory. Rapid development of productive forces in the era of industrial capitalism made it possible to increase considerably the numerical strength of armies, recruited on the basis of military conscription. The use of railroads for mass transport made it possible to concentrate large military masses quickly in specific regions, and promptly provide them with everything necessary for life and battle, while employment of the electric telegraph helped to implement continuous control of joint actions by large force groupings deployed over a considerable distance and often isolated from one another. All this resulted in military operations acquiring considerably broader scope than formerly, with respect to time and space, and in other consequences. Under conditions where opposing armies of great numerical strength began to deploy on fronts numbering tens and hundreds of kilometers, the mission of destroying the enemy's armed forces could no longer be resolved in one so-called "general engagement." It became necessary to seek resolution of this problem in a whole series of battles and engagements, conducted both simultaneously and at various times on a relatively large territorial expanse, but guided by an overall operational plan for the achievement of a single aim.

The embryo of this new phenomenon could already be observed in the war Russia fought against Turkish aggression in 1811, and especially in the Patriotic War of 1812. Thus, for example, the elements of an operation could be seen in the actions of Russian armies during their shift to the counteroffensive under the command of the great Russian military leader

M. I. Kutuzov, in their pursuit of enemy forces, in combat actions at the Berezina River, and in the 1813 campaign conducted by Russian forces in Western Europe. However, it should be noted that, although the necessity for organizing and conducting operations had already arisen, the factual ability to execute them was still inadequate. These potentials became more real during the Franco-Prussian War of 1870–71. Thus, during the defeat of the French Army at Metz, the elements of an operation could already be clearly identified. In six days, 1st and 2d Prussian Armies conducted three engagements in succession – at Colombey and Noueille, at Mars-la-Tour, and at Gravelotte and Saint Privat – completing a 90-kilometer wheeling around the left flank and enveloping the French Army, which was densely concentrated at Metz. These successively conducted engagements were also united by a general plan and subordinated to the single general aim of defeating the French Army's main forces concentrated in Metz. It must be noted, however, that the opposing armies' higher command personnel little understood the essence of the operation, and often acted contrary to the plan and situation.

The increase in the numerical strength of armies and their fire power in the beginning of the twentieth century increased the independence of formations and conditioned the widening of the front of combat operations and a considerable increase in the duration of engagements as early as the Russo-Japanese War. Other actions were undertaken between battles and engagements, of a supporting nature or preparing for subsequent, more dynamic army operations. The engagement itself began to be divided in time and space into separate parts or stages, each of which pursued a specific aim, conditioned by the general engagement plan. Thus, for example, combat operations of the Russian Army deployed on a 54-kilometer front in the engagement at the Shakhei River began on 5 October 1904 with an offensive that lasted five days. The offensive, conducted indecisively, was unsuccessful, and on 11 October Kuropatkin issued an order to shift to the defense. The Japanese, who had shifted to the offense against the center and on the right flank of the Russian forces, took advantage of this. Attacks and counterattacks by both sides followed one another, accompanied by dynamic unit and formation maneuver. Fierce two-week battles along the Shakhei resulted in no noticeable advantage for either side, but demonstrated that the achievement of a specific, large-scale result required prolonged and varied combat actions unfolding over considerable territory. Here, both sides used the offense and defense, regrouping and maneuver, and all this within the framework of a single plan.

The clearest prototype of future First World War operations, with their broad combat fronts and positional forms of struggle, was the Battle of Mukden in 1905. Three Russian armies, deployed on a front of up to 150 kilometers, opposed an almost equal force of four Japanese armies, deployed on a front of 110 kilometers. Frontal attacks from both sides, penetrations of the front and envelopments, a dual-axis operational envelopment of the defending Russian armies' flanks by forces of 5th and 3d Japanese Armies, and massive regroupings to counter the flank envelopment continued without interruption for 20 days, from 18 February to 10 March, not only during the day, but also often at night, ending with the general withdrawal of Russian armies to occupy defensive positions prepared in the rear.

Thus, the practical combat experience of the Russo-Japanese War demonstrated the further growth of new phenomena of armed struggle, objectively ensuing from the massive size of armies and the development of combat equipment and control means. Extensive use of smokeless powder, rapid-fire artillery, and magazine rifles, and the employment of machine guns, albeit in small quantities, the telephone as well as the telegraph, and railroads for strategic transport – all this imparted an intense, prolonged nature to armed struggle. The achievement of a decisive aim – the defeat of the enemy's main forces – was possible only as a result of conducting a series of engagements requiring special preparation and extended over time and space. Each engagement pursued its particular aims, which ensued from the overall aim of the armed struggle in a theater of military operations. The problem of controlling combat operations by several army large formations, consisting of all combat arms outfitted with increasingly more combat equipment, was quite apparent. This problem was resolved in the Russian Army even before the commencement of the First World War by organizing *front* directorates. The French and German commands arrived at a similar solution during this war, organizing army group directorates.

In the First World War, the massive size of opposing armed forces reached unprecedented proportions. The developed railroad network made it possible to deploy each state's armed forces strategically on a broad front. Although in nineteenth century wars it was already necessary to divide the armed forces into several independent armies, during the First World War such a division of armed forces was developed further. In the Western Theater, the French and British deployed seven armies on a 340-kilometer front. The Germans also deployed as many armies in this theater. On the Eastern Front, the Germans, together with Austro-Hungarian forces, deployed five armies and one army group, while the Russians deployed six armies. During the war, the number of armies on the Russo-German front almost doubled.

The largest engagements of the first period of the 1914–18 war (in the east – in Eastern Prussia and the Battle of Galicia; in the west – the border engagements and the Battle of the Marne) were strategic in nature. However, in essence they were predominantly army operations conducted independently. *Front* operations became widespread in the Russian Army only in 1916, and army group operations in the West only by the end of the First World War.

The attempt to achieve decisive war aims in a short time – the complete defeat of the enemy's armed forces by extensive maneuver operations – experienced insurmountable difficulties. Neither the forces nor their leaders were ready to resolve their assigned missions under altered armed combat conditions. New objective factors, such as armies of massive numerical strength, the great costs of operations, enormous requirements for ammunition and other materiel, increase in scope of the armed struggle, especially its duration, and a number of other reasons, were not fully understood or considered. Inadequate forces and means, as well as materiel resources necessary to resolve strategic missions confronting the warring countries in the initial period of the First World War, the slow shift of industry from a peacetime to a wartime footing, and the inability to wage armed combat under altered conditions led to the stabilization of fronts and the formation of a continuous positional defense line, resting, on the one hand, on the sea and, on the other hand, on the borders of a neutral state.

During the First World War, the emergence of a continuous armed combat front was accompanied by force echelonment into the depth and development of a multi-belted defense, with allocation of large reserves to important axes. If under conditions of maneuver actions the content of operations was determined by an attempt of both sides to conduct an offensive jointly and, by maneuvering, to strike the enemy, then the shift to positional combat forms necessitated preparation and conduct of a penetration of the enemy defense as the first and most important task of planned offensive operations. Seeking methods for resolving this problem, each side improved existing means and introduced new combat means into their forces' armaments, thereby attempting to find new combat methods under altered conditions.

The task of penetrating a continuous defensive front was not an end in and of itself. It was associated with more profound missions, namely defeating a large enemy operational grouping and capturing important objectives, regions, and lines in the depth of the defense, which would create favorable conditions for subsequent combat operations. However, the insurmountability of the defense increased more rapidly than the change in the methods of penetration or the increase in ability to conduct the offensive into the depth of the defense.

To overcome a deeply echeloned defense, the attacking side was compelled to conduct a series of battles to capture defensive positions and belts successively; to maneuver committing fresh reserves from the depth to strengthen the shock force and replace divisions exhausted in an engagement lasting many days; and to shift from one engagement to another without interruption in combat actions or with a pause necessary to create a new grouping, which could once again ensure achievement of superiority over the enemy on the attack axis.

At the same time, the defender, conducting intense battles to hold his defensive positions and belts and intensifying his resistance power by maneuvering army and *front* (army group) reserves to the region where enemy penetration had been observed, organized and conducted powerful counterstrokes against the attacker's combat formation, attempting to stabilize the front on a new defensive line. In the overwhelming majority of cases, an ongoing offensive was thwarted as a result of inadequate forces and means to suppress the defense, and of the defender's dynamic maneuver during the operation and counterstrokes by reserves which had just arrived from the depth of the defense. Essentially, the problem of penetrating a deeply echeloned defense and developing a tactical penetration into an operational penetration was not resolved during the First World War.

Nevertheless, it can be ascertained that in armed struggle which developed over enormous expanses during the First World War, features of the operation as a form of action inherent to specific large formations such as armies and *fronts* (army groups) began to appear distinctly.

The basic content of an operation was the engagement as a totality of army formation combat actions. An operation was composed of a long period of preparation for penetration, during which the enemy defense was reconnoitered, the staging area for the offensive prepared, the necessary force grouping, taking up a specific operational structure, created, and materiel and personnel reserves gathered. An increasingly greater quantity of means of suppression – artillery and aviation, and then chemical weapons and tanks – was used for the penetration. These means were massed on selected offensive axes, and then introduced into the engagement by various methods. The necessity of achieving the overall aim conditioned the organization of painstaking cooperation among forces and means, formations and large formations, designated to conduct the engagement. Troop control became complex, army combat actions were increasingly more coordinated, and the prerequisites for conducting *front* operations appeared.

Inadequate armed forces development, poor combat capabilities of operational large formations, and the backwardness of military theory hindered resolution of the problem of operational development of the penetration into the depth of the defense. First World War operations usually bore a linear character, although linear forms of combat actions contradicted new phenomena of armed struggle. This lack of accord resulted in the great spatial scope of combat actions and insignificant results.

Attempts, however, to employ artillery and aviation massively to strike the enemy defense more deeply, and to use cavalry and tanks to develop the penetration into the depth attested all the same that by the end of the First World War the rudiments of deep forms of the operation were, to a certain degree, objectively expressed.

The operation developed considerably during the Civil War in the USSR, and even more so during the Second World War.

The appearance of new combat means in mass quantities, and the considerable improvement of those which existed earlier, conditioned the further development of the operation and the enrichment of its forms, which, in turn, led to great qualitative changes in separate combat arms and armed forces services, especially by the beginning of the Second World War.

As a result of completely outfitting rifle forces with varied weapons and equipment, their fire and shock power, mobility, and maneuverability increased sharply. Infantry had, to a great degree, developed its ability to fight under any terrain and weather conditions, day and night, and, co-operating in battle with all other combat arms and aviation, defeat the enemy in close battle. It was best able of all forces to hold defensive terrain stubbornly. Under modern conditions, rifle formations have great independence in conducting combat actions and can resolve large-scale tactical and operational missions in battles and operations.

Transforming rifle formations into powerful, mobile, and maneuverable combined-arms organisms, and (the main thing) reinforcing combined-arms armies with an enormous number of technical combat means, especially artillery and tanks, have made it possible to have a smaller number of rifle formations as part of army large formations than in First World War armies. All this has resulted in some narrowing of large operational formation combat sectors in comparison with First World War operations, which is especially noticeable when studying Great Patriotic War operations.

The increase in fire power, rapid fire, and range of artillery guns and mortars, together with the growth in mobility and maneuverability of all artillery systems and improvement of fire control equipment and methods, made artillery the main fire shock force under modern combat conditions. The appearance of new means with great destructive force has in no way diminished artillery's role at present as the principal means for penetrating a deeply echeloned enemy defense and accompanying attacking forces. The presence of artillery formations having great fire power and mobility makes it possible to maneuver artillery extensively and quickly to create decisive fire superiority on the most important offensive and defensive axes, creating necessary conditions for improving combat efficiency and achieving large-scale operational results in an operation.

The quantitative and qualitative growth of tanks resulted in armor and mechanized forces being used during the Second World War not only as a means for accompanying infantry, but also as part of highly mobile operational formations and large formations. Under contemporary conditions, these forces, on the basis of improved armaments and an increase in operational mobility, are still, to a great degree, capable of conducting independent combat actions in the operational depth at considerably greater distances from combined-arms large formations than previously. Mass participation of armor forces, in combination with aviation, accords great scope to modern operations, and dynamism and swift development to combat actions.

Aviation, whose development proceeded especially swiftly, had already been designated an independent armed forces service by the beginning of the Second World War. It consisted of various types: fighter, bomber, ground attack, transport, and special aviation. Aviation was one of the most powerful factors affecting the nature of armed struggle and imparting new characteristics to modern operations.

The increase in flight speed and altitude of modern airplanes, together with the improvement of aviation weapons and self-piloting instruments, makes it possible to increase the radius of action for air forces, conduct intense air battles and engagements against enemy aviation, and carry out missions with great effectiveness in the interest of assisting ground and naval forces. The organizational arrangement of aviation into formations and operational large formations consisting of various aviation formations makes it possible to conduct combat actions not only jointly with ground or naval forces, but also independently.

Increased aviation capabilities resulted in the emergence of air-assault forces. During Second World War operations, air assaults were already landed on tactical and larger scales. The modern development of airborne forces opened prospects for conducting airborne operations, considerably widening the scale of armed struggle.

In connection with the rapid development of aviation, the significance of protecting forces and rear area objectives from enemy air strikes has sharply increased, which, in turn, has led to the rapid growth of air defense methods and means. Dynamic actions by air defense forces and means have become a typical feature of every modern operation, and the successful resolution of air defense missions affects, to a considerable degree, the success of operational plans.

Engineer forces play a considerable role in modern operations; offensive tempos and defensive stability depend, to a great degree, on their efforts. Various auxiliary technical and special forces are appearing in increasingly greater number in formations and large formations.

Thus, in contrast to the uniform composition of First World War armies and *fronts*, consisting basically of purely tactical infantry and cavalry formations, organizationally part of army corps, and a small number of artillery reinforcement units, during the Second World War operational large formations of much more complex and varied organization operated in the armed forces of all countries, which imparted an especially intense nature and enormous scope to operations as a form of armed struggle.

Second World War experience clearly demonstrated that the operation was an increasingly complex manifestation of armed struggle – the totality of various combat actions of operational large formations, united by a single plan, pursuing concrete aims of defeating an enemy grouping on an operational axis, and having operational or strategic significance. Under modern conditions, operations are characterized by mass employment of a variety of combat equipment and vehicles, and by wide scope with respect to both space and time, and to the quantity of materiel expended to conduct them.

The Great Patriotic War not only enriched operational forms, researched and generalized in the prewar years, but also gave rise to and defined operational characteristics of various types and scales.

Regardless of type and scale, the operation, as an objective phenomenon, has an entire series of features and natural regularities inherent only to it, distinguishing it from battle on the one hand, and from a military campaign and war as a whole on the other. This circumstance also makes it possible to examine an operation within the framework of a relatively independent scientific theory, that is, the theory of operational art.

It is apparent that, under conditions of the machine era of warfare, the limits of an operation, as a manifestation of armed struggle, are determined by the size of the armed forces participating in the operation, its aims and operational objectives, and the results, whose repetitiveness gives us the right to determine several law-based characteristics and add this phenomenon to the investigated field of armed struggle.

If we examine operations with respect to the composition of the armed forces used to conduct them, we can divide them into army and *front* operations, and operations of a group of *fronts*. The aim of these operations is, in the first order, to defeat large enemy groupings having operational or strategic significance, that is, those capable of conducting their own operations. An operational aim may also be to capture operationally important regions and positions. Most often these aims coincide, since the enemy usually creates large operational groupings to defend such regions and positions.

Under modern conditions, an offensive operation conducted independently by the forces of a single army is a rather rare, atypical event, for in this instance an army can resolve limited missions. The Great Patriotic War provides a few examples of such operations. They either were conducted on small independent operational axes (the April 1944 offensive operation of Separate Coastal Army in Crimea, and some others), or were to achieve partial operational aims, such as seizure or elimination of a bridgehead, capture of some important objective in the immediate operational depth of the enemy defense, or delivery of a retaliatory strike. Army defensive operations can be distinguished by greater independence.

During the last war, both offensive and defensive army operations were usually conducted within the framework of a *front* operation. In this instance, army operations achieved the greatest results and, in addition, during a *front* offensive they created favorable conditions for conducting successive operations. The objective of an army operation was most often part of an enemy grouping operating on a given axis, as well as regions and operational positions having great significance for the successful development of the *front* operation. Army operational aims were achieved within relatively restricted temporal and spatial limits. *Front* operations grew immeasurably in comparison with operations during the First World War, and had greater scale than army operations with respect to participating forces and means, as well as greater temporal and spatial scope and more decisive results. The objectives of such an operation may have not only operational, but also strategic significance, and its results may effect a change in the situation on the entire strategic axis and, consequently, on the course of the campaign. The result of such an operation, whatever it is, depends on the *front* large formation's composition, which can change considerably.

The results of combat actions of air force or naval formations and large formations and airborne forces can be fully used within the framework of a *front* operation. Therefore, a *front* operation is not simply the sum of several simultaneous and successive army operations, but a more complex phenomenon, in which the actions of large formations and formations of different armed forces services achieve a result which considerably exceeds the capabilities of these large formations, were they to operate independently.

Finally, operations conducted by several *front* large formations whose efforts are coordinated with respect to aims and time are the largest, with respect to scale, and most effective, with respect to results. These operations are essentially capable of not only changing the course of a campaign, but also predetermining the subsequent outcome of the war; this was exemplified by the results of the Stalingrad, Kursk and Berlin operations and a number of others.

The results of an operation determine its significance to a greater degree than other factors. Sometimes a successfully conducted and concluded army or *front* operation can create a more favorable situation on a strategic axis or in a theater of war than an operation conducted by larger forces, but which has not been developed.

Thus, the Korsun-Shevchenskiy operation of 1st and 2d Ukrainian Fronts, which resulted in the defeat of a large enemy operational grouping, was, nevertheless, not considered a strategic operation.

On the other hand, the Petsamo–Kirkenes operation, despite the limited scale of forces employed, achieved rather large-scale strategic results.

However, inasmuch as the expected result depends, to the greatest degree, on the quantity of forces and means allocated for conducting an operation, the possibility arises to classify operations mainly according to this specific indicator. For example, operations by a group of *fronts* are relied on to achieve a result capable of affecting the course of the campaign, and some-times of the war as a whole; thus, these operations, as a rule, have strategic significance. The Iassy–Kishinev operation of 2d and 3d Ukrainian Fronts, and the Berlin operation of a group of *fronts* were just such operations.

As a result of conducting each of the above-mentioned operations, strategic enemy groupings were defeated. In addition, the successful conduct of the Iassy–Kishinev operation resulted in the withdrawal of Romania and Bulgaria – two of Nazi Germany's allies – from the war; the Berlin operation forced Fascist Germany to capitulate quickly, that is, both these operations had large-scale political consequences and major strategic results. Generally, such operations pursue the aim of defeating the main enemy grouping on a strategic axis and ensuring a fundamental military-political change in the situation on a given strategic axis, and sometimes in the entire theater of military operations.

If the principal content of an army or *front* operation is the engagement, usually developing in the operational sector of a given large formation, then there can be no single engagement within the framework of an operation of a group of *fronts*, for each of the *front* large formations or large formations of other armed forces services can begin an engagement independently, and only during the development of the operation are the efforts of the *fronts*, coordinated by the general operational plan, directly combined. Operations of a group of *fronts* are usually implemented according to plan and under the leadership of the Supreme High Command.

So-called joint operations, conducted on coastal axes in cooperation with ground, air, and naval forces, and with participation of airborne and air defense forces, most often have strategic significance.

For the sake of research convenience and practical realization of operational regularities, joint operations can be examined according to types of combat actions and types of armed forces conducting a given operation.

Offensive operations correspond to the most decisive type of combat actions, the offensive. The enemy can be completely defeated only by conducting offensive operations with decisive aims. However, by nature it is true that in a number of cases it is also necessary to conduct defensive operations on separate axes. The principal aim of defensive operations always includes repelling the offensive of superior enemy forces by inflicting upon him the greatest losses possible in personnel and combat equipment.

Defensive operations may be undertaken to hold important operational-strategic objectives, regions, and lines, and to gain time necessary to regroup and create conditions to support shifting to a counteroffensive.

The counteroffensive, as an operation with inherent distinguishing features, is a special type of offensive, essentially different from the conventional offensive operation. The counteroffensive is an operational-strategic phenomenon, arising during transition from the defense to a decisive offensive along a strategic axis or in a theater of war. This transition usually occurs in a situation of fierce fighting for operational initiative on land and in the air, as well as at sea in coastal regions. The counteroffensive pursues the aim of not only defeating the enemy's main forces engaged on a given axis, but also creating conditions to shift to a decisive offensive. Therefore, if offensive and defense operations can be conducted by large formations of any scale, beginning with an army and ending with several *fronts*, then a counteroffensive is most often possible on the scale of several *fronts*, although it can sometimes be conducted by the forces of a single *front*. An army-type large formation cannot conduct a counteroffensive independently, since it does not have adequate forces.

The withdrawal operation is a special type of operation. It is usually conducted after unsuccessful defensive actions, when, under pressure of superior enemy forces, it is necessary to abandon one's own territory so as to retain forces, occupy more favorable lines in the depth of one's disposition, and create a new strong grouping for subsequent operations.

During the Second World War, each of the armed forces' main services – ground forces, air forces, and naval forces – to a certain degree conducted independent operations, resolving operational missions usually within the framework of a larger-scale joint operation. Sometimes these independent operations acquired strategic significance.

Swift penetration of a prepared enemy defense and a deep strike against his operational formation require not only that ground forces deliver a powerful attack, but also that aviation be effective to a considerable depth of the enemy deployment, and that it continuously assist its attacking forces for the duration of the entire operation.

An increase in offensive tempos by intensifying the shock force to encircle and destroy large defensive groupings was achieved most effectively when resistance by defending forces was broken by attack not only from the front, but also from the rear. This ability to deliver attacks from the rear was ensured by landing airborne forces in the operational rear (and, during operations along the sea coast, by landing amphibious assault forces).

The landing of airborne and amphibious assaults requires that enemy resistance be overcome in the air and at sea. The actions of these assault forces in the enemy rear take place during intense fighting against his ground forces, aviation, and naval forces. The totality of engagements unfolding in the air, at sea, and on land, subordinated to a single plan and to the interests of achieving an overall aim, provide us with complete justification in stating that the landing of large airborne and amphibious assaults and their combat actions in the enemy rear are operations, each of which has its own specific features and relatively independent significance.

The scope of amphibious assaults and airborne operations can be widened to dimensions in which they will be able to resolve independently a particular strategic mission, for example, opening a new combat front in a new theater, capturing large islands, etc.

The landing of a large amphibious assault in the enemy rear requires considerable efforts by the navy and aviation, and often a simultaneous landing of airborne assaults. Therefore, an amphibious assault operation is a joint operation of ground, naval, and air forces. The surprise of an assault landing, penetration of a coastal area's anti-assault defense on a wide front, gaining of superiority in the air and at sea in the region where the operation is being conducted, and rapid establishment of cooperation between the amphibious assault, air forces, and ground forces attacking the formation are all necessary conditions – as Second World War experience shows – on whose basis the greatest success of amphibious assault operations was achieved.

The anti-assault operation is also associated with joint operations. The necessity of continuously protecting the coastal flank of ground forces is completely obvious. The anti-assault defense of a coastal area is organized for this purpose, for which part of the forces or the main *front* and naval forces are allocated. Their main mission is to repel an amphibious assault landing and destroy enemy forces which have landed ashore.

In the case where defensive forces are able to deliver powerful strikes against an enemy assault force in ports where they are being loaded and on their sea crossing, the scope of an anti-assault operation increases significantly. A defensive engagement of ground forces in a coastal area anti-assault defense, in which naval and air forces also are taking part, will be only the concluding stage of an anti-assault operation.

Among new operational phenomena emerging during the Second World War are independent air force operations. It was quite clear that ground and naval forces could operate successfully only with air superiority. Air forces play a major role in gaining this superiority, destroying enemy aviation at its airfields and in air engagements. Air superiority is achieved by a series of air engagements and strikes against enemy air bases, comprising in their totality an independent air force operation. Inflicting substantive losses on the main enemy air grouping creates a favorable correlation of air forces, ensures the most favorable conditions for operations by one's own ground, naval, and air forces, and restricts the actions of enemy aviation. It is necessary to bear in mind, however, that aviation, having an exceptionally high degree of maneuverability, can quickly concentrate its efforts on decisive axes, and if appropriate measures are not taken, then the correlation of air forces at a specific moment may change as a result of intensification of enemy air forces, and the air superiority gained will be lost. Therefore, the struggle for air superiority and maintaining it are indissoluble, and are a constant mission for aviation in any operations.

Modern aviation's great radius of actions creates conditions for conducting independent air operations to hit important objectives or enemy groupings located in his deep rear area. Such operations as air operations to destroy strategic enemy objectives and to thwart amphibious and airborne assault operations may also not be associated directly with operations prepared by ground or naval forces. Positive results of such air operations will significantly influence the overall course of armed struggle, thereby predetermining subsequent success of ground and naval operations, especially if they are correctly coordinated.

In naval combat operations there can also be independent operations, whose aim is to gain superiority at sea or to weaken enemy naval forces considerably; operations to destroy enemy naval forces at sea and at bases; operations to blockade straits and enemy naval bases or to penetrate a naval blockade set up by the enemy; operations to disrupt his maritime lines of communication; and operations to protect one's own maritime communications.

Independent naval operations require the organization of efforts of various naval and air forces. As with operations on ground forces axes, these are the totality of a series of engagements and battles, as well as maneuver undertaken at sea in their interests, united by an overall plan.

These are the principal types of operations, objectively arising under conditions of modern armed struggle.

The nature and forms of combat operations change in connection with changes in combat means. This itself is also conditioned by changes in the nature of operations. The postwar development of artillery, tanks, and aviation makes it possible to strike the enemy at a greater depth than was possible during the Second World War. The appearance in army weaponry of new combat means with enormous destructive force, and their deployment in modern operations make it possible to conduct operations with greater scope and with even more decisive results.

Under the above-mentioned conditions, shock force and high offensive tempos result in sharp and rapid changes in the situation, which increases the significance of dynamism and surprise actions, and the struggle for the initiative.

The increase in depth of offensive operations is a logically natural result of the increase in depth of the operational formation of defending enemy forces and the increase in range of combat means.

To achieve the aim of a modern offensive operation, a *front* is required to defeat not only the opposing operational grouping echeloned at a depth of 120–150 kilometers, but also operational and sometimes strategic reserves approaching from the depth, that is, march formations whose depth may be as much as 200 kilometers. This requires that *front* forces continually conduct an offensive to a depth measuring hundreds of kilometers.

As experience teaches, the most decisive results in offensive operations are achieved by encircling and completely destroying large enemy groupings, while simultaneously attempting to develop the offensive into the depth to defeat his approaching reserves piecemeal before they can concentrate and form a sufficiently powerful new force grouping.

The enemy will strive for defensive stability by preparing defensive belts in the depth beforehand. The latter can be occupied in advance by defensive forces, or hurriedly occupied during the operation by forces withdrawing under the attacker's blows, reserves advancing from the depth, or forces regrouping from axes not under attack. Consequently, when organizing an operation it is necessary to be prepared to overcome increasing enemy resistance in accordance with the expected nature of his actions and possible conditions.

Success of offensive operations under modern conditions depends, even more than in the past, on how swiftly superiority in forces and means over the enemy is achieved on the main axes during the offensive.

The duration of an offensive operation depends directly on its tempos. To deprive the enemy defense of the ability to intensify forces during the struggle for the tactical zone, where engineer preparation of the terrain is most developed and the density of forces and means is highest, it is necessary to penetrate this zone with the greatest speed possible for the concrete conditions, simultaneously striking enemy reserves before they arrive and intensify resistance of forces in the tactical defense echelon.

Second World War operational experience demonstrates that this problem was resolved completely successfully. As a result of a precisely organized and effectively conducted artillery and aviation offensive, a continuous defensive front was penetrated in a short period. Commitment of mobile groups into the penetration on the first day of battle made it possible to develop it to the entire depth of the tactical defense zone and advance up to 16–20 kilometers a day, and sometimes even more. This tempo was successfully maintained, and was often considerably exceeded in the final days of an operation. Offensive tempos were lower on separate axes only when the enemy, having freedom to maneuver reserves, was able to deliver strong counterstrokes.

The contemporary level of development of suppression means, and the high degree of force motorization are creating prerequisites for penetrating the entire tactical defense zone even more swiftly on the first day of the operation, despite a certain increase in defensive stability and increased maneuverability of its forces and means.

To realize these capabilities, however, measures are necessary which will make it possible to achieve precise and continuous cooperation among forces and the entire set of varied combat equipment participating in the penetration. The achievement of surprise and destructiveness of the preliminary strike, and the securing of freedom of maneuver for one's forces for the duration of the operation, especially those designated to strengthen the blows, play a very substantive role.

Consequently, resolving the problem of offensive tempos reduces to the art of organizing combat actions in an operation, based on operational foresight of the most probable development of the operation, and to assurance of stable and continuous troop control during the operation.

An attack against a weak area of the defense along a high-speed axis to vulnerable areas of the defending grouping, together with decisive massing of forces and means to deliver a powerful blow against the entire depth of the defense's operational formation, creates conditions for the successful defeat of the main defensive forces.

In turn, the rapid defeat of the designated grouping makes the subsequent defeat of deep operational and strategic defensive reserves advancing to the offensive sector easier. If the forces of the attacking large formation are calculated correctly and combat operations against the new grouping can begin swiftly, without spending time to regroup, then the attacker has grounds for not only maintaining, but even increasing offensive tempos.

The duration of an offensive operation under modern conditions tends to be somewhat reduced in comparison with that of Second World War operations, because of significant reductions in time for regrouping during an operation, and for overcoming enemy resistance in defensive belts in the operational depth. Organization of combat actions from the march, which ensures seizure of defensive belts in the operational depth, has decisive significance.

While during an offensive operation there is a real possibility of planning offensive tempos and duration, the duration of a defensive operation cannot be precisely determined beforehand, since it is impossible to specify the temporal framework of a defensive engagement. The duration of a defensive engagement is particularly affected by the capability for maneuvering forces and the rapidity of strengthening efforts to consolidate the defense on the most important axes or creating a counterstroke grouping. Under conditions where the tempo of transferring defensive reserves significantly exceeds the advance tempo of attacking forces, the defender will be able, to a certain degree, to increase the duration of the engagement, forcing the attacker to capture each defensive belt in succession. Moreover, the defense will gain time to introduce into the engagement forces at the disposal of a higher authority.

Under modern conditions, freedom of movement is acquiring exceptionally great significance. It is achieved, first and foremost, by reliable air defense of forces and use of the terrain's protective properties against enemy atomic strikes. Under modern conditions, the constant threat of enemy atomic attack requires the organization of anti-atomic defense; otherwise, force combat actions will not achieve necessary swiftness.

Organizing cooperation and control facilitates the employment of radar means of detection and guidance. In addition, however, it is necessary to take into account that the enemy's employment of these very means poses most keenly the question of measures for combatting his radar reconnaissance and his organized radio and radar jamming.

In conclusion, it is necessary to emphasize once again that, under modern conditions, a relatively new phenomenon of armed struggle – the operation – continues to develop and become more complex. Armed forces development on the basis of the continuous growth of military equipment extremely complicates armed struggle, and provides it with a prolonged character and great intensity. The final result of armed struggle – the complete defeat of enemy armed forces – can be achieved only as a result of many repeated blows, each of which is distinguished with respect to aim, scale, nature of employed forces and means, temporal and spatial scope, and results. Objective phenomena of armed struggle such as the battle, operation, campaign, and war as a whole, with their inherent natural regularities, are distinguished according to aims and results. The content and facets of these phenomena are not, however, constant; they change, depending on the level of armed forces development and conditions of armed struggle. For convenience of investigating and realizing the natural regularities inherent in each of the above-mentioned phenomena, the current need has arisen to categorize them and develop appropriate theories.

The division of military art into a theory of strategy and theory of tactics, which existed up to the First World War, became obsolete. In connection with combat operations of large operational formations giving rise to a new phenomenon in forms of armed struggle which did not fit into the framework of either strategy or tactics, a special theory – the theory of preparing and conducting operations, that is, the theory of operational art – was created in Soviet military art. This theory's appearance and its further development is completely natural and logical; moreover, it was successfully verified by the practical experience of the Soviet Armed Forces, especially during the Great Patriotic War.

Under modern conditions, operational art as the study of operations, together with strategy, is acquiring very important significance for revealing and realizing in practice the natural regularities of operations, and for commanding large operational formations.

Soviet operational art reflects the objective reality of armed struggle, and is being developed and enriched continually; operational forms are also becoming enriched, and their organization more complex. Success in conducting modern operations lies in the high moral-combat qualities of Soviet soldiers, further improvement of army expertise of generals and officers, improvement of the qualities of combat equipment, and knowledge of equipment and ability to master it.

Operations, as the basic form of conducting military actions under modern conditions of armed struggle, in their totality and consistency lay the foundation for successfully conducting a campaign.

Knowledge of natural operational regularities, mastery of theory, and development of skills for its successful preparation and conduct are one of the most important steps in the growth of military expertise of generals, admirals, and officers of the Soviet Army and Navy.

NOTES

1. A. Tsvetkov, "Operatsiya, yeye sushchnost' i znacheniye v sovremennoy vooruzhennoy bor'be," *Voyennaya mysl'* [Military thought], 3 (1955), pp. 39–52.

Operational Art as an Integral Part of Soviet Military Art

COLONEL V. VASIL'YEV[1]

Over the centuries-old history of the existence of a class society, forms of armed conflict have changed many times, and continue to change even now. At the basis of these changes are objective conditions of society's material life and, above all, the development of its productive forces, as a measure of whose growth means of armed conflict correspondingly develop, with its forms simultaneously becoming more improved and complex. Military operations are encompassing an increasingly wider expanse; not only forces fighting on fronts, but also the populations of the warring sides are participating in armed conflict on increasing scales. It can be said that in our time, in connection with the appearance of new means of mass destruction which, undoubtedly, will lead to further sophistication of forms of armed conflict and an even greater disappearance of the boundary between front and rear, military art is entering a new, higher phase of development.

Over an extended period, while the level of the development of production and the nature of productive relations were inadequate to create mass armies and their rears, and to supply them with everything necessary during a prolonged armed conflict, wars bore a local character, and their outcome was often determined as a result of a single or several general engagements. The overall plan for waging war, the selection of the time and place for conducting general engagements, and the quantity of forces allocated to participate were determined by strategic considerations and the degree of readiness of a given country for war.

As a result of the relatively small size of armies, the poor technical outfitting of forces, and the inadequate might of armaments, general engagements developed in limited terrain sectors. Forces lacked adequate mobility or capability for rapid restructuring during an engagement. Therefore, it was very important before the commencement of the engagement to select a structural force formation which would provide the ability to intensify efforts without serious restructuring until the end of the engagement, thereby ensuring an outcome to one's advantage. In other words, the outcome of an engagement depended, to a very significant degree, on how well the commander of one of the two sides was able to select and implement the correct tactical plan of action for a given engagement. Strategy's role was expressed in the overall leadership of the war and, mainly, in the correct use of tactical success achieved; tactics were the direct executor of strategic plans.

Thus, in the past, the division of military art into strategy and tactics was completely logical. The development of its theoretical foundations, as well as independent tactical and strategic theories, was conducted accordingly.

The increase in the scope of armed conflict, conditioned by the rapid development of productive forces, led to sophistication in its methods and resulted in the appearance of a new form of struggle, that is, the military operation, which was a set of combat actions and, above all, the totality of engagements and battles conducted simultaneously or successively according to a single plan, directed toward the defeat of a large enemy grouping. Accordingly, changes also took place in the organizational structure of the armed forces. Large operational formations such as the army and *front* appeared on the battlefield.

Operational art could not be born in the early stages of the development of military art, but appeared only when mass armies appeared in the area of struggle and society's productive forces were able to provide them with everything necessary during a war, when conditions for conducting armed conflict qualitatively changed, and when it had acquired new, more complex forms.

The emergence of a new form of struggle in military art – the operation – naturally required the creation of a corresponding theory – the theory of operational art. Thus, operational art as the theory and practice of preparing and conducting operations, was a reflection of objectively existing reality; it emerged as a result of the entire course of military art's historical development.

If the tasks of strategy before had consisted of selecting the time for the commencement of a war, depending upon the readiness of one's armed forces, and determining the main attack axis, quantity of forces and means, and place and time to conduct individual general engagements, and if tactics resolved the problem of planning and directing troop actions during these engagements, then strategy did not now deal with individual engagements, but determined the aims, forces, means, time, and place for conducting large operations interconnected by an overall war or campaign plan. The resolution of the problems of planning operations and troop leadership during such a war was assigned to operational art. It remained for tactics to resolve problems of troop leadership during the preparation and conduct of separate battles.

Shifting to an examination of the content of the principles of the theory of operational art, it should be said that, as any genuine scientific theory, it represents the generalization of experience in preparing and conducting operations amassed by armed forces under specific historical conditions. Basing itself on this experience, as well as using the latest achievements in various fields of science and technology, this theory should provide a substantiated prognosis of future development of operational art, and illuminate a path for its practice.

The theory of operational art was not created all at once, and its development cannot cease. We will try to trace how conditions for conducting operations have changed, and how this has affected the development of the theory of operational art.

The operation, as a new phenomenon in military art, had already appeared in the wars of the last century.

The evolution of the operation as an objective phenomenon was summarized quite completely in Lieutenant General A. Tsvetkov's article.[2] Therefore, without going into detail on this question, it should only be mentioned that some elements of the operation had already appeared during the Fatherland War of 1812, during combat actions to rout Napoleon's Army in Western Europe, and during the Russo-Japanese War. However, its most characteristic features were clearly expressed only during the First World War. But even during this war the operation still did not receive full development, mainly because right up to the concluding stage of the war the opposing sides were unable to use their available means to turn tactical success into operational success. Thus, despite the large quantity of cavalry in the armies of the warring states, they were used to resolve only tactical missions. At the end of the war there appeared a new combat arm – tank forces, which could have been a powerful means for developing operational success. However, firstly, the war ended before sufficient experience could be accumulated in their combat employment, and, secondly, the Allied military command was unable to assess this new weapon or develop methods for employing it.

Soviet military art took into account the experience of the First World War and already used it during the Civil War. Since at that time young Soviet Russia's industry did not have the ability to mass produce tanks, the issue of the development of operational success was resolved by creating large formations, and then large operational cavalry formations in the form of cavalry armies, which were a means for developing tactical success into operational success and supporting the conduct of operations to great depth with decisive aims.

The operational use of large, highly mobile, and, for that time, powerful cavalry formations for actions in the enemy's deep rear, in combination with attacks by rifle formations advancing from the front, changed the nature of Soviet Army operations, which led to a sharp increase in offensive tempos and mobility of combat operations.

After the Civil War, on the basis of taking into account its experience and previous war experience, the formulation of operational art into an independent theory commenced in Soviet military art. In the mid-1930s, the theory of the deep operation was created, and it received further development during the Great Patriotic War and in the postwar period.

The most important prerequisite for the creation of this theory was the strengthening of the Soviet state as a result of the correct course by the Communist Party and the Soviet government for the industrialization of the country, which made it possible to provide our Armed Forces with all modern technical combat means.

The Great Patriotic War and Second World War were a new stage in the development of the theory of operational art. During these wars the air forces developed especially swiftly, and forces were equipped with more tanks, which made it possible to create not only traditional formations, but also large operational armored and mechanized formations, and to increase considerably the quantitative and qualitative outfitting of forces with artillery. Rocket artillery emerged and was widely employed on battlefields, the function of the navy broadened, mainly in the area of its cooperation with ground forces and aviation, and airborne and national air defense forces began to play an increasingly greater role during combat actions.

All this was most widely reflected in the theory of operational art. During the Great Patriotic War such issues as preparation and conduct of airborne and amphibious-assault operations, operational cooperation, and troop support had already been developed quite fully; the content of the concept of forms of conducting operations, operational maneuver, and methods of developing operational success broadened considerably. Preparation and conduct of a large offensive operation by the forces of several *fronts,* a very important problem of operational art, received theoretical and practical resolution, as a result of which the strategic situation in the theater of military operations often underwent significant changes. Such operations were conducted by the Soviet Armed Forces for the first time in the history of military art. In view of the great scope of the results of such operations, they received the name "strategic offensive operations."

Finally, during the Great Patriotic War there emerged new types of operations and associated concepts in the theory of operational art, such as the air and air defense operation, and joint operations involving ground forces, air forces, and the navy.

After the Second World War, a new concept appeared in our operational art: the anti-assault operation, which very much widened the content of combat operations for the defense of maritime axes and increased their dynamism. The content of the struggle to win and maintain air superiority was much more fully developed. In addition, other problems of operational art were also fully or partially resolved.

Such, in most general terms, was the path covered by the development of the theory of operational art in Soviet military art until the present.

Looking into the future, it can be said that prospects for further development of the theory of operational art are very extensive. The appearance of weapons of mass destruction, rapid development of technical combat means, increase in aviation speed and range, improvement of tank armaments, and further mechanization of armies is leading to an augmentation in the scope of offensive operations and increased defensive stability. In addition, the depth of force deployment in the defense must be increased and the ability to shift forces swiftly from the defense to a counteroffensive must be broadened; operational art is once again confronted with issues of troop control, and a number of other problems are being raised.

Because the framework of this article does not allow us to discuss these problems concretely, we can only briefly express our opinion on the probable paths of further development of operational art.

In our opinion, this development will proceed along the path of both improving existing forms and methods of conducting operations, and, especially, finding new means, which will have a greater effect on conditions for conducting armed struggle. Changes in these conditions may be expressed, as already mentioned, by an increase in scope and tempos of conducting offensive operations, mobility of combat actions in the offense and defense, the emergence of more frequent meeting battles and meeting engagements, an increase in the significance of the factor of surprise, complexity of troop control and cooperation, an increase in the quantity and complexity of measures for all types of troop support in an operation, and an increase in the significance of reliable security and defense of the rear.

In examining the evolution of the theory of operational art, it is easy to observe that both its content and the very concept "operation" have gradually broadened and become more complex, and this is completely logical.

In truth, if we can already observe an army operation in a sufficiently clearly expressed form at the very beginning of the First World War, and if its emergence dates to an even earlier period, the *front* operation only began to develop during the First World War and acquired more or less precise expression only in the offensive of Southwestern Front forces in 1916.

Even then, however, it bore the character of the sum of separate army operations, since the organizing and guiding influence of a *front* had still not sufficiently appeared in it. And only during the Great Patriotic War did the *front* operation acquire its ultimate, fully independent character. In addition, during the last war the concept "operation" was broadened, since it included combat actions of several *fronts* conducted according to a single plan.

What, then, is the subject and content of the theory of operational art at the contemporary stage of its development?

To answer this question briefly, it can be said that the subject of study of the theory of operational art is the following: *the means*, that is, the operational formations of various armed forces services, and various formations [*soyedineniye* and *ob"yedineniye*] of combat arms temporarily detached from the reserve of the Supreme High Command to reinforce *fronts* and armies; and *the methods and forms* of preparing and conducting operations of all types and scales, depending on the conditions under which they are employed, that is, in concrete theaters of military operations and operational axes, the probable enemy in a particular theater, the time of year, etc.

We would like to state our point of view concerning a very important issue: we cannot agree with the very widely disseminated opinion that the operations of several *fronts* should be examined not within the theory of operational art, but within the theory of strategy, because the conduct of these operations during the last war frequently led to strategic results, and their leadership was executed by the Supreme High Command. In examining this issue, it is necessary to take into account the following circumstances. First: participation of several *fronts* is not always necessary to achieve strategic results in an operation. In separate cases, such a result may be achieved by even fewer forces; everything depends on the theater of military operations and the nature of the objectives having strategic significance in it. Second: under conditions of the Great Patriotic War, the Supreme High Command was able to execute direct operational control of several *fronts* because the war proceeded on one, albeit very wide, strategic front, which encompassed several adjoining and strategically interconnected theaters of military operations. One cannot help but take into consideration, however, that war in the future may develop simultaneously on two or more strategic fronts. Under these conditions the Supreme High Command will hardly be able to cast its attention on the direct leadership of individual operations, no matter how large, separated by enormous expanses. It can be assumed that direct leadership of such operations will possibly not be executed by the Supreme High Command. Third: leadership of even the largest-scale operations represents the resolution of a sum of problems of a narrow military nature, so that strategic leadership of the entire war, which emerges from state policies, cannot be restricted only to the resolution of purely military issues. Consequently, operational leadership is only one of the functions of wartime strategic leadership. This function basically consists of specifying the aims which should be achieved as a result of conducting an operation of strategic significance. Questions concerning the preparation and conduct of any operations should be examined not in the theory of strategy, but in the theory of operational art. Fourth: the concrete content itself of operations and their elements, such as the operational formation of forces and their make-up, force missions, forms of maneuver, and the nature of cooperation, are common for operations conducted by the forces of an army and *front* or several large *front* formations.

The methodology of analyzing operations is closely associated with their scales. Despite there being general foundations and principles for all operations, the operations of an army, *front*, and group of *fronts* have substantive differences, which arise from situational conditions. The larger the scale of the operation, the greater the degree of its singularity. In reality, army operations, even those conducted in a single theater of military operations, normally do not resemble one another. The matter is even more complex with *front* operations, and especially with operations by groups of *fronts*, which are more unique and in each separate case require a broad, innovative approach to solving a series of new problems. Inasmuch as the conditions and nature of all these operations will always be different, no stereotypical patterning is permissible in their organization and conduct.

The content of the theory of operational art at the contemporary stage of its development is determined by the wide variety of types of operations. It was mentioned earlier that the Second World War resulted in the appearance of a series of new concepts in operational art. In this connection, we will attempt to enumerate the basic types of operations modern armed forces can conduct, to determine the actual content of the theory of operational art.

As is known, the overwhelming majority of modern operations are conducted by the joint forces of various armed forces services in ground forces sectors of theaters of military operations. There is no need to prove that ground forces alone cannot conduct fully independent operations. They will always need powerful support from air forces and, in a number of cases on maritime axes, naval forces, protection by air defense forces and means against attacks by enemy aviation and pilotless assets, and often participation of airborne forces in an operation.

The same can be said about the navy when they conduct operations on the maritime expanses of theaters of military operations. However, this does not mean that naval combat operations can be conducted only jointly with ground forces. The contemporary situation does not exclude, and, on the contrary, even requires that the navy be able to organize and conduct independent operations on the open sea or ocean.

The role of air forces has also immeasurably increased. They are capable not only of actively participating in ground forces and naval operations, but also of independently conducting operations of strategic significance.

Despite the broad participation of different armed forces services in modern operations, when classifying the primary types of operations one should proceed from whichever armed forces service is playing the main role in the particular operation.

Guided by this, the following primary types of operations can be established. Above all, we will examine ground forces operations, or, more precisely, operations conducted on ground expanses of theaters of military operations. Among these are offensive and defensive operations, the counteroffensive, operations to break out of encirclement, and withdrawal operations. Joint operations conducted by ground forces with the navy may be assault and anti-assault operations to capture naval bases and support the maritime flank, etc.

Among naval operations are those to destroy an enemy navy at sea, disrupt his maritime communications, blockade an enemy navy at its bases, support one's own maritime communications, protect one's own naval bases against enemy naval strikes, and strike enemy bases and objectives located in coastal regions.

Operations to gain air superiority, destroy strategic enemy objectives and take-off areas for his pilotless assets, thwart transport and concentration of enemy forces, and prevent amphibious and airborne operations are among air force operations.

Airborne forces can conduct operations to capture and hold important objectives in the enemy rear until the arrival of ground forces, capture and hold bridgeheads on the sea coast to support the landing of an amphibious assault, and capture individual enemy islands.

Air defense forces conduct air defense operations of varied scale.

It is natural that with such a wide variety of types of operations, a general theory of operational art alone will not suffice; this requires concretization, making it possible to delve thoroughly into elaborating operational problems of different armed forces services in accordance with their development.

Presently, the independent significance of the theory of naval and air force operational art has been precisely specified in the general theory of operational art. This is completely logical, since operations conducted by the navy on maritime and oceanic expanses, and by aviation in the air or against objectives located in the enemy's deep rear, are sharply different, with respect to their aims, content, and nature, from operations conducted in ground sectors of theaters of military operations. They have their own features which are inherent to them alone, and, consequently, problems of the theory of their preparation and conduct require independent categories of the theory of operational art.

Regarding the rapid growth of air forces and the even wider development of pilotless means for long-range air attack, capable of carrying weapons of mass destruction, air defense, especially of military objectives in the country's rear, has acquired great significance, as a result of which the importance of operations conducted by air defense forces has also increased. The nature of these operations has become increasingly more sophisticated, and their scope has increased. In the overall system of armed struggle these operations have acquired a much more independent significance. Air defense means are becoming increasingly more varied, their control is becoming more complex, and ever greater demands are being made of air defense forces with respect to their constant combat readiness. This is leading to air defense operations acquiring specific features, which are difficult to examine in an overall theory of operational art. The necessity to develop an independent theory of air defense operations is arising.

As for the theory of preparing and conducting airborne operations, in our opinion there is still no need to allot it an independent category of operational art theory. From the cited list of operations conducted by airborne forces, it is apparent that the latter conduct operations only in the interests of ground or naval forces. Undoubtedly the role of airborne forces in the overall system of armed conflict is continuously growing; however, in our opinion there is insufficient justification to anticipate in the immediate future serious changes in the nature, content, and designation of operations they conduct. Therefore, questions concerning the preparation and conduct of airborne operations can be placed within the framework of the overall theory of operational art and partially examined in the section on the operational art of air forces.

Thus, it can be said that the theory of operational art at the modern stage of its development contains the following sections:

- an overall theory of operational art, which examines conditions under which an operation arises, its content, role, and place in the overall set of military operations, methods and means of conducting operations, characteristic features inherent to operations of all types and scales, and problems of the operational use of armed forces services and principles of their independent operations, conducted in the interests of each of them and of the armed conflict as a whole;
- a theory of naval operational art, which examines problems of preparing and conducting naval operations on maritime expanses of theaters of military operations, and operations conducted primarily by the navy or jointly with ground forces;
- a theory of air force operational art, which examines problems of preparing and conducting independent air force operations, and operations they conduct in the overall complex of ground forces and naval operations.

In addition, in our opinion there is a need to develop an independent theory of preparation and conduct of air defense operations, in which it is necessary to examine problems of the content and nature of these operations, especially problems of controlling air defense forces and means and their maneuver during an operation, taking into account that here the factor of surprise will hardly play the most important role, in comparison with all other operations.

Since each armed forces service contains different combat arms (for example, rifle forces, artillery, armored and different special forces are part of the ground forces; air forces are divided into fighter, bomber, reconnaissance, transport, and other types of aviation), each category of the theory of operational art accordingly examines problems of the operational use of corresponding combat arms.

Thus, we have presented the principal content of the modern theory of operational art. As a component of Soviet military art, operational art encompasses the theoretical investigation of the problems of preparing and conducting military operations and the practical activity of command and staffs in leading wartime combat operations of large armed forces formations.

What place does operational art occupy in Soviet military art? In our opinion, this is determined by the place of the operation in the overall system of armed conflict. It is known that the operation took the place of the general engagement when, because of conditions which developed historically, the latter no longer could resolve strategic missions of the war as a whole, or of one of its campaigns.

Recent war experience, especially that of the Great Patriotic War, demonstrated that to achieve an intermediate war aim, that is, the resolution of some strategic mission, it was necessary to conduct not one, but a series of large-scale operations. For example, the turning point in the Great Patriotic War was conditioned by the entire preceding course of the war, and was the result of several campaigns in which a series of operations were conducted, including such large ones as the Battles of Moscow and Stalingrad.

However, if it was necessary to conduct a series of large-scale operations to resolve such an important strategic mission as the achievement of a turning point during a war, then, in their turn, some of these led to the achievement of a strategic aim, although not as significant. For example, after the Battle of Moscow, Hitler's command could no longer count on blitzkrieg, that is, the operation achieved a strategic result.

Consequently, during armed conflict a campaign, and sometimes even a separate large-scale operation, leads to the resolution of some strategic mission. This manifests the interconnection between strategy and operational art.

This association found more concrete expression in the fact that strategy, proceeding from the campaign plan or war plan as a whole, planned the sequence of conduct of the most important operations, established the aims for them, and determined the forces and means, and sometimes the main attack axis, for conducting operations. The guiding role of strategy, with respect to operational art, also included the organization of strategic cooperation among large operational force groupings, as well as among the different armed forces services. Strategy, in fulfilling its guiding role with respect to operational art, must take into account the latter's capabilities as well, so as not to assign it missions beyond its power. Thus, operational art, as the theory and practice of conducting operations, closely joined to strategy on the one hand, fulfills the latter's missions and is subordinate to it. On the other hand, the operational aim is achieved as a result of conducting a series of engagements, which, in turn, include separate battles, marches, and regroupings, albeit connected by a single plan. From this it is clear that, in the final analysis, the operational aim is achieved as the result of a set of tactical troop actions. Consequently, in this respect operational art is closely joined to tactics, but occupies a guiding position with respect to it, analogous to that which strategy occupies with respect to operational art.

As a component of Soviet military science, operational art is developing on the basis of natural laws, inherent to operational art on the whole. Within the framework of operational art, however, these laws are, to a certain extent, qualitatively different, and this is expressed, above all, in the greater concretization of military art's basic principles as applied to operational art. For example, the known principle that strategy's correct choice of main attack axis predetermines, for the most part, the fate of the entire war does not always have concrete spatial expression: it may mean that the main attack at a given stage of a war is directed, let us say, toward undermining the enemy's economic might, so as to create subsequently the most favorable conditions for defeating his armed forces. This principle, when applied to operational art, will always have a concrete spatial expression. The main attack axis in an operation is always defined by concrete terrain locations at a depth specified beforehand, in accordance with the enemy grouping, by the aim of the given operation, and by the situation as it actually unfolds.

In addition, in operations and, consequently, in operational art, the role of such temporary factors as surprise, the degree of force combat readiness, favorable terrain conditions, and the profile of the front line are growing respectively. This is understandable, since under modern conditions it is very difficult to achieve full surprise at the commencement of military operations; operational surprise can be achieved relatively more easily by skillfully concealing preparations for an operation and attacking on those axes where the enemy least expects it. The duration of an operation is also insufficient for temporarily operating factors to forfeit their significance completely. Therefore, operational art should focus much attention on the study of the influence of temporarily operating factors on the course of combat operations and the methods of achieving superiority in them.

Other basic principles of military art, such as the significance of reserves and centralization of control, are also fully applicable to operational art, within the framework of which they are becoming more concrete.

To sum up, the following conclusions can be drawn.

Operational art could not have appeared at earlier stages of the development of military art, when the outcome of military operations, despite the considerable duration of some wars, was determined by the defeat of the enemy's armed forces in one or several general engagements.

Operational art arose in the period when, on the basis of the development of society's productive forces, the potential was created to deploy mass armies and satisfy the needs of a *front* for all types of armaments and supplies during a war, and when, in connection with the growing combat might of forces, it became impossible to resolve the mission of defeating the enemy's primary forces in one or several general engagements. To destroy each more or less large enemy grouping, it was necessary beforehand to plan combat operations at a great depth and rout the enemy successively, overcoming his resistance on several lines. Operational art was also the result of the change in the nature of armed conflict, when the necessity arose to create large military organisms such as armies and *fronts*, coordinate their efforts during the armed struggle, and centralize leadership of troop actions on large territories.

The designation of operational art as a component of Soviet military art, together with strategy and tactics, reflects most correctly the development of new forms of struggle, and serves as an indicator of the progressive nature of Soviet military science.

The most important component of Soviet military art is strategy. Operational art, occupying a subordinate position with respect to strategy and guided in its resolutions by the requirements of strategy, simultaneously advances new demands for the development of tactical procedures for conducting battle, thus promoting the development of tactics. This reflects the interconnection of all three components of military art.

Operational art is evolving on the basis of general laws of development of military art, and interprets their tenets in a more concrete form, applicable to the actions of large operational troop formations under conditions of a situation as it actually unfolds.

The primary task of operational art is to study the laws and natural regularities of modern operations of all types and scales; develop, on this basis, the most efficient methods of preparing and conducting them in the interests of executing missions advanced by strategy; and present demands for tactics, with respect to developing the most perfected tactical procedures for conducting battle in the interests of resolving missions assigned for the operation.

The theory of operational art under modern conditions, in connection with enormous changes in the technical outfitting of forces and in the field of their organization, and also relating to the further improvement of the forms and methods of armed struggle, must be improved continually and objectively reflect changes taking place in military affairs. The improvement, deepening, and broadening of the theory of operational art is one of the major duties of Soviet military cadres.

NOTES

1. V. Vasil'yev, "Operativnoye iskusstvo kak sostavnaya chast' sovetskogo voyennogo iskusstva," *Voyennaya mysl'* [Military thought], 6 (1956), pp. 3–13.
2. A. Tsvetkov, *Voyennaya mysl'* [Military thought], 3 (1955).

On Modern Soviet Military Art and its Characteristic Features

MARSHAL OF TANK FORCES P. ROTMISTROV[1]

Historical experience convincingly confirms the correctness of the Marxist thesis on the dependence of forms and methods of armed struggle on the level of development of productive forces and on the socio-economic system. This thesis has fundamental significance for Soviet military science, assisting it in both analyzing military history and forecasting the nature of future war.

The continuous development of society and, above all, its productive forces has introduced substantive changes into military art and the methods of preparing and conducting military operations. The successive increase in the scope of wars, and the intensified dependence of a country's armed forces on its rear area and economic and moral potentials the country or a coalition of countries possesses are a clearly defined natural law.

Analysis of the developmental process of military art demonstrates that its tempos of development were not uniform: over the course of time they continually accelerated in accordance with the tempos of development of productive forces and with scientific and technological progress. Thus, if in the feudal era, between the time firearms were invented and the Napoleonic wars, that is, over four centuries, military affairs developed extremely slowly, then with the advent of capitalism and the period of rapid development of productive forces and associated socio-economic changes, each major war signified a new step in the development of military affairs. As examples one can cite the Franco-Prussian War (1870–71), the First World War (1914–18), and the Second World War (1939–45). These wars unquestionably were qualitatively different from one another, but the continuous increase in their scale, intensity, and degree of destructiveness should be noted as conforming to natural laws.

One of the features of military art in our time is that its development occurs without interruption, even in peacetime. In the past, the level of military art in intervals between major wars was almost unchanged. This made it possible for states and armies to prepare for a new war, making full use of previous experience, and to begin a new war with essentially the same methods and means used at the last stage of the preceding war. Beginning with the second half of the nineteenth century, this picture sharply changes. In connection with the continuously accelerating tempo of development of productive forces, not only wars, but also the intervals between them have been important steps in the development of military affairs. We recall that tanks, which first appeared during the First World War, were only the embryo of those armored forces which developed and were formed into an independent combat arm during the 20 years separating the Second World War from the First. The same expansion occurred within aviation, perhaps to an even greater degree. It is also characteristic that it was in the interim between these two wars that a new branch of Soviet military science – operational art – emerged and was developed.

Over the 12 years since the end of the Second World War, serious qualitative and quantitative changes have taken place in military art. During the first five or six postwar years further development and improvement of the theory of Soviet military art occurred on the basis of war experience. At the same time, atomic weapons were being developed and tested, and their properties studied.

During this time Soviet military thought did enormous work studying and generalizing war experience on the basis of the further development of the armed forces.

The gigantic development of productive forces, unprecedented scientific and technological progress in the postwar period, and, in particular, mastery of atomic energy could not help but affect military art. With the beginning of the 1950s, our theory began to develop new methods for conducting military operations using means of mass destruction; considerable results have been achieved in this direction.

The probability of extensive use of thermonuclear and atomic weaponry in an armed conflict compelled us to reexamine viewpoints on the nature of future war, organization and technical equipping of the armed forces, and fundamental principles for conducting combat operations, established on the basis of experience of the last war and taking into account the appearance of atomic weapons as the latest word in the theory of military art.

What, then, is characteristic now for Soviet military art and its components, that is, strategy, operational art, and tactics?

Modern Soviet military art is based on a lofty material foundation created by the latest scientific and technical achievements, and on our socialist state's powerful economy.

The scientific elaboration of questions of the theory of military art is inseparably associated with concrete changes in the technical outfitting of the armed forces. From the moment that new means are transferred from laboratories and experimental ranges to the armed forces, and sometimes even before that, there is a reexamination of theoretical views and positions and practical methods of troop operations.

There are still many questions associated with the employment of atomic weapons in armed conflict not fully investigated, and, even more so with thermonuclear weapons, but the fact that this has already become the property of military thought attests to new principles of modern military art. A fundamental reexamination of a number of basic principles of military art is taking place under the influence of the introduction of powerful means of destruction into the armed forces and their complete outfitting with new combat equipment. The result of this reexamination is often the emergence of completely new views on the nature and methods of preparing and conducting armed conflict, and on the use in it of armed forces and combat arms.

We have undoubtedly entered a new era of military art, whose development should cover not only (and not so much) the path of interpreting the lessons of the last war and the development and improvement of methods by which it was conducted, but rather the path of consistently and steadfastly searching for principally new methods, making it possible to exploit new opportunities created by developing combat means and improving organizational structures of the armed forces on this basis.

However, it should be kept in mind that new methods and procedures for conducting combat operations cannot be invented immediately. They are created over years, on the basis of acquired experience and a profound knowledge of those opportunities which new combat means give.

Formerly, before the First World War in particular, it was considered that the appearance of a new weapon or new combat means affected, above all, methods and forms of conducting battle, that is, tactics, and, through this, strategy. This tenet was correct while the range of new weapons was limited to the battlefield, and their destructive force was comparatively modest. Tanks and aviation, which emerged during the First World War and whose further development during the Second World War was very rapid, began to affect not only tactics, but also operational art directly. The situation is otherwise with atomic weapons, which possess enormous destructive force, and with their carriers in the form of intercontinental ballistic rockets, long-range aviation, and surface ships and submarines with rockets, which make it possible to deliver annihilating strikes against objectives hundreds and thousands of kilometers away; this also applies to rockets of operational-tactical significance and atomic artillery. The effect of these new combat means is felt simultaneously by strategy, operational art, and tactics.

As is known, strategy encompasses questions of the theory and practice of waging war and conducting military campaigns. Soviet strategic leadership determines, on the basis of state policy, the forms and methods of organizing, preparing, and employing armed forces in war to achieve victory over an enemy.

When resolving assigned missions, strategy proceeds from the country's economic, moral, and military potentials, and takes into consideration those of the enemy.

In the postwar period, Soviet strategy has been undergoing specific changes. This is taking place as a result of the direct influence of the development of military equipment, outfitting of the army and navy with new combat means, and large-scale achievements of Soviet science and technology, radically changing the overall conditions for waging war.

Formerly strategy, lacking its own means for pressuring the enemy directly, was compelled to achieve its aims only by having the various armed forces services conduct a series of operations. Now strategy has acquired additional powerful means for directly influencing strategic objectives in an enemy country. These means are long-range aviation and, especially, long- and super-long-range rocket weapons equipped with atomic and thermonuclear warheads, as well as submarines armed with similar weapons.

Comrade N. S. Khrushchev, in answering questions from W. R. Hearst, head of the U.S. newspaper and publishing trust, indicated that

> if war is unleashed by the aggressive circles of the US, then it will take place not only in Europe, Asia, and Africa; this war will immediately shift to the territory of the United States of America, because now intercontinental ballistic rockets make it possible to strike targets in any region of the globe. Here, the American people will suffer enormous losses. All assets – intercontinental ballistic rockets, submarine rockets, and other assets which we now have – will be used in an armed conflict.

Aviation and rocket strikes delivered against the enemy's military and economic objectives will widen the zone of military operations immeasurably, eliminate the line between front and rear, and attach to armed struggle an all-inclusive and exceptionally decisive nature.

The use of rockets of various designation with atomic and thermonuclear warheads, long-range aviation, and submarines makes it possible to destroy strategic objectives on enemy territory, regardless of the distance from the front line. The destruction or disruption of normal activities in the enemy's important economic and entire industrial regions, transport centers, and political and administrative centers during the war can place him in very difficult circumstances and seriously affect the course and outcome of the war as a whole.

The employment of super-long-range means of destruction will inevitably entail an intercontinental struggle of military coalitions and lead to the emergence of armed struggle simultaneously in many theaters of military operations.

Possessing powerful means of destruction, Soviet military strategy is now capable of resolving large-scale missions in a short time and achieving sharp changes in the military-political situation.

Victory or defeat in war depends, as is known, not only on economic, but also on socio-political conditions of public life, inasmuch as now millions of people participate. The awareness and will of the people, their ideology, and the attitude of the state toward policy directly affect a war's course and outcome. The level of the state's military might is determined by the totality of moral, economic, and military potentials. It should be especially stressed that modern armed forces and their successful actions depend, as never before, on acquiring enormous quantities of various types of combat equipment, arms, and other materiel, that is, on the successful operation of the country's rear area.

Strategy is now faced with a whole series of new problems, whose resolution will give it a new character and direction. The success of preparing our armed forces for war will depend, for the most part, on the completeness of the development of a theory of strategy.

In addition to the direct influence of new, super-powerful means of destruction on strategy, changes in operational art and tactics, once again taking place under the influence of changes in the materiel base of armed conflict, are also seriously affecting the development of strategy.

Soviet operational art has amassed rich experience, making it possible to make further steps, theoretically and practically, in the development of this important branch of military art. It will be necessary, however, albeit difficult, to reject several principles of operational art from the last war. Now, 12 years after the end of the Second World War, when science and technology have made enormous leaps forward, one cannot be guided by principles which correspond to the conditions of the last war, many of which already do not meet the requirements and conditions of new war. It is necessary to develop principally new tenets on preparing and conducting operations.

The theory of operational art, as mentioned earlier, was created before the Second World War, but until now the confines of this theory, in particular with respect to its junction with the theory of strategy, have not been defined precisely. There is not complete clarity as to the extent of the questions with which operational art deals. For example, even now one encounters statements in our military literature to the effect that operations of a group of *fronts* must be associated with the sphere of strategy, while operations of a *front* and army are within the sphere of operational art.

Differentiating operations with respect to scale, as we seem to do, still does not serve as an adequate foundation for their distinct division into two groups – non-strategic and strategic – with association of the latter with the theory of strategy. Apparently this occurs because until now we have not scientifically established what operational art treats.

An examination of operations differentiated according to their scale, partly as the theory of strategy and partly as the theory of operational art, makes it difficult to investigate them profoundly and thoroughly. Dividing one and the same phenomenon between two theories is damaging not only to the theories of strategy and operational art, but also to military art as a whole.

In our opinion, any operation, regardless of its scale, should be organized and conducted according to theoretical principles of operational art. Strategic leadership can only assign a mission to a group of *fronts* or one *front*, or a large air force or naval formation. All operations conducted by the forces of a large army or *front* formation or group of *fronts*, and operations conducted by armed forces services, both independently and jointly, should be examined in the theory of operational art.

Operational art is the connecting link between strategy and tactics. It specifies methods of preparing and conducting army and *front* operations, operations of groups of *fronts*, and independent and joint operations of combined armed forces services, in accordance with the requirements of strategy, to achieve strategic aims. At the same time, operational art assigns missions to tactics and directs tactical actions of formations and combat arms in the interests of an operation.

New combat means are the necessary material prerequisites for conducting operations in a new manner. They will not, however, provide the required effect in and of themselves, if their employment is paralyzed by old forms of conducting operations, which do not correspond to their capabilities. New weapons also require new forms and methods of troop actions.

Extensive employment of modern combat equipment has sharply increased shock force and troop mobility, imparted to operations a maneuver, extremely decisive, and deep character, and made it possible to execute complex forms of operational maneuver. All this, together with the large size of modern armies, leads to an increase in the scope of operations and growth in the quantity of forces and means participating in the operation, with a simultaneous reduction in its duration.

Modern offensive operations, under the influence of new combat means and changes in force organization, are acquiring qualitatively new traits in comparison with the Second World War, which require a search for different methods and procedures for their organization and conduct.

One of the most important features of the modern offensive operation is the very powerful simultaneous pressure on the entire depth of the defending grouping's operational formation. Enemy forces – not only those defending in the tactical zone, but also operational and even strategic reserves – and areas where control organs are located, as well as regions of concentration for weapons of mass destruction, aviation bases, road junctions, crossings, and other important operational objectives, will be subject to powerful strikes of atomic and other means of mass destruction. In addition to aviation, rocket weapons, and long-range artillery, powerful armored groupings, airborne forces, and, on maritime axes, the navy and amphibious assaults will take part in delivering deep strikes.

Strikes against enemy objectives in the depth of the defense were made in the last war as well; however, because of the limited capabilities of available means of destruction, the results of such strikes were insignificant. The presence of new means which have enormous destructive force is imparting a new quality to strikes delivered against objectives in the operational rear.

Powerful fire and shock pressure against the defense's entire operational depth will make it possible to suppress forces in a short period, so as to make them incapable of stubborn resistance or swift and effective maneuver on the battlefield, and to disorganize control.

Deep annihilating attacks by large armored groupings operating in the operational formation's first echelon, delivered simultaneously along several axes in combination with strikes by aviation and other long-range means against reserves and other important defense objectives, will lead to swift penetration of the tactical depth of the defense and a considerable increase in offensive tempos of forces in the operational depth. Attacks by large armored groupings and employment of tactical and operational airborne forces will increase the force of simultaneous pressure against the entire depth of the enemy force's operational formation and deprive him of the ability to maneuver his reserves promptly and implement other operational measures, which will make it possible to rout the enemy piecemeal and demoralize him completely. Troop actions in an operation should be planned and organized so that shock groupings are not tied down by the execution of incidental missions, but rather are able to advance swiftly into the depth and defeat advancing enemy reserves without halting.

Simultaneous and successive blows against the entire depth of the enemy deployment, which increase in their strength, make it possible to enlarge breaches in the defense and conduct an operation at high tempos until the enemy is completely routed and destroyed.

Modern offensive operations are characterized by the great intensity of the struggle for air superiority. This struggle cannot, as before, be restricted to single blows against an enemy air force grouping located in a large operational formation's offensive zone and on its flanks. Modern aviation's high degree of mobility makes it possible for the defender to concentrate aviation forces swiftly on the necessary axis and re-establish the air situation. Therefore, gaining air superiority requires defeating enemy aviation at least within the bounds of the given theater of military operations; the aviation of one, and even several large operational formations may not always be up to the task. Certain resolution of this task can be realized only on the strategic scale by all armed forces services, with the participation of several large operational formations' aviation, the main command's aviation, and rocket forces.

Having begun before, or simultaneously with the shift of ground forces to the offensive, the fight against enemy aviation does not cease during the entire offensive operation. The defender who has a strong air force and atomic and nuclear weapons will not only stubbornly resist the actions of the attacker's aviation, but will also strive to deliver retaliatory strikes against it in the air and at airfields. As a result, the struggle for air superiority will ensue under difficult conditions and require considerable efforts on the part of the attacker.

The change in the nature of modern operations has led to considerable complexity in the process of encircling and destroying large enemy groupings. As a result of the increase in the width and depth of defensive belts, and the considerable dispersal of defending forces and their high degree of mobility, it has become more difficult to encircle a large grouping of defenders in a small area, as was done during the last war. A more expedient form may be the simultaneous suppression of the defense's entire operational formation and rapid penetration into its depth by armored forces, making it possible to cleave enemy groupings into separate units and destroy them rapidly, using second-echelon and reserve forces. In this instance, the first echelon, which is not tied down in battles to destroy encircled groupings, will maintain its strength longer and be able to develop the offensive at high tempos and to great depth.

Of course, we are not thinking of disavowing the expediency and potential of encircling and destroying large enemy forces. Such a form of conducting operations under specific favorable conditions is also possible.

The growing significance of the fight against enemy reserves is characteristic of the modern offensive operation. The defender, making use of the high degree of troop mobility, will attempt to conduct extensive maneuver with his operational and strategic reserves to slow down the offensive and subsequently re-establish his lost position. The struggle against defensive reserves should be at the center of the attacker's attention for the extent of the entire operation. Offensive success is impossible without the prompt and complete rout of enemy reserves.

The conduct of modern operations does not depend on the time of year or day. During the last war, the Soviet Armed Forces demonstrated high-level skill in conducting large-scale offensive operations in winter's severe cold, in summer, and during the spring thaw. Equipping forces with combat and transport vehicles with high cross-country capability, together with extensive use of military-transport aviation to convey forces and cargoes, expands force capabilities even more in this respect. Skillful conduct of combat operations at night by large formations and formations of all combat arms and armed forces services has acquired special significance. Unlike the last war, such operations have turned into a common occurrence.

Offensive operations can commence under the most varied conditions, ensuing from the nature of military operations in a given theater, the correlation of opposing forces, their overall military-political and strategic aims, and the military-geographic features of the theater of military operations.

During a war, when a pause occurs between two consecutively conducted offensive operations, both sides can create a series of defensive belts at considerable depth in a short time, making use of modern engineer equipment, prepared reinforced concrete, fast-drying cement, and other technical achievements in the construction of field defensive structures. Forces will occupy part of these belts. Considerable time is required to organize a penetration of such a prepared defense, and concentration of sufficient forces and means, including atomic weapons, is required to execute it.

With the rapid development of military operations, the enemy will often be compelled to use his withdrawing forces and reserves to occupy defensive belts hastily. The degree of readiness of the engineer preparation of these belts and their development into the depth can be varied: in some cases they will be completely insignificant. Penetration of such a defense must be executed most often during the development of an offensive operation or at the very beginning of consecutively conducted operations. As a rule, penetration of a hastily occupied defense will be executed from the march, using powerful armored forces attacks in cooperation with aviation and airborne forces, with or without the use of atomic weapons, which will subsequently make it possible to conduct the entire offensive operation at high tempos and achieve its aim quickly.

In a number of front sectors, attacking forces may encounter fortified regions, constructed in peacetime or during war on natural lines having operational and strategic significance, and on operational axes leading to important objectives. The construction of new fortified regions is facilitated by using modern, powerful construction equipment. The conduct of offensive operations with the penetration of fortified regions may require longer preparation, use of enormous forces and means, and employment of special procedures and methods of troop actions. The presence of a sufficient quantity of atomic weapons facilitates considerably the suppression of fortified regions; however, the conduct itself of combat operations, in regard to the enormous destruction from atomic blasts and the high degree of radiation, will entail serious difficulties.

An offensive operation can begin immediately following or during the conduct of a defensive engagement. If the defender has inflicted considerable losses on the attacker, bled him dry, and stopped the offensive in all sectors or on important axes, then he can shift to a counteroffensive, but only if during the defense he has maintained the necessary forces and means or received them from the Supreme High Command. Considering that skillful use of a sufficient quantity means of mass destruction makes it possible for the defender to change rapidly the correlation of forces to his advantage, it can be assumed that under modern conditions the counteroffensive will be used more frequently than previously.

A counteroffensive can be conducted by the forces of several *fronts* or one *front*, and even by a single army in mountain and desert regions and under other special terrain conditions. It is advantageous to begin a counteroffensive while successfully developing counterstrokes by introducing fresh forces from the march or after a brief pause, following the end of a defensive engagement. Having routed the attacker's principal forces, one can reckon on conducting a counteroffensive at high tempos, since at this time, in the majority of cases, the attacker will not have strong reserves at his disposal.

Offensive operations in a number of cases may begin with a meeting engagement, in particular when both sides are advancing large reserves along separate operational or strategic axes to achieve decisive aims. Such a situation may be created at the beginning of and during a war when new *fronts* emerge. Forestalling the enemy in deploying one's forces on favorable lines, surprise, and mass use of means of destruction will make it possible, with dynamic and forceful operations, to seize the initiative, win the meeting engagement, and further develop the offensive at high tempos.

Meeting engagements can occur rather often in the operational depth, during a fight against approaching enemy reserves. They will be characterized by the participation of large aviation, rocket, and armored forces from both sides.

Front offensive operations under modern conditions will have large scope with respect to frontage and depth. In this regard, in some sectors the commencement of an offensive operation and its development may ensue under conditions which sometimes sharply differ from the situation in other sectors. This requires an innovative approach when determining methods of troop actions on different axes, and extremely flexible troop leadership during the operation.

The modern defense, while retaining many of those characteristics exhibited during the last war, acquired a number of new features during the postwar period. Speaking about theoretical principles for organizing and conducting the defense, above all the difficulty in working them out should be noted. If such difficulties arise even when establishing some general principles for conducting offensive operations, each of which results from peculiar conditions inherent to the given operation, then the matter is considerably more complex with a defensive operation in which, in addition to the variety of conditions, initiative belongs to the attacker.

The modern defensive operation is characterized by the extreme intensity of defending forces' combat actions against superior offensive forces, and by the necessity of repelling mass blows by enemy artillery, armored forces, aviation, and rocket means.

The attacker's employment of weapons of mass destruction and large armored groupings to penetrate the defense inordinately complicates the organization and conduct of defensive operations and requires great intensification of the moral and physical strength of defending forces. Modern defense successfully carries out its assigned missions only if it can withstand massive strikes by the attacker's atomic weapons and prevent him penetrating the tank groupings. Consequently, a most important characteristic feature of the modern defense is its high degree of anti-atomic and antitank stability.

The defender's attempt to protect his forces against atomic weapons strikes necessitates troop dispersal, which leads to an increase in the width of the zones of defending formations and operational formations. In addition, the depth of the defense's operational formation also increases, since only a deep defense will be able to withstand enemy blows. Skillful engineer preparation of the terrain, especially in an anti-atomic and antitank respect, has acquired exceptionally great significance. However, this should not allow the attacker to discover the defensive formation and the concept of the defensive operation.

Echeloning of defending forces has also undergone drastic changes. If previously the defender, as a rule, attempted to stop the offensive in the first defensive belt and concentrated his main forces to hold it, then today such an operational method will not always be expedient. After employing mass atomic weapons strikes, the attacker can hit forces occupying the first belt and swiftly penetrate the tactical depth of the defense. Under modern conditions it will often be more advantageous to concentrate the main efforts in the depth. In these circumstances the defender should have strong second echelons and reserves.

The principle of fighting against the enemy long before he goes over to the offensive, with the simultaneous conduct of combat operations in a large region, whose boundaries are determined by the range of various types of weapons, is characteristic of the modern defensive operation.

During the enemy's preparation for an offensive operation, when he is regrouping and concentrating his forces and means, the defender's aviation and rocket weapons, using weapons of mass destruction, systematically strike the attacker's principal group concentrations, his large bases, his primary lines of communication, and his aviation grouping. Such continuous action against important enemy objectives causes disorganization and leads to the premature exhaustion of his forces.

The employment of atomic weapons and other means of mass destruction increases the stability and dynamism of the defense, and creates conditions for decisive rout of the attacker. The conduct of a counterpreparation has acquired great significance under modern conditions.

In comparison with the last war, the counterpreparation has acquired new qualities. The range and power of modern means of destruction fully support a strike against the first-echelon main force of the attacker's operational formation and his most important objectives. A counterpreparation executed suddenly by aviation, rocket, and artillery forces using weapons of mass destruction against the enemy's main force grouping can weaken his initial attack and thwart his offensive.

Under favorable conditions, after the counterpreparation, specially allocated forces can conduct particular offensive operations with limited missions: the rout of part of the main grouping's forces during its concentration, capture of staging bridgeheads or lines favorable for the enemy, etc.

Destruction of the enemy begun by the counterpreparation continues during the defensive operation by different means, depending on the operational situation.

From the moment the enemy goes over to the offensive, the defender's mission is to stop his main forces and prevent penetration of the tactical depth of the defense. If, according to the defensive operational plan, the principal forces are concentrated in the depth of the defense, then the mission of forces defending in the first belt will be to prevent the attacker's main forces from capturing it from the march, and to inflict maximum losses on him.

If the enemy penetrates into the tactical depth, counterstrokes, as a higher form of defense dynamism, must play a decisive role in routing him. Counterstrokes are usually executed by second-echelon forces and reserves of large operational formations, using units of first-echelon forces directly conducting the defensive engagement. Skillful employment of atomic weapons and other means of mass destruction in the interests of the counterstroke makes it possible to change rapidly the correlation of forces in favor of the defender and, under these conditions, to assign forces delivering counterstrokes a decisive aim: the rout of the attacking grouping and re-establishment of the earlier occupied position.

Under modern conditions, it is inadmissible for forces delivering the counterstroke to remain in deployed positions for a long time. It is more expedient, as a rule, to conduct the counterstroke by deploying forces from the march on a line prepared beforehand. It is necessary for forces to arrive quickly at the line of deployment from various directions to create a grouping which will ensure a powerful blow against the enemy; this is a very important concern of command and staffs.

Under specific conditions, when, as a result of successful counterpreparation and during the defensive engagement, the attacker's forces are sapped and his reserves exhausted, while the defender has maintained his second echelon or received new forces from the reserve of the High Command, a counterstroke can, as already mentioned, develop into a counteroffensive.

The defensive engagement may not even conclude with a counterstroke. If the situation develops unfavorably, the higher command can decide to withdraw and organize a defense on a new line in the operational depth.

During the postwar period, the theory of the operational art of armed forces services – air forces, navy, and national air defense forces – was developed quite considerably. This development was a result of the rapid progress in combat equipment and armaments for these services.

Air force operations are substantively different from operations of other armed forces services. Their peculiarities are explained by the specific conditions of the air milieu, the traits of objectives to be hit, the combat and technical capabilities of aviation equipment and weapons, and special air force operational methods and procedures.

The basic method of aviation action is delivering surprise mass strikes against the enemy's main force grouping and other important objectives, whose destruction has a substantive influence on the course and outcome of the operation. When executing missions in an operation, preliminary strikes should be extremely powerful, using means of mass destruction.

Air superiority maintained for the duration of the entire operation is the most favorable condition for the successful conduct of air force operations.

Under modern conditions, air operations to hit the enemy's deep strategic objectives have acquired extremely important significance.

Naval operations, as with air force operations, are conducted either in direct cooperation with other armed forces services and in their interests, or independently, in the interests of the armed struggle as a whole.

Thanks to the employment of new combat means, naval operations are characterized by the conduct of combat actions at a great distance, with decisive aims, and mass participation of underwater means and aviation, which is especially important.

Among naval operations, operations on oceanic and maritime lines of communication and those to destroy strategic objectives on enemy territory occupy a special place. These operations pursue the aim of undermining the enemy's military and military-economic might, by which their significance in armed struggle is determined. Underwater forces and aviation are the principal forces conducting such operations.

National air defense (PVO) operations are conducted to repel an enemy air attack against industrial-economic regions, political and administrative centers, and other important objectives located on the country's territory. To achieve more decisive results, these operations, as a rule, are combined with bomber and rocket strikes against enemy attack means.

National air defense is structured on the composite employment of modern fighter aviation armed with rockets, antiaircraft and rocket weapons, and antiaircraft artillery, with the wide automation of control means.

The prepared grouping of air defense forces and means should ensure concentration of their main efforts promptly on the primary air axes to the most important regions, and maneuver of forces during the operation.

Tactics are also currently undergoing considerable changes. We have already indicated that in the past the appearance of new combat means have affected, in the first order, tactics, and through them operational art and strategy. As new combat means have further developed qualitatively and quantitatively, their use has left the realm of tactics and they have begun to be used to resolve operational missions. This was so, for example, with tanks, which changed from a means for only direct infantry support on the battlefield into a powerful operational means. The influence of aviation on all components of military art was manifested even more clearly.

We observe a completely different picture with the appearance of atomic weapons. These weapons developed as a strategic means, and only as they improved were they gradually introduced into the area of operational art, and then tactics.

Modern combined-arms battle is characterized, above all, by the use of atomic weapons and mass employment of various combat arms with varied combat equipment and aviation. All this has sharply energized combat operations, which are acquiring special decisiveness, high maneuverability, and speed.

The simultaneous participation of different combat arms in battle and the use of means of mass destruction in the interests of formations and units is imparting special significance to the organization of continuous and reliable cooperation among combat arms, subunits, units, and formations, when combat formations are dispersed.

Previously it was thought that only the steadfastness of infantry in the defense and its decisive advance in the offense made it possible for other combat arms to execute their missions successfully. Now this situation appears to be somewhat different. Of course, infantry has not lost its great significance in battle and operations, especially since it has now acquired new qualities. Overall success of combat operations still depends now, to a considerable degree, on its successful actions. In addition, infantry's success, in turn, depends more than ever on other combat arms, especially armored forces.

The problem of successfully conducting modern battle is resolved, as before, by the combined efforts of all combat arms; now, however, such a consolidation of efforts is acquiring special significance. Annihilating blows against the enemy leading to his complete defeat in a short time can be delivered by decisive, skillful, and timely use of new weapons and armored forces in cooperation with other forces.

Mass employment of atomic weapons and other means of mass destruction, and the complete outfitting of combined-arms formations with tanks and other combat equipment are conditioning rapid and sharp changes in the situation. Forces now must be able to concentrate swiftly to deliver a powerful attack against the enemy, and disperse swiftly so as not to subject themselves to attack by his atomic means. High troop mobility on the battlefield is one of the most important features of modern combined-arms battle.

As a result of the dispersal of both defensive and offensive forces' combat formations, battle will often reflect a fragmented character; rather large gaps between units and formations may occur, covered only by fire. In this situation some formations, where the defense is reliably suppressed, will be able to burst forward swiftly, while others, which have encountered enemy resistance or have been subject to his atomic strikes, will be forced to stop. All this will lead to the front line seldom being continuous, but interrupted and rather twisting, and its configuration changing rapidly. Regarding the extensive use of aviation and airborne forces in battle, it will be necessary to conduct combat operations more intensely than before, not only frontally against a ground enemy and his aviation, but also in his rear against his airborne forces, in the tactical zone, or directly outside its boundaries.

The employment of atomic weapons and other means of mass destruction can very often lead to a large number of personnel and their equipment being put out of action. Remaining subunits, units, and sometimes even formations will lose their combat capability for a time. The necessity of conducting combat operations continuously will require the introduction of fresh forces and means to replace units and subunits which have lost their combat capability, and to intensify efforts. Therefore, under modern conditions the presence of sufficiently strong reserves of all combat arms in combat formations is acquiring great significance.

The fact that modern battles on land, at sea, and in the air will be conducted not only during the day, but also at night is characteristic.

While during a night offensive operation not all first operational echelon forces will usually participate, but only individual formations specifically allocated for this purpose, during night combat for a prepared defense all first-echelon force formations and units participating in the penetration will, as a rule, take part, and the night battle will be no different from a day battle, with respect to intensity.

The employment of modern combat means and associated further development of troop operational methods have resulted in the appearance of new types of combat and operational support, such as protection against means of mass destruction [*ZOMP*] and radio countermeasures, have led to a qualitative change in existing types of combat and operational support, and seriously influenced force organization.

It is known that armed forces organization is changing in accordance with changes in the material base. The more qualitative the leap in the development of armaments and combat equipment, the more significant the changes in force organization. Modern force organization must conform to the nature of armed conflict and correspond to new weapons requirements. It also must ensure the most complete use of all the strong aspects of combat arms and armed forces services, and the capabilities of new means of destruction, as well as protection against the latter.

Among the most important features of ground forces organization, ensuing from the nature of modern armed conflict, are their full motorization, which ensures high mobility; the appearance of military organisms outfitted with rocket equipment; an increase in the importance of armored forces; and, together with this, the further equipping of combined-arms formations with tanks. An attempt to simplify combined-arms formations and impart to them qualities which support great operational independence is also characteristic.

In examining characteristic features of Soviet military art in this article, the author has attempted to identify only a point of departure, which is now the initial foundation for further development of questions of military theory.

Today, all factors of armed struggle have sharply grown, not only quantitatively, but even more so qualitatively. Its success on the whole depends, above all, on the correct use in the armed forces of the latest weapons, combat training, and the moral state of the troops. Here, despite unprecedented progress in the technical equipping of forces with the latest weapons, the significance of the moral factor has not only not decreased, but, on the contrary, it is increasing. Without a high moral state of the troops and their high level of preparation, not even the latest equipment can provide positive results.

Soviet military art, having absorbed many centuries of the Russian nation's combat experience, the best traditions of the Russian army's national military art, and all that was progressive in the history of other nations' military art, has developed along its own independent and distinctive path on the basis of the principles of Soviet military science, inseparably associated with the political and economic conditions of our socialist society. At all developmental stages, Soviet military art, as a genuinely scientific theory, has always moved forward and occupied a leading position with respect to various foreign schools, demonstrating more than once its superiority on the fields of battle.

NOTES

1. P. Rotmistrov, "O sovremennom sovetskom voyennom iskusstve i yego kharakternykh chertakh," *Voyennaya mysl'* [Military thought], 2 (1958), pp. 82–95.

CHAPTER FIVE

The Revolution in Military Affairs, 1960–64

In general terms, the revolution in military affairs did not appreciably alter the Soviet definition of operational art. It did, however, diminish the importance of operational art in regard to questions of strategy, and, in particular, it lessened concern for conventional operational techniques and increased concern for strategic nuclear concepts.

The ensuing period encompassed two distinct stages. The first, lasting from 1960 until roughly the time of Khrushchev's removal from power in 1964, was marked by extensive concern for global nuclear war. Best characterized by Colonel General S. V. Sokolovsky's work *Voyennaya strategiya* [Military strategy], during this period Soviet theorists discounted the likelihood of conventional war and argued that future war would be inherently and globally nuclear. This belief was underscored by a restructuring of the military to deemphasize operational (ground) forces and instead emphasize nuclear (strategic rocket) forces. Clearly this policy was not altogether acceptable to military circles.

The article by Major General B. Golovchiner typifies Soviet attitudes toward operations in a nuclear context. Stressing the increased importance of joint operations, he emphasized the emerging role of atomic weapons, rocket delivery systems, and radio-electronics in modern combat. These new systems, in turn, placed an even greater premium on depth of operations and the concept of simultaneous engagement of enemy forces.

Colonel I. Mariyevsky's 1962 piece traces in detail the pre-1920s roots of operational art and is notable for its partial rehabilitation of the concepts of A. Svechin, the long-ignored father of operational art. Mariyevsky provides a wealth of material on developments during the interwar years hitherto unavailable in print and, in particular, candidly addresses the damage done to Soviet military thought by Stalin's excesses.

To demonstrate further the process of de-Stalinization and the new period of *glasnost'* under Khrushchev, in 1963 *Voyenno-istoricheskiy zhurnal* (*VIZh*) [Military-historical journal] republished a 1932 exposition by Red Army Chief of Staff A. I. Yegorov on operational art and tactics. Publication of the article by Yegorov, who had died a victim of the purges, marked a new Soviet commitment to reinvestigate the impact of the purges on operational thought and assess the role repression had on the disastrous initial stages of the Great Patriotic War. Set within the context of Soviet fixation on nuclear matters, this new preoccupation with the failures of the late 1930s had the added effect of revitalizing Soviet concern for operational art. The subsequent removal of Khrushchev from power in 1964, in part prompted by Soviet senior officer dissatisfaction over the reduction of the ground forces' influence (and the concomitant deemphasis of operational matters), set the stage for a fundamental reassessment of military doctrine and renewed concern for conventional war and operational art.

Some Questions of Modern Operational Art

MAJOR GENERAL B. GOLOVCHINER[1]

As is generally known, operational art is a component of military art and deals with the development of the theory and practice of organizing and conducting operations. It investigates both joint operations with the participation of large operational formations of armed forces services, operating according to a single plan to achieve specific operational or strategic aims, and independent operations by large formations of armed forces services. Operational art defines coordination in large operational formation operations and directs their efforts toward the execution of missions in accordance with the operational plan and proceeding from the actual capabilities of forces and means participating in it.

As the study of operations, operational art under modern conditions is acquiring, together with strategy and tactics, very important significance for revealing and practically implementing those natural laws which occur in armed struggle.

A distinctive feature of Soviet operational art is its development in full accordance with the continuous growth of the country's economic and moral potentials. It proceeds from consideration of objective developmental tendencies of means and methods of armed struggle, and from consideration that the influence of rapidly improving combat means is changing not only the nature and methods of conducting modern operations, but also the operational role and significance of each armed forces service.

There is no doubt that modern means of armed struggle and, above all, rocket-nuclear weapons are sharply increasing the combat capabilities of all armed forces services and introducing fundamental changes in the content of missions they are resolving and methods for their combat employment, making it possible for large formations of armed forces services to achieve independently very important operational results.

In addition, under modern conditions the role and significance of joint operations conducted by large operational formations of armed forces services in a theater of military operations are increasing. As a rule, large-scale operational or strategic results cannot be achieved without the combined efforts of all armed forces services and their direction against the principal enemy forces and, above all, means for nuclear attack, aviation, air-craft carrier and rocket carrier forces, and the main ground forces groupings located in a given theater of military operations.

Soviet operational art covered a large developmental path, over whose expanse the theory and practice of conducting operations changed and improved. The progress of operational art, as well as military art on the whole, was conditioned by continuous economic, scientific, and techno-logical development. The modern period is characterized by the appearance and rapid development of qualitatively new means of armed struggle, princi-pally different from those employed during the last war. As is generally known, the main place among new combat means is occupied by nuclear weapons, rocket technology, and radio-electronics. These means are decisively influencing further development of the structure of the armed forces and the theory of military art.

In connection with the appearance and rapid development of nuclear weapons and various types of rockets, and with qualitative and quantitative changes in the composition of large operational formations of armed forces services in a number of developed countries, views on the conduct of operations have become different. New weapons and the variety of improved combat equipment employed on a massive scale have fundamentally affected the nature of operations. Large-scale transformations have occurred in the organizational structure of armed forces services and in views on their use in an operation. The theory and practice of organizing and conducting operations have undergone and continue to undergo significant changes.

The development of the theory of operational art, as with all military art, is based on an assessment of the possible nature of war. Operational art proceeds from the fact that future war, which may be unleashed by aggres-sive imperialist circles, will become a coalitional, intercontinental world war of states which belong basically to two opposing systems – capitalist and socialist. With respect to its political essence, war will be a decisive armed encounter of these systems; with respect to the combat means employed, it will be a rocket-nuclear war.

Imperialists will most probably attempt to begin a future war by a surprise attack using the maximum number of rocket-nuclear weapons. Here, the employment of extremely destructive and long-range combat means in all armed forces services and their increasing strike force will lead to the emergence of completely different conditions for organizing and conducting operations by large operational formations in a theater of military operations.

One of the important conditions influencing the organization and conduct of an operation will be the possible nature of the enemy's military actions. Therefore, it is necessary to know the probable enemy, continuously study his views on conducting military operations, and objectively assess and consider the combat potentials of the enemy's armed forces services and prospects for their development, to investigate correctly questions on the theory of operational art and their practical application in an operation.

In each theater of military operations, independent strategic axis, and even important operational axis, one side's forces may be opposed by groupings from the other side which differ in composition, combat capability, and technical outfitting. In addition, each theater of military operations or axis has its own specific military-geographic features. Because of this, operational aims on each axis may also be different.

The significance and nature of the operational aims determine its scale and predominant type of combat actions. An attempt to rout and destroy principal enemy armed force groupings in a theater of military operations and capture operationally or strategically significant regions and objectives or hold them in the defense will obviously be an overall aim in modern operations. The primary mission on the path to achieving an operational aim will be to destroy the enemy's means of mass destruction.

Modern operations are, in the first place, characterized by nuclear weapons employed in them being the principal and decisive strike means. The possibility of mass employment of nuclear weapons in an operation makes it possible to hit the enemy's main groupings and various objectives effectively and quickly, inflict heavy losses on him, and thus create favorable conditions for swift and decisive operations. Rapid exploitation of the results of nuclear strikes against enemy objectives by large operational formations of armed forces services, especially ground forces, is a very important condition for the successful conduct of operations.

The development of various types of rockets and their employment during combat operations by formations and large formations of various armed forces services are broadening the potential for effectively using nuclear weapons against the enemy within the framework of an operation. These new types of weapons, combining enormous power and practically unlimited range, are capable of hitting the enemy's groupings, leading to the rapid achievement of large-scale operational or strategic results.

The decisiveness of the war's political aims and the employment of extremely powerful combat means predetermine the decisive nature of operations, expressed in an attempt to destroy completely and swiftly corresponding enemy armed forces groupings, and to stifle his will to resist.

It is completely natural that operations conducted with such decisive aims require great intensification of moral and physical strength, because new combat means, above all, rocket-nuclear weapons, are capable of exerting a considerable effect on the morale of armed forces personnel, not to mention physical effects.

Modern operations are characterized by increasing maneuver capabilities of all armed forces services. These capabilities should be directed, above all, toward effectively exploiting the results of rocket-nuclear strikes against enemy objectives, to complete assigned missions in the shortest time.

The correct and timely exploitation of maneuver capabilities of formations and large operational formations makes it possible to shift efforts from one axis to another, depending on the situation.

Maneuver – a very important condition for ensuring success in an operation – makes it possible for whoever is able to gain time in tempos for maneuvering forces and means, thereby forestalling the other side, to achieve victory on battlefields. In modern operations, large radioactive zones, which the enemy can specially create at the commencement of and during an operation, and which also arise as a result of both sides' mass employment of nuclear weapons, will have a substantial effect on maneuver of forces and means, especially ground forces formations. Maneuver of rocket weapons, which can be implemented, above all, by trajectories, will play a principal role in the maneuver of forces and means. Strikes by rocket weapons in a very short time can be concentrated or redirected toward decisive axes and delivered against the most important enemy objectives, thus supporting the operations of different armed forces services groupings and their execution of operational missions.

The principle of delivering deep simultaneous and successive blows against the enemy, which was successfully implemented during the Great Patriotic War, has even greater significance in modern operations. This is the most effective method of disrupting the stability of different enemy armed forces services groupings.

Delivering deep blows against the enemy became important, thanks to the presence of powerful and long-range means of destruction in all armed forces services. The necessity of using combat means to exert pressure at a great depth is conditioned as well by the increased depth of concentration of forces and means of different enemy groupings, and by the presence of important objectives in the depth of his deployment, such as nuclear attack means, aviation groupings, and naval forces (on maritime axes). Rocket-nuclear strikes play the main role in suppressing the enemy depth. They are delivered, allowing that their results should be exploited in the interests of rapid execution of subsequent missions of large operational formations. Here, the unexpected and annihilating force of preliminary strikes in each concrete operation has especially important significance. Subsequent strikes must be delivered for the complete rout of the enemy and achievement of the assigned aim.

The conditions and sequence of maneuvering forces and means in modern operations substantively differ from similar conditions and operations in the past. At present there is no need to have large and dense force groupings, aviation, or navy, since now it is not so much the quantitative, but the qualitative composition of the groupings which has acquired great significance.

Mass use of nuclear weapons on decisive axes against main enemy groupings and most important objectives, with maximum dispersal of groupings of the different armed forces services, is acquiring decisive significance. It is necessary to concentrate forces and means of formations and large formations, as the operational structures permit, above all to create favorable conditions for their rapid use on decisive axes and against the main objectives.

The principle of conducting combat actions in operations by joint efforts of large operational formations of various armed forces services is still very important for modern conditions. The combat capabilities of formations and large operational formations make it possible to effect cooperation among all forces and means participating in the operation, on the basis of more extensive maneuver than in the past. A very important aim of cooperation among operational formations of different armed forces services and combat arms formations and units is to ensure coordinated employment of nuclear weapons in combination with other means of destruction, and rapid realization of the results of these strikes by ground forces, aviation, and the navy.

At present, the acute and intense struggle to seize and hold the initiative is the most characteristic feature of operations. To seize and hold the initiative for itself, each side will strive for surprise employment of means of armed struggle. This will make it possible to inflict heavier losses on the enemy in a very short time, sharply reduce his combat capability, swiftly change the correlation of forces and means to one's favor, paralyze his will, and deprive him of the ability to render organized resistance. In this way favorable conditions can be created to achieve the greatest results in an operation using fewer forces and means, with the fewest losses and expenditures.

When conducting an operation, it is necessary to exhibit initiative on the basis of a correct and thorough understanding of assigned missions and a complete analysis of the situation. Its essence consists of an attempt to find the best methods and to use promptly available forces and means in an operation; the skillful use of favorably developing conditions to attack the enemy; and promptly taking measures against an impending threat. It is necessary to strive to make use of any possibility to seize the initiative, and after this to hold it stubbornly during the entire operation.

Under modern conditions, combat operations develop on both sides with the greatest rapidity, and if available potentials are not promptly realized, then they may be irretrievably lost. This is why the struggle to gain time in an operation plays a very large role. The fact is that what occurred in the last war in 24 hours, for example, may now take place within several hours, even minutes.

The side which is able to employ appropriate forces and means in the necessary location and in a specific period of time will be able to achieve a decisive operational result. Modern operations must be conducted at rapid and increasingly faster tempos, using various and unexpected methods of combat actions.

The achievement of continuousness in combat operations has very important significance. They must be developed along the most important axes, continually forestalling the enemy in delivering strikes using means of mass destruction. Continuousness of combat operations makes it possible to keep the enemy continually under dynamic pressure, and this inhibits his initiative, while simultaneously being an important condition for successful resolution of missions in an operation.

Modern operations are characterized by great spatial scope, which is conditioned by the increased fire, strike, and maneuver capabilities of formations and large operational formations, and mainly by the appearance of powerful, long-range means, above all, rockets with nuclear warheads, which make it possible to strike successfully various enemy objectives in a short time and at practically any depth. The high mobility of ground forces and the increasing strike force of formations of other armed forces services are creating favorable conditions for rapid exploitation of the results of nuclear strikes, which is also leading to an increase in the scope of an operation.

Under the influence of improved combat means and increased capabilities of large operational formations, with respect to conducting operations at a great depth and at high tempos, a further reduction in the time for their conduct is occurring.

A characteristic feature of modern operations conducted by large ground forces operational formations is the conduct of combat actions along separate axes and under conditions of the absence of continuous fronts. Here, combat actions by forces of large operational formations can be conducted in separate regions, sometimes isolated from one another, and they can develop unequally on a wide front at various depths. The varied nature and high dynamism of combat actions developing simultaneously over a very large area are also important features of operations. The wide use of nuclear means of destruction, high force mobility, varied scale, and varied nature of actions will, undoubtedly, lead to sharp, frequent, and rapid changes in the situation. Forces of large operational formations on some axes may successfully develop the offensive, while on others they may conduct meeting battles and engagements; on others they may repel enemy counterattacks and counterstrokes, and on others they may temporarily shift to the defense or even withdraw.

Such, in general terms, are the nature and most important of the principles of conducting modern operations.

Subsequent development of the theory and practice of operational art should proceed, above all, from the capabilities of those means of armed struggle which large operational formations on both sides have and will have at their disposal in the immediate future.

The potential for armed forces services to conduct joint and relatively independent operations is conditioned by the necessity for developing both *a general theory of operational art and a theory of operational art for the armed forces services*, to perfect existing methods and find new, more expedient forms and methods for conducting an operation, and to use more effectively large armed forces services operational formations and combat arms formations.

Armaments, equipment, and the organization of armed forces services formations and large formations are being improved continuously. In this connection, the types and content of operations and their nature and scale are also continuously developing and changing. Proceeding from the modern condition of development of means of armed struggle, however, the organization of armed forces services, and the nature of future war, operational art can determine the types, nature, and scale of operations for some specific period of time. This will make it possible to study more thoroughly the theory and practice of organizing and conducting operations.

Depending on the primary share of participation of the armed forces services and the sphere of their employment, operational art examines and studies operations of ground forces, air forces, the navy, and national air defense forces. In each of these operations, a decisive role belongs to nuclear weapons. Under modern conditions, the overwhelming majority of operations are joint, since different, or even all, armed forces services participate in them. Independent operations of one armed forces service can be conducted by large air force, naval, and national air defense operational formations. It should be remembered, however, that the concept of an independent operation is relative, for operations of one armed forces service are also, to some measure, connected with operations of another armed forces service, and they undoubtedly have a definite influence on one another. An operation by large formations of one armed forces service can create favorable conditions for another armed forces service to conduct an operation. For example, an independent operation conducted by air forces or national air defense forces ensures, to a certain degree, the success of operations being conducted by ground forces or the navy. In turn, ground forces or naval operations have a specific positive influence on the conduct of operations by air forces and national air defense forces.

Air defense forces, having successfully repelled a surprise enemy air attack, eliminate the danger of being struck by groupings of other armed forces services. In sum, favorable conditions are created for these groupings to resolve their assigned operational missions. In turn, the timely execution of operational missions by ground or naval forces, associated with the rout of enemy aviation groupings, especially his rocket groupings, creates a very sound situation for large air defense operational formations to organize and conduct operations.

The role and significance of any armed forces service during a war and in its individual periods can substantively change, depending on the aim of the armed struggle, the strategic situation, and the nature of the theater of military operations. However, in the general system of armed struggle, those armed forces services able to achieve the best results in war more rapidly than others obviously occupy a leading position. In addition, it should be taken into account that positive results can be achieved only by a system of mutually coordinated operations conducted by large operational formations of all armed forces services to achieve a single strategic aim in a theater of military operations.

The theory of operational art examines operations in all the varieties of their characteristic features. The uniqueness of operations conducted by various large operational formations of armed forces services is especially great.

Each operation conducted in a specific theater of military operations, either by joint efforts or independently by one of the armed forces services, has a character inherent to it alone, which is conditioned by the operational aim, the quantity and quality of forces and means of both sides participating in the operation, materiel and technical support, and the theater of military operation's physical and geographic conditions.

In addition, modern operations, independent of the aim for which they are being conducted, their nature, and the participating armed forces service, have common principles of organization and conduct, which ensue from the nature of modern war. The general theory of operational art examines the characteristic features and principles of organizing and conducting operations which are inherent to operations of all armed forces services of any scale, as well as operations of large ground forces formations and the principles of joint operations of large formations of armed forces services.

At the basis of joint operations lie coordination of actions in carrying out overall missions, and correct combination of air force, naval, and national air defense efforts with ground forces operations. Such operations usually adopt a many-faceted character, encompassing large land, sea, and air expanses, where operations are developed jointly by large operational formations of some or all of the armed forces services. Here, the theory of operational art must take into account the significance and standing of each armed forces service in the armed struggle, the missions of the formations and large formations comprising them, and the expected nature of the probable enemy's actions.

Together with general principles of organizing and conducting operations, it is necessary to investigate their use of air, naval, and air defense forces in close mutual association. The necessity of developing the theory of operational art for each armed forces service is dictated by the great variety of operations and characteristic features inherent only to them, which have no place within the framework of a general theory of operational art.

Thus, the theory of air force operational art is characterized by peculiarities of using large aviation formations to achieve aims in air operations associated with destroying enemy armed forces groupings and demolishing various enemy objectives. Naval operational art investigates the use of naval forces and means for conducting operations at sea. National air defense operational art is characterized by the specifics of using appropriate forces and means to repel enemy air strikes. This struggle is viewed as air defense, which is directed toward the destruction of enemy aviation and rockets only in the air.

As is generally known, Soviet military art examines different methods of conducting armed struggle. However, it considers that only a decisive offensive directed toward the defeat of enemy armed forces will bring victory. Therefore, offensive operations conducted by the Soviet Armed Forces will be, as before, the main type of operations, and actions of all armed forces services will be organized to achieve these aims.

Initial offensive operations occupy an especially important place in operational art, inasmuch as the course and outcome of the war depend, to a considerable degree, on their results.

A ground forces offensive operation under modern conditions can be structured, in our opinion, so that, following rocket nuclear strikes, these forces swiftly shift to a decisive offensive, in cooperation with air forces, and in a short time achieve very effective results on the most important axes.

Operational art also focuses required attention on defensive operations, which, under modern conditions, are also employed in armed conflict. Rocket-nuclear strikes are a very important part of these operations. Defensive operations are usually conducted under conditions where an offensive in separate theaters of military operations and axes is, for some reason, inexpedient or impossible, and when it is necessary to support an offensive in other theaters of military operations and operational axes which are more important at the given time. Modern defensive operations should be structured on the basis of effective use of rocket-nuclear strikes and wide maneuver of forces and means, directed toward thwarting the enemy offensive or weakening his groupings, and toward firmly holding occupied territory. The main aim of defensive operations, then, is obviously to create conditions necessary for subsequent offensive operations by large operational formations.

Operational art views the counteroffensive as a basic form of the offense. A ground forces counteroffensive, in cooperation with other armed forces services, is conducted with the same goals as offensive operations in general. However, the counteroffensive has its own features, the essence of which is that it is executed against an enemy who is conducting an offensive or who has been stopped, but still has not successfully shifted to the defense. The counteroffensive differs from the usual offensive in its complexity of preparation and the specific conditions under which large ground forces operational formations shift from defensive to offensive operations. Here, its characteristic feature is its direct dependence on the conditions and results of preceding defensive engagements.

During an armed struggle, ground forces can conduct a withdrawal maneuver, which most often will be the result of unsuccessful defensive engagements. Under specific conditions, a withdrawal maneuver can even be conducted on the scale of a large formation. Obviously, the aim of such a maneuver will be to remove one's forces out from under strikes and place them in the best position with respect to the enemy, thereby ensuring that the enemy will subsequently receive a decisive blow.

Large ground forces operational formations, in cooperation with formations and large formations of other armed forces services, can conduct airborne, amphibious assault, and anti-assault operations. Usually such operations are a component of offensive or defensive operations.

The navy can conduct operations to destroy enemy naval shock forces, demolish naval bases, ports, and other important shore objectives, disrupt maritime communications, and support its own maritime communications. The navy also participates in operations conducted by large ground forces operational formations operating on coastal axes. During an offensive by large ground forces operational formations along the coast of closed maritime theaters, the navy's mission will be to assist ground forces in the capture of straits or in their defense.

Air forces can conduct operations to demolish and destroy the enemy's operational or strategic objectives, disrupt ground, air, and maritime communications, rout enemy operational and strategic reserves, and thwart his airborne and amphibious assault operations. In addition, air forces can participate in operations conducted by large air defense and ground forces, and sometimes even naval, operational formations.

Air defense forces conduct operations of various scales, the content of which is always associated with the protection of armed forces groupings and other objectives against enemy air strikes. The complexity and importance of these operations consist of the growing potentials for the enemy's mass use of pilotless means for air attack, capable of delivering nuclear weapons and other means of mass destruction.

With the development of combat means, the content, nature, and scales of operations conducted by large operational formations of armed forces services can change and acquire new form and content in the overall system of armed conflict.

The appearance and further development of combat means, especially rocket-nuclear weapons, require new resolutions of many issues in the theory of organizing and conducting operations. Based on the rich accumulated experience of organizing and conducting operations, and mainly making use of contemporary achievements of science and technology, the theory of operational art must develop uninterruptedly and find more modern forms and means of conducting operations.

NOTES

1. B. Golovchiner, "Nekotoryye voprosy sovremennogo operativnogo iskusstva," *Voyennaya mysl'* [Military thought], 10 (1961), pp. 41–9.

Formation and Development of the Theory of Operational Art (1918–38)

COLONEL (RET.) I. MARIYEVSKY[1]

Operational art is the theory and practice of preparing and conducting all types of military operations on all scales. Operational art as a military-theoretical discipline arose comparatively recently. The birth of the theory of operational art dates from the beginning of the twentieth century. The history of operational art has been insufficiently illuminated in our literature. The latest work in this field is Major General V. A. Semenov's, *Kratkiy ocherk razvitiya sovetskogo operativnogo iskusstva* [A brief essay on Soviet operational art].[2] Even with this, however, one cannot trace the history of the development of the theory of operational art. In this article the author attempted to illuminate some issues concerning the formation and development of the theory of Soviet operational art.

The existence of the Soviet Army's theory of operations began with selection, accumulation, and systematization of data on the First World War and Civil War operations. The first printed works which provided a more or less systematized account of operational knowledge appeared in 1919–20.[3] These works stated the most general principles for conducting ground forces operations. After the Civil War, a significant amount of research was published which generalized the experience of the last wars on the issue of operational and tactical troop actions.[4]

The works of B. Barsky and N. Suleyman presented problems of the materiel support of operations and ways of resolving them.[5] The broadening of operational knowledge was made possible, to a large extent, by the military-historical work of A. Svechin, V. Novitskiy, A. Zayonchkovskiy, N. Kapustin, A. Bazarevskiy, N. Kakurin, and V. Melikov, whose works illuminated concrete data on operations in the First World War and the Civil War.[6]

The works of Ludendorf, Falkenhayn, Kuhlman, and others were translated into Russian to study the experience of the German and French Armies in the First World War, to which the Higher Military-Editorial Council of the Republic attached serious significance.[7]

In 1923, the works of Clausewitz, one of the most thorough writers on military issues, were published in Russian.[8] The following year, under the editorship of A. Svechin, the first volume of *Strategiya v trudakh voyennykh klassikov* [Strategy in the works of military classics] came to light, in which the views of many famous military theorists and practitioners were set forth with extensive commentaries by the editor.[9]

In many theoretical and military-historical works, the operation was treated in the most varied manner: a grouping of battles for the achievement of strategic aims, the "totality of strategic and tactical actions directed toward the achievement of the one mission of a given war, being concluded in large part by a large combat encounter of both sides";[10] the "totality of maneuvers and battles in a given sector of a theater of military operations directed toward the achievement of the overall ultimate assigned aim in a given period of a campaign";[11] "an act of war, during which troop efforts are directed without any interruption on a specific area of the theater of military operations toward the achievement of a specific intermediate aim";[12] "the sum of various actions directed for the achievement of one of the aims set forth by strategy".[13]

The theory of operations was usually included in strategy (more rarely, in tactics) and was marked by the terms "operational leadership of troops", "operational matters," "operational technique," "tactics of mass armies," "tactics of a theater of military operations," "strategic art in an operation," "conduct of an operation." The term "higher command" was also used. Thus, it was called "Official guidance for commanders and field control of armies and *fronts*," as stated by M. V. Frunze in 1924.

The inclusion of the theory of operations, now in strategy, now in tactics, and the mixed nature of the terms which designated this theory created more than a few difficulties and resulted in lively arguments.

The two-part formula "strategy – tactics" had, over a number of centuries, contained all the substance of the art of conducting military operations. Until the middle of the nineteenth century, forms of conducting operations resulted from the small numerical size of armies, their armament properties, the availability of free maneuver area in a theater of military operations (the absence of broad strategic fronts), free (open) flanks, and a rear (communications). The fate of a war was often decided by a single operation or campaign. At that time an operation consisted of two parts: maneuver, whose purpose was to place an army's main forces in a favorable position, and the general battle, that is, a battle in which the main forces of both opposing sides took part. Hence, military art was divided into strategy and tactics. Thus, it was considered the "ideal of military art in general and strategy in particular . . . to resolve the war by a single, 'general' battle, that is, in the first days of military operations, in the first encounter to destroy (or take prisoner) all enemy armed forces."[14]

In the last quarter of the nineteenth century and at the beginning of the twentieth century, as a result of rapid growth in society's productive forces, conditions for conducting armed combat became significantly more complex. By this time, compulsory military service was introduced in all major European countries.[15] This made it possible to prepare cadres beforehand and draft large numbers of trained reservists into an army during a war. Mass armies appeared.[16]

Together with the numerical growth of armies, rapid quantitative and qualitative development of arms and combat equipment occurred. Rifled weapons, including new types (machine guns) had been significantly improved by the beginning of the twentieth century, and the attempt to exploit fully the maximum power of their fire (long range, rapidity of fire, accuracy, close grouping) resulted in a widening of the scope of armed conflict, never before seen.[17]

The rapid development of railroads facilitated the resolution of force mobilization readiness problems and made it possible to deploy mass armies and supply bases on a wide front and maneuver troops and materiel during the war; the appearance of telegraph made easier control of mass armies possible.

New conditions of armed combat gave birth to new methods and forms of conducting it. The general battle declined. There was no longer one "center" of battle; rather this changed into a "combination of a multitude of smaller battle centers scattered in space and time," not linked tactically, but requiring unification and leadership in aim, place, and time.[18] This was a new phenomenon in armed combat. Russian military thought at first called such combat actions army battle (*armeyskiy boy*), "battle in large masses,"[19] and then used the term "operation."

Historically, the Mukden operation in the Russo-Japanese War of 1904–05 can be considered the first new type operation. This operation is characterized by a broad front (more than 100 kilometers) and depth of deployment (as much as 60 kilometers), unprecedented duration (two weeks), combination of various actions (offense, defense, withdrawal), and great quantity of forces and means enlisted to participate in it (approximately 300,000 soldiers and 1,000 guns on each side). In this operation, troops maneuvered on the battlefield and beyond its limits, were replaced and replenished, and rested. Battle as a means of operations began to change in its essence as well, turning into a combination of fire and movement. In 1912, Russian military theorists, who noted the new phenomena in armed combat, expressed their views on the necessity to create a new theoretical discipline for studying operations – *operatika*. In reality, the changed nature of the operation, the mass of troops and equipment used to conduct it, the organization of movement of large troop masses, the great depth of columns and difficulty in deploying them for battle, maneuver in the course of the operation (battle), the difficulty in organizing the operational rear, and many other things required a specific theoretical base. Now a certain theoretical foundation was necessary to develop a plan of operation.

The First World War introduced serious changes in the nature of armed combat. This war most fully demonstrated that it was impossible to count on finishing off the enemy's entire active army with a single blow, that is, a general battle, even though it be in a gigantic strategic operation. Henceforth, war began to be composed of a series of campaigns, and each campaign of a series of operations organized in time and space. To carry out these blows, to control continuously large troop masses assigned to inflict them, and to organize troop supply, a definitive period was required to divide the operating army into partial armies, rather than separate ones, and to combine them into *fronts*[20] or army groups. The organization of armed combat in a theater of military operations or in a large part of it was assigned to the *front*, while the armies making up the *front* were assigned the organization of armed combat on operational axes. *Front* and army operations arose. During the Civil War this regularity was manifested with even greater force. The war was conducted on an unprecedented broad front (more than 8,500 kilometers in 1919), at various times by the forces of 12 *fronts* and four separate armies. Its conduct consisted of the sequential defeat of the principal enemy strategic groupings. The rout was achieved as a result of continuous implementation of successive operations until the enemy's complete liquidation. Operations were characterized by unusual mobility of *fronts* and maneuver of troops.

Thus, in the First World War and the Civil War new traits in military art, not encompassed by the old formula "strategy – tactics," were manifested. One of the first to come out against this formula was Professor A. Svechin.[21] In an introductory lecture for the strategy course given at courses of the Administration of Military Commandants at the Frunze Military Academy on 1 September 1924 on the subject "Integral Understanding of Military Art," he said: ". . . we suggest that maintenance of the old division of military art into strategy and tactics at the present time is absurd, since, in reality, the general battle, which earlier served as the basis of this division, has disappeared."[22]

With the appointment of M. N. Tukhachevsky (who also held the post of Chief Director for Strategy of All Academies) that very year as Chief of Staff of the *RKKA* [Workers' and Peasants' Red Army], the Frunze Military Academy's Department of Strategy began its work on researching questions of the conduct of war and operations. The subject of "conduct of operations" included only operational techniques, and was understood as the totality of procedures for organizing and supporting troop operational activities. Professor K. Berends in his work *Strategicheskiye vekhi* [Strategic landmarks], which, according to his modest admission, was only an honest transmission of the views and thoughts of the Department of Strategy and Military Art, wrote on this question, "Operational techniques in our understanding are only that part of strategy which comprise the subject of conduct of operations," while "the operation is a combination of combat actions to achieve a specific aim."[23]

The study of army operational activities at this time often took the form of general discussions which did not have great practical significance. Therefore, Frunze's demand for "less general discussion, more work on details and techniques of conducting operations" was not an indiscriminate one.[24]

The study of the literature of the 1920s shows that right up until 1926 the formula "strategy – tactics" remained unchanged. Moreover, as Tukhachevsky noted, the terms "strategy" and "tactics" were treated differently by everyone, and often contradictorily.[25] Such a situation was intolerable. And here it was not only a question of terminology, the significance of which is important in theory, but of the fact that after the First World War and the Civil War the theory of military art had ceased to reflect the fundamental qualitative changes which had occurred during those wars. Previously the theory of military art was developed only as a theory of techniques for conducting armed combat. The experience of those wars, however, especially the Civil War, showed that now a single technical theory was completely inadequate. Success in war, as never before, began to depend on proper political inculcation of the masses, on their understanding of war aims, and also on the country's economic condition. Hence, the leadership of armed combat began in practice to include not only the technical art of its conduct proper, but also the art of political leadership of the masses and the art of managing all the country's resources for economic support of the war. The existing theory of military art was not able to encompass the content of armed combat in a future war the imperialists were preparing against the Soviet Union.

A way out of the existing situation with the theory of military art, or out of the crisis, as A. V. Golubev called it, was found in the following.[26] Tukhachevsky expressed the idea about the necessity of creating "a science concerning war, which until now did not exist."[27] In his opinion, none of the First World War participants were prepared for its dimensions and forms, and only in the period of a "groping" development did their combat capabilities evolve, in particular because they did not have a science concerning war.[28] This science had to be a synthesis of the axioms of modern war, both as a socio-political phenomenon and as a process of armed combat and its economic support. Tukhachevsky proposed to call this new science concerning war "polemostrategy."[29] The principal task of polemostrategy was to be the higher generalization of the art of conducting modern war and the theoretical solution of the problems of war as armed combat on the whole. As for military operations, according to Tukhachevsky they were to comprise a subject in the study of strategy, while the study of battle up to a corps inclusive was to be in the study of tactics. Svechin, who more than once stated the necessity of a new classification of the theory of military art and who gave it a foundation in his book *Strategiya* [Strategy], proposed that the study of the conduct of war be made the subject of strategy, the conduct of operations the subject of operational art, and the conduct of battle of up to a division, inclusive, the subject of tactics. He explicitly emphasized that "the study of the methods of conducting operations is a task not of strategy, but of operational art."[30] Tukhachevsky did not insist on the term "polemostrategy" and agreed with the classification suggested by Svechin, although he criticized him on many other issues. It was admitted that the formula "strategy – tactics" had become obsolete in all respects. Therefore, the division of military art into three parts – strategy, operational art, and tactics – was confirmed in the Soviet Army from the mid-1920s.

Thus, in a brief sketch: armed combat as a whole – operation – battle, as the three levels of conducting war in the Soviet Army, corresponded in the theory of military art to strategy – operational art – tactics.

It cannot be said that the term "operational art" more fully reflected the content of the theory and practice of operations. This term was called into question earlier and even now has its opponents. However, it has firmly entered into the literature and we have become accustomed to it.

In this connection it is appropriate to note that some foreign military writers censure Soviet military theorists for the fact that they "wedged in" operational art between strategy and tactics. Thus, the American military writer Walter Jacobs in his article "Operational Art," published in November 1961 in the journal *Army* indicates that the purpose "of such an innovation is unclear," and that "in Western military science operational art as a theoretical concept is completely rejected." In his article's conclusion, the author says that "The West should not add this concept to its armory, simply because it does not allow for the development of its military art."

Is this so?

Soon after the First World War, in some foreign armies attention was also turned to the fact that the modern operation, on the strength of its inherent features alone, was a new phenomenon subject to thorough study. In Western European countries questions on the conduct of war were examined in strategy, questions of the preparation and conduct of operations in lesser strategy (Britain) or higher tactics (France), and battle in tactics. Thus, in some Western armies the question of conducting operations became a subject of study in a special discipline.

Operational art, which in the Soviet Army was formed into an independent theory of military art, encompassed the organization and leadership of armed combat in a theater of military operations, usually within the framework of a *front* (army), to execute missions assigned by strategy.

The essence of the interrelationship of operational art with strategy and tactics at this time was represented in the following way. As an intermediate level between strategy and tactics, operational art contained elements of both. Golubev wrote:

> If strategy groups and organizes operations for the achievement of the war aim, then operational art, within its limits, organizes and groups the immediate combat efforts of the forces in order to achieve those aims which strategy places before them. Thus, in the very essence of operational art are presented those elements which comprise the essence of strategy (the overall routine of the conflict and the grouping of force combat efforts to achieve specific intermediate war aims, not on the scale of the war as a whole, but rather on the scale of its separate parts).[31]

The conclusion was reached that inasmuch as war is a unified process for the use and actions of armed forces, there exists a dialectical interconnection and interdependence between operational art, tactics, and strategy. "Battle," wrote Varfolomeyev, "is the means of the operation, tactics is the material of operational art; the operation is the means of strategy, operational art is the material of strategy."[32] This meant that the more effective the battles, the more successful the operation. Therefore, the more tactics and their means improved, the more dynamic and decisive the methods of conducting operations could be, all else being equal. Hence, operational theory could not be created in isolation from tactics; it would be impossible to understand operational art without a thorough understanding of the sphere of tactics. Strategy had such a dependence on the capabilities of operational art, despite the fact that strategy determined the operational aims, and the forces and means for their implementation. Consequently, the theory of operational art is a whole whose integral parts are organically connected, conditioning one another in a specific way. V. Melikov correctly wrote, "One cannot build a watershed or construct a wall between strategy and operational art, since here one flows from the other, supplementing one another, that is, the same way as operational art and tactics."[33]

The study of ground military operations is included in the subject of the theory of operational art. At the time being examined, the term ground operations was understood as the activities of ground forces in a theater of war jointly with aviation, and jointly with a river flotilla along large rivers, having as their aim the rout of a specific enemy grouping or opposition to this grouping. With respect to types of force actions, ground operations were divided into offensive and defensive; with respect to scale they were divided into army and *front* operations.

The combat actions of troops making up an army and their materiel support, implemented in time and space into the execution of the mission assigned by the *front*, comprise the essence of an army operation. The concept of *front* operation was understood as the *front's* execution of a series of strategic missions into which the main command subdivided the current stage of the war. Keeping this mission in mind, the *front* determined its ultimate operational aim, broke it down into intermediate missions, and assigned their execution to component armies. Within the limits of these missions and the forces and means allotted by the *front* in accordance with the situation, each army conducted its own operation.

Thus, a *front* operation, encompassing an entire theater of military operations or a large part of it, consisted of army operations connected by an overall mission and close cooperation between one another on the basis of the overall *front* operational plan.

The art of conducting an operation (*front* and army) was perceived as the ability to mass forces and means on important axes. This assumed the existence of several groups in the operational force formation, namely a shock (countershock) group designated for operations on the main axes; a holding (auxiliary) group with the mission of working together with the shock group; and feint groups created to divert enemy attention. These groups were created chiefly by internal regroupings of army and *front* forces. Here it was emphasized that "maneuver is successful only when personnel and technical combat means are skillfully distributed (into indicated groups), achieving a ram-like massing on decisive axes at decisive moments."[34]

Everything stated above was included in most general form in the content of the theory of operations and determined its tasks. Chief among these were: investigating the operational nature of a future war; determining the role and place of combat arms (armed forces services) in a ground operation and requirements for their organization and combat training; determining the theoretical foundation of the *front* and army operation – aim, scope, operational support techniques,[35] and control (work of command and staff); developing a methodology for calculating forces, means, time, and space necessary for the operation; developing foundations and techniques of maneuvering such as march-maneuver,[36] and railroad and automobile maneuver; and investigating questions connected with the organization and work of the operational rear.

The formation of the theory of Soviet operational art proceeded under conditions of critical discussion, since various points of view on the nature and content of the theory of operations were discovered.

Many old military specialists based their judgements concerning the nature of future operations only on the purely military experience of past wars, while the social and class nature of the opposing states and the rapid growth of technical means of combat were not sufficiently taken into account. They presented the theory of operations in the form of a system of general ideas emerging primarily from the so-called "eternal and unchanging principles of war," irrespective of the Red Army, irrespective of where, irrespective of with whom, and irrespective of under what conditions it would have to fight. Girs wrote: "The field of military-scientific research includes mainly an examination of issues concerning the adaptation of conditions which are, in and of themselves, unchanging to conditions connected with a specific, concrete situation."[37] The metaphysical nature of similar views is obvious.

M. V. Frunze, M. N. Tukhachevsky, A. I. Yegorov, V. K. Triandafillov, I. E. Yakir, A. I. Sedyakin, I. P. Uborevich, N. Ye. Varfolomeyev, and others were in favor of developing a theory of operations for a concrete war in defense of the only socialist state in the world. In their opinion this theory would serve as the foundation of a specific system for conducting operations and a guide specifically for the Red Army. Above all, the theory of operations would have a distinct research task proceeding from the military-political aim of a future war, that is, to repel the aggressor overwhelmingly. This aim could be achieved only by means of implementing broad offensive operations directed toward the complete rout of the enemy. Therefore, they considered it necessary to develop, above all, offensive operations. The predominant attention to offensive operations was also explained by the complexity and difficulty of organizing and implementing them.

Possible forms of operational maneuver in offensive operations were considered to be the following: a *frontal* attack, an attack along converging axes (double penetration using a favorable *front* configuration), a combined attack – the organization of several attacks of various strengths on a broad front (the so-called blasting attack), envelopment (of one or both flanks), and encirclement. All these operational maneuver forms were widely employed during the Great Patriotic War. Defensive operations were not ignored, but they were viewed as subordinate to the interests of the operational offensive.

The first All-Union Congress of the Military-Scientific Society, in 1926, played a large role in the formation of operational art. At the Congress, in whose work M. I. Kalinin participated, basic issues on the country's defense and the development of the armed forces and theory of military art were discussed. There were 16 reports given, including those by Tukhachevsky (*Voprosy sovremennoy strategii* [Problems of modern strategy]), Triandafillov (*Razmakh operatsiy sovremennykh armiy* [The scope of operations of modern armies]), and Kamenev and Tsiffer (*Osnovnyye zadachi taktiki* [Basic tasks of tactics]). In his presentation Tukhachevsky emphasized that the theory of operations had to pursue the aim of developing "the art of destroying enemy armed forces" as the most economical method of conducting war. This had to be viewed as the foundation for educating the Red Army; it had to be studied in full, grasped entirely, and implemented.[38] This was stated in an address to those old specialists who, basing themselves on the experience of the First World War, asserted that in a future war it would be impossible to place before oneself the aim of routing the enemy's armed forces. In the collection *Grazhdanskaya voyna* [The civil war] it was pointed out that

> the aim of an operation can be either the seizure of enemy lines of communication or the penetration of his front or, finally, an attack with the envelopment of one or both flanks. One could not place before one-self the aim of "destroying" the enemy. Such a statement of the issue expresses nothing. This is a dream which cannot be fulfilled

and, therefore, "in the majority of cases remains empty noise."[39]

The positions stated by Tukhachevsky concerning operational aims were supported by the majority of Congress delegates. They had great theoretical and practical significance, since, henceforth, the varied treatment of operational aims was replaced by a clear and solid requirement: in all instances the operational aim was solely the destruction of enemy personnel and equipment, after whose achievement any other operational mission could be resolved. Tukhachevsky also emphasized that "operations should not be conducted anarchically or without principles. We must be permeated by a single, overall method."[40] Each operation should have an aim and plan which determines the actual method of action. The basis of the plan should consist not of "repelling the enemy," "capturing his flanks," but of encircling and destroying the specific enemy operational grouping. The operational form, which henceforth was to be determined depending on the main attack axis, had to correspond to the operational plan. The aim, plan, and form of the operation had to be worked out carefully and formulated extremely clearly and concretely. To achieve the operational aim, it was recommended to create powerful shock groupings (rams).

To theoretically solve the complex problem of "What must we immediately prepare for?"[41] in the field of conducting operations, the "eternal and unchanging principles of war" could not be taken as initial data. Advocates of a concrete theory of operations considered initial material to be the political aims for whose sake the war was necessary; the human material from which the Red Army and the armies of probable enemies were created; the organization, tactics, combat training, and probable numerical composition of the Red Army and that of its probable enemies; military equipment and prospects for its development, nature of theaters of military operations and possible enemy operational activities; and operational experience of the past, especially the last war. While attempting to determine scientifically the nature of operations in a future war, Soviet military thought searched for answers to such questions as the possible density of an armed front (at the initial period and during the war), probable scope, tempos, materiel needs and methods of satisfying them; what changes to expect in former ways and means of conducting operations, and the possibility of substituting them with new means (and, if so, which ones specifically); in what direction must the technical outfitting, organization, and combat preparation of the Red Army develop in order that these methods provide the greatest effect, etc. In searching for answers to these questions, very great significance was attached to military history and its lessons.

In the course of fulfilling the first five-year plan for the Soviet Army, a new materiel-technical base began to be created, the period of the army's technical reconstruction ensued, and the army began to receive the most modern weapons. All this fundamentally changed the old impression about operations.

The newest combat means indicated that a new stage in operational art was beginning, where the essence of the operation was the centralized inter-action of new means of destruction which possessed various combat (shock) and maneuver capabilities. In this connection, Tukhachevsky pointed out:

> we, of course, cannot remain at the former level of our military-theoretical thinking . . . we cannot fail to consider the five-year plan in the theory of military affairs of the Red Army . . . or react to it with an appropriate restructuring of military-theoretical tenets.[42]

A new orientation in the field of Red Army analytical thought was pro-vided by the Chief of Staff of the *RKKA*, A. I. Yegorov, in a welcoming address at the Frunze Military Academy in connection with its fifteenth anniversary. "The main and fundamental task of military art," he wrote, "is not to allow the formation of a continuous front, by giving operations and battle a crushing blow and a rapid tempo."[43] For the theory of operational art this meant that it was necessary to find the most effective method of crushing the entire enemy operational defense and subsequently routing the main operational grouping.[44] In his work *Udarnaya armiya* [The shock army], Varfolomeyev demonstrated that operations at the end of the First World War were conducted in linear forms, that is, combat was conducted the whole time on the line of direct contact with the enemy on the principle of "wall to wall"; the offensive was conducted in one "operational wave" (echelon) primarily composed of infantry divisions, which often had been used in overcoming the tactical defense. Where breaches were successfully formed at some point in time, there was no one to take advantage of them, since the infantry, if it was there, could not, in view of its mobility and fire power, be a means for developing a tactical penetration into an operational one. The defenders' numerous reserves, not pinned down by the attackers, maneuvered freely and always succeeded in closing the breaches, which had usually been made with a great deal of effort. The defensive front was pressed in or moved back, remaining operationally invulnerable. Operations developed very slowly, exhausting terribly the advancing armies both materially and physically.[45]

Soviet analytical thought reached the conclusion that in future wars a continuous strategic front was inevitable and it would have to be penetrated. The tactical capability of rapidly opening a breach in the enemy's tactical defense, thanks to the principles of deep battle, made it possible to reject maneuver before the enemy front, as was done in the war of 1914–18, but rather to carry it through these breaches beyond the enemy front into the operational depth. The theory indicated that it was namely here that it was necessary to direct new combat means – a mass of tanks, motorized infantry, mechanized cavalry, and aviation. Their great mobility, fire power, and shock force would make it possible to break an immobile front from within, and this would make it possible to develop wide maneuver actions. The basic principles of such an operation were not linear, but deep attacks of enormous penetrating force. Inflicting a deep attack was understood as simultaneously destroying, suppressing, and pinning down not only those defending forces designated to repel an attack from the front, but also those located behind the front in its operational depth; operations would also be directed against rear areas, headquarters, railroad junctions, etc. Requisite principles for success of the deep attack were the gaining of air superiority, isolation of the battle area from approaching enemy reserves, and interdiction of materiel being sent to his attacking troops. This method of conducting operational actions was called the deep operation.

The development of the theory of the deep operation is a great achievement of Soviet military-theoretical thought. An account of the foundations of this operation is not the subject of the current article. Here we will only point out its essence. It was conceived to carry out the simultaneous destruction of the operational defense by an attack from the front to penetrate the enemy's tactical defense and form a breach in it, and an attack in depth through this breach to penetrate the operational depth, implemented in close cooperation with aviation. The operational formation of the attacker's shock group should accordingly consist of a penetration echelon (chiefly infantry reinforced with tanks and artillery), an echelon for developing the penetration (a mechanized corps, cavalry, and motorized infantry), and an aviation group.[46] The art of conducting an operation began to consist of the actions of shock, holding, and feint groups, as well as those of penetration echelons, echelons for developing the penetration, and aviation, while tactically not interconnected, being consolidated along the front and in the depth, on the ground and in the air, into an attack mechanism which would provide single, purposeful, and continuous action against the enemy operational grouping until he was completely routed.

An extremely important role in the development of a correct methodological approach to studying operations, based on a Marxist-Leninist understanding of the specific nature of armed combat, belongs to V. K. Triandafillov. He was the first to attach important significance to the study of the nature of operations in political-economic, materiel-technical, operational-tactical, and strategic respects. Therefore, it is not by chance that he called his eminent work *Kharakter operatsiy sovremennykh armiy* [The nature of operations of modern armies]. "The book influenced many minds," said the editorial preface to the second edition, "and changed the conventional thinking of very many operational workers."[47]

Triandafillov's enormous merit consists also of his correctly posing the question concerning the necessity of basing the art of conducting operations not on the "intuition" and "feeling" of the military leader, but on a specific calculation of forces and means with respect to time and space. "Operational art," he wrote, "not only should, but can, give way to a certain calculated foundation."[48]

Stating that operational art does not exist outside specific norms, Triandafillov was far from the sense of "viewing operational art as a type of bookkeeping . . ."[49] In his opinion the art consisted of correctly taking into account the operational significance of all, usually changeable, elements of the situation, correctly determining those forces and means necessary for resolving a given concrete mission, and properly distributing them to formations [*soyedineniye*] and large formations [*ob"yedineniye*].

The theory of deep operations was developed for the first time in the Soviet Union. In the mid-1930s, not a single army in the world had a military theory so completely developed as did our Soviet Army. It corresponded to the nature of a future great war as a conflict between massive armies, abundantly outfitted with the latest technical means, whose use on an operational scale would be expedient only in the form of a deep operation. In connection with the unjustified repressions of 1937–38, many tenets of the theory of deep operations were questioned, inasmuch as military figures subject to the repressions had actively participated in its development.

In essence, our thinking was turned back to linear forms of armed combat on an operational scale as a result of this circumstance, and also as a result of incorrect conclusions drawn from the experience of the limited war in Spain in 1936–39, the implementation of which led to the disbanding of mechanized corps in 1939, the limitation of aviation to a tactical framework of actions on the battlefield, etc.

Thus, the highest achievement of our military-theoretical thought was temporarily consigned to oblivion. The experience of the first year of the Second World War demonstrated that the Germans were using our scientific achievements in the field of the theory of operational art most fundamentally and successfully. We quickly began to reexamine our views and introduce serious changes into the organizational force structure. But there was little time. Soon the Great Patriotic War began. Enormous efforts were required to eliminate these tremendous shortcomings.

In complete contradiction to historical truth, German Field Marshal Erich von Manstein states that during the war the Soviet command seemed to learn from the Germans the expedient organization of tanks into tank and mechanized corps and simultaneously adopted the German method of deep penetration.[50] Although we are not able to deal with this issue in detail, we point out the following.

It is known that the main source for judgement on operational-tactical procedures of one army or another is usually their regulations. The German regulations, *Troop Leadership*, adopted in 1933, contained not a hint of deep battle or operations in the sense in which these were treated in the book by Soviet researcher G. S. Isserson, *Evolyutsiya operativnogo iskusstva* [The evolution of operational art], which appeared in autumn 1932, as well as in the lectures on tactics given that year in the operations department of the Frunze Military Academy.

Because of its original posing of the question on new forms of armed combat on an operational scale, Isserson's book attracted the attention of German military researchers. Thus, a 1935 article, "A Modern Genghis Khan," published in the journal *Militaer Wochenblatt*, pointed out the novelty of the ideas stated in Isserson's book and recommended that they be regarded in all seriousness; moreover, it indicated that Soviet industry could support these ideas with appropriate armaments. It must be said that beginning in the 1930s and especially after the publication in 1936 of the new *Field Regulations of the Soviet Army*, in which the fundamentals of deep tactics were expounded, German military thought took in Soviet ideas of new forms of armed combat. One could find them, for example, in the works of German Generals Ludwig, Ehrfurt, and others. Most characteristic was the work of General-Lieutenant Tausen, *Problems of the Tactical and Operational Use of Tanks*, published in 1939. It examined questions of penetrating the entire enemy front by all modern combat arms, and throwing into the penetration large tank and motorized formations to completely crush the enemy being attacked.[51]

Thus, in the Soviet Army the theory of operational art was naturally assigned to an independent branch of military knowledge. Its history is the systematic, thorough, and multi-sided study of the continuously developing social and materiel-technical base and military thought of both the Soviet Army and the armies of probable enemies. Investigation of these issues was conducted in order to determine, promptly, in what direction and how the development of the theory of operations could proceed, what would be its ideological content, and which tasks would be the major and decisive ones for it. The creators of the theory of operational art (Tukhachevsky, Triandafillov, *et al.*) attempted to bring to light and master the new axioms of war; creatively develop corresponding ways and means of destroying enemy armed forces in a theater of military operations, that is, in *front* and army operations; systematically verify theoretical tenets already developed; and replace the obsolete with the new. The scientific or progressive nature of one or another theory of operations is usually judged according to how much its prognoses are justified, while the forms and methods developed by it for conducting operations passed a practical wartime verification. Despite some inadequacies (insufficient development of the operational defense, especially the withdrawal), the Soviet Army's theory of operational art passed the test of the Great Patriotic War and continues to be enriched by new tenets corresponding to modern conditions.

NOTES

1. I. Mariyevsky, *Voyenno-istoricheskiy zhurnal* [Military-historical journal], 3 (March 1962), pp. 26–40.
2. V. A. Semenov, *Kratkiy ocherk razvitiya sovetskogo operativnogo iskusstva* [A brief essay on Soviet operational art] (Moscow: Voyenizdat, 1960).
3. *Grazhdanskaya voyna. Sbornik I. Soobshcheniya po strategii grazhdanskoy voyny, chitan-nyye sotrudnikami shtaba 5-y armii. Inspektsiya voyenno-uchebnogo otdela 5-y armii Vostochnogo fronta, 1919; Tekhnika vedeniya operatsiy. Zapadnyy front, 1920; Boyevoye primeneniye strelkovoy divizii i vysshikh kavaleriyskikh soyedineniy* [The civil war. Collection I. Reports on the strategy of the civil war given by workers of 5th Army Headquarters. Inspection of the military-academic department of the 5th Army of the Eastern Front, 1919; Techniques of conducting operations. Western Front, 1920; Combat use of a rifle division and higher cavalry formations]. This work is in the personal library of V. I. Lenin in the Kremlin. On the title page of the book is the inscription "Copy of V. Lenin, 24 April 1920."
4. S. Kamenev, *Ocherednyye voyennyye voprosy* [Latest military issues] (Moscow: VVRS, 1922); M. Tukhachevsky, *Voprosy vysshego komandovaniya* [Problems of the higher command] (Moscow: 1924); M. Tukhachevsky, *Pokhod za Vislu* [Campaign for the Vistula] (Smolensk: 1923); A. Neznamov, *Sovremennaya voyna* [Modern war] (parts 1 and 2) (Moscow: Gosizdat, 1921–22); A. Verkhovsky, *Obshchaya taktika* [General tactics] (parts 1 and 2) (Moscow: VVRS, 1922); M. Batorsky, *Podgotovka plana voyny i operatsii* [Preparation of a plan for war and operations] (Izdatel'stvo upravleniya VUZ Zapadnogo fronta, 1921); N. Varfolomeyev, *Tekhnika shtabnoy sluzhby* [Techniques of staff service] (Moscow: VVRS, 1924); N. Shvarts, *Ustroystvo voyennogo upravelniya* [Setting up military control] (Moscow–Leningrad: Gosizdat, 1927).
5. B. Barsky, *Organizatsiya i upravelniye tylom* [Organization and control of the rear] (Moscow: Gosvoyenizdat, 1926); N. Suleyman, *Tyl i snabzheniye deystvuyushchey armii* [Rear and supply of an active army] (parts 1 and 2) (Leningrad: Gosizdat, 1927).
6. A. Svechin, *Evolyutsiya voyennogo iskusstva* [Evolution of operational art] (vols 1 and 2) (Moscow–Leningrad: Gosizdat, 1927–28); V. Novitsky, *Mirovaya voyna* [The world war] (Giz: 1928); A. Zayonchkovsky, *Mirovaya voyna. Manevrennyy period 1914–1915 godov na russkom (evropeyskom) teatre* [The world war. Maneuver period of 1914–1915 on the Russian (European) theater] (Moscow–Leningrad: Giz, 1929); A. Bazarevsky, *Mirovaya voyna 1914–1918* [The world war 1914–1918] (Moscow–Leningrad: Giz, 1927); N. Kapustin, *Operativnoye iskusstvo v pozitsionnoy voyne* [Operational art in a positional war] (Giz, 1927); N. Kakurin, *Kak srazhalas' revolyutsiya* [How the revolution was fought] (vols 1 and 2) (Moscow–Leningrad: Gosizdat, 1925–26); N. Ye. Kakurin and V. A. Melikov, *Voyna s belopolyakami 1920* [War with the White Poles, 1920] (Moscow: Gosvoyenizdat, 1925); V. Melikov, *Marna – 1914 goda. Visla – 1920 goda. Smirna – 1922 goda* [The Marne – 1914. The Vistula – 1920. Smirna – 1922] (Moscow–Leningrad: Giz, 1928).

7. E. Ludendorf, *My Recollections Of The War 1914–1918 (Vols 1 and 2)* (Moscow: Gosizdat, 1923–24); E. Falkenhayn, *The Supreme Command 1914–1916 In Its Most Important Decisions* (Moscow: VVRS, 1923); F. Kuhlman, *Strategiya* [Strategy] (Giz, 1927).

8. K. Clausewitz, *Fundamental Tenets On The Study Of War* (*The Most Important Principles Of The Conduct Of War*) (Moscow: Voyennyy Vestnik, 1923); *Principles Of Strategic Decision* (Moscow: VVRS, 1924).

9. *Strategiya v trudakh voyennykh klassikov* [Strategy in the works of military classics], Vol 1 (Moscow: VVRS, 1924) (in this were extracts from the works of Lloyd, Napoleon, Medem, Vilizen, Leval, Verdi du Vernois, von der Holtz, Foch, Schlieffen); Vol 2, (Voyenizdat, 1926) (in this were extracts from the works of Bulow, Archduke Karl, Jomini, Moltke, Scherf, Leer).

10. *The Civil War, Collection 1. Reports on Strategy,* p. 50.

11. N. Ye. Varfolomeyev, *Konspekt lektsiy po operativnomu iskusstvu* [Conspectus of lectures on operational art] (Frunze Military Academy, 1928), p. 3.

12. A. Svechin, *Strategiya* [Strategy] (Moscow: Voyennyy vestnik), 1927, p. 15.

13. Ibid., p. 200.

14. A. Neznamov, *Sovremennaya voyna* [Modern war] (SPB, 1912), p. 10.

15. The first compulsory military conscription was introduced in Prussia in 1813, in Austro-Hungary in 1868, in France and Japan in 1872, and in Russia in 1874.

16. The result of introducing compulsory military service and the shift of armies to a cadre system was clearly obvious in the example of Russia. In two centuries, from 1700–1900, Russia conducted 35 wars, which covered a total of 128 years, in which 9,810 soldiers participated. By 1 August 1914 its cadre army numbered 14,375 men; in all, the army numbered 15,978 fighting men. Thus, in the three years of the First World War the number of men engaged in battle was almost twice that of the 128 years of war mentioned above.

17. In 1812 the French and Russian armies met at Borodino on a front of 6–8 kilometers; in 1914, the French and German armies deployed on a front of 340 kilometers, while the Russian army deployed at that time against the German and Austro-Hungarian armies on a front of 1,057 kilometers.

18. N. N. Golovin, *Vvedeniye v kurs taktiki* [Introduction to a course in tactics] (SPB, 1911), p. 9.

19. V. V. Marushevsky, *Upravleniye voyskami na teatre voyny i na pole srazheniya* [Troop control in a theater of war and on the battlefield] (SPB, 1912), p. 124.

20. A *front,* as a higher formation (*ob"yedineniye*) of armed forces on a theater of military actions, was created in Russia for the first time in 1900 in the plan for strategic deployment of the Russian army against Germany and Austro-Hungary.

21. A. A. Svechin (1879–1941) – general-major of the Russian army, in the Red Army from 1918. He was the military leader of the Western Screen (Front), chief of the All-Russian Main Staff, chairman of the military-historical commission, professor in the Department of Strategy, War History, and Military Art at the Frunze Military Academy.

22. The journal *Krasnyye zori* [Red Dawns], 11 (1924), p. 23.

23. K. Berends, *Strategicheskiye vekhi* [Strategic landmarks] (Moscow: Frunze Military Academy, 1925), pp. 52, 61.

24. M. V. Frunze, *Izbrannyye proizvedeniya* [Selected works] Vol. 2 (Moscow: Voyenizdat, 1957), p. 35.

25. M. Tukhachevsky, *Voyna. Sbornik Voyennoy akademii RKKA im Frunze* [War. Collection of the Frunze Military Academy of the *RKKA*], book 1, 1926, p. 1.

26. A. Golubev, *M. V. Frunze o kharaktere budushchey voyne* [M. V. Frunze on the nature of future war] (Moscow: Gosvoyenizdat, 1931), p. 8. Golubev was a colonel (retired), member of the CPSU from 1917. On the eve of the Great Patriotic War he headed the department of operational art at the Higher Military Academy.

27. Tukhachevsky, *War,* p. IV.

28. Ibid. Tukhachevsky not only came forth with a suggestion for the creation of a "science concerning war", but soon after set about developing it in a monograph entitled *Novyye voprosy o voyne* [New issues concerning war]; see *Voyenno-istoricheskiy zhurnal* [Military-historical journal], 2 (1962).

29. From the Greek "polemos" – "war" and "strategiya" – "troop leadership."

30. Svechin, *Strategy*, p. 200.
31. A. V. Golubev, *Voprosy frontovoy i armeyskoy operatsii* [Questions on the *front* and army operation] (Moscow: Military Academy For Tank Troops), 1940, pp. 5–6.
32. N. Varfolomeyev, *Strategiya v akademicheskoy postanovke* [Strategy in an academic formulation] in *Voyna i revolyutsiya* [War and revolution], 11 (1928), p. 84. N. Ye. Varfolomeyev (1890–1941), staff-captain in the old Russian army; in the Red Army from 1918. He held the posts of chief of army staff, deputy chief of *front* staff, deputy chief of the strategy cycle at the Frunze Military Academy of the *RKKA*, and district chief of staff.
33. V. Melikov, *Problema strategicheskogo razvertyvaniya* [The problem of strategic deployment], Vol. 1 (Moscow: Frunze Military Academy, 1935), p. 32.
34. *Vyssheye komandovaniye* [Higher command] (Moscow: VVRS, 1924), p. 3.
35. In the concept of "operation support technique" are included reconnaissance, security (mainly the air defense of the area of the operation), engineer support, communications, military communications, supply, outfitting, and medical and veterinary services. In the guide *Higher Command* it is emphasized that operation support techniques "are the basis of strategic maneuver," (p. 6) and that they should "have specific norms and permanent methods" (p. 4).
36. March-maneuver is the movement of an army from landing points toward the enemy, or any shift of several large formations.
37. G. Girs, *Zadachi nauki i voyennaya doktrina v svyazi s perezhivayemoy nami revolyutsionnoy epokhoy* [The tasks of science and military doctrine in connection with the revolutionary epoch which we are experiencing], book 1, 1921, pp. 50–51.
38. Tukhachevsky, *Problems of modern strategy*, p. 19, 20.
39. *Grazhdanskaya voyna*/The civil war, collection 1, p. 34, 35.
40. Tukhachevsky, *Problems of modern strategy*, p. 20.
41. Ibid., p. 11.
42. M. N. Tukhachevsky, *O kharaktere sovremennykh voyn v svete resheniy VI kongressa Kominterna* [On the nature of modern wars in light of the decisions of the VI Comintern Congress], notes, Vol. 1 (Komakademiya, 1930), p. 20.
43. *XV let Krasnoznamennoy Voyennoy akademii RKKA im. M. V. Frunze (1918–1933)* [Fifteen years of the Red Banner Frunze Military Academy of the *RKKA* (1918–1933)], 1934.
44. N. Varfolomeyev, *Udarnaya armiya* [The shock army] (Moscow: Voyenizdat, 1933), p. 178.
45. Anglo-Franco-American troops in the four months of the offensive in 1918 advanced 100 kilometers.
46. Several mechanized corps could form a motor-mechanized army, and a formation of mechanized corps with cavalry – a mounted-mechanized army or group.
47. V. K. Triandafillov, *The Nature of Operations of Modern Armies*, p. 11.
48. Ibid., p. 224
49. Ibid., p. 225.
50. Erich von Manstein, *Verlorene Siege* [Lost victories] (Bonn, 1955).
51. *Voyennyy zarubezhnik* [Military foreigner], 8 (1939).

Tactics and Operational Art of the Workers' and Peasants' Red Army at a New Stage

A. I. YEGOROV[1]

The theses of the report by Marshal of the Soviet Union A. I. Yegorov, published for the first time by the editorial staff in abbreviated form, are of considerable interest. They sum up the results of scientific-theoretical research carried out in the Red Army at the beginning of the 1930s, connected with the technical reconstruction of the armed forces.

Although the report's theses are called *Taktika i operativnoye iskusstvo RKKA na novom etape* [Tactics and operational art of the *RKKA* [Workers' and Peasants' Red Army] at a new stage], their content encompasses a number of strategic questions. In particular, the theses raise questions such as strategic deployment, views on the nature of the initial period of a future war, views on the use of types of armed forces, and other matters.

The history of this document's creation is interesting.

The outfitting of the army and navy with new combat equipment sharply posed the question of the course of further armed forces development and creation of a military theory which responded to the requirements for the technical reconstruction of the *RKKA*. In view of the urgency and importance of this matter, the USSR Revolutionary Military Council [*RVS SSSR*], in its meeting of 11 March 1932, charged the *RKKA* staff with developing a report on operational-tactical problems associated with the reconstruction of the *RKKA*. On 20 April 1932 the *RVS* heard Yegorov's preliminary observations on the question and decided on a special meeting for 20 May to examine the final version of the report. The *RKKA* Chief of Staff was tasked to work out fully by this time the report's theses and distribute them to all members of the *RVS SSSR*.

At the beginning of July, the report's theses were distributed to military district commanders, deputy people's commissars, and chiefs of military academies. In comments received, the theses' basic tenets were approved. The former (at that time) commander of the Ukrainian Military District, I. Ye. Yakir, wrote that the report's theses raised a number of new tenets in the field of tactics and operational art in a timely fashion in connection with the widespread introduction into the army of motorization and the development of aviation. He proposed to conduct a series of exercises and games to verify in practice the theoretical tenets formulated in the report's theses.

The commander of Leningrad Military District forces, I. P. Belov, in analyzing the content of the stated tenets on strategy, pointed out that they were a new contribution to the development of Soviet military doctrine. The former (at that time) *RKKA* Chief of Combat Training, A. I. Sedyakin, also warmly supported the report's theses. In a letter to Yegorov he wrote that he fully shared the basic positions on tactical and operational art which were stated in the theses of the *RVS* report.

The report's theses, opinions, and observations were used to develop *Vremennyye ukazaniya po organizatsii glubokogo boya* [Temporary Instructions for Organizing Deep Battle], sent to the troops as an official manual in 1933.

The ideas stated in the report's theses are of great scientific interest. It should be taken into account that the report's theses were written in the first half of 1932, that is, at the dawn of Soviet Army mechanization and motorization, when not a single army as yet had experience in using large masses of armored and mechanized forces or massive use of aviation with qualitatively new aircraft combat characteristics.

This was a turning point, when many tenets of military art, confirmed after the First World War, were recognized as obsolete; searches for new forms of conducting operations and battles corresponding to the new level of armed forces development were carried out. At that time, the old views, which relied on First World War and Civil War experience, were still unusually tenacious. They exerted considerable influence on the development of military theory. Therefore, in the published report's theses, together with bold and correct conclusions which emerged from the qualitative and quantitative development of the armed forces, there were also erroneous tenets, obsolete for that time, on the nature of conducting armed struggle and the role of combat arms.

On the basis of analysis of armed forces development after the First World War, new content was added to the concept – the initial period of war. This was not a period of passive concealment of armed forces mobilization, strategic concentration, and deployment, but one of dynamic actions with far-reaching aims. In the report's theses, the possible nature of force actions during this period was stated. Second World War experience basically confirmed the correctness of the tenets advanced in this document.

In addition, several questions concerning the conduct of combat operations during the initial period of war were subject to subsequent reworking. The experience of strategic games and exercises conducted in the 1930s demonstrated that invasion groups were not able to fulfill their assigned missions in the first strategic stage of the struggle. They were weak in composition, and directed toward operations along isolated axes, which could lead to their subsequent defeat by the enemy. Instead of groups, initially it projected the creation of invasion armies or shock armies; then it recognized that it was necessary to assign the fulfillment of the missions of the invasion armies to the entire first strategic echelon of the armed forces.

After a brief summary of opinions on the nature of the initial period of war, the theses examined individual problems concerning strategic concentration of the Soviet Armed Forces. A special place in the report's theses was devoted to analysis of the nature of operations which would take place in future wars, and also of the place and role in them of types of armed forces and combat arms. A reevaluation of the role of cavalry was noted in the theses, although extensive introduction of automatic weapons into the forces and development of aviation already in the First World War had led to a significant reduction in the role of cavalry in battle and operations. With the appearance, then, of tanks and the transformation of aviation into an independent armed forces branch, the significance of cavalry as an army shock force was, in essence, reduced to naught.

The theses emphasized increased demands for troop control, and mentioned that "the new form of operation requires extensive use of radio, aircraft, communications, and combat vehicles (on a tank chassis)," that is, radio and mobile means of communication occupied first place. The Great Patriotic War confirmed the viability of these demands.

While elaborating on tactical questions, of which in the published material only a section on the meeting engagement was inserted, the report's theses examined in particular the sequence of using aviation and armored troops in the offensive, with a penetration of the enemy defense on to entire depth.

A model operational plan for tanks jointly with combined arms formations was presented in the following manner. After the artillery preparation, operations were begun by long-range action [DD] tanks as a means of the rifle corps or division commander. This tank group was to suppress artillery in the depth of the enemy position, control points, and reserves. Following this, long-range support [DPP] tanks went into the attack as a means of the division or regimental commander; these were to suppress enemy infantry fire means in the depth of the defense. Finally, direct infantry support [NPP] tanks as a means of the rifle company commander followed directly with the infantry. Each rifle corps in the offensive battle was reinforced by one brigade and two to three tank battalions of the Reserves of the High Command [RGK]. However, combat operations conducted by Soviet Army forces at the end of the 1930s forced a reexamination of this model for using tanks.

The increasing density of defensive antitank means made it impossible for long-range action tanks to operate independently in the deep enemy deployment. Being of no use, long-range action and long-range infantry support tanks in the majority of cases suffered great and unwarranted losses.

Increased artillery range and creation of light and assault aviation made it possible to suppress more effectively and reliably the tactical defensive zone to its entire depth. Therefore, with the beginning of the Great Patriotic War, only direct infantry support tank groups were created for cooperation with infantry.

The report's theses ended with conclusions which concisely reflected the opinions of Soviet military theory at the beginning of the 1930s on the conduct of battles and operations and on the organizational principles of Soviet Armed Forces development.

The publication of the theses of A. I. Yegorov's report opens yet another page in the history of the development of Soviet military theory.

The published document is kept in the Central State Archive of the Soviet Army.

I. INTRODUCTION

1. The plan, accepted by the *RVS* for the development of Air Forces and mechanized units, and the introduction of mechanization and motorization into rifle and cavalry units and formations in the next one to two years not only radically change the *RKKA*'s organizational structure, but also pose a number of new problems of a strategic and operational-tactical order.

2. In 1933 we will have powerful formations, such as aviation and mechanized corps. With respect to means of suppression, we can support a shock group of corps and several shock armies by considerable additional means of attack (aviation, tanks, artillery, etc.), which make it possible to pose the problem of the nature of the battle and operation in a new way ...

II. TACTICAL ISSUES

1. At this stage of the development of the *RKKA*, in view of the saturation of forces with the newest technical means of combat and control, a whole series of tactical questions (the offense, defense, pursuit, etc.) acquires a completely different nature of activity.

Modern means of destruction, on the strength of their great power (aviation, Armies of the Reserve of the High Command/*ARGK*), rapid movement (tanks, aviation), and range, make it possible to strike the enemy simultaneously to the entire depth of his deployment, as opposed to present forms of battle and attack, which can be characterized as successive suppression of separate elements of the combat formation.

These assets are used so as to paralyze the fire of all defensive means, independent of their depth of deployment, isolate one part of the enemy from the other, disrupt cooperation between them, and destroy them piecemeal.

The following should be attached to troop formations to inflict a blow and execute an attack against the entire depth of the enemy combat deployment:

(a) aviation – to suppress artillery and rout reserves;
(b) additional artillery – to suppress infantry and infantry fire means, the antitank defense, and artillery;
(c) tanks – to suppress infantry fire assets and artillery, and to rout reserves.

Meeting Engagement. The presence of a large quantity of tanks, artillery, and aviation is undoubtedly reflected in the nature of the meeting engagement as well. There is the opportunity to have the advance guard stronger in artillery support, approximately three or four artillery battalions per rifle regiment (not including regimental artillery), tanks for accompanying infantry, and approximately one battalion per rifle regiment. Taken together, this reinforces to a higher degree the advance guard's offensive strength and makes it possible for it to achieve the outcome more rapidly against enemy security units.

The presence of combat aviation and fast-moving tanks makes it possible for the chief of a column to produce the first effects against the enemy by using these longer-range and faster-moving means.

Aviation initiates the battle. It executes the first attacks against the enemy. By its operations it can upset the columns of the enemy's main forces, isolate one column from the others, and isolate the advance guard from the column's main forces. This is achieved by repeated operations by separate detachments or squadrons.

In all probability, fast-moving tanks will be put into action immediately after the deployment of the advance guard's artillery, so that their actions can be supported by sufficiently strong artillery.

The object of both artillery and fast-moving tank actions should be one and the same, that is, breaking up the enemy march formation: deploying enemy artillery, separate battalions or regiments still located in the column or already moving in open formations. Usually artillery subjects these objectives to concentrated fire, while fast-moving tanks attack and annihilate them from the flanks and the rear. Aviation is enlisted for repeated strikes either against the same targets or against neighboring ones, so as to isolate the objectives being attacked.

An attack by fast-moving tanks against separate elements of the march formation will precede the transition to the offensive by the advance guard's main forces, since the infantry physically cannot manage to deploy simultaneously with tanks; to surrender the opportunity to attack the enemy while the infantry is formed in a column would be a mistake.

The advance guard, under cover of these actions, swiftly deploys, and with its accompanying tanks attacks enemy security units.

During this period, regiments of the main forces column with accompanying attached tanks will be located in the approach stage and along column roads, or they will reach the deployment area dispersed along separate approaches. Their final attack axis should be determined in accordance with the results achieved by aviation, tank, artillery, and the advance guard actions as a whole until the moment these tanks arrive in the deployment area.

All column forces, all infantry, artillery, tanks, including those which until this time took part in one or two attacks, and all aviation should participate in this general new phase of the meeting engagement. This attack by united forces is organized as an advance against a defending enemy (with long-range action, long-range infantry support, and direct infantry support tanks and air assault detachments thrown into the enemy's rear area), and should lead to a complete rout of the enemy.

Here, questions concerning control are new and most formidable.

Reliable and continuous communications with airfield aviation obviously is required; such communications can be supported on the march only with the help of radios and aviettes,[2] and duplicated by motor vehicles.

Reliable communications are required between ground and air forces, between commands on the ground and airborne aviation; obviously, here only radio can provide control. All communications means will find a place in the organization of communications between commands, tanks, artillery, and infantry. With tanks engaged in battle, communications is by radio and combat vehicles (small tanks, armored vehicles).

A broad network of command observation posts with responsible staff workers is required for observing troop activities along the entire front and to the entire depth. In all probability, this will not be successful without special observation aircraft with radio stations for reception and transmission mounted on them. Special command combat vehicles, which are sent with tank echelons together with communications delegates, can help . . .

III. OPERATIONAL ISSUES

1. New means of armed conflict (aviation, mechanized and motorized formations, modernized cavalry, air assault forces, etc.) and their qualitative and quantitative growth are raising new questions concerning the initial period of war and the nature of modern operations.

2. *The Initial Period of War.* Opposing sides will attempt as early as possible, with the help of covert mobilization methods, to amass more quickly those forces and means, with whose help they can invade enemy territory and forestall enemy mobilization in border areas and concentration of forces.

All combat aviation, motor-mechanized units, and mounted masses will be used for this . . .

It is impossible to determine precisely the nature of initial operations, but operational landmarks can and must be laid.

Aviation, by air actions and air-assault landings in conjunction with diversionary acts from within, can hinder railroad transport to a depth of 400–600 kilometers, inflict considerable damage on enemy air and naval forces, and destroy the most important supply depots and bases supplying his army.

Large motor-mechanized units interacting with mounted masses and aviation, supported in the first days of border engagements by infantry units, penetrate into enemy territory.

The primary aims of invasion groups are the following:

(a) destroying covering units;
(b) thwarting mobilization and new formations in border areas;
(c) capturing and annihilating enemy reserves formed for the conduct of war, and holding areas of operational significance, indicated in the mission as one of the principal aims of the deep invasion into enemy territory;
(d) forcing the enemy to withdraw his positions deeply into the rear area.

The depth of penetration of invasion groups will be determined by the correlation of forces at the moment of invasion, the distance to the largest water barriers, the fortification of areas, and calculations of provisions . . .

It is necessary, however, to take into account that invasion groups will be able to create only a number of crises and inflict a series of strikes against covering armies, but will not be able to resolve the issue of concluding the war or delivering a decisive strike against the main forces. This is the mission of the subsequent period of operations, when the operational concentration will be complete.

3. *The Problem of Concentration.* Two principal factors determine the situation of the initial concentration:

(a) aviation, whose location depends on its quantitative and qualitative state;
(b) the presence of motor-mechanized formations, which combine great shock and fire power with great mobility.

These data are reflected in the following way in the process of the *RKKA's* initial concentration.

Enemy aviation, by air actions and air-assault landings, can actively hinder transportation to a depth of up to 600–800 kilometers (Moscow–Khar'kov meridian), forcing maneuver along the railroads both in bypassing the destroyed sectors and in changing the direction of flow and areas of concentration.

Large motor-mechanized units interacting with cavalry can interfere with *RKKA* transportation and concentration by means of ground operations.

Under our conditions, in the presence of river lines along the border (Dnestr, Sluch) and a number of fortified areas, the danger of disrupting railroad transportation and *RKKA* deployment by ground forces troop actions is insignificant. With the reinforcement of fortified areas by garrisons in peacetime and by antitank defense, this danger can be eliminated.

The principal and sole threat to the railroad transport plan and, at the same time, to the deployment plan by the first operation, will be from enemy aviation.

In this regard, planning, control, and support of the process of concentration, as distinct from the World War, acquires a special character. These features are reduced to the following:

(a) the railroad transportation plan should be flexible, allowing the opportunity for changing the flow in bypassing a destroyed sector in case of disruption of movement on one railroad axis;
(b) it is necessary to pose in a new way the problem of reserves and the location of means necessary for reestablishing destroyed railroad sectors. These means should be concentrated in peacetime at railroad centers and other points of probable enemy attack (in the vicinity of railroad bridges, railroad sidings, and unloading stations).

The principal guarantee of the capability for continuous fulfillment of the concentration plan is the presence of a powerful air fleet, air defense means, powerful mechanized groups, and mounted units, appropriately located in peacetime. Control of the concentration process within the limits of principal trends and ideas should be centralized. Thus, the following are tasks for the High Command:

(a) control of railroad maneuver;
(b) maneuver by means of changing points and periods of time for loading units (outside of the zone of control of *front* command);
(c) maneuver of reserve means for restoring the railroad;
(d) change of lines of concentration and deployment;
(e) change of groupings by means of redistribution of forces between *fronts* . . .

4. *The Nature of Modern Operations.* The modern operation will consist of combat actions unfolding on a large expanse, both along the front and in the depth.

The depth of a modern operation will depend on the depth of the enemy's operational deployment, which will reach 100–120 kilometers, taking into account as well reserves maneuvering with the help of vehicular transport, airfields with aviation (including heavy) deployed on them, distribution railroad stations with reserves of combat goods, etc.

The penetration of such a deployment presently entails great difficulties and a great expenditure of time. This is conditioned by the fact that:

(a) the tactical stability of the defense in connection with the presence of a large number of infantry machine guns is so great that the rate of the advance from the front is very slow. It is considered that, with battles, an average of 8–10 kilometers can be covered on the day of an operation, and only as a maximum will this reach 12 kilometers;

(b) the presence of reserves in the rear, and the ability to maneuver by vehicular transport and railroads make it possible to bring forward new forces into the area relatively swiftly; these can easily cover the breach which has been formed.

The Imperialist War knows many instances of penetration of the enemy's defensive belt, but these penetrations amount to the tactical breakthrough of a front. The development of efforts into the depth to transform tactical success into an operational achievement did not take place. The reason for this is disclosed in the absence of mobile operational echelons capable of developing the penetration, annihilating approaching reserves in its path, disrupting control and supply system, etc. Operational art of the Imperialist War did not demonstrate the ability to implement an operational penetration (on the Western Front).

To transform a tactical penetration into an operational breakthrough of the entire enemy defensive belt, it is necessary not only to attain a higher rate of offensive development from the front (which is now achieved with the help of tanks, artillery, aviation, and motorization of rear areas), but also to find means which would make it possible, simultaneously with a strike from the front, to attack enemy reserves, his aviation, and supply units even more deeply, and to deprive him of the ability to maneuver extensively both these reserves and those new troops which can arrive by railroad or with the help of vehicular transport. Means are required which would make it possible to create heavy traffic congestion in the enemy rear area, thus cutting off the path of enemy withdrawal; this would lead to his complete tactical "encirclement."

These opportunities are opened by the following:

(a) correct operational use of contemporary (modernized) strategic cavalry;

(b) appearance of new means permitting rapid penetration into the enemy rear area – large motorized and mechanized force formations (mechanized corps, mechanized brigades, and motorized divisions);

(c) large-scale development of combat aviation, which has obtained, thanks to this, the capability of powerful and extended action against objects located in the enemy's deep rear area;

(d) prospects of extensive use of air-assault forces in the enemy's deep rear area . . .

6. *Organization of an Operation on a Decisive Axis.*[3] The central question in organizing an operation on a decisive axis (shock army) and its planning is the *correct combination* of frontal attacks with strikes to the depth of the enemy's operational position. This combination of blows should lead to a possible *swift* penetration of the entire enemy front, and encirclement and annihilation of his forces occupying the front sector being attacked; as a result, this should open a new opportunity – the development of decisive operations on the flank and in the rear area of forces occupying the remaining sectors of the enemy front.

In organizing an operation and when directing forces, it is necessary to strive so that at the end of the first, or in an extreme case at the beginning of the second day of the operation, *ground* forces attack the depth of the enemy's operational position, whose overcoming would lead to complete penetration of the enemy front. This depth will usually be determined by the deployment area of his army reserves and heavy-aviation airfields. This is achieved roughly by the following plan for organizing the attack.

With the disruption of the enemy's defense system (upon penetration by infantry 6–10 kilometers into the enemy's position), the following are thrust forward:

(a) motor-mechanized units (mechanized corps, brigades) in combination with aviation and air assaults to attack the deepest objectives (supply stations, rear lines, etc.), army reserves, airfields, heavy aviation, etc.

   The depth of the penetration during the first day is up to 80–100 kilometers. Mechanized units, in advancing into the enemy's deep rear area to the indicated objective, annihilate approaching reserves, withdrawing units, and transports in their path;

(b) cavalry, with aviation support, are sent to attack reserves and light aviation airfields which are not as deep, and to destroy withdrawing logistic support elements. The depth of penetration during the first day is up to 50–60 kilometers;

(c) motorized units sent to destroy reserves approaching or being transferred into the penetration area, or to operate along the rear areas of sectors not being attacked, to widen the penetration. Heavy and light bomber aviation attack railroad centers (destroy them) on major lines leading to the penetration area to prevent transport of reserves from the depth of the country. The depth of operation is up to 400 kilometers . . .

Further attacks occur simultaneously from the front and rear until full tactical encirclement is achieved.

From the commencement of enemy withdrawal, the army shifts to the pursuit. Here, motor-mechanized units and cavalry pursue along parallel roads and break out, striving, if possible, to form a "Cannae" on the withdrawal route.

To organize such an attack, an army combat formation is structured in the following way:

(a) in front are rifle corps, with a depth of combat deployment of up to 6–8 kilometers;

(b) behind, on the army's main attack axes, are motor-mechanized units and cavalry, ready to be thrust forward;

(c) aviation is echeloned as follows: light combat aviation from 40–60 kilometers, and heavy aviation from 80–200 kilometers.

7. *Control.* Control of a modern shock grouping is complicated by the following facts:

(a) various units being sent into the enemy's rear area require that their operations be closely coordinated among one another, not only at the commencement, but also during the operation itself and in the first period of actions, as in a corps. The army commander should provide a timetable by which combat operations of all units are coordinated to the entire depth of the battle;

(b) the great separation of forces being sent into the enemy's rear area makes it difficult to provide continuous communications with these forces and to supply them.

Therefore, the new form of operation requires extensive use of radio, communications aircraft, and combat vehicles (on a tank chassis).

The use of code should be simplified and introduced into the army so that it can also be used in normal conversation.

Control in a modern operation is organized based on the prerequisite that command of all units attacking one and the same objective is unified in the same hands. Motor-mechanized formations, air assault-motorized forces, and aviation operating against deep enemy objectives are united by the mechanized corps commander.

Strategic cavalry and aviation operating against the enemy's administrative rear area are subordinate to the cavalry group or cavalry army commander.[4] All units attacking rear objectives should not be connected by demarcation lines.

At the beginning of the operation, aviation functions according to the direct task of the army commander, and with the beginning of the advance of mechanized and cavalry units it is attached to the latter at the prerogative of aviation groups . . .

IV. AIR FORCE

1. The modern development and state of aviation equipment and the country's existing powerful aviation base provide for the rapid growth of our air force.

Our air force has reached a new developmental stage, which, based on its increasing combat significance, requires new points of departure in using both separate types of aviation and the Air Forces as a whole.

2. During the first period of war, all available combat aviation (including naval and army) is massed for independent operations to achieve air superiority, disorganize the rear, disrupt mobilization and concentration of the army, and destroy enemy naval forces.

The basic principles for combat use of massed aviation should pursue the resolution of the following tasks by *RKKA* air forces:

(a) to have air superiority, both for attack and immediate protection of the Soviet Union's territory, and especially the most important economic, political, and military areas, regions, and centers;

(b) in the event of an attack against the Soviet Union by one of the capitalist powers or a bloc of such states, to thwart at the very core their armies' mobilization and concentration and to disrupt the administrative and economic life of whole areas, mainly with respect to military production;

(c) interacting with naval forces, to break up and destroy any enemy navy which would operate in waters adjacent to the Soviet Union;

(d) to land motorized air-assault forces in the most revolutionary areas to organize and develop armed combat in the enemy rear area and on operationally advantageous sectors of enemy territory.

3. In the process of war, all light combat aviation is subordinated to the field command of armies and *fronts* and interacts with ground forces. As a rule, heavy combat aviation remains in the hands of the High Command to resolve independent missions as a long-range air fleet, to operate against enemy political and economic bases . . .

CONCLUSIONS

The principal contemporary problem is the simultaneous deployment of combat operations to great depth. This problem is central, both in tactics and operational art.

In tactics, its resolution is planned along the line of penetrating the entire depth of the enemy defense (area of artillery positions and tactical reserves), with the help of fast-moving tanks, artillery, infantry transports, and by assault aviation actions.

In operational art, this is achieved when large cavalry masses and motor-mechanized formations, with the support of powerful aviation, reach deep into the enemy's rear area or penetrate into this rear area, if there are no open flanks. The forces of these formations (both cavalry and motor-mechanized forces) are counted on not only to create congestion in the enemy's rear area, but also to be able to *attack* independently his large reserves or withdrawing forces. Operations should develop simultaneously from the front and the rear.

The problem of operational control presently includes the correct combination and continuous control of forces fighting from the front and forces advancing from the deep rear against the enemy's deep rear areas.

The following issues are most correctly resolved by means of planned organizational measures:

(1) organization of air forces and mechanized units;
(2) strategic cavalry – sufficiently outfitting cavalry divisions and corps with technical combat means;
(3) organization of forces operating from the front – rifle corps receiving additional means of suppression on the main attack axes.

With respect to motorized forces, the internal structure and content of such formations as the motorized division have not yet been determined; the broad question of transporting troops on motor vehicles has still in no way been posed.

The problem with means of controlling battle has still not been resolved in all aviation units or among all troops.

The existing internal structure of headquarters, the number of their personnel and means of control are not capable of controlling the battle and operation immediately developing to great depth. It is necessary to implement immediately the planned reorganization of the control apparatus.

Only our cavalry has some experience in actions in the spirit of new demands on the operational scale.[5] However, it has no experience with actions in the enemy's deep rear area jointly with tanks, aviation, and other combat means.

As for deep combined-arms tactics, tactics of mechanized formations, and mass combat use of aviation, we not only have no experience, but the basic tenets of the new equipment and operational art have also not been theoretically worked out.

All this requires rapid organization of extensive research work, with the help of organized experimental exercises and large ground forces and air maneuvers.

NOTES

1. A. I. Yegorov, "Taktika i operativnoye iskusstvo *RKKA* na novom etape," *Voyenno-istorich-eskiy zhurnal* [Military-historical journal], 10 (October 1963), pp. 30–9.
2. Editor's note: an aviette is a small-powered or light motor aircraft which appeared after the First World War in connection with the attempt in various countries to create a simple, cheap, economical type of aircraft. Later, aviettes were widely used in the Soviet Union as exercise aircraft, e.g., the UT-1 and UT-2.
3. Translator's note: the article has no point No. 5, but goes directly from No. 4 to No. 6.
4. Editor's note: in the given concrete instance, an attempt is made to transfer mechanically the experience of the Civil War into new conditions, where aviation, tanks, and artillery have become the decisive force for conducting deep operations.
5. Editor's note: Here the cavalry is clearly idealized as a combat arm.

Index

air assault, 95, 96, 245, 275–6, 320, 321, 324, 325, 326
airborne forces, 117, 203, 245, 247, 248, 249, 250, 259, 262, 264, 277, 283, 296, 320
Alba (Duke of), 12
Amiens, 11, 126
amphibious assault, 249–50, 259, 263, 296
Anglo-Boer War, 144
Anglo-French Army, 13
annihilating battle *see* annihilation
annihilating engagement *see* annihilation
annihilation, 2, 8–12, 13, 14, 15, 18, 22, 54, 69, 72, 87, 125, 144, 145, 147, 155, 157, 159, 162, 173, 192, 202, 211, 212, 214, 215, 220, 227, 231, 233, 271, 275, 282, 290, 319, 321, 323, 324
anti-assault operation, 250, 259, 263, 296
army defensive region, 102–7
Arnold, 208
artillery offensive, 179, 184, 187, 194, 202, 252
artillery preparation, 105, 114, 124, 126, 134, 135, 138, 170, 175, 179, 194, 317
Asian Russian Corps, 15
Aspern (Battle of), 9
atomic attack (strike), 253, 279, 283
atomic weapons, 237, 270, 271, 274, 279, 280, 283, 285
attrition, 2, 8, 11, 12–16, 18, 54, 75
Augustow Forests, 20
Austerlitz, 28

Balaton Operation, 195–6, 216
Balkan Wars, 144, 148
Baltic Sea, 20, 215
Barsky, B., 298
Bazarevskiy, A., 298
Bazin, 58
Belebey Operation, 172
Belgorod Operation, 185, 230
Belorussian Operation, 191–2, 195
Belorussian–Polish Theater, 21
Belov, I. P., 316
Benedek, L. von, 58
Berends, K., 301

Berezina River, 26, 43, 44, 240
Berlin Operation, 247, 248
Bernhardi, 68
Black Sea Fleet, 16
blitzkrieg, 155, 207, 208, 222, 265
Blume, Wilhelm, 7
Bobruisk Operation, 158
Bock, 134
Borodino (Battle of), 56
Brezhnev, vii
Brossait, 127
Brusilov, 15, 21, 110, 150, 160, 170–1
Bug River, 44
Buguruslan Operation, 172

Cambrai (Battle of), 126, 133, 149
Cannae, 144, 158, 159, 325
Chataldjin Battles, 148
Civil War (Russian), 2, 3, 19, 33, 35, 36, 40, 41, 42, 49, 127, 151–2, 167, 171–2, 206, 211–12, 214, 243, 258, 298, 301, 302, 316
Clausewitz, 1, 7, 23–4, 49, 52, 53, 55, 57, 70, 207, 208, 298
cleaving strike (attack), 152, 160
Cold War, viii
Colombey-Nuilly (Battle of), 60, 240
concentration (of forces), 85, 137, 145, 168, 184, 193, 196, 197, 225, 290, 291
Congress of Paris, 16
correlation of forces (and means), 27, 45, 70, 108, 129, 170, 175, 176, 188, 195, 198, 204, 219, 231, 250, 280, 291, 321

Danube River, 215
deep battle, 2, 4, 78, 91, 309, 311, 316
deep echelonment, 80, 87, 216, 228, 242, 243, 244
deep operation, 2, 4, 78, 81, 86, 88, 92, 93, 154, 155, 167, 172, 173, 212, 214, 220, 223, 224, 259, 309, 310, 311
deep pursuit, 42, 43
deep strategy, 80, 89
Demiansk Operation, 184
Denikin, 43, 152, 172, 212
Desna River, 188

Devez Line, 132
Dnepr River, 157, 184, 188, 230
Dnestr River, 157, 322
Don River, 181
Dubenet, 75, 85
Duffeur, 74
Dunkirk, 133, 139
Dvina River, 70, 82
Dyle River, 133

East Prussian Operation, 192
Ehrfurt, 159, 311
En River, 133
encirclement, 27, 136, 139, 140, 147, 148,
    152, 154, 157, 158, 159, 160, 164, 172, 174,
    175, 182, 184, 187, 189, 190, 191, 192, 199,
    200, 201, 202, 204, 213–14, 215, 220, 223,
    224, 226, 227, 232, 233, 234, 235, 249, 251,
    263, 306, 307, 323, 324, 325
Engels, F., 54, 57, 59, 64, 66, 67, 123
Entente, 48, 76, 153
envelopment (enveloping maneuver), 27, 28,
    83, 86, 145, 147, 154, 155, 170, 172, 174,
    182, 191, 192, 200, 202, 222, 240, 306, 307

Falaise "sack", 214
Falkenhayn, 298
Finnish War *see* Russo-Finnish War
First World War *see* World War, First
Flanders, 21
flank strike (attack), 27, 145, 148, 172
Foch, 14, 76, 146, 153
foresight, 228, 253
Fort Eben-Emael, 132
fortified region, 96, 128, 133, 322
forward base(s), 42, 97
forward belt of resistance, 105–6
forward operational zone, 102, 103
forward security detachment, 60
Franco-Prussian War, 269
Frederick the Great, 12, 55
French Revolution, 1, 49, 55
Frunze, M. V., 81, 152, 156, 299, 302, 306
Frunze Academy, 3, 4, 301, 308, 311
Fuller, 50

Galicia, 10, 24, 147, 241
Gambetta, Leon, 12
General Staff (Soviet), 92, 166
General Staff Academy, 3, 4, 33–47, 166
German–Polish War (1939), 129–31, 140–1
Girs, G., 306
Golovchiner, B., 285, 287–97
Golubev, A. V., 302, 304
Gorev, B. I., 40
Gotchin (Battle of), 59
Grandmaison, 146

Gravelotte and Saint Privat (Battle of), 60, 63,
    72, 240
Great Patriotic War, xi, 150, 152, 155, 156–
    64, 166, 176, 179, 180, 186, 197, 198, 202,
    206–7, 212–17, 218–36, 244, 246, 254, 259,
    260, 261, 265, 286, 290, 306, 310, 312, 317,
    318
Groener, 50
Guderian, 131, 134, 137

Hannibal, 144, 145, 148, 158
High Command *see* Supreme High Command
Hitler, Adolf, 218, 221, 222, 223, 224, 225,
    228, 230, 231, 233, 236, 265
Hoth, 131, 134

Iassy–Kishinev Operation, 158, 192, 195, 232,
    247, 248
Immanuel, 50
Imperialist War *see* World War, First
Initial period of war, 86, 87, 91, 166, 220,
    242, 307, 315, 316–17, 320–1
initiative, 291, 292
intercontinental ballistic rockets, 272
Isserson, G. S., 3–4, 48–77, 78–90, 311

Jacobs, Walter, 303
Jena Operation, 11
Joffre, 149
Jomini, Henri, 1, 8

Kakurin, N., 298
Kalinin, M. I., 306
Kalisha, 26
Kamenev, 306
Kant, Emmanuel, 7
Kapustin, N., 298
Karelian Isthmus, 96, 101, 103
Kenny, 208
Khalkhin-Gol River, 123, 155
Khar'kov Operation, 230
Krushchev, N. S., 272, 285, 286
Kiev Operation, 152, 160
Kinburn, 16
Kitchener Program, 15
Koenigratz (Battle of), 61
Kolchak, 42, 172
Korkodinov, P. D., 92, 124–42
Korsun–Shevchenkovskiy Operation, 158,
    232, 247
Kuhlman, 50, 76, 81, 298
Kuropatkin, 240
Kursk Operation, 184, 185–7, 195, 216, 218,
    220, 227–30, 247
Kutuzov, M. I., 168, 239–40

Lama River, 178

La Manche, 20
Leer, G. A., 8, 12, 62
Leipzig (Battle of), 56
Lenin, V. I., 53, 88, 140
Leningrad Military District, 316
Leningrad Operation, 177, 184
lightning war *see* blitzkrieg
linear strategy, 58–9, 61, 63, 67, 69, 70–2, 76, 77, 89
Lloyd, Henry, 7
Lodz Operation, 147
Lotharingia, 20, 30
Lucas, 145
Ludendorff, Erich, 5–6, 11, 14, 20, 26, 49, 50, 298
Ludwig, 311
Lys River, 133, 138

Maas River, 132, 133
MacMahon, 58
Maginot Line, 96, 97, 101, 121, 134, 139
Main Army Directorate, 46
Manchuria, 15
maneuver, 20, 22, 23, 24, 26, 28, 38, 63, 67, 78, 81, 82, 83, 85, 86, 87, 96, 100, 102, 107, 135, 145, 146, 147, 148, 149, 150, 152, 153, 154, 155, 156, 158, 159, 160, 161, 164, 169–70, 171, 172, 173, 174, 175, 176, 177, 178, 179, 181, 182, 183, 185, 186, 188, 189, 190, 191, 192, 193, 194, 195, 196, 197, 198, 200, 201–2, 204, 205, 211, 212, 215, 216, 220, 221, 222, 223, 224, 225, 229, 230, 231, 232, 233, 234, 235, 240, 242, 243, 244, 251, 252, 253, 259, 261, 264, 282, 289–90, 291, 292, 295, 296, 299, 300, 301, 305, 306, 308, 309, 321, 322, 323
maneuver war, 19–22, 82, 83, 96, 126, 153, 154, 211
Mannerheim Line, 97, 100, 101, 121, 141, 155
Manstein, Erich, 183, 310–11
Marengo (Battle of), 56
Mariyevsky, I., 285, 298–314
Marne River (Battle of the Marne), 18, 21, 30, 65, 69, 71, 72, 82, 225, 241
Mars la Tour (Battle of), 60, 240
Marshall Plan, 208
Martel, 126
Marxism-Leninism, 172, 209, 217, 219, 309
maskirovka, xii, 46, 184
Maurice of Saxony, 12
meeting battle, 56, 60, 136, 140, 260, 292
meeting engagement, 121, 260, 278, 292, 317, 319–20
Melikov, V., 298, 304
Metsch, 50
Metz (Battle of), 61, 240
military doctrine, xiii, xvi, 41, 129, 175, 176,

207, 208, 286, 316
military science, xiii, xvi, 94, 182, 209, 210, 211, 212, 213, 217, 219, 226, 230, 235, 265, 267, 269, 270, 284
Minsk Operation, 232
Moltke, 8, 9, 10, 11, 23, 24, 51, 52, 57, 58, 59, 60, 61, 62, 63, 64, 65, 67, 68, 79, 84, 143
Moscow Operation, 177, 178, 179, 181, 182, 183, 186, 215, 216, 218, 220, 221, 222, 223, 225, 229, 265
Mukden (Battle of), 64, 240–1, 300

Nachod (Battle of), 59
Nancy, 20
Napoleon I, 1, 1, 8, 9, 10, 11, 12, 14, 16, 18, 22, 23, 24, 37, 52, 55–7, 58, 59, 60, 51, 62, 65, 67, 68, 70, 143, 144, 146, 168, 169, 258, 269
Napoleon III, 58
Nara River, 178
Narev River, 70, 192
Naroch (Lake), 15
Narva, 22
NATO, vii
Neman River, 70
night operation, 283
Nivelle, R., 5–6, 21
Normandy, 213
Novitskiy, V., 298
nuclear strike, 289, 290, 292, 295
nuclear war, 237, 288
nuclear weapons, xvii, 275, 276, 277, 287, 288, 289, 290, 291, 293, 295

Oder River, 157, 160, 193, 195
Odessa Operation, 177
Oka River, 178
operational aim (objective), 5, 6, 16, 19, 22, 23, 24, 26, 27, 28, 42, 45, 66, 117, 154, 157, 161, 171, 173, 174, 182, 189, 191, 197, 199, 200, 201, 206, 209, 211, 213, 214, 220, 231, 232, 239, 245, 246, 247, 248, 251, 257, 258, 265, 266, 281, 287, 289, 294, 295, 302, 304, 305, 307
operational deployment, 21, 22, 23, 24, 25, 28–9, 30, 323
operational depth, 54, 60, 65, 88, 98, 99, 118, 136, 154, 155, 161, 174, 176, 178, 183, 187, 190, 194, 200, 202, 220, 243, 251, 253, 278, 281, 285, 309
operational depth of the defense (enemy resistance), 101, 106, 109, 118, 119, 149, 154, 155, 173, 174, 183, 191, 195, 204, 246, 253, 279
operational plan, 5, 26–7, 30, 45, 65, 119, 184, 196, 197, 199, 200, 201, 209, 210, 220, 226, 228, 229, 231, 239, 245, 248, 251, 257, 265,

280, 287, 300, 305, 307, 317
operational reserves, 15, 30, 70, 95, 98, 114,
　116, 135, 149, 161, 173, 178, 181, 191, 195,
　197, 200, 201, 251, 253, 296
Orel Operation, 185, 230

Paris (Battle of), 61
Patriotic War (1812), 239–40
penetration, 27, 28, 72, 75–6, 78, 95–6, 97,
　99, 109–14, 116, 118, 119, 121, 123–4,
　126, 127, 128, 129, 130, 134, 135, 136,
　137, 138, 139, 144, 148, 149, 150, 151,
　152, 153, 154, 155, 157, 158, 159, 160,
　161, 164, 170, 171, 173, 174, 175, 179,
　182, 183, 184, 187, 189, 190, 191, 193,
　194, 195, 196, 198, 199, 200, 201–2, 204,
　213, 215, 216, 220, 223, 227, 228, 233–4,
　235, 240, 242, 243, 244, 249, 250, 251,
　252, 279, 280, 283, 306, 307, 308, 309,
　311, 317, 321, 323, 324, 326–7
penetrative force of the attack, 79, 80–1, 83,
　86, 87, 88, 229, 309
Petsamo–Kirkenes Operation, 247
Port Arthur, 16
positional defense, 102–3, 170, 176, 198, 233,
　242
positional front, 19, 20, 21, 48, 75, 76, 78, 86,
　123, 148, 149, 150, 157, 173
positional war, 19–22, 81, 82
Prasnysh Quadrille, 21
pursuit, 22–3, 30, 42, 116, 128, 136, 140, 158,
　161, 190, 191, 192, 197, 199, 201, 203, 230,
　325

ram attack, 29
Recken, 50
Red Army, 3, 10, 33, 34, 35, 36, 39, 41, 43,
　91, 92, 94, 96, 97, 98, 127, 141, 150, 152,
　155, 156, 157, 158, 159, 160, 161, 162, 163,
　164, 167, 184, 301, 305, 306, 307, 308, 315,
　316, 318, 321, 322, 326
Regensburg (Battle of), 56
Rennenkampf, P. K., 28
Revolutionary Military Council, 315
Rhine River, 82, 84, 153
RKKA *see* Red Army
rocket-nuclear strike *see* nuclear strike
rocket-nuclear war *see* nuclear war
rocket-nuclear weapons *see* nuclear weapons
Rostov-on-the-Don Operation, 177
Rotmistrov, P. A., 237, 269–84
Russian Pacific Fleet, 16
Russian Revolution, 35, 41
Russo-Finnish War, 91, 92, 155
Russo-Japanese War, 2, 3, 16, 24, 38, 64, 143,
　144, 148, 240–1, 258, 300
RVS *see* Revolutionary Military Council

Rzhev Operation, 184

Sakhalin (Expedition), 16
Samsonov, A. V., 28, 48
Sarykamysh Operation, 147
Scheffer, 147
Schlichting, 54, 55, 59, 62, 144
Schlieffen, 1, 50, 63, 67, 71, 72, 144–5, 158
Schlieffen Plan, 13, 20
Sedan, 23, 60, 61, 62, 133, 139
Sedyakin, A. I., 306, 316
Seine River, 214
Semenov, V. A., 298
Sevastopol, 16
Seven Years' War, 7, 12
Shakhei River, 240
Shamil, 16
shock army, 109, 116, 117, 118–19, 174, 317,
　318
shock group (grouping), 79, 80, 109, 121, 172,
　178, 179, 182, 184, 186, 187, 189, 200, 203,
　215, 224, 228, 229, 275, 305, 307, 309, 318,
　325
Siegfried Line, 126, 138
Silesian Operation, 193
Sluch River, 322
Smith, Adam, 7
Sokolovsky, S. V., 285
Somme, 15, 21, 100, 109, 114, 133, 134
Soviet–Finnish War *see* Russo-Finnish War
Sozh River, 188
Spanish Civil War (1936–39), 310
Spichern (Battle of), 59, 60
staging area, 86, 137, 140, 243
Stalin, I. V., 70, 92, 93, 94, 95, 141–2, 151–2,
　166, 167, 171, 172, 176, 178, 179, 180, 181,
　182, 184, 188, 197, 209, 210, 211–12, 213,
　214, 216, 217, 218, 219, 220, 222, 223, 224,
　225–7, 228, 230, 231, 232, 233, 234, 235,
　236, 237, 238, 285
Stalingrad Operation, 157, 158, 159, 180–5,
　186, 187, 190, 215, 216, 218, 220, 221,
　223–5, 226, 227, 228, 229, 230, 234, 247,
　265
Stalyupenin, 29
Stavka (of the Supreme High Command), 163
strategic rocket forces, 285
successive operations, 2, 3, 10, 11, 42, 44, 45,
　65, 70, 108, 109, 162, 172, 212, 246, 247,
　275, 301
Suleyman, N., 298
Supreme High Command, 91, 92, 157, 162,
　179, 181, 182, 188, 189, 199, 213, 224, 248,
　261, 278, 322, 326
surprise, 91, 126, 132, 135, 138, 166, 167,
　176, 184, 197, 198, 205, 215, 219, 221, 237,
　250, 252, 260, 264, 266, 278, 281, 288, 291

Suvorov, 146
Svechin, Alexander, 2, 3, 5–30, 38, 39, 285, 298–9, 301, 302–3

tactical depth of the defense, 73–4, 154, 155, 171, 173, 183, 279, 280
tactical defense zone (belt), 101, 104, 149, 155, 198, 202, 252, 318
Talenskiy, N., 92–3, 143–65
Tausen, 311
theater campaign, 22, 23
theater of military operations, xi, 5, 8, 20, 27, 28, 37, 38, 58, 61, 62, 79, 81, 83, 85, 86, 87, 97, 108, 116, 122, 135, 141, 151, 169, 172, 173, 201, 204, 207, 209, 241, 248, 259, 261, 262, 263, 264, 272, 287, 288, 289, 294, 295, 299, 301, 303, 305, 307, 311
theater of war, 5, 7, 59, 65, 88, 108, 111, 141, 144, 146, 147, 153, 247, 248, 304
thermonuclear weapons, 269, 271
Timoshenko, S. K., 92, 94–123
Torna, 26
Trautenau (Battle of), 59
Triandafilov, V. K., 51, 162, 306, 309–10, 311
Truman Doctrine, 208
Tsiffer, 306
Tsusima, 16
Tsvetkov, A., 237, 239–55, 258
Tukhachevskiy, M. N., 2, 36, 39, 301, 302, 303, 306, 307, 308, 311
Turenne, 9

Uborevich, I. P., 306
Ufa Operation, 172
Ukrainian Military District, 315
Ulm (Battle of), 56
U.S. Army Command and General Staff College, viii
U.S. Army War College, viii

Varfolomeyev, N. Ye., 2, 3, 33–47, 304, 306, 308
Vasil'yev, V., 237, 256–68
Velikie Luki Operation, 184

Verdun, 15, 21
Vetoshnikov, L., 167, 168–205, 206–17
Viaz'ma Operation, 184
Vistula–Oder Operation, 192–3
Vistula River, 33, 43, 44, 69, 70, 71, 82, 157, 160, 193
Vitebsk Operation, 158
Volga River, 218, 225
von Rundstedt, 134
Voroshilov, 92

Wagram (Battle of), 9
Warsaw (Operation), 26, 43
weapons of mass destruction, 238, 260, 263, 279, 280
Werth (Battle of), 59, 60
Western Bug River, 131
Western Dvina River, 157
Weygand Defensive Line, 99, 101, 133–4, 138, 139
White Finns, 103, 141
White Guards, 211
White Poles, 33, 41, 44, 172, 212
Wilhelm II (of Germany), 16
Willisen, 7
Workers' and Peasants' Red Army *see* Red Army
World War, First, 2, 3, 6, 13, 15, 20, 21, 22, 36, 40, 42, 48, 49, 50, 53, 54, 62–77, 79–80, 81, 82, 83, 86, 87, 89, 95, 96, 101, 106, 114, 123–4, 127, 128, 143, 144, 145, 146–51, 152, 153, 154, 155, 156, 159, 160, 161, 162, 168–71, 173, 204, 206, 207, 211, 212, 213, 233, 240, 241–3, 244, 245, 247, 254, 258, 260, 269, 270, 271, 298, 301, 302, 303, 306, 308, 309, 316, 317, 322, 323
Wrangel, 43, 172

Yakir, I. E., 306, 315–16
Yegorov, A. I., 285, 286, 306, 308, 315–28

Zayonchkovskiy, A., 298
Zhilinskiy, Ya. G., 28
Zlobin, V., 167, 168–205, 218–36